M000199567

BETWEEN THE LINES

SOUTH ASIANS AND POSTCOLONIALITY

In the series
Asian American History and Culture,
edited by Sucheng Chan,
David Palumbo-Liu, and
Michael Omi

BETWEEN
SOUTH ASIANS AND POSTCOLONIALITY
THE LINES

EDITED BY
Deepika Bahri
AND
Mary Vasudeva

Temple University Press   Philadelphia

Temple University Press, Philadelphia 19122
Copyright © 1996 by Temple University (except Chapter 6, copyright ©
M. G. Vassanji). All rights reserved
Published 1996
Printed in the United States of America

⊗ The paper used in this book meets the requirements of the American
National Standard for Information Sciences—Permanence of Paper for
Printed Library Materials, ANSI Z39.48-1984

Text design by Will Boehm

Library of Congress Cataloging-in-Publication Data

Between the lines : South Asians and postcoloniality / edited by
  Deepika Bahri and Mary Vasudeva.
      p.   cm. — (Asian American history and culture)
    Includes bibliographical references.
      ISBN 1-56639-467-8 (cloth : alk. paper). — ISBN 1-56639-468-6
  (pbk. : alk. paper)
      1. South Asian Americans. 2. South Asian Americans—Ethnic
  identity. 3. South Asians—Canada. 4. South Asians—Canada—Ethnic
  identity. 5. Oriental literature (English)—History and criticism.
  6. Decolonization in literature. 7. Culture conflict in literature.
  8. Ethnicity in literature. 9. South Asia—Civilization—20th
  century. 10. South Asia—Colonial influence. I. Bahri, Deepika,
  1962–   . II. Vasudeva, Mary, 1966–   . III. Series: Asian
  American history and culture series.
  E184.S69B48   1996
  973'.04914—dc20   95-52972

CONTENTS

ACKNOWLEDGMENTS

We thank all those who helped in the compilation of this anthology, our contributors, families, friends, and collaborators at Temple University Press: David Palumbo-Liu, Janet Francendese, Patricia Sterling, and Joan Vidal. For institutional support, we thank Bowling Green State University, Georgia Institute of Technology, and Emory University. We were fortunate to have had the support and encouragement of many; most useful, perhaps, were their insightful criticism and input. We especially thank our spouses, Joseph Petraglia-Bahri and Vivek Vasudeva, for their encouragement, flexibility, and patience as we worked on this project.

BETWEEN THE LINES

SOUTH ASIANS AND POSTCOLONIALITY

CHAPTER 1

Introduction

Deepika Bahri and Mary Vasudeva

This volume brings together the voices of South Asians in the Anglo-American academy on the construction and representation of the "post-colonial."[1] Combining interviews, literary criticism, commentaries, and cultural studies, *Between the Lines: South Asians and Postcoloniality* suggests the diversity and complexity of what one might designate the "postcolonial" subject. Further, even within the narrower parameters of specifically South Asian post-colonial subjectivities and their representation in the language and framework of the academy, the quest for a stable South Asian identity is a daunting venture; hence, the varied articulations presented here offer an understanding of identity as the product of complex interactions and negotiations. Enunciated variously, identity emerges as a dynamic process without primordial fixity, ultimately making it impossible to view this collection as a representative profile of the groups invoked in its title. Rather, the categories "postcolonial" and "South Asian" become tools for reconfiguring our understanding of identity and culture in light of an intricate mesh of social, economic, and historical events in the past and present.

Our focus on South Asians is motivated by several considerations. First, ours is an attempt to record the growing South Asian presence in the United States and Canada and to explore the intercultural dynamics that result from it. The historical and cultural specificity of South Asian experiences is often obscured or omitted within the discourse of "Asian" studies in Anglo-America, requiring expression in a space explicitly devoted to them. This volume is thus also an effort to disaggregate the group "Asian" by focusing on a subgroup that is not often recognized or represented, because that term is commonly thought to connote a Sinitic constituency. In the introduction to her "South Asian American Studies Bibliography," Rosane Rocher observes that a 1976 collection on the Asian American experience included a piece titled "The Forgotten Asian Americans: The East Indian Community in the United States." "Twenty years later," she continues, "it remains the case that the Indian American experience in the United States has received less attention than that of some other Asian Americans."[2] Jane Singh's foreword to *Our Feet Walk the Sky* (1993) underscores the same problem: "As one of the least studied groups in the United States, people of South Asian origin have been overlooked by historians and social scientists as well as by scholars of Ethnic and Women's Studies."[3] But just as there may be sound historical reasons for the unimportance of South Asians in Anglo-America thus far, relative to other Asian and minority groups, particular configurations in the present oblige us to turn our attention to the role they have begun to play in the sociopolitical life of Anglo-America.[4] Much postcolonial discourse, for instance, has been the province of critics, theorists, and writers from the part of the world described as South Asia. Their work, although prolific and represented in various postcolonial collections, has yet to be brought together in dialogue.

Readers will find in this collection a sampling of perspectives from South Asian writers and critics in the Anglo-American academy on broad questions of identity, representation, and postcoloniality. Previously unpublished, the pieces attempt to address these issues within a contemporary frame of several compelling realities that invite a reexamination of the past and the present. Of particular note are these: economic and cultural, some would argue political, globalization; increasingly contentious relations in the United States and Canada between majority and minority as well as within minority groups; escalating religious fundamentalism in South Asia with resonances and support abroad; growing awareness in the academy of the need to unpack and complicate such categories as "Third World woman" and "postcolonial," even as the academic and popular market's demand for a consumable Other shows no signs of abating; and the mounting need to address in more nuanced ways the abiding issue of class differentials and privilege. Discussions on the "postcolonial" and "South Asian" proceed to unfold prismatically into a varied set of concerns that nevertheless converge as often as they diverge. The complexity and density of issues and concerns remind us that even though these critics and writers speak sometimes as "South Asian" and sometimes as "postcolonial," these labels are discursive and contingent as well as descriptive.

What are the discursive or particular contingent features that prompt us to acknowledge and assert a South Asian presence? For that matter, one may well ask, just who does "South Asian" refer to?[5] The term is most often used to describe people who either come directly from or can trace an origin to the Indian subcontinent. The synonymity of "South Asia" with "India" is usually explained, though perhaps not justified, by that nation's historical sway in the region; more important, perhaps, it is a reminder of the roots of the tradition of study about South Asia in colonial India. Although scholars often use it interchangeably with "India," editors of collections in South Asian Studies tend to mention by name all the countries represented (or at least seen as legitimate members of the group). Customarily, "South Asia" would include Afghanistan, Bangladesh, Bhutan, India, Myanmar, Nepal, Pakistan, Sri Lanka. These are countries that share contiguous or close borders and claim some modicum of cultural overlap—in language, religion, cuisine, or certain attitudes and practices—and a shared history of colonization before their evolution into modern nationhood. Yet it is rare to find all or even most represented in the available literature. Between the Lines reflects the views of those who responded to our call for all these constituencies to participate. That these voices predominantly derive from India and Pakistan may be a factor of their greater visibility and larger numbers within the academy. Even in this limited group, one observes with little surprise, the contributors show tremendous diversity of background and perspective.

Largely an academic configuration maintained to cope with the accidents of history that fractured what appeared to be a unitary peninsular entity, "South Asian" is a term that has long been in circulation to describe studies of the region dating from colonial times. Interest in South Asia has therefore as much a traditional and colonial as a contemporary, diasporic, and postcolonial dimension. The first South Asian Studies program in the United States began in the early 1940s at the University of Pennsylvania, taking its place among earlier programs of Oriental and Indic Studies in the United Kingdom and elsewhere.[6] The branch of academic inquiry referred to as South Asian Studies carries the undeniable legacy of the political and economic maneuvers of colonialism, themselves buffered by Orientalist scholarship. Although the number of South Asian Studies programs in Anglo-America remains small, those in existence share in this legacy, which continues to pose persistent challenges for students and scholars attempting to transcend Orientalist visions of South Asia. In contemporary collections in South Asian Studies, the encyclopedic coverage of topics—ranging from discussion of ancient religious epics to their televisualization in the last decade, from Dravidian linguistics to language policies under colonialism to the changing curricula in English Studies with greater attention to "native" writers at the turn of this century—suggests the continuing coexistence of more traditional kinds of study with a recognition of the new face of South Asia in an age of advanced technology and continual quest for cultural self-determination in the face of new challenges to its identity.[7]

The mobilization of the term "South Asian" in Anglo-America in the context of diasporic Anglo-American identity is a quite different and significantly more recent phenomenon than that of South Asian Studies programs, although both presuppose an interest in South Asia(ns). The latter may include some examination of the diasporic in the study of South Asia, and the former may share the study of topics found in South Asian Studies programs, but the "South Asian" that has begun to emerge on the academic and sociopolitical scene more recently is the result of the intersection of past histories with present conditions arising from the more pronounced South Asian presence in the West in general and Anglo-America in particular.

In a general climate of multiculturalist identity formation, it seems less apt to ask, why the emphasis on South Asian in Anglo-America *now*, than to wonder why—despite the success of similar identitarian maneuvers by African Americans and other Asian Americans—there has been so little emphasis on South Asians. Both questions oblige us to turn to history. Although, according to the last census, the number of Asian Indians in the United States has increased to 815,477 and that of all South Asians to 925,803, while the number of people of South Asian origin in Canada increased from 314,040 to 420,433 (486,433 if one includes the number of those responding to the South Asian multiethnic category) between 1986 and 1991, the growth of South Asian populations in Anglo-America is a discontinuous and sporadic phenomenon.[8] In numerical terms, South Asians did not register a significant demographic presence in Anglo-America till the 1960s, when the Canadian government removed racial and national immigration restrictions (immigration regulations of 1967) and President Lyndon B. Johnson signed the Act of 3 October 1965 (amending the Immigration and Nationality Act), which eliminated race, religion, and nationality as criteria for immigration and phased out the quota system in the United States.[9] The scanty nature of the early Asian Indian presence in the United States is catalogued by Surinder M. Bhardwaj and Madhusudana Rao: "From 1820, when a solitary Indian was admitted to the United States, through the next half a century, fewer than ten Asian Indians arrived per year on average. . . . This trickle of Indians, all told, amounted to fewer than 700 over a period of 80 years from 1820 to 1900."[10] Before the Johnson-Reed Immigration Act of 1924 stemmed any further influx, no more than 6,400 Asian Indians had come to America, as opposed to about 430,000 Chinese, 380,000 Japanese, and 150,000 Filipinos.[11] By contrast, the post-1960s South Asian influx in both countries demonstrates a dramatic increase in volume. In 1966–72, for instance, "immigrants from India [to the United States] totaled 50,990, a number equivalent to more than seventy percent of all the East Indian immigration over the last one hundred and fifty years." In Canada "approximately 200,000 South Asians immigrated between 1971 and 1982, with their numbers growing to over 300,000 by the end of 1982. Since then the Canadian government has reduced the flow of immigration, but the numbers of South Asian immigrants to Canada remain proportionately high."[12] In the early 1970s, Idi Amin's expulsion of Ugandan Indians brought "some 70,000 Indian refugees from business and professional classes . . . under a special clause" to the United States; moreover, "many overseas Indians also immigrated from other countries, particularly the Caribbean Islands and the British Commonwealth countries."[13]

In broad terms, South Asian immigration to both the United States and Canada is best understood as a distinctly two-phase phenomenon, one phase dating from the early years of this century and another heralded by the immigration reforms of the 1960s. Small numbers and staggered, discontinuous patterns of immigration until the 1960s are not the only factors that must be acknowledged in accounting for the slow advent of the South Asian constituency on the social and political scene, however, since the difference between the two phases is not merely quantitative but qualitative as well. For one thing, "after nearly six decades of Punjabi-dominated immigration a more balanced and varied mix of South Asian peoples took up residence throughout the country [United States]" in the second phase. Moreover, the early wave of South Asian immigrants would have belonged (barring a very small number of middle-class students, elites, and political refugees) to the laboring and farming class without the advantage of much education.[14] Conversely, the typical profile of the second wave of South Asian immigrants suggests that "they were highly educated, English-speaking, had come to the United States for economic reasons, and had immigrated together as a family."[15] Sheth comments that "the new Indian immigrants consist mainly of college-educated, urban, middle-class professional young men and women of religious, regional and linguistic diversity." Although the earlier influx was from rural areas, "post-1965 Indian immigrants have generally come from large cities in all parts of India," and "most of them are fluent in English."[16] Well-educated and cosmopolitan for the most part, this group of immigrants would begin to attain visibility by virtue of numbers as well as their greater preparation and ability to enter the cultural, social, and political mainstream. The changing composition and numbers of South Asians seem to have had a definite impact in recent years: "All but ignored between 1930 and 1965, the South Asians in the United States and Canada are now starting to write and research their own social and historical role in North America's cultural mosaic."[17]

Actively discriminated against and discouraged from developing connections with their adoptive countries by laws restricting citizenship, marriage, and landownership, early immigrants were understandably prone to assume a "sojourner" rather than a settler stance. By and large they would have remained isolated and fragmented, practically invisible in the Anglo-American context.[18] Even during this phase, however, there is evidence that early immigrants did participate in forming ethnic organizations, sometimes to gain leverage in their fight for greater civil rights, but more often to support the cause of independence from the British in India.[19] With increasing immigration and a more liberal environment in the wake of the Second World War, South Asians began to register their presence more aggressively. In the first half of the 1960s many South Asians had children who "were beginning to attend school at all levels"; it was at this time that "cultural pluralism and ethnic identity were concepts that gained great attention as a result of civil rights movements and a growing consciousness of minority lifestyles."[20] The rise of Asian American activism during this period, with Chinese, Japanese, and Korean Americans at the forefront, obscures the burgeoning consciousness on the part of South Asian communities, one that would become more noticeable in years to come.[21] Although a more marked presence would await the coming of age of a more sizable South Asian population, during this period "second-generation South Asians began to move slowly into mainstream politics, educational institutions, and to participate in American social life. A notable example was Dalip Singh Saund, an internationally known India-born member of the U.S. Congress . . . 1959–1962 and the first Asian to be elected to this legislative body."[22]

In more recent years, significant concentrations of South Asians in Anglo-American urban centers has brought them increasing attention. New York, Chicago, Los Angeles, Washington, San Francisco, Houston, Philadelphia, and Detroit, for instance, featured Asian Indian populations from 10,000 to 55,000, according to the 1980 U.S. census.

> In the urban areas the sheer numbers of South Asians have attracted the attention of local politicians, city government, and the press as South Asians have grown to become an identifiable and sizable ethnic group within a heterogeneous milieu. Since many are from mercantile or professional classes their involvement in U.S. and Canadian life is in marked contrast to the relative obscurity of their predecessors; they are a more visible segment of their communities. As engineers, professors, doctors, lawyers, and businessmen, they have entered North American professional organizations and, sometimes, social groups.[23]

Professional and often highly educated, they have also become increasingly visible in workplace areas "such as high technology firms, hospitals, universities, and hotels/motels in or around metropolitan areas or along state highways," and "Asian Indians have started imprinting their culture on American schools, residential streets, and marketplaces," with the support of local politicians, by giving Indian names to areas where they live or do business; they also donate funds to universities, politicians, and hospitals, "which help to increase their clout."[24] The Canadian counterpart of the South Asian movement has a somewhat older history than the American, and the proliferation of South Asian materials emanating from Canada (films, music, cultural events, journals, anthologies) has yet to be matched in the United States. Rocher notes that "the South Asian American experience in the United States has been less studied than that in Canada, a fact that is at significant variance with other strands of Asian American Studies and which stems from a British imperial—now 'commonwealth'—past."[25] Other relevant factors include the significantly larger concentrations of South Asian populations in large Canadian metropolitan centers such as Toronto, Vancouver, and Montreal. A considerable history of attacks against racial minorities and the unconscious promotion of ethnic identitarianism through Canada's declared "mosaic" policy in multicultural affairs have also, one might venture to suggest, contributed to the development of "South Asianism" at a somewhat earlier stage there than in the United States.[26]

The label "South Asian" is today deployed in Anglo-America for various purposes: to gain visibility in the sociopolitical arena; to speak against racism and misrepresentation from a position of collectivity; to initiate social action for the economically depressed and systemically alienated among the group; to open an avenue for the exploration of lost or receding cultural ties with the country of origin; to provide a forum for expressing and investigating experiences and feelings of displacement, alienation, and other forms of cultural anxiety; and to gain a more equal footing, perhaps even an advantage, in market value and economic opportunity. It has been noted, however, that those we may describe as "South Asian" tend to identify with smaller microcommunities based on religion, language, sexual orientation, or gender; these intimate groups are more immediately appealing than the denatured category "South Asian," which for the most part has enjoyed academic rather than popular success. Naheed Islam observes that "the term is not even used by members of the different communities for self-reference."[27] Although most South Asians, Asian Indians in particular, continue to coalesce more commonly around cultural interests than political and economic issues, awareness of economic, social, and gender-based inequities within the population and discrimination from without have in recent years prompted a significant growth in South Asian organizations that have a more significant sociopolitical agenda. Apart from a mushrooming of groups promoting the business and professional interests of South Asian men and women and activist organizations supporting the cause of women, gays, AIDS patients, and victims of civil rights abuse in most major cities in Anglo-America, publications from educational institutions—such as *SAMAR* (South Asian Magazine for Action and Reflection), with an editorial collective of academics and activists; *COSAW Bulletin* (published by the Committee on South Asian Women); and *SAGAR* (South Asia Graduate Research Journal)—have been attempting to educate the South Asian and larger community about current issues both in South Asia and in Anglo-America. In New York City, where as many as 60 percent of cab drivers are new immigrants of South Asian origin, a show of community-based strength in the recent dismissal of charges against Islamabad-born Saleem Osman has been attributed to "community pressure" on the district attorney's office to drop a racist and weak case. Osman, a staff organizer for the Lease Drivers Coalition of the Committee against Anti-Asian Violence, plans to continue his fight for justice, and the committee has been active in protesting the "significant harassment and violence [toward cab drivers of South Asian origin] at the hands of police."[28]

Although many South Asian educators have been involved in organizing community service and activist groups, perhaps the most significant impact of South Asian presence for those in the academy has been its influence on literary and cultural theory as well as on hiring and pedagogic practices in Anglo-America. The increased visibility of academicians of South Asian origin in the field of cultural criticism and the ready transfer and exchange of Third World and postcolonial discourse between South Asia and the growing ranks of South Asian academicians resident in Anglo-America have served to consolidate the status and currency of postcolonial literature and theory considerably. At a time when there is no more than a handful of South Asian Studies programs in the two constituent countries of Anglo-America, literature and theory of South Asian origin nevertheless feature prominently in the curricula of their educational institutions.[29] In response to our questions, "Why is this 'the' postcolonial moment? Why have the term and field gained so much currency in the last few years?" Gauri Viswanathan says in her interview included in this collection, "It's probably not accurate to say it has come into its own now; the ground has been prepared over the last couple of decades. When the doors for immigration opened up in 1965, whole groups of South Asian professionals flooded into the country. Their presence and intellectual activity were bound to have some kind of impact on the restructuring of the curriculum."

This impact has been noted by other critics as well. Arif Dirlik suggests only somewhat facetiously that the prominence of postcolonial studies is a function of the presence of Third World, largely Indian, intellectuals in Western academia. Ella Shohat contends that the "postcolonial," while being associated with Third World countries that gained independence following World War II; and after "spreading from India into Anglo-American academic contexts," also "refers to the Third World diasporic circumstances of the last four decades—from forced exile to 'voluntary' immigration—within First World metropolises."[30] In fixing on the diasporic and translocal development of postcolonial theory and studies, Dirlik and Shohat remind us of the diminishing importance of historical and locational particulars and the emergence of a new global tide in the affairs of the world. As an increasingly complex and interactive global market erodes old boundaries, and national and cultural enclaves can no longer be self-contained, new rubrics and new theories of power relations have become necessary. Arjun Appadurai's analysis of global cultural flow in terms of ethnoscapes, mediascapes, technoscapes, finanscapes, and ideoscapes reveals a vision of the contemporary world mired in a cultural "chaos" that remains to be adequately theorized.[31] The opening of new and more fluid labor and intellectual markets in the current global order makes it possible for the First World as cultural, economic space to be unmoored from a physically spatial site and for Third World intellectuals to be displaced from what used to be a geographical location and yet to speak as if still within it. This condition of betweenness, the spatiotemporal confusion of what is believed to be a shrinking world, has become a hallmark of postcoloniality.

The hybrid, the exiled, the dislocated, the multi-located—the "postcolonials" in many metropolitan definitions of postcoloniality—have stepped nimbly into the breaches and the flows of the new economic and cultural order, occasioning and creating a theory woven from myriad strands of thought to explain and themselves exemplify a plexus of disconcerting intricacy. The postcolonial has thus become a matter both of the chronology of a certain phase of imperialism and of a supercession of the historio-chronological in favor of an imaginary space of contemporary global relations—a continual condition of postcoloniality that seems to apply across the particulars of history and geography.[32] Regardless of the current amorphous and indeterminate parameters of postcolonial theory, the colonial encounter remains a reference point of sorts, reflected in the continuing popularity of a term reminiscent of it and subsisting as a ghostly palimpsest when the term is redefined more expansively.

Because of the confluence of various factors, intellectuals of South Asian, particularly Indian, origin have played an important role in consolidating the importance and currency of postcolonial theory, although postcolonial status and credentials are clearly not confined to them alone. Their prominence in the field might be linked to the historical importance of the countries of the Indian subcontinent within the colonial empire and the special attention accorded the education and training of the natives of a region considered the "jewel in the crown." To explain divergent colonial educational policies in African and Indian situations, Michael Adas speculates that policy decisions were made to accord with an "imagined hierarchy of peoples and cultures." While "the study of India's ancient mathematical and scientific learning by . . . 'Orientalists' did much to elevate Hindu and, to a much lesser extent, Muslim civilization in the eyes of the European observers," David Hume's damning pronouncements on the lack of achievements by Africans "further reduced an already low estimate of the Africans' capacity for acquiring European learning or devising their own."[33] The status of Indian intellectuals might be ascribed at least in some measure to this older historical bias.

A more or less continuous tradition of curiosity about India, bolstered by the movement of educated Indians into the Western academy, has also contributed to their dominance. Early interest in the histories of the colonies and specifically of India was embodied in schools of Indic and Oriental Studies; today it abides in a general investment in multicultural issues throughout much of the West as well as in the shape of institutional awards, such as the Booker Prize in England and the Governor General's Award in Canada, which favor postcolonial literature. Graham Huggan sees it as hardly a coincidence that "of the twenty-seven Booker prize winners to date (in 1974 the prize was shared), no fewer than seventeen deal with Empire." The commodified exoticism provided by postcolonial literature and the theory generated by highly educated intellectuals—often British or otherwise Western trained and residing in or in contact with the West—both serve as a mirror in which the Empire continues to reflect its past in some form and also hint at its neocolonial avatar in the shadow of contemporary Western influence and hegemony in ex-colonies.[34] As the realities of colonialism begin to fade in many countries now peopled by a generation increasingly distanced from it, postcolonial literature and theory continue to be sustained by other, more contemporary realities: the availability of postcolonial literary texts in the West because they are either produced there or have entry into Western markets through Western-based publishing houses and the presence of a metropolitan circuit of intellectual and literary exchange; the reception of these texts as tokens of acceptable and unthreatening difference because often they evoke the otherness that is located "elsewhere";[35] the actual presence of "postcolonials" in the West with the ability to teach and discuss those texts while exerting an influence on the educational and cultural ideoscapes of Western countries (their presence reinforced by a growing student population of minority and South Asian origin);[36] the postcolonials' own investment in keeping the memory of colonial dominance alive to continue to pose a continuing challenge to Eurocentrism, to warn of the dangers of neocolonialism in the context of globalization, and in part to retain their own position; Western investment in maintaining and encouraging a corps of qualified and trained "multiculturals" who can educate the current generation and expand its appreciation of the rest of the world while also equipping it to understand the "language of the [prospective] customers" in a globalizing economy. Gayatri Chakravorty Spivak suggests that the study of Third World texts in the West is at least partially grounded in a question facing capitalist multinationals: "How are we to sell our products in a global economy when we are yet to learn the language of the customers?"[37]

The popularity of postcolonialism in the specific context of "transnationalism" has given rise to considerable speculation and concern. Transnationalism is marked by the movement of labor and capital (physical, economic, and cultural) between nations in unprecedented volume, the emergence of multinational corporations such as AT&T, Dow, Exxon ("those are the nations of the world today," as a character in the film Network remarks), the opening of new channels of communication between the citizens of the world (albeit often with certain class-specific restrictions), and the concurrent growth in new technologies of representation and exchange. With its inevitable impact on global culture, transnationalism has also contributed to the politicization of identity in the shape of communalism and fundamentalism as well as multiculturalism, a term amply familiar to those in Western nations. In its ideal form, says Benjamin Lee, critical multiculturalism is believed capable of addressing the "cultural dimensions of globalization." Lee reports that a gathering of American and foreign intellectuals in 1990 at the Center for Transcultural Studies in Chicago had hoped that such a critical framework with "a mix of Marxism, deconstructionism, and post-colonial theory would provide a theoretical foundation for an international vision that, in the name of the study of contemporary culture, could articulate cultural difference as the ground for an internationalized, liberal political critique."[38] That promise would seem to have been belied, despite the crucial conjunction of corporate and liberal interests in the "age of transnationalism," and the deployment of postcolonial theory and literature within this junctural construction. Caren Kaplan remarks sardonically that the notion of a "world without boundaries . . . appeals to conservative, liberal, and progressive alike—the multinational corporation and the libertarian anarchist might choose to phrase their ideal world in just such terms."[39] As big business and the multiculturalist both "reinvent the periphery" for consumption within transnationalism, one cannot absolve the latter alone of participating in an essentially commercial enterprise.[40] Roger Rouse complains that "both corporations and universities have used an emphasis on diversity much less to engage the problems suffered by citizens of color, especially those from the lower reaches of the class structure, than to license the creation of a cosmopolitan professional-mangerial class by recruiting researchers, managers and academics from a global pool of talent."[41]

Difference within the consumer culture of transnationalism, critics warn, succeeds in masking the operation of power relations.[42] The inevitable focus on the present (at the cost of a broader sense of history) and the privileging of the registers of postcolonial transnationalism (reflected in the language of diaspora, hybridity, alterity)—as opposed to the narratives of micropolitical resistance to globalization or the material particulars in the postcolony—have limited the potential and utility of postcolonial discourse. Moreover, focus on "geopolitical and corporeal identity," as Rouse argues, has served to depress discussion of exploitation alongside "questions of prejudice and discrimination."[43] The flattening of postcoloniality into a transnational condition obscures the economic and social particulars of the postcolony in the past as well as in the present; at the same time it creates for postcolonial immigrants a liminal zone that diverts attention from the fact that not all of them have entered "transnational" space on the same terms.

Discussions of postcolonial literature and theory these days are heavy with discontent. There is concern over the use and abuse of both, their distance from the historical particulars of postcolonies, and their function in a world riven by cultural politics, general social discontent, and economic complications. Dissatisfaction has been registered on several counts: that increasingly, the business of postcolonial discourse is business—the booming Otherness industry threatening to dissolve any radical charge in the field; that the "postcolonial" is simultaneously undergoing overworlding and deworlding, each phenomenon carrying its own problems; that the abstractions of postcolonial theory raise questions of relevance and accountability and fail to distinguish its concerns clearly from those of postmodernism; that in attempting global applicability, postcolonial theory has lost its ability to inform about the local; that the term "postcolonial" has obscured the operations of neocolonialism, deflected attention from the decolonization project, absolved the postcolony and the postcolonial of responsibility, and robbed them of agency; that prominent among the conditions accounting for its success is the unacknowledged coterminous rise of global capitalism; that in being mobilized for the culture wars and economic aspirations of the West, postcolonial literature has itself been immobilized and restricted, being mostly valued for its ability to "play up squarely on the green summer pitches of the Imperium in its neo-colonial phase," in Stephen Slemon and Helen Tiffin's memorable analogy.[44]

The connection between the emergence of the "postcolonial" and the context of Anglo-American identity politics indicates the convergence of discourses of postcolonialism, identity, and ethnicity and reflects on the tangled web of socioeconomic and historical realities that bring them together.[45] Simultaneously of Indian (or, say, Pakistani or Sri Lankan) and of metropolitan Western space, the South Asian in Anglo-America slides between identities, illustrating the transnational reality of migration and hybridity. The seamless and unannounced shifting of this individual between the left side of the composite configuration South Asian–American/Canadian—as well as between national and larger South Asian affiliation—while also occupying the national, economic, historical space evoked by the right side bespeaks the particular situation of these new immigrants even as it invokes a more global condition of lost or eroding boundaries. Rouse notes that "the tendency of newer groups to move between particular communities of origin and specific settlements in this country and, in so doing, to establish important links between them is not, in itself, particularly novel. But their growing access to telephones, electronic banking, videorecorders, fax machines and computers has brought a significant shift, making it possible for the first time for (im)migrants to operate more or less simultaneously in the different settings they inhabit."[46]

Not surprisingly, then, the impact of the presence of these individuals is similarly manifold. If we examine their influence on curricular matters, we will see that it has generated attention both to their immigrant history and to the history of their nation(s) of origin. On the one hand, for instance, it is telling that "the state-adopted History/Social Sciences (H/SS) Framework—the California State Department of Education's (CDE) guideline to schoolteachers—advises that all sixth grade students in California learn about India as part of its "West Meets East" curriculum."[47] On the other, textbooks such as *From Beyond the Western Horizon: Canadians from the Sub-Continent of India* and *The East Indians and the Pakistanis in America*, texts for secondary school social science courses, focus attention on the displaced and diasporic South Asian now entering the fabric of Anglo-American life.[48] Similarly, the South Asian use of computers and the internet in Anglo-America involves services and software that introduce Indian classics, languages, and history; provide high-tech job referral services; create a forum for discussions of Indian religions and culture; and attempt manifestly to link both worlds, the originary and the diasporic.[49]

The conception of "home" for the South Asian immigrant is thus not sharply divided between homeland and diaspora. Nor, it must be admitted, is the divide between diasporic and domestic concerns necessarily sharp. Purnima Mankekar suggests that "diasporic subjects can (and do) forge coalitions based on a politics of location and accountable engagement with struggles in both the homeland and the diaspora," since "the political lives of diasporic subjects are not insulated from events in the homeland."[50] The question of identity is particularly vexed for the diasporic individual caught between different notions of "home," varying and multiple loyalties to various causes in all the "homes," and the options of "assimilating" and retaining (or being obliged to retain) a sense of difference from the mainstream culture. English race relations scholar Anthony Richmond argues that "the varied role sets characteristic of modern societies call for multiple, overlapping and sometimes conflicting definitions of personal identity and group membership."[51] On the one hand, it would seem that the diasporic home demands loyalty from its new denizens; on the other, the stresses of diaspora can intensify considerably the subject's identification with the originary homeland. Identity, always "conjunctural," as Mankekar puts it, rather than "stable and unified," takes shape in response to varied stimuli; prominent among these are xenophobia in the new homeland, the perceived or real need to struggle for economic ground, and anxiety at the loss of tradition. Through the operation of complex factors, the immigrant may simultaneously be made to feel different and perceive a need to self-identify as separate from others. The imperatives of choice, obligation, and interpellation by mainstream narratives can operate more or less concurrently, each sustaining and strengthening the others. Thus the immigrant both exercises and has no choice. Peter van der Veer remarks that "those who do not think of themselves as Indians before migration become Indians in the diaspora. The element of romanticization which is present in every nationalism is even stronger among nostalgic immigrants, who often form a rosy picture of the country they have left and are able to imagine the nation where it did not exist before."[52] Appadurai notes that diasporic communities, "safe from the depredations of their home states . . . become doubly loyal to their nations of origin and thus ambivalent about their loyalty to America."[53] At the same time, diasporic groups may discover (or find reinforced) narrower communal and linguistic identities. Not surprisingly, then, many separatist and fundamentalist movements in South Asia have found monetary and propaganda support among the ranks of expatriate communities. Shifting between multiple and dynamic identities, South Asians, like many other minority groups, "seek to define both their historical legacies and their present geographic and social realities."[54] Diasporic communities find themselves exemplifying multiple realities: reaffirming the nation of origin, marking the erosion of the nation-state, or responding to a new global order—or sometimes engaging in all three.

Despite the real-world implications for both public policy and sociopersonal perceptions of the self and other, it would be accurate to say that the configuration "South Asia"—whether used in its diasporic or homeland or geographical sense—is a construct, created as a manageable category for the purpose of discussion and study and accepted by scholars and activists as a necessary fiction. This is not to say that the regions encompassed by this nomenclature do not have a great deal in common but to alert ourselves to the constructed nature of such configurations and the limits to which one can generalize about them.

The real and perceived advantages of such grouping, some clearly more innocuous than others, have served to expedite identity-based moves. But identitarianism, we might pause to note, can be a double-edged sword. The use of "South Asian" to make visible a political constituency is likely to lead to unproductive generalizations, suggesting a false homogeneity, already compromised by more specialized community affiliations and ludicrous in the face of its highly constructed and expedient nature. The many available axes of mobilization and coalition have complicated identity politics tremendously. The unity of often disparate communities implied by the term "South Asian" does not exist; there is no South Asian essence. Conjured up as a generic category, it may actually obscure important differences based on individual experience, class, religion, history, sexuality, or politics. This is not to deny the emotional and instinctive attachment many feel to homeland cultures and histories but to forestall the extrapolation of these connections to narratives of reductive and unproductive generalizations within and about the group. Often it is precisely such misleading narratives that create the need for identitarian moves in the first place.

Moreover, identitarian moves, seeking to define and stake political ground, can have the pernicious effect of creating their own minoritized Others while demonizing the equally fictional, dominant Other. Naheed Islam acknowledges the currency of South Asian studies within the academy today but adds that "a new hierarchy has emerged in which certain voices have been privileged and have developed their own hegemonic power. Multiculturalism participates in this process by its uncritical approach to the positioning of subjects and groups within the new categories."[55] We have also heard distinctions made by South Asians proud to be perceived as part of the model minority: "We" aren't "lazy" like other minorities; we are able to come to the United States and not be dependent on welfare, and so on. Predictably, policymakers base their decisions on funding and entitlements on the same specious distinction, often pitting minority groups against one another.[56] Also inherent in the Manichean politics implied here is the mechanism both for registering one's own oppression (and, therefore, moral high ground) against a constructed and undifferentiated white Other, and for colluding in the existing marginalization by convincing "marginals" to continually reinscribe themselves as marginal. Needless to say, also elided within this kind of politics are issues of privilege, gender and class differences, alternative sexual preference, conflicts among minorities, internal colonialism and oppression within South Asian postcolonial states, and the very significant ideological conflicts among South Asians at home and abroad.

We raise this long catalogue of potential problems to resist hypostatizing the category of "South Asian" even as we invoke it. The extent to which our use of the term participates in its reification is a consideration we weigh against the concomitant need to address a category already in currency and the promise of its emerging as less rather than more intact through attention to the differences within it. While stressing differences, we reiterate that the investigation of "South Asian" as an aggregate category does not deny the presence of shared cultural and historical memories; it undertakes, rather, the task of sifting through various situations in which they may be less or more relevant. This task also entails an examination of the extent to which these memories are shared, and their susceptibility to being harnessed within nationalist projects. The challenges in an effort like ours are many: to represent without seeking to be representative; to suggest diversity without resorting to formulaic representations of it—trotting out the gay, the female, the underclass perspective, for instance; to raise the important questions of gender and class without denying persons with more rather than less privilege—academicians, for instance—the right to speak; to privilege polyvocality without lapsing into particularism; to retain a sense of productive difference without particularizing "South Asian" to the point of irrelevance; and to recognize the contingent and discursive nature of "South Asian" without losing the ability to use the term in meaningful discussion. Ultimately, we invite the reader to view this construction as a point of departure rather than arrival.

* * *

The contributions to this volume address the questions raised above and others relevant both to South Asian and Postcolonial Studies. These dense and overlapping concerns and the multiple critical methods employed by our contributors provide rich and textured responses but have made it difficult to group the chapters in discrete sections. Our strategy has been to develop an arrangement reflecting their genres: interviews, commentaries, studies in the media, literary criticism, and, in the concluding section, experimental critiques—pieces that not only challenge the limits of more established genres but signal the need for a continuous undoing of categories, of genre boundaries, of economic and social divisions, of lines between the academic and nonacademic.

In conducting the interviews that make up Part I, we set out to explore a similar set of questions from multiple perspectives. Although our agenda was to focus on the scope and purpose of postcolonialism and the responsibility of the South Asian critic and writer inside and outside the academy, each interview revealed further avenues for discussion. Yet notwithstanding their varied perspectives, all three respondents express a conviction that the strategy underlying postcolonial theory needs to be questioned and, further, that issues of marginality and representation deserve considerable reexamination and increasingly subtle nuancing.

The interview with Meena Alexander, "Observing Ourselves among Others," proceeds like a personal meditation as she talks about multiple displacements: her early years on three continents and her current career in New York. In pointing to the "joints between personal experience and cultural narrative," she provides an introduction to the purpose that recollection can serve in post-colonial discourse, as demonstrated in later pieces. The conception of living on and between borders as "postcolonials" begins to take shape in her vignettes of the daily life of persons not residing in the academy but living on the borders we do not always recognize: those inhabited by cab drivers, newspaper vendors, sex workers—a distinct "underclass" that one observes from within academic discourse. The postcolonial problem, as she insightfully notes, is to stitch together the different narratives in the postcolonial experience, "recognizing both the sex worker and the academic, with the seams revealed so that the labor shows." For those in the academy struggling to find a responsible and relevant politics, Alexander's ironic comment that "the academy is always belated: It always gets things after they've happened on the street," is mediated by the reminder that "belatedness can be an advantage; it can give you time to meditate or to ponder."

Particularly valuable in Gauri Viswanathan's interview, "Pedagogical Alternatives: Issues in Postcolonial Studies," are her strategies for a more reflective pedagogy within the study of literature in English. Her discussion of the role of South Asian academics in the field provides a useful historical frame for all readers; her subsequent remarks on its problems and possibilities will be of interest to teachers of postcolonial literature and theory. Bemoaning the lack of "contextual focus" in the study of non-European literature, she suggests a "postcolonial method" of reading even canonical texts as "a healthy way to counterbalance the ahistorical functions that postcolonial literature has acquired over the past years." Although Viswanathan offers less than Alexander in the way of the personal, her discussion of the experiences of South Asians—particularly as they are "Orientalized" in the United States while also participating in that process—also recalls the lives of those outside the academy. Her views on the representation of minority communities in popular media and their collusion in such representations raise at least two important questions for those within the academy: How can we resist neo-Orientalizing in our critical productions and studies? and what responsibilities do we bear to make our critiques meaningful beyond the academy? Viswanathan's advice is to interact more closely with the popular media, to turn literary criticism into "a viable tool for analyzing contemporary cultural trends in cinema, literature, the arts, and so on, that can speak to a broad audience." The strategies used by such critics as Cornel West and bell hooks are useful examples of the kinds of intervention Viswanathan recommends. The relevance of African

American theory and activism to the "postcolonial moment," acknowledged by Viswanathan and discussed in a later selection by Amritjit Singh, suggests the importance of viewing the expatriate South Asian experience within the larger frame of the experiences of other minorities in Anglo-America.

Gayatri Chakravorty Spivak's interview, revealingly titled "Transnationality and Multiculturalist Ideology," also invokes these connections. She examines the "formula of subjection" implied in the epithet "postcolonial" and juxtaposes the experience of African Americans with that of a displaced South Asian academic like herself, thus foregrounding the issues that postcolonialism grapples with while also calling into question the motives and intentions of its practitioners. Spivak makes pointed reference to the plight of South Asians who are not part of the Western academy and shows that postcolonial discourse cannot be useful if it ignores those outside the academy. The failure to examine how imperialism and neocolonialism operate in the critic's own work constitutes a denial of the complexity of the relationship between colonizer and colonized. As Spivak makes clear here and elsewhere, Postcolonial Studies must make the effort to recognize that those we would label "colonized" or "neocolonized" are also "agents of knowledge," not merely "objects of investigation."[57] Her ranging observations offer incisive comments on private and public space, responsible pedagogy, and the role of belletristic literature in making visible the limits of rational speculation.

Spivak is particularly trenchant in explicating the conditions of postcolonialism's rise within economic transnationalism and the important questions it leaves unaddressed. Especially useful is her relentless examination and critique of the underlying assumptions that we, as editors, have made in compiling this collection. Her persistent question as to why there is a need for such collections was one we found difficult but useful; her own response provides a reflective investigation of the framework of global capitalism within which multiculturalist projects have been validated: "Our claim to be included, and the claim outside, 'get off our backs,' in the context of development and transnationality, are two different kinds of claims. It seems to me that if we are going to think of ourselves as agents in this situation, then in fact we must think of ourselves as Americans—in fact, acknowledge that we have come to be Americans. And that American is hyphenated." Dispatching the dominant-marginal split of much postcolonial discourse, Spivak points out that "having thrown in our lot with a northern economy—an exploitive economy, in fact—whether we like it or not, we are . . . agents of exploitation. . . . If we are addressing an academic need, the academic's duty is to understand the big picture." Encouraging us to keep the big picture in frame, Spivak reinforces Alexander and Viswanathan's exhortation to bear in mind the responsibilities of those in the academy. All three interviews remind us of the breadth of the population included in the labels "postcolonial" and "South Asian" and the evidence for calling those labels into question. Viswanathan's adamant "Obviously" in response to the question "Should we be trying to make postcolonial theory more accessible?" underlines Alexander's portrayal of the taxi drivers of New York City to whom our locutions may be meaningless and even irrelevant, and Spivak's reference to villages in developing countries where there are not only no books or newspapers but no one who could read them if there were.

Explanations and observations on a wide range of topics evoked by the terms "postcolonial" and "South Asian" appear in Part II under the rubric "Commentaries." In registers ranging from the journalistic and personal to the more academic and theoretical, these pieces theorize and explain critical situations confronting the constituencies important to this collection: nonacademic and academic, expatriate and homeland. In "African Americans and the New Immigrants," Amritjit Singh examines conflict politics among minorities in the United States, focusing on inter-minority tensions particularly between African Americans and South Asians (a theme that reappears in Binita Mehta's essay). Singh points out that identitarian coalitions and groupings take place not simply against dominant groups but against other minorities as well: "The real perils of balkanization lie most probably not in . . . new conceptions of immigration or multiculturalism but in the giant-size failure of all Americans—white, black, or brown—to make a difference in the way racism, poverty, unemployment and underemployment, drugs, and crime continue to plague the lives of our largest community of color: African Americans." His implicit call to "South Asians" to see themselves as agents rather than victims with regard to their responsibility to other groups in Anglo-America is reminiscent of Spivak's questions, "Why should I make myself representative as a colonial subject rather than make myself representative as a female employer of female servants? Which one do you choose? Victim or agent?" Singh's call for a responsible treatment of issues of race, caste, gender, and class is rendered particularly profound by his weaving in of a personal experience: the chance racist comment by an Indian friend's granddaughter, which gives rise to an intense feeling of despair and his subsequent meditations on the future of America.

Canada and the status of its nonwhite immigrants command M. G. Vassanji's attention in "Life at the Margins: In the Thick of Multiplicity." Meditating on expatriate identity and the growing ethnic and communal tribalism around the world, Vassanji observes that "South Asian" is a term "purely geographic, artificial, and recent." As he muses on the dangers of tribalism and the fragmentation of national identities, he also draws the reader's attention to the tendency of media forces to construct and maintain the notion of marginality,[58] recalling

Viswanathan's admonition that "this is the moment, in the academy, to enter the broadcasting media." Eroding the idea of marginal identity itself, Vassanji undermines the notion of "Indian" and "South Asian" identity through glimpses of his own checkered past (which has included both India and Tanzania, Hindu and Muslim influences) and conflicted present in yet another "home." Canada, straining to find its own identity, now hopelessly complicated by those who will not allow it a univocal Anglo sense of itself, must decide whether it can yield a hospitable space for its various peoples. Vassanji speaks from his position as both a South Asian and an African, with affiliations to Canada and India as well as the Third World at large. His acceptance of multiple affiliations and his mistrust of those who espouse religious, national, and ethnic purity lead him to announce his own credo, one he seems to be urging Canada also to consider: "Life at the margins has its comforts, and in multiplicity there is creativity and acceptance."

Sohail Inayatullah's "Mullahs, Sex, and Bureaucrats: Pakistan's Confrontations with the Modern World" is another commentary on the question of identity, this time involving another national future: Inayatullah examines the multiple and conflicted possibilities that confront Pakistan at the close of the twentieth century. Observing the forces of fundamentalism pitted against incipient technological modernization and economic and cultural globalization (often identified with Western encroachment), he speculates on the implications for the position of women. Inayatullah, himself an expatriate Pakistani who adopted American citizenship to facilitate his movement across borders throughout the world, observes with a mixture of detachment and concern the fate of a country torn by conflicting impulses as it struggles to define itself.

Deepika Bahri's "Coming to Terms with the Postcolonial," in identifying and explaining the ideological premises and limitations of postcolonial discourse, attempts to project for the field a future characterized by rigorous reexamination and the courage, in the words of Santiago Colás, to "mark failures, shortcomings, distances to be traversed, and pockets of domination in thought that remain critically unexamined, let alone eradicated in their practical form."[59] Discussion unfolds to reveal the crises of signification invoked by the term "postcolonial," a dense web of contradictions and unacknowledged, perhaps even unknown, complicities. Bahri comments on the constraints of the definitional and the problems of casual or careless usage, urging ever more reflective theory and more responsible practice. "It is too early," she concludes, "to be satisfied with the condition of Postcolonial Studies and too late to dismiss their impact."

Written in the style of much postcolonial theory, Bahri's essay is somewhat different from the other pieces in this section but is equally an attempt to understand and explain a critical situation. The other selections comment on the condition of Postcolonial Studies by appraising conflicts that arise within certain geographical spaces; this one surveys a different sort of "territory" with equally nebulous and conflicted boundaries. What unites them is the similarity in approach—aggregating annotations on a series of related topics in order to study them from various angles. These are pieces driven less by one clear thesis than by the need for accumulating layered perspectives that will thicken the texture of the interpretation and exegesis. Together, through theoretical and personal explorations, they raise questions that have become central in the postcolonial project: What is home? Where is home? What is nation? What is one's identity in a state of diaspora, of postcoloniality? How is the self to be defined? And who defines it? If these questions return with disconcerting regularity for the expatriate postcolonial, they are no less significant for the postcolony struggling to define itself against a colonial past, a neocolonial present, and a future that seems threatened by the divisive forces of communalism and nationalism.

Part III, "Studies in the Media and Popular Culture," provides a lens through which to view the media's relationship to postcolonial identity, offering discussion of current popular articulations of South Asian identity in film and television. Ranita Chatterjee's analysis in"An Explosion of Difference: The Margins of Perception in *Sammy and Rosie Get Laid*" not only adds to the very limited critical work done on Hanif Kureishi and Stephen Frears's film but also explores in more general terms the place of "alterity" in producing identity. Her reading of "one of the first films to paint a manifold portrait of South Asian experiences in the diaspora" reinforces Kureishi's sense of the absurdity of identity-based categories and demonstrates that notions of black and white, Pakistani and Indian, South Asian and Anglo are consistently undermined by a powerful nexus of other factors: class, privilege, gender, and sexual orientation. Chatterjee's claim that "being nonwhite or nonmale or nonheterosexual does not exempt one from replicating yet another hierarchy of privilege" is a potent admonition to those who wish to romanticize the other and view him or her as spectacle for metropolitan consumption, instead of allowing that other a measure of complexity and contradiction.

Binita Mehta's "Emigrants Twice Displaced: Race, Color, and Identity in Mira Nair's *Mississippi Masala*" refers back both to Chatterjee's sensitive treatment of the topic of representation and to Singh's contentions with regard to interminority relations in Anglo-America. Within a framework of recent disputes among minority groups in the United States, Mehta's discussion emphasizes that "contemporary debates on race and color . . . must necessarily include relations between nonwhite minorities." Against useful background information on Indo-black relations in Uganda, Mehta examines *Mississippi Masala*'s portrayal of minority cultures in interaction and conflict in Greenwood, Mississippi. One unduly severe critique of the film, Mehta suggests, fails to account for Nair's often successful attempts to present a "complex, nuanced" treatment of the vexed topics of representation, identity, and displacement. While recognizing that the film is ultimately a limited effort to tackle highly complex and conflicted race relations in the United States, Mehta reminds us of the useful range of issues addressed by Nair. In terms reminiscent of Alexander, Vassanji, and Singh, her analysis resurrects the perennial predicaments of the diasporic postcolonial: What constitutes identity for the doubly, multiply displaced migrant? How long before the migrant's ties to "home" have receded beyond recuperation? And how long before the migrant learns that a new "home" must be imagined where the assumption of compelling responsibilities may not be deferred?

Sanjoy Majumder moves to a more culturally influential piece within India, the prime-time dramatization of the *Mahabharata* as shown on Indian television. From Mehta's and Chatterjee's focus on Anglo-America, Majumder's shift of venue reveals that questions of representation and identity are equally troubled in the postcolony. In "From Ritual Drama to National Prime Time: *Mahabharata*, India's Televisual Obsession," he documents the power of the media, highlighting the impact that technology can have on culture by its use of a narrow Hindu religious identity to create a national one. Emphasizing the text's "tremendous ties to popular memories and personal histories," Majumder suggests that its study as a "multivalent text" can usefully counter its appropriation by nationalist and hegemonic forces through televisualization. The cultural critic, he insists, must carefully consider "the discourses of class, caste, and religion which invariably intersect the site of cultural presentation." Acknowledging that a popular text like the *Mahabharata* "can be appropriated for both hegemonic and subversive purposes," he suggests an analytic method through which nation and national culture emerge less as "a way of life" than as "ways of struggle."

Mahasveta Barua's "Television, Politics, and the Epic Heroine: Case Study, Sita" reiterates the power of telecommunications technology. Barua shows how a traditionally oral history—the *Ramayana*—made into a popular cultural event can result in major political and social changes, given a television serial's ability to transform characters into cultural artifacts. In particular, this analysis reveals that the confluence of narratives of nation and woman continues to create oppressive positions for Indian women in the newest technologies of representation: Sita, the sacrificial heroine of the *Ramayana*, Barua suggests, has been cast in symbolic rather than real forms to serve male rather than female history. In contemporary terms, the idealistic representation of Sita reinforces the power of the patriarchal state. Barua ends by asserting that "it is not she but her representation in Indian literary, oral, and now audiovisual and political tradition that has been counterproductive to the women's movement and the achievements of contemporary Indian women. If Sita were recast as woman, perhaps the ideal Indian woman and the modern one would not need to be at such odds."

In this set of studies the issues of identity and representation deemed so crucial to postcolonials in exile and diaspora are revealed as equally important within originary postcolonial societies and nations, even though the contexts and variables differ widely. Clearly, identity and culture are intimately tied to our cultural productions—both as we produce them and as they produce us. Since literature has always played an integral part in this relationship, Part IV, "Literary Criticism," features critiques of many major authors of South Asian origin who write about the postcolonial, including Salman Rushdie, Anita Desai, Bharati Mukherjee, Mahasveta Devi, Bapsi Sidhwa, Khushwant Singh, and Sara Suleri. These contributions use the works of such authors to unveil and disrupt postcolonial assumptions and engage in the issues relevant to a study of "new" literatures. They show how major authors of South Asian origin represent themselves and how those representations are fielded by other South Asians.

Sukeshi Kamra's "Replacing the Colonial Gaze: Gender as Strategy in Salman Rushdie's Fiction" brings feminist concerns into dialogue with postcolonial work while also challenging prevailing Rushdie criticism. Again, we are pulled back to the discussion of "Orientalizing" broached by Viswanathan and others as Kamra asks Rushdie's text to justify its Orientalist practice: "Good intentions and isolated feminist passages aside, Rushdie's fiction is problematically riddled with familiar patriarchal modes of containment such as fetishism, signaling more clearly than ever the absence of the very subject the texts are largely about. . . . One might very well ask . . . 'Is there a female in these texts?' " If colonial narratives that Orientalized both the subject nation and its women can be charged with giving women no speaking position, and if Rushdie appropriates the feminine, "already a patriarchal construct, . . . to express the male postcolonial writer's subjectivity," Kamra asks, "how are Rushdie's texts any different from the scores of texts that violated both nation/Orient and Oriental female?"

Samir Dayal in "Style Is (Not) the Woman: Sara Suleri's Meatless Days" also highlights issues of gender. Even as he commends Suleri's work as suggestive of alternatives for Third World writing that resist assimilation into reductive categories, Dayal notes that her (dis)articulation of the category of Third World woman, her claim that "there are no women in the third world," could well carry the danger of yet another "flaccid negativity, and once more a silencing of the Third World subject/woman." If her style is remarkable, her antiessentialism is significant for its figuration of (female) subjectivity as nothing more than a style of being. Dayal's essay traces Suleri's complex and quirky experiment in autobiography in light of current theoretical approaches, noting some of the questions raised by Suleri's method but also emphasizing its importance as an example of a postcolonial discourse that troubles conceptualizations of nation, race, gender, class, and everyday life in the so-called Third World. Perhaps most enlightening is Dayal's questioning of the category of Suleri's work and, by suggestion, other postcolonial texts. If the work is interesting for its highly personalized and extremely individualistic (even idiosyncratic) representation of subcontinental diasporic subjectivity, in departing from both Western feminist models of antiessentialism and received notions of Third World representations of women grounded in their quotidian materiality, *Meatless Days* also offers an exemplary instance of the possibilities for subcontinental diaspora writing.

Dayal brings attention to the privileged position occupied by Suleri while arguing that her work ignores this vital part of postcoloniality: "Her perspective cannot be unproblematically assimilated to a neatly defined Third World woman's minority perspective, at least not without acknowledging the privileges accruing to such a diasporic intellectual," he notes, recalling Spivak's point that women who have the luxury of problematizing the "questioning subject" are in "privileged positions in the geopolis."[60] Effectively destabilizing the categories of "postcolonial," "marginal," and "Third World (woman)," Dayal reminds us that both those who write from the position of the postcolonial and those who critique them from postcolonial perspectives often occupy decidedly privileged positions within the academy.

Pushpa Naidu Parekh's "Redefining the Postcolonial Female Self: Women in Anita Desai's *Clear Light of Day*" develops yet another perspective on the formulation of the category "Third World women." Desai's novel, in Parekh's reading, serves to complicate a Western understanding of these women as a homogeneously marginalized group. Contending that "class and caste intersections operate as significant constitutive forces in colonial and postcolonial representations of Indian women," Parekh illustrates that the novel's class-privileged heroines, Bim and Tara, "inhabit a space where privilege and agency for educated, upper middle-class women is mounted on the silence and erasure of poorer and often socially ostracized women. . . . Within a society constrained by caste, class, and patriarchy, operating on the principles of colonial institutions, the presence of some women implies the absence of many others."

The last two essays in this section move us into an area of particular interest in postcolonial discourse: the question of history. Since colonial and neocolonial narratives might be said to install the colonized as object rather than maker of history, postcolonial preoccupation with remaking and reinterpreting history surfaces in theory and in literature as well as in nationalist narratives in the political life of the postcolony. Indrani Mitra's "Luminous Brahmin Children Must Be Saved: Imperialist Ideologies, 'Postcolonial' Histories in Bharati Mukerjee's *The Tiger's Daughter*" focuses on one of the most popular and most provocative South Asian writers. Mitra moves beyond the available scholarship on Mukherjee to reevaluate her place in the growing postcolonial canon. The essay is especially useful because it critiques its own critical framework by calling into question the use of its terminology, mainly that of postcolonial theory. Framed by these larger postcolonial issues, Mitra's piece examines the formulation of East-West relations "encoded in the novelistic representation of one definitive moment in the history of contemporary India, the Naxalbari uprising of the 1970s." Critical of Mukherjee's participation in an Orientalist view of the homeland, Mitra notes with surprise both her stature in the postcolonial canon and the absence from that canon of politically activist and resistive South Asian and postcolonial literature: "Compare the paucity of critical interest in a Premchand or an Ismat Chugtai or a Manik Bandyopadhyay (to name just a few Indian writers available in translation) to the spurt of scholarly papers generated annually on . . . 'the metropolitan celebrities.'" Mitra urges a scrupulous examination of those who like Mukherjee trifle with the complications of Indian history, and urgently recommends a rigorous reconsideration of the purpose of Postcolonial Studies before "postcolonial," like "Third World," becomes "another 'shapeless sack into which one could simply dump peoples, classes, races, civilizations and continents so that they might more easily disappear.'"[61]

Huma Ibrahim's "The Troubled Past: Literature of Severing and the Viewer/Viewed Dialectic" examines the literary treatment of another historical event—the partition between Pakistan and India in August 1947. Although discussions on the violence of colonialism abound in postcolonial discourse, this violent moment in postcolonial history continues to confound those who suffered its most horrific excesses. The varying perspectives from the Hindu and Muslim sides, Ibrahim argues, often become ways of evading and blaming instead of taking responsibility. She finds the effects of partition not only portrayed within the literature she discusses but evident in the ways the authors approach the subject because of their own response to the event. Arguing that a certain squeamishness and sense of shame have prevented any real dialogue between those who experienced it, Ibrahim illustrates the inability of various authors to confront its brutality squarely; they are forced to retain the perspective of detached observers. Echoing Spivak's concern that "the generation with the memory will never be able to write the 'history' of partition," Ibrahim concludes that the violence of that moment, with its devastating implications for the violence of the present moment, thus remains inadequately theorized and ultimately unnegotiated.

Finally, Part V, "Experimental Critiques," challenges traditional notions of literary and theoretical criticism. Each piece displaces in a different way our sense of the borders usually found between the theoretical and the personal. Amitava Kumar, in "Jane Austen in Meerut, India," combines a critical essay with a short story. While ostensibly looking at the work of Upamanyu Chatterjee in conjunction with that of Mahasveta Devi, Kumar locates himself within the cultural narratives these works invoke. Even as he commends Chatterjee's *English, August* for its newness and satirical wit, Kumar notes with concern the foreclosure of paths of resistance against multiple oppressions: Although it lampoons the elitism and stale officialese of the bureaucratic upper class, in its celebration of the carnivalesque, the novel is unable to move beyond its consistent portrayal of the poor as sullen and of women as silent. Kumar locates an alternative articulation of social realities and conflict in the journalism of the well-known playwright and novelist Mahasveta Devi. Her public writing is also pitted against the arrogant officialdom of the ruling class, but her accounts provide a more powerful counternarrative, linking "tales of woe and exploitation on the one hand" to "the pulse of resistance mounting on the other." Devi's accounts, gleaned from travel and work among tribal men and women, who also appear in Chatterjee's *English, August*, provide a radically different possibility for building critical solidarities and effecting change. As a way of repeating that impulse but by returning to the fictive, this essay extends into the short story "The Monkey's Suicide," which also offers a tribute to those who don't find a worthy place in Chatterjee's universe: "writers, critics, mothers, sisters, and other activists." Linking the female characters in the story with other agents of resistance, the story makes "overt what has remained implicit throughout: the process of finding in the politics of place (in Ara, a postcolonial, post-independence site of peasant resistance and class war in which women have played no small role) the possibility not only of sharing struggles but also of overturning extant divisions between private and public, the home and the world, the party and the family."

Each of the two selections that follow might be described in Nancy Miller's terms as "personal criticism," or "an explicitly autobiographical performance within the act of criticism."[62] Shantanu DuttaAhmed's "Border Crossings: Retrieval and Erasure of the Self as Other," positioning the author as a gay, South Asian academic within the dominant culture, gives voice to the belief that the personal is an integral part of a discussion of marginality and difference and that personal disclosure can work well within a theoretical framework. It attempts to implicate the personal in a politicized criticism and to define an otherness that resides within the self, both disrupting and forming that self's possibility. Combining gestures of retrieval—acts of memory—with a willed, strategic erasure of the self, DuttaAhmed proceeds to discuss the dynamics of cultural visibility versus invisibility. His timely examination of the "real" border crossing between California and Mexico brings the issue of marginality out of the South Asian framework and into the more universal hegemonic structures underlying both real and figurative borders; it also attempts to reveal the imagined threats, perceived by the dominant culture, which inscribe border realities. By skillfully weaving the personal into a theoretical discussion, Dutta-Ahmed reminds us that "it is in fact disrupted selves, multiple selves that the border posits rather than the singular, identifiable Other who is then configured in opposition to the Western subject."

Using journal entries and a deliberately personalized style, Uma Parameswaran, in "I See the Glass as Half Full," challenges "the depersonalized voice of authority institutionally favored by academia." Linking her badminton injury with a discussion of the threat of neocolonialist appropriations of postcolonial discourse, Parameswaran warns that "while acquiring the tools of scholarly discourse, we just might have let our cultural tendons atrophy and may be strutting on ankle supports fashioned by the tools." As she examines a series of crucial issues—identity, (mis)representation, hybridity, cultural (mis)appropriation—Parameswaran's ability to see the glass as half full is not compromised but complemented by a recognition that the glass is also half-empty: "We have to live," she notes, "in a plane of many truths." It is a politics of victimhood and helplessness that valorizes the "half-empty glass," the jargon often taking over to "trivialize both real victimization and real heroism." Allowing that scholars must have the "right to choose their glasses," Parameswaran herself opts to "step in with [her] half-full glass" when such jargon limits her students' ability to respond more thoughtfully to Indian English literature. If the glass is half empty, the response must be "to contribute toward filling it to the top." Her own project is no less than to "bring the Ganga to the Assiniboine." The racism that thwarts this attempt, notwithstanding, Parameswaran insists that "it is an exciting time to be in Canada, where we are shaping a new national culture that will be a composite of many heritage cultures, not the least of which will be the aboriginal culture that is experiencing a renaissance." Despite experiences that leave her troubled and despondent, she resolves to reject the pessimism inherent in reinforcing lines between insider and outsider: "So what do we do? Erase all lines, those phallic symbols of patriarchal oppression? Better," she suggests, "bend them into circles." Parameswaran's critique of unimaginative and narrow politics in the academy ultimately issues a powerful challenge to her audience to envision a more liberating future of enablement and hope.

The concluding section of this volume, then, presents the interaction of the personal "I," the collective "we," and the world beyond. The critiques offered by Kumar, DuttaAhmed, and Parameswaran are integrally connected to the narrative forms of their pieces. Refusing the split between the personal and the political, each chooses to write the text of personal engagement into the usually impersonal narratives of theory and critique. If these final selections manage to offer a performative enactment of an aesthetics and a politics that promulgate a breakdown of crude dichotomies, they will have complemented the other pieces in this volume in going some way toward providing a more inflected and subtle understanding of the issues under scrutiny.

NOTES

1. We have used the term "Anglo-America" as a collective designation for the United States and Canada. Elsewhere in the collection, some contributors use the term "North America" in its popular sense (see Uma Parameswaran's response to our usage). *The Concise Columbia Encyclopedia* (New York: Columbia University Press, 1991) defines "North America" as "third largest continent, . . . usually considered to include all the lands and adjacent islands in the Western Hemisphere located N of the Isthmus of Panama (which connects it with South America)". It goes on to list "the countries of the continent," including "the U.S. and Canada, known as Anglo-America." If "Anglo-America" should also invoke and include the "English" (as in "of England") context, perhaps that slippage is not entirely unintentional, since for the postcolonial all these spaces function synecdochically to suggest the Center, the metropole, and the West.

2. See the bibliography contributed by Rosane Rocher to *SAGAR: South Asia Graduate Research Journal* 2.1 (1995): 64–95. Rocher's conflation of "Indian" with "South Asian," pointing to the preponderance of "Indian" within the construct, is fairly common in South Asian discourse but should not be taken to imply an exclusion of other constituencies. For a discussion of the historic reasons for the relative unimportance of South Asians in "Asian" America, see Deepika Bahri, "With Kaleidoscope Eyes: The Potential (Dangers) of Identitarian Coalitions," in a forthcoming collection titled *Closing the Gap: South Asians in Asian America*. On the lack of attention to Indian and South Asian Americans, see also P. K. Nandi, "The World of an Invisible Minority: Pakistanis in America," *California Sociologists* 3 (1980): 143–65.

3. Jane Singh, foreword to *Our Feet Walk the Sky: Women of the South Asian Diaspora*, ed. Women of South Asian Descent Collective (San Francisco: Aunt Lute Books, 1993), vii.

4. Recognizing a growing consciousness among and about South Asians, Rocher offers her bibliography of South Asian American Studies "as a testimony to the coming of age of South Asian American Studies and as an incentive for further development" (64).

5. For a corresponding discussion on "who is the postcolonial?"—the rise of postcolonial studies and the questions that confront postcolonial critics—see Deepika Bahri's "Coming to Terms with the 'Postcolonial'" (Chapter 8 in this volume).

6. Carol A. Breckenridge and Peter van der Veer, eds., *Orientalism and the Postcolonial Predicament: Perspectives on South Asia* (Philadelphia: University of Pennsylvania Press, 1993), vii–viii.

7. See, e.g., the breadth of coverage in a compilation such as *Contact between Cultures: South Asia*, ed. K. I. Koppendrayer, vol. 2 (Lewiston, N.Y.: Edwin Mellen, 1992).

8. Bureau of the Census, *1990 Census of Population: General Population Characteristics, United States* (Washington, D.C., 1992); Statistics Canada, *Census of Canada*, 1986 and *Census of Canada*, 1991. See also Manju Sheth, "Asian Indian Americans," in *Asian Americans: Contemporary Trends and Issues*, ed. Pyong Gap Min (Thousand Oaks, Calif.: Sage, 1995), 169–98; Ronald D'Costa, "Socio-Demographic Characteristics of the Population of South Asian Origins in Canada," in *Ethnicity, Identity, Migration: The South Asian Context*, ed. Milton Israel and N. K. Wagle (Toronto: University of Toronto, Centre for South Asian Studies, 1993).

9. See "South Asians in North America," in *South Asians in North America: An Annotated and Selected Bibliography*, ed. Jane Singh et al., Occasional Paper Series 14 (Berkeley, Calif.: Center for South and Southeast Asia Studies, 1988), 5–14.

10. Surinder M. Bhardwaj and Madhusudana Rao, "Asian Indians in the United States: A Geographical Appraisal," in *South Asians Overseas: Migration and Ethnicity*, ed. Colin Clarke, Ceri Peach, and Steven Vertovec (Cambridge: Cambridge University Press, 1990), 197. References to the importation of Indian servants to New England as early as in the late eighteenth century have not been confirmed in the sources we were able to find.

11. Ronald Takaki, *Strangers from a Different Shore: A History of Asian Americans* (New York: Penguin, 1989), 62, 65.

12. Gary R. Hess, "The Forgotten Asian Americans: The East Indian Community in the United States," in *The Asian American: The Historical Experience*, ed. Norris Hundley Jr. (Santa Barbara, Calif.: Clio, 1976), 78; "South Asians in North America," 11.

13. See Sheth, "Asian Indian Americans,"173.

14. "South Asians in North America," 10; Sheth, "Asian Indian Americans," 171. See also Takaki, *Strangers*.

15. Amarpal K. Dhaliwal, "Gender at Work: the Renegotiation of Middle-class Womanhood in a South Asian-Owned Business," in *Reviewing Asian America: Locating Diversity*, ed. Wendy L. Ng, Soo-Young Chin, James S. Moy, and Gary Y. Okihiro (Pullman: Washington State University Press, 1995), 84 n 5.

16. Sheth, "Asian Indian Americans," 169, 174.

17. "South Asians in North America," 11.

18. See Hugh Johnston, "Patterns of Sikh Migration to Canada, 1900–1960," in *Sikh History and Religion in the Twentieth Century*, ed. Joseph T. O'Connell, Milton Israel, and Willard G. Oxtoby, with visiting editors W. H. McLeod and J. S. Grewal (Toronto: University of Toronto, Centre for South Asian Studies, 1988), 296–313.

19. Such organizations were vital in influencing the passage of the Luce-Celler bill in 1946, which allowed citizenship to people of South Asian descent and permitted family reunification; because of the reestablishment of quotas, however, the bill did not allow unlimited immigration. See Sheth, "Asian Indian Americans" and "South Asians in North America."

20. "South Asians in North America," 9–10. See also Arthur M. Schlesinger Jr., *The Disunity of America: Reflections on a Multicultural Society* (New York: Norton, 1992).

21. For excellent histories of Asian American activism, see Takaki, *Strangers*; *The State of Asian America: Activism and Resistance in the 1990s*, ed. Karen Aguilar–San Juan (Boston: South End Press, 1994); Sucheng Chan, *Asian Americans: An Interpretive History* (Boston: Twayne, 1991); and William Wei, *The Asian American Movement* (Philadelphia: Temple University Press, 1993).

22. "South Asians in North America," 10.

23. Ibid., 11. For more details, see Bhardwaj and Rao, "Asian Indians in the United States."

24. Sheth, "Asian Indian Americans," 176. See also Arthur W. Helweg and Usha M. Helweg, *The Immigrant Success Story: East Indians* (Philadelphia: University of Pennsylvania Press, 1990); and Jayjia Hsia, *Asian Americans in Higher Education and at Work* (Hillsdale, N.J.: Erlbaum, 1988).

25. Rocher, "Bibliography," 64.

26. M. G. Vassanji explains its appearance in Canada thus: "In response to the marginalization and racism suffered by the immigrants, and partly also because of the presence of strongly identified groups such as the 'Blacks' and 'Natives' and the racial politics and political advantages perceived for them, in Canada there have been attempts to formulate an entity called 'South Asian'" (Chapter 6, this volume).

27. Naheed Islam, "In the Belly of the Multicultural Beast I Am Named South Asian," in Women of South Asian Descent Collective, *Our Feet Walk the Sky*, 243.

28. "Charges Dropped: DA's Office Backs Down under Community Pressure," *India Currents* 9.10 (1995): 19.

29. According to *Peterson's Guide to Graduate Programs in the Humanities, Arts and Social Sciences*, 1995 ed., and *Peterson's Guide to 4-Year Colleges*, 1995 ed., a total of twenty-one institutions in the two countries offer specializations in the field of South Asian studies.

30. Arif Dirlik, "The Postcolonial Aura: Third World Criticism in the Age of Global Capitalism," *Critical Inquiry* 20 (Winter 1994): 328–56; Ella Shokat, "Notes on the Post-Colonial," *Social Text* 31–32 (1992): 102.

31. Arjun Appadurai, "Disjuncture and Difference in the Global Cultural Economy," in *Colonial Discourse and Post-Colonial Theory: A Reader*, ed. Patrick Williams and Laura Chrisman (New York: Columbia University Press, 1994), 324–39.

32. Consider, e.g., Homi Bhabha's contention that "the postcolonial perspective resists the attempt at holistic forms of social explanation. It forces a recognition of the more complex cultural and political boundaries that exist on the cusp of these often opposes realms" (*The Location of Culture* [London: Routledge, 1994], 173). Or Stephen Slemon's observation that the concept of the "post-colonial" is most useful "when it locates a specifically anti- or post-colonial discursive purchase in culture, one which begins in the moment that the colonising power inscribes itself onto the body and space of its Others and which continues as an often occluded tradition into the modern theatre of neo-colonialist international relations" ("Modernism's Last Post," *Ariel: A Review of International English Literature* 20.4 (1989): 6).

33. Michael Adas, "Scientific Standards and Colonial Education in British India and French Senegal," in *Science, Medicine, and Cultural Imperialism*, ed. Teresa Meade and Mark Walker (New York: St. Martin's, 1991), 7.

34. Graham Huggan, "The Postcolonial Exotic: Salman Rushdie and the Booker of Bookers," *Transition: An International Review* 64 (1994): 26. Consider Huggan's observation (24) that "the Booker McConnell Co. has evolved into a postcolonial patron; through its sponsorship it celebrates the hybrid status of an increasingly global culture."

35. In speculating on the unprecedented success of two first novels by Canadian "ethnic authors," Smaro Kamboureli suggests that these novels "exemplify the expectations multiculturalism has generated from ethnic writing" by "importing otherness into Canadian literature as otherness," ensuring that it is uncontaminated by Canadianness, and thus

retaining the foreign ("Of Black Angels and Melancholy Lovers: Ethnicity and Writing in Canada," in *Us/Them: Translation, Transcription, and Identity in Post-Colonial Literary Cultures*, ed. Gordon Collier [Amsterdam: Rodopi, 1992], 55). Diana Brydon notes that "the post-colonial literatures represent that genuine difference which an imperialist culture fears. The establishment must therefore ensure that post-colonial self-representations continue to be ignored, while representations of them are reconstructed within the academy as safe alternatives to their real threat" ("Commonwealth or Common Poverty? The New Literatures in English and the New Discourse of Marginality," *Kunapipi: Special Issue on Post-Colonial Criticism* 11.1 [1989]: 12).

At the same time, note that the South Asian immigrant experience is also beginning to be seen as concrete presence rather than abstract "foreignness": "The South Asian story is slowly finding a place in public school textbooks" ("South Asians in North America," 11).

36. By virtue of the empire's early investment in the education and training of Indians, perhaps it is felt that the educated Indians found in Western universities bear out Thomas Macaulay's prediction that government support for English education would create "a class of persons, Indian in blood and colour, but English [and by extension, Western] in taste, in opinions, in morals and intellect" (quoted in Adas, "Scientific Standards," 13).

37. Gayatri Chakravorty Spivak, "Teaching for the Times," *Journal of the Midwest Modern Language Association* 25.1 (1992): 7.

38. Benjamin Lee, "Critical Internationalism," *Public Culture: Society for Transnational Cultural Studies* 7.3 (1995): 579–80.

39. Caren Kaplan, "A World without Boundaries: The Body Shop's Trans/National Geographics," *Social Text* 43 (Fall 1995): 45.

40. Note Rey Chow's observation: "The production of the native is part of the production of our postcolonial modernity" (*Writing Diaspora: Tactics of Intervention in Contemporary Cultural Studies* [Bloomington: Indiana University Press, 1993], 30).

41. Roger Rouse, "Thinking through Transnationalism: Notes on the Cultural Politics of Class Relations in the Contemporary United States," *Public Culture: Society for Transnational Cultural Studies* 7.2 (1995): 384.

42. Jonathan Rutherford, cited in Kaplan, "A World without Boundaries," 50. "In a world where nation-state power is eroded yet intact," as our diasporic communities with their multiple loyalties and displacements suggest, Kaplan warns that "the myth of a 'world without boundaries' leaves our material differences intact and even exacerbates the assymetries of power that stratify our lived experiences" (60).

43. Rouse, "Thinking through Transnationalism," 385.

44. Stephen Slemon and Helen Tiffin, "Introduction," *Kunapipi: Special Issue on Post-Colonial Criticism* 11.1 (1989): ix–xxiii. See also comments in Brydon, "Commonwealth or Common Poverty?" 1, on the persistently marginal status of postcolonial productions that are appropriated by "a new form of cultural imperialism."

45. Critics—Arjun Appadurai, Homi Bhabha, R. Radhakrishnan, and Gayatri Chakravorty Spivak, among others—have raised many of the central issues in the discourse of identity and ethnicity.

46. Rouse, "Thinking through Transnationalism," 367–68.

47. Rashmi Sharma, "Teaching India: Bureaucracy Limits Access to Better Teaching Materials on India," *India Currents* 9.6 (1995): 7.

48. Francis C. Hardwick and Philip Moir, *From Beyond the Western Horizon: Canadians from the Sub-Continent of India*, Canadian Culture Series 4 (Vancouver: Tantalus Research, 1974); Leona B. Bagai, *The East Indians and the Pakistanis in America* (Minneapolis: Lerner, 1972).

49. See "Multimedia Panchatantra" in the software review section of *India Currents* 9.4 (1995): C70; "Software Comes of Age: Multimedia Titles Tackle Indian Subjects" (review of *Gyana: Multimedia Introduction to India* and *Akshar Animations: Multimedia Software for Teaching the Hindi Alphabet*) *India Currents* 8.12 (1995): 22; Pran Kurup, "Job Hunting on the Internet," *India Currents* 9.3 (1995): 22; the list of bulletin boards in Amit S. Rai, "India On-line: Electronic Bulletin Boards and the Construction of a Diasporic Hindu Identity," *Diaspora* 4.1 (1995): 31–57; Rajiv Kumar, "Linking Indians Worldwide," *India Currents* 9.3 (1995): 23.

50. Purnima Mankekar, "Reflections on Diasporic Identities: A Prolegomenon to an Analysis of Political Bifocality," *Diaspora* 3.3 (1994): 350, 365.

51. Quoted in Noel Jacob Kent, "When Multiethnic Societies Work: Notes on an Ethnic Relations Model in Balance," in *New Visions in Asian American Studies: Diversity, Community, Power,* ed. Franklin Ng, Judy Yung, Stephen S. Fugita, and Elaine H. Kim (Pullman: Washington State University Press, 1994), 135.

52. Peter van der Veer, ed., introduction to *Nation and Migration: The Politics of Space in the South Asian Diaspora* (Philadelphia: University of Pennsylvania Press, 1995), 7.

53. Arjun Appadurai, "Patriotism and Its Futures," *Public Culture* 5.3 (1993): 424.

54. Calvin Reid, "Caught in Flux: Transatlantic Aesthetics in the Museum," *Transition: An International Review* 5.1 (1995): 133.

55. Islam, "In the Belly of the Multicultural Beast," 242.

56. Neil Gotanda suggests that "the term 'model minority' . . . includes references to three distinct and different levels of racial status—a three-tier racial stratification. At the top, there is the White majority. In the middle are the Asian Americans, role models for another racial group in need of exemplars for their own conduct. At the bottom are African Americans, who are directed to emulate Asian Americans with the goal of someday achieving a higher racial status" ("Reproducing the Model Minority Stereotype: Judge Joyce Karlin's Sentencing Colloquy in *People v. Soon Ja Du,*" in Ng, Chin, Moy, and Okihiro, *Reviewing Asian America*, 95). See also Amritjit Singh's "African Americans and the New Immigrants" (Chapter 5 in this volume).

57. Gayatri Chakravorty Spirak, "Feminism in Decolonization," *Differences: A Journal of Feminist Cultural Studies* 3.3 (1991): 171.

58. Content analyses of the CBC, *Toronto Sun*, and *Globe and Mail* reveal a large number of editorials and columns that are prejudiced and racist, according to Effie Ginzberg, "Power without Responsibility: The Press We Don't Deserve. A Content Analysis of the *Toronto Sun,*" *Currents* 2 (1986): 1–5.

59. Santiago Colás, "Of Creole Symptoms, Cuban Fantasies, and Other Latin American Postcolonial Ideologies," *PMLA* 110.3 (1995): 392.

60. Gayatri Chakravorty Spivak, "Strategy, Identity, Writing," *Journal of Politics* 18 (1986–87), rpt. in Spivak, *The Post-Colonial Critic: Interviews, Strategies, Dialogues*, ed. Sarah Harasym (New York: Routledge, 1990), 42.

61. Regis Debray, quoted in Barbara Harlow, *Resistance Literature* (London: Methuen, 1987), 6.

62. Nancy Miller, *Getting Personal: Feminist Occasions and Other Autobiographical Acts* (New York: Routledge, 1991), 1.

PART I

INTERVIEWS

CHAPTER 2

Observing Ourselves among Others

Interview with Meena Alexander

Deepika Bahri and Mary Vasudeva

This interview was conducted at Meena Alexander's home in New York City on 12 November 1993. Settled in front of the picture window in her apartment, we began our discussion over chai (tea) and cookies. We sat on the edge of a covered futon (no American sofa or La-Z-Boy here), surrounded by Wordsworth, Anita Desai, Günter Grass, works by Alexander herself, and other books too numerous to count. We felt for a moment as if we had stumbled into a library in a home in Delhi, but the view from a window overlooking the Hudson River provided a reminder that we were, in fact, in a flat in New York City. The only interruptions were our frequent requests for more tea and Alexander's repeated returns to the kitchen to refill her glass with seltzer water. The two hours passed quickly and comfortably.

DB: The book we are compiling is an exercise in observing ourselves and attempting to theorize what we see, which also seems to be the business of postcolonialism. Since this term occasions endless debate, however, could we talk about working toward a postcolonial theory of sorts?

MA: Let me puzzle through this by relating a "New York experience." Picture Forty-Second Street—I'm walking around, looking into shops and getting some curious glances, and I see a piece of site-specific art, say, by Karen Finley or Jane Dickson, and right next to it there's a sex shop where they're renting adult videos for a quarter, which in this age of inflation is quite something. Then they have peep shows. But the point is that on one hand there is this whole issue of buying and selling desire, right next to an "art" object, and on the other hand there is the business of having South Asian men working in that shop—it's one of the few jobs that easily available to them, like selling newspapers in the subway, or driving cabs. In fact, South Asians are involved in some of the most dangerous jobs in the city. Here is where the postcolonial dilemma comes in.

MV: So, the conflation of art, buying desire, and South Asian "sellers" draws you in but also asks you to position yourself as an observer?

MA: Yes. It relates to what you were saying about positioning yourself as an observer and being drawn in, because you need to be drawn in in order to play the postcolonial; I think there's always that edge of unsettlement in doing that. I think it should make us very wary of overarching theories. To that extent the kinds of insights we develop should be a stitching together of multiple pieces, recognizing both the sex worker and the academic, with the seams revealed so that the labor shows. It reminds me of that wonderful line in Yeats's "Adam's Curse." He says, "A line will take us hours maybe; / Yet if it does not seem a moment's thought, / Our stitching and unstitching has been naught." I think that when one works on a piece of art, it should be a fine woven piece so the seams don't show. But in the kinds of meaning-making that postcolonial analysis attempts, the seams have to show very, very deliberately if it is to make any sense.

DB: You were saying we have to do away with the notion of suturing things together so the seams don't show, which is the problem we're having with this whole project. How do we give the project the unity that a compilation demands while also exposing the absolutely necessary seams between pieces? The observer position, which is ours, whether we like it or not, needs to be acknowledged because ultimately our entire project is a version of auto-voyeurism. I realize that.

MA: What do you mean by auto-voyeurism?

DB: It's looking at yourself in the mirror, projecting yourself in a particular way, and studying the image that's reflected.

MA: And looking at how we fit in into what might be going on. I think this auto-voyeurism you are talking about is a very American thing. So is the whole issue of autobiography, which you also have to place in the context of contemporary American culture. It is a very American thing to try to define one's self and to think that in the defining there would be a germ of some kind of essential meaning. This is not the Indian way, if there is an Indian way. There are multiple Indian ways, so I think I shouldn't posit the Indian as opposed to the American. But I think this focus on the self is very peculiar to the culture of North America, and generally, so is the desire to create "autobiography." A constant attempt to vivify what one thinks of as identity by redefining one's self is a very American project. The interest in postcoloniality and what you're saying about looking at one's self is also part of the current wave of the culture. I see that as part of what afflicts us at the end of the century.

DB: This desire to look at ourselves, this desire for the East, is produced by Western academic discourse. This is the hoped-for postcolonial moment, right? We have been sanctioned by the academy.

MA: It seems appropriate at a time when the world is splintering into ethnicities. Look at the erstwhile Soviet Union, the former Yugoslavia.

MV: Your discussion about the genre of autobiography is very interesting. In the first volume of *Women Writing in India*, there is mention of one woman who did write an autobiography, and the editors discuss how unusual it was to find an autobiographical selection by a South Asian woman, particularly before the nineteenth century.[1]

MA: Yes, quite. The first autobiography in Bengali was by a woman, and there's also a lot of material in Marathi. There are actually a number of women's autobiographies in Marathi, and others have been discovered in Malayalam. But it is by no means a very common genre for Indian women.

MV: How did you feel about writing in the autobiographical mode in creating *Fault Lines*?[2]

DB: Was self-disclosure difficult for you?

MA: I think it was a very curious thing. I remember a number of years ago, in 1987, I was a UGC [University Grants Commission] visiting professor in Kerala, and someone published an interview with me in *Kala Gomati*, which is a Malayalam magazine that is sold on newsstands and also publishes stories about the lives of film stars, that sort of thing. I was actually in New York when it came out, and my mother called me and said, "Everyone's read it, including the woman who's cutting the grass outside next to the mango tree." I can't read Malayalam, so I asked my mother, "What does it say?" And she said, "It's not for you to know."

Now this is very interesting to me because my mother's quite traditional, although she's gone to college and so on. In what she said there was a resolute sense that if you're a woman, you should not be committed to self-disclosure because that's not appropriate. Kamala Das, whom I'm very fond of, wrote her autobiography [*My Story*] and got into a lot of trouble. And I remember her warning me. I suspect that if I had lived in India I would never have written a book like *Fault Lines*. And I have tried to walk a delicate line between self-disclosure and self-knowledge. Not that I have any clear answers. The whole issue of what it means to speak out is occasioned, I think, by the pressure of living in America, of doing my version of what you said you were doing with your project—looking at myself and how I fit in relation to others. Particularly as a writer. I think that for a number of years the fact that I had moved so much in my life was a source of difficulty for me, because I felt that for a writer it's terribly important to be in one dear, well-rooted place. I think my memoir was born in my coming to New York. I emphasize New York particularly because the pressure of multiple ethnicities is always present here. Coming here and trying to make some sense of what one might be moved me toward this self-disclosure. I think a postcolonial writer definitely draws upon different strands to find some kind of self-definition.

DB: Is your book a positioning of sorts? You talk about yourself as a nowhere creature. This is very telling. Yet, at the same time that you say you're a nowhere creature, Fault Lines is clearly an exercise in trying to see where you are.

MA: Yes, I suppose it is. Although one does draw some sort of comfort from the thought that there may be millions like me. I'm interested in how one's relationships to others defines where one is. One has to be aware of issues of class and of the complexities involved in examining different experiences, aware that both I and the man selling the stuff are standing on Forty-Second Street. He probably was a Gujarati, but I wasn't sure. He could've been a Malayali. He may have come from the village next to my father's, So I think an encounter like that, if it had developed into an encounter, could be quite an extraordinary moment for reflection. Here's a whole world struggling for voice. My story is only one among the many others that connect with it. At the same time, my world and that of the cab driver seem so far apart. Those are the seams I was talking about earlier.

DB: You're saying a very important thing. When we started our project, we thought it should address the needs of the community as well as the academy, and soon we found that we were not going to be able to locate the voices of people outside the academy. Their issues don't fit here, but we need to be aware of them.

MV: How do you see the community fitting into the academy, particularly regarding postcolonial issues?

MA: That is a very difficult question that I'm not sure I can answer. I know, though, that we have to make an effort to include the community. Let me just explore some of the ways I see South Asian experiences within the community. I know that there are some South Asian organizations that deal with violence against women. There's "Sakhi" in New York City, and "Manavi" is active in New Jersey. These are very important groupings of people interested in resistance to what it means to be assimilated into mainstream America. There is so much to look at. I mean there's a difference between the immigrant who comes into law school and then lives in a suburb in Jersey and the one who sells newspapers in the subway. One is drawn to America and to New York by a certain idea of bettering oneself—that's the American dream—but of course most Indians who have come here, until the recent waves of immigration, have been middle class, whereas the pattern of immigration in Britain, for instance, has been quite different; a lot more working-class people have moved there.

A few months ago I was invited by the Arts Council of Great Britain to go on a reading tour with three other Indian writers. We began in London at the Royal Festival Hall and read to a very literary audience. We traveled all over the country and then went to Bradford. It has large, urban, postindustrial population—heavily Asian with a very strong Muslim community. The Arts Council had distributed posters saying, "Come and hear four contemporary Indian writers talk about contemporary issues, sex, politics, art"—you know how they try to draw a crowd. A representative from the Arts Council gave the poster to a local Muslim leader, who said, "This is out of the question; we will definitely not distribute it." The Arts Council was hoping for some kind of community outreach, but inevitably, if you modulate it in such a manner, you are bound to lose some sections of the community. I mean, there were plenty of people in the audience, but they were not the people the Arts Council was hoping to draw. Just as there are plenty of people in the community, but you may not be able to draw them to or into your work. But you have to be aware that they are out there.

DB: Do you see the same divide, then, between the academic and that working-class community which comes over from the Indian subcontinent?

MA: Well, it's an economic divide. If you drive a taxicab from nine in the morning to nine at night, you're not going to have leisure to sit down and write your great novel. I sometimes take a cab back from Hunter College, and often the cab driver is from India—if the driver is a Sardar, he'll say he's from Punjab rather than India, or sometimes he may be Malayali—and so we get into a conversation. By the same token, I have cousins who live in Pennsylvania who are terribly well off compared to me, and my aunt, who is my father's sister, came to visit me and looked at all my books and said "Don't worry, everyone begins like this; in a few years you'll settle down." So I said to her, "I shall end like this." But as far as she was concerned, I haven't "made it" because I don't have three cars and we live very modestly.

DB: If you did have three cars, who knows where you would park them in New York?

MA: They'd probably be stolen! [Laughter]

MV: Do you think that we have some responsibility to make our work somehow more accessible? To bridge the gap between classes? Should we be out there getting the voices of the South Asians on Forty-Second Street?

MA: It would be a challenge to do that kind of work because the material is raw; it hasn't already been processed by the academic mills. You cannot footnote some famous author five times and cross-reference it. The question then is how to draw that raw material into very particular ways of making sense.

MV: And if you do a translation into academic discourse so that it's more acceptable to the academy, then how does what you've written about them reach the persons who can't read?

MA: They may not even be particularly interested, but the fact of speaking is important. It's a very complicated thing to figure out first of all what it means to make a picture, and second, what it means to make a picture of somebody else. There's something almost magical involved in it, even if the picture is just in words. There's iconic power in stringing words together in a certain fashion, which can be wonderfully empowering, but it can also be dangerous. We have to be wary. There is one sense in which the academy is always belated: It always gets things after they've happened on the street. But I think at the same time that belatedness can be an advantage; it can give you time to meditate or to ponder.

A few days ago Cornel West was speaking at Hunter. I went to listen and I was quite moved. He was talking about the prophetic tradition in the black and Jewish traditions—you know there's been a lot of racial trouble in the city—and I was thinking there's a prophetic tradition in India that's been lost. I was thinking of Gandhi in particular, and I thought this is what I should do when I finish the novel I'm working on: I should read Gandhi's autobiography again, and maybe I'll read some of Martin Luther King. I'm very interested in the way in which issues of power—I think this might be relevant to what you call the postcolonial moment—can be transmuted into something that illuminates the ordinary condition and so offers some kind of resistance. There is this connection with nonviolence. My grandparents were Gandhians, and I was very much influenced by Gandhi, and I thought it would be interesting to think about that intellectually but also creatively. I'm not sure what the result might be.[3]

DB: You mention Faiz Ahmed Faiz in *Fault Lines* and refer to his comment that "poetry must be like bread."[4] And you ask, how is that so? Do you have an answer to that question yet, or is that where you're heading? Does your poetry play into this project of illumination?

MA: I think it must, but it would be very presumptuous to say how; I don't know how. It's a very good question because I think the kind of clarity I'm talking about does have to do with words, since that's what I work with. I really don't have a good answer for you, except that when you crystallize something and it's out there, one is able to read one's thoughts through it. And it's possible that in the reading-through there's a momentary release. One couldn't say it is permanent, because nothing is. I think that in the act of making sense, the world as we apprehend it makes available to us some kind of breathing space for self-understanding. This might, in fact, permit certain sorts of action.

I remember when I was at Jawaharlal Nehru University in Delhi, some students invited Günter Grass. And he said something I've never forgotten in response to the question, "What do you do as a writer?" The good old question, "What is the role of the writer?" And he said, "You know, I'm a social democrat." Of course, there were lots of people who admired Trotsky, and they were upset. There was a lot of muttering. He went on to say, "I have this Volkswagon van, and I pick people up and take them to a voting booth to help people to vote. When I drive, I drive following the yellow lines like a good citizen. But you see, when I'm writing in my room, I question those yellow lines, but when I drive, I don't, because there'd be terrible accidents if I did." I thought, how very wise. What a wonderful thing to say. And that stayed with me even though it was almost twenty years ago. It made a whole lot of sense.

MV: Audre Lorde says you can't use the master's tools to dismantle the master's house. But we do use the tools. We are driving along within the yellow lines and criticizing the yellow line. You've mentioned Audre Lorde . . .

MA: Audre taught at Hunter for many years, and she was a very powerful influence there. I knew her personally also, but then she left for the Virgin Islands. I think the African American experience in this country is terribly significant, and we haven't worked out a way of talking about that experience in terms of the vision of the postcolonial. We may not have made sufficient connections within our postcolonial theory, because if you think about the issue of radical democracy, India and the United States are the two largest, most populous democracies in this world, and both are in straits as far as democratic processes are concerned. I mean votes are bought and sold in both countries. The Republican Party may have paid huge sums of money in New Jersey to suppress black voter registration, or so it is alleged. It happens, of course, in India too. It's very important for our cultural understanding to think of some of these political dimensions that might provide connections. I think there is this pressure of ethnicity, which turns into fascism. Look at what's happening in Bosnia and what happened in Ayodhya.

DB: Yes, it's more important now than ever to form coalitions. Were you thinking of Mouffe and Laclau when you talked about radical democracy?[5]

MA: I wasn't thinking of them in particular, but certainly there are connections.

DB: They also talk about realigning coalitions, shifting and so diversifying the centers of power.

MA: You know, I think a lot of people are thinking along those lines. It's difficult because we really don't have a set of overarching principles. And I think spiritually that's a loss. What do you tell your children when they're growing up? Be nice to your friends? It isn't quite enough. But maybe that's the best you can do? I don't think it is, but these are very difficult issues. They have to do with questions of community, and whether art is relevant in the affirmation of some kind of humanly possible, livable world.

Talking about trying to stitch things together, there's a very interesting anthology coming out called *Blood into Ink*. The collection has Middle Eastern and South Asian women's writing about war and is edited by Roshni Rustomji and Miriam Cooke; I've written a preface for it, about women and violence and colonialism.[6] It was a painful yet necessary task for me to read these writings by women living in wartime. Many of the writings are from Beirut—you know I used to speak Arabic, so I have an emotional commitment to that culture. I located my essay in the particular moment of the Gulf War. An important fact is that it really was an Asian war, and a lot of the people displaced were South Asian.

MV: Can we go back to your earlier comment that maybe we haven't formalized a way of talking about ethnic Americans in terms of the postcolonial? What are your thoughts on the debate about what exactly is postcolonial? Is it always something "over there"?

MA: I keep hearing about this debate. What exactly is the debate?

MV: The major debate centers on the question, is "postcolonial" a referent to theoretical discourse that doesn't exist anyplace else in the world, or is it in fact a referent to a place? And if it does refer to a physical space, is it the space we term the Third World? Can we have postcolonial theory without a discussion of people who live in the United States, for instance?

MA: It seems to me that in the United States there is one people that has really been colonized: the Native Americans. Look what has happened to their culture, and the kinds of terrible pain and voicelessness that you find. How can they not be included when we speak of the postcolonial? These are important questions. What does it mean to talk about the postcolonial experience in Sudan or Ghana or India or Sri Lanka? I mean, can we talk about them all in the same breath? Should we? We have to be aware that there are crucial differences.

MV: And similarities—places where experience connects?

DB: You seem to have a very clear sense of a global alliance with writers, and in *Fault Lines* you mention Audre Lorde, Claribel Alegria, Kamala Das, Jayanta Mahapatra. It almost sounds as if you have detected a common purpose in all these voices.

MA: Well, I never thought of it that way. But you know, it's almost like making the kind of mesh we talked about. I think part of it is because living as I do here, I don't have a face-to-face community except a very small one of people who read my work, but that's different from knocking at a friend's door and saying, "Look at this." I mean I have one or two friends I can do that with, but less and less do I do it. Let me just give you an example. My long poem *The*

Storm, which was published as a book, is coming out in Malayalam translation, and I can imagine a face-to-face community of poets talking about it.[7] When it came out here, it was a very different kind of setting; certainly, I gave readings and people talked about it, but I think it's still different because in Kerala, say in Trivandrum, there is a small group of writers who get together—not that there aren't terrible splits, but you know who the other person is. The thing about the different kind of postcolonial mesh is that there isn't necessarily the face-to-face community, even though one has met and talked to these people.

DB: The whole idea of meshing is an important factor for us. To go back to what you were saying, should we be and how can we be talking to the African American experience?

MA: Well, it may be difficult till, say, one has a more crystallized sense of what it means to be a South Asian here. It may be difficult till then; that may be the next step, you know?

MV: Do you think we are close to developing an idea of what it means to be South Asian in the United States?

MA: In the last two or three years I've been traveling a lot, reading poetry to students. They've invited me, not faculty—now this is important—and students have said that they liked my poems. It's not like having a colleague saying come and give a lecture. Often these student-sponsored readings are quite large events, because the students are better funded; they have their own sort of mechanism. And they're young women and men who've been born here, perhaps, but who are part or wholly Asian—Korean, Chinese or Japanese, some Indian, but very few Indians have joined in these groups. And there we struggle to make sense of things together, though sometimes making sense happens in a very private mode.

I'm going to Carleton College in January and speaking at a convocation. I got a message on my machine from someone who said they'd be assigning Fault Lines to seven hundred students. It's funny, because I think there's this whole generation of people, maybe a little bit younger than the two of you—I imagine you are both in your mid-twenties, but I may be wrong.

DB: Mary is in her twenties and I'm in my thirties.

MA: People from, say, sixteen to about twenty-four who come from Pakistan, India, East Africa, or wherever, are going through enormous struggles about how to make sense. On the one hand, they might want to assimilate; on the other hand, because of the racial formation of this country—it's a racialized society here—they're rejected. And it's interesting to me that I have an audience there I never would have imagined. The people of my generation who read me—that's a little bit different, or people like yourselves, but I think this audience is not something that I could ever have predicted. It has been terribly important in terms of my own imagination and what it means to live here, because I think that these issues of imaginative displacement that I'm talking about can have a very real ground-level effect on the lives of many of us.

MV: Do you have an audience in mind when you write? Or is it, in a way, yourself?

MA: I always find that a hard question.

DB: Do you have an ideal audience? You talk about being surprised to find an audience among very young South Asians.

MA: No, I'm delighted. I'm actually deeply honored, and I feel grateful that my work makes sense to young people, because I think that's a very critical time of life. I suspect that part of what's driven you both up here are things that happened to you when you were that age. You spend many, many years working on questions that first come in very raw, brutal form without the sophistication of the tape recorder and computer technology, and I think these are things that drive us as human beings. These questions have resulted in my writing this long work [Alexander's novel in progress]—it wouldn't seem long to someone who'd been writing prose all their lives. It's quite a complex book, and within it are one or two references to the *Mahabharata*, to Thoreau's *Walden*, to Billie Holiday's music. I throw in little things that please me. Is the ideal reader someone who gets an elliptical reference but reads the work with a certain distance, or is the ideal reader one for whom that book makes a kind of visceral sense? I don't know. I mean I really don't know. All I can say is that one is grateful for readers. Because one writes in solitude, one is grateful to be read.

MV: Can you imagine a following from among people who aren't relating to the immigrant experience at all? Say, second- or third-generation immigrants?

MA: Oh sure. For instance, my memoir is coming out in India this month—and I wonder how people will respond. It'll be a very different audience, and for some of them it may have more immediacy—certain parts of it. Then again, my novel *Nampally Road* came out in German—I don't read German—and I'd be interested to know about the reaction of that audience, because the audience that one does compose in one's head is in some ways a part of one's self.[8] I think we write to enlarge our sense of the world, but I think the world is often composed in some measure of those one values deeply. I don't mean one particular individual. I think it's very dangerous to say "I write for an audience"; it becomes dangerous because you might start to censor yourself. It's hard enough not to be scared of what one is writing, worrying about who to satisfy—your mother or God or your husband or somebody—particularly for women.

DB: You started talking about women writing the body, in a sense, and in *Fault Lines* you speak of the English language as a "pale skin that has covered up

. . . [your] flesh, the broken parts of . . . [your] world"—the challenge being to break through.[9] How does one do that? Do you feel that, like the women Romantic writers you've written about in the past, you put your bodily self into your writing?[10] Too, is it the condition of the female writer that the body enters the space of writing—does that just happen?

MA: It always does, whether one is male or female, but that does not necessarily have to be foregrounded as a theme. I think for me it's become more of a concern precisely because of the sorts of histories that I've experienced. I've never been in a war; I've been at the edge of war. It seems to me that the kinds of upbringing one has as a woman do impose certain constraints, and in order to be aware of these constraints one does have to have a sense of what bodily being is. I mean the idea might be to write free of the body entirely. I remember saying to a friend at the MacDowell Colony this summer, "When I write I'm not male or female, I just write." Except having said that, I think this writing the body business is almost the last surface of resistance. What happens if we don't have the sofa, *chai*, coffee, table, chair? What is it that one works with? I think one does need clothing, food. The way in which the body links up to language has been for me an important, informing issue in my writing—after the age of maybe twenty-seven.

When *Ms.* magazine was planning a profile, someone called me for a fact check—something I had said about language and shame. That wasn't there, I think, in my very early writing, because then I believed in the Romantic imagination. I still do, and that's what provides the tension; without the imagination we simply cannot make sense. I talked about what happens when everything else is taken away. Of course, the body isn't just the body, it's also the spirit—one can construct a powerful anti-Cartesian argument in the late twentieth century at least. I've been reading Shankaracharya's *Vivekachudamani* and learning that one has to free oneself—all the knowledge that comes from the body is suspect. It's *maya*, it's *avidya* if you wish. What one should strive for is the *chinmayadeha*, the level beyond the gross body. This is very attractive to me at the same time that the notion of being without the body seems unreal.

DB: Since you are a Romanticist too, would the aeolian harp be an apt metaphor for us to consider for the body and the spirit being played by our experience?

MA: Have you ever heard this instrument being played? It's like a wild animal. I first heard it when I went to Grasmere to look at Dorothy Wordworth's papers when I was working on *Women in Romanticism*. Apropos of which, here's an interesting story: My son was about four when I was doing my research on Dorothy's papers. He had heard a lot about Dorothy Wordsworth, and one day he asked, "Mama, is there a boy Wordsworth?" [*Laughter*] A boy Wordsworth! I was quite amused. I reassured him. Of course, by the time he was five he was beyond that stage. Anyway, back to the question. I'm not really sure that the aeolian harp captures "the body" or "the spirit" in its entirety, but certainly in many ways it is apt.

MV: If we can make a jump here to teaching—I'm interested in you as a teacher. How is your teaching influenced by feminist and postcolonial theory or any other theories?

MA: I teach two different sorts of classes, and I think I learn from both differently. This semester I'm teaching a poetry workshop and a seminar on Romanticism and Colonialism. In these writing workshops the material we look at is produced by the students themselves—we use one or two books, but the basic material of the workshop is the production of the participants. It's difficult at times, because these are very personal pieces of writing. Then you get into it, and you hear comments from people, and you sit around and talk.

When I teach my postcolonial classes at the City University of New York Graduate Center or at Hunter, I start with the history of colonization, European expansion, look at Panniker's *Asia and Western Dominance*, Columbus's journals. Then we would enter into a complicated discussion about language. I've used Michelle Cliff's essays and Ngugi Wa Thiong'o's *Decolonising the Mind*. There are times even in my graduate class when I try to get students to do an exercise whereby the issue of access to language becomes autobiographical. I do request people to make this connection, even if they end up writing a very theoretical final paper or focus on literary issues.

Of course, the autobiographical mode can enter into criticism, and I try to make that connection, because access to language is also access to imaginative power. One needs to speak in many tongues to live in the world today. This is relevant to postcolonial analysis, because it's not like saying I'm going to write a Ph.D. on one of Wordsworth's minor poems and look at the textual material. What is the textual material? Yes, you can look at Nawal al-Saadawi, Mahasveta Devi, and so on. But what sense does it make to a Hispanic immigrant living in New York City? Is it like teaching Wordsworth in Hyderabad?

DB: In the preface to *Women in Romanticism* you mention that you had to learn Wordsworth's poem "Daffodils" as a child. You comment that you "had no idea what the flower looked like." Do you think that children or adults in the postcolonial world should continue to study absent referents? Should they still be reading "Daffodils?"

MA: Oh sure, that is if you want to. I wouldn't make it a requirement. I think we should read Wordsworth but read him in different ways. He's an extraordinary poet, although I hate much of what he stands for. Once you get into the aesthetic issue it gets very complicated, but it's also freeing in a way. You should go for what you love, and you should go for what is excellent in it. But you should also be able to say that I disagree with this and don't want to read it because I don't have time for it. You ought to have those possibilities available to you, and I think that part of pedagogy must necessarily question the kind of language we use. One cannot have a rich postcolonial analysis without thinking about language, about English.

I take it very differently from the old Commonwealth attitude. When I was a young writer in India, there was an anxiety about authors not being "Indian" if they wrote in English, but that is not what it's about. Now there is a greater sense of liberation, since English is seen as an Indian language. So I think that particular element of scrutiny, at a very basic level, could be brought to bear on the kind of investigation postcoloniality seems to work with. Of course, at some point you need to master certain bodies of knowledge and think about history and so on, but that particular connection is important, and the other is the question of the traditional canon—the two are not unrelated.

DB: We see a lot of South Asian women doing work in the area of Postcolonial Studies. Do you think their stakes are different? Do they have a greater need to be defining themselves?

MA: The whole issue of self-disclosure as it plays into postcolonial culture is a difficult one, but it may be more attractive to women because of the possibilities it offers of inventing a space for oneself. That may not be quite as necessary for men. I don't know, I'm thinking out loud. This whole idea of talking about oneself is harder for men. Not that there haven't been extraordinary male autobiographers.

DB: We had wanted to ask if you saw the genre of autobiography or cultural narrative as particularly potent for the field of Postcolonial Studies, as opposed to straight, theoretical, academic essays.

MA: Well, if I could use Wordsworth one more time—if you were writing a thesis on Wordsworth, it would be a bit harder to say, well, here I am and this is my testimony. On the other hand, I think that with something like this there is both the enticement and the danger. One could be slipshod or one could be rigorous. The whole issue of weaving personal narrative is a very exciting one, but it has to be done with great care and great attention. It shouldn't just be that "I'm wearing a sari, so this should be my right." In fact, anything that you claim for yourself as a tradition has to be honored, but there's discipline involved in it, and the joints between personal experience and cultural narrative need to be examined very closely. They haven't been; they need to be. So I think this field is very much beginning. Any area that has this immediate connection with personal experience, such as Black Studies, can yield exciting material. Our approach to Postcolonial Studies needs to be refined. You need to identify areas to be foregrounded in terms of study and in terms of analytical procedures.

MV: You were talking about the need to earn the right to be able to speak. How does one earn that right? Who should speak about postcolonial experience?

MA: How does one earn the right to speak as a postcolonial or an American or a citizen? What do these questions mean? I guess you have to speak as yourself. If certain issues and problems can be attached in some way to you or stand in resistance to certain definitions that count culturally, then you should speak. But you cannot speak as a postcolonial, as such. Someone else may say, X is speaking as a postcolonial, and I may really be speaking as a woman, but for me that has very different valency. I might say I am speaking as a woman who had a postcolonial education and give some specific details, and then it would work. But to say I'm speaking as a postcolonial makes me very nervous because of the multiple uses of that word.

DB: It seems as if we've come back to the question we asked earlier: How should we define "postcolonial?"

MA: Well, it has to be rooted in very specific issues of injustices, imbalances, and cultural self-understanding that have resulted from taking apart what was put in place by colonialism. I think there's a very specific burden to that term. It can of course be enlarged, but what does it mean for somebody who was born after independence to say I speak as a postcolonial? It's correct in a way, but is it just a fashionable way of saying you should listen to me? Because I've something different to say? Or is something else happening? In some sense everybody has a right to speak. What it reminds me of is the phenomenon of the African caps and shawls worn by young people here, including Indians. The term "postcolonial" must not become in the academy like that.

DB: Like a badge . . .

MA: If you want to wear a shawl, theek hai [it's okay], that's fine. I dress all sorts of ways. I was doing a reading at Tufts one time and someone asked me, "My God, can you do that, can you wear a sari?" I said, "Sure." She said they told her mother she would lose her job if she wore a sari. Her mother is a doctor on Staten Island. It made me stop and think about the whole idea of resistance. One of the things that happened in New Jersey is that some women stopped wearing the sari after the Dotbuster Skinhead attacks.[11] Then I remember meeting this wonderful woman, a medical doctor, who was talking about mobilizing people, and she said "We wore our saris." Wearing a sari in New Jersey has a whole different meaning from wearing it in, say, Hyderabad. I think it's fine to use the word "postcolonial," that's the beauty of language, but if you put it in terms of an academic discipline or an area of study, it's very exciting that this is a field of multiplicities.

MV: How do you see yourself in relation to Postcolonial Studies?

MA: You've come here to talk to me as a postcolonial, which also means Indian as far as I'm concerned. People sometimes will speak of me as an Asian American writer. This is the other part of my communal identity. What does it mean to be an Asian American writer? people ask. I say, I'm not sure. How do you fit in with other Asian American writers? they want to know. I write, and then subsequently people will say she's an Asian American writer. Of course I am, but that's a very different taxonomy from that of postcolonial, because postcolonial presupposes a previous history, or it should, whereas Asian American has to do with the constitution of an ethnicity that is very broad ranging in the United States. What is the connection between a Korean and a Japanese writer? There may be strong connections, but they are formed under the pressure of being in America. I bring this up because I think of things being read in many different ways. When my novel came out in India, the reviews were quite different than they were here.[12] It was being compared with other Indian novels, whereas here if it was compared with something, it would be a novel from the so-called Third World, whatever that means. That's very different from saying, look, someone wrote a novel in Kannada, and it was translated. I'm not deliberately complicating it for you, but I think you will be interviewing people who think of themselves as being in a field as such. As a writer, I'm always outside the field. My identity is as a writer. I *happen* to work in the academy.

DB: We need to hear from people who think "postcolonial" is being used as an academic label that is part of a specialized, manufactured discourse. After all, postcolonialism is also an academic industry.

MA: It's like the term "South Asian," which really was born in the academy; it's used a lot now.

DB: There is a great deal of discourse coming out under these labels.

MA: What's exciting about those attempts and what you're doing is that you're trying to make sense of something that isn't already crystallized; it's important to hold on to that as part of the boundary of what you're doing. How does race play into this? That's something I talk about in my memoir. What does one pass for in the street?

DB: Indeed, which of us can say we're passing for Americans? What's American to you?

MA: I don't know. If you look at what I've written in the last few years, I don't think I would have written it if I hadn't been living here. My identity is formed by the pressures I've mentioned.

MV: *Fault Lines* suggests the many "fractures" of identity that you have experienced and will continue to experience, including your early experiences in India, growing up in Africa, and moving to the United States. There are times when you're Asian American, times when you're South Asian, and then again you're Indian.

DB: Is *Fault Lines* an academic text?

MA: It's been taught in several seminars. It was hardly out before it was taught at Sarah Lawrence in a course called "Exile and Autobiography," along with texts in Francophone African literature and other texts dealing with issues of language and translation. There are all these worlds of readers.

DB: In what ways do you think it is useful to produce a "document" that chronicles a variety of South Asian positions and experiences, as we are attempting to do? Is it valid to engage in this kind of "representation," however aware we may be of the provisionality of these produced identities?

MA: I remember I was giving a reading at the University of Michigan and talking about writing my memoir, and a graduate student, an Indian woman, said to me, "Please don't do it. You know what they do to Maxine Hong Kingston; they say this is what Chinese is. If they read your memoir, they'll say this is what Indian is." She got very nervous, and it was very sweet of her. But people need to know this isn't what Indian is; this is what I am. Still, it's interesting that this woman was facing her anxiety, for me and for herself.

DB: We're very concerned with the issue of representation in the collection we're putting together. Are people going to think it is a representative South Asian text?

MA: There seem to be several South Asian anthologies in the making. Obviously, people don't do this unless there's a real interest, which is wonderful.

MV: The more such collections come out, the less chance there is that any one text will be frozen as representational.

MA: That's right, there is less danger of codification. It's an excellent thing.

DB: You weave in references to your family in your work. That's clearly very important to you.

MA: It *is* important to me. I remember being brought up with this idea that writers had an immaculate life. They were mostly male, and other people did the work. They did not take care of their children if they had them, these great men we are taught to revere. And here I am trying to be a writer. Nobody does my cooking; I do it myself, and I take care of my children. I don't see why this should not be part of my identity. It's absolutely appropriate that it should be so. Elevating the writer to a rarefied level makes the work seem less relevant. Indians are much better in this regard. I've learned a lot from being in India and meeting and getting to know some wonderful Indian writers. My children know that I write poems. They would prefer that I be baking cookies sometimes, but it's something their mother does. I don't have the means to set up a separate life.

MV: Would you like to talk about your future projects?

MA: I'm working now with two women's lives, twining them together in this novel: one a woman raised in India who has come to America, and the other a woman of Indian origin whose parents are from Trinidad but who was herself born in upstate New York and now lives in Manhattan. Their lives intersect. The woman who comes from India, Sandhya, is a housewife, and the American-born one, Draupadi, is a performance artist who lives in an artist's housing area; she lives a very downtown sort of existence and does performance pieces. The novel began as the story of sexual passion, but then the whole world entered into it—the assassination of Rajiv Gandhi, the Gulf War. I'm deliberately putting two narratives together; this is my way of making sense of what postcolonial means. There's also a scattering of intellectual characters—there's one from Egypt, a real postcolonial. So it's a world made up of . . . I suppose people like us of no special merit, but we live our lives. That's what the novel is.[13]

DB: The unfreezing of postcolonial identity and this problematization of what is postcolonial is very interesting here.

MA: I think this novel is the underbelly of Fault Lines. There are limitations to any genre, to an autobiographical one for that matter, but maybe it frees up certain fictional elements. A key point in the novel is that one of the women tries to kill herself, and the other one rescues her.

DB: Which one?

MA: Sandhya, the woman from India, tries to kill herself. It's as if she has to earn the knowledge necessary to live in this world. Then too, one time there was spate of suicides by young girls in India on account of the dowry issue. I'm very concerned about this whole issue of female identity and what it means to annihilate oneself, because the promise of America is often held to be the promise of a fresh start in a new world. And passion comes into it.

DB: You talked about sexuality and desire in Fault Lines, topics not often broached by South Asian women.

MA: Back in 1987 there was a woman in Kerala who warned me, "Don't talk about eroticism." But I think I'm becoming more interested in this issue now. When you're twenty, twenty five, it has such a terrible power that you can't talk about it. In a way I'm at an age when I've earned my spurs. I'm becoming very interested in the issue of desire. I once wrote about the rape of a woman. One talks about violation; it's very difficult to write about desire in the same breath, but I think great writers do it. I think one of the reasons why Mahasveta Devi is so extraordinary is that she does both. I'm trying to talk, in a very limited way, obviously, about female desire and what happens if it's not within the set boundary and what violation means and how these things are internalized. I once thought of writing a poem about a woman being raped in a bar, a poem with a grotesque element—there's that whole thing about the exotic Asian woman and then the debate about the sacred and the profane. You remember that horrible incident, the woman who was dancing in a bar who was gang-raped on a billiard table by seven men in Rhode Island? It was a very big case, because almost no one in the bar had protested. It was cast as a "she was asking for it" thing.

DB: You mention violation and desire in the same breath, and I'm thinking of Indian cinema as I was growing up. I only noticed this when I went back to India with my ex-husband, and he commented that the only sex one sees on the Indian film screen is rape. You never see any sexual interaction between people who love each other. Any desire is kept under wraps, and the lesson we learn is that desire equals violation.

MA: I never thought of it that way, but it's true. That was the paradigm, wasn't it?

DB: I don't know that it has changed much.

MA: Hmm. There was a box office feminist movie *Swati*, and my daughter's called Svati, so we got the video. The film starts off really well, but about halfway through the film-maker changes his mind, and she's about to be raped. It's the formula; it has to happen. That's a postcolonial issue. But where is that discussion in our discourse?

MV: We did not give you the opportunity to touch on areas that are of particular interest to you.

MA: I want to show you some poems. I don't talk as well as I write; I deal with the questions you're asking in my poetry for the most part. Perhaps this one is relevant, "Brown Skin, What Mask?" Let me show it to you. Could you read it aloud?

MV: Of course.

Brown Skin, What Mask?

Babel's township seeps into Central Park
I hunch on a stone bench scraping nightingale-bulbuls
Cuckoo-koels, rose gulabs off my face

No flim flam now; card sharp, streetwise
I fix my heels at Paul's Shoe Place for a dollar fifty
Get a free make-over at Macy's, eyes smart, lips shine.
Shall I be a hyphenated thing, Macaulay's Minutes
and Melting Pot theories not withstanding?

Shall I bruise my skin, burn up into
She Who Is No Colour whose longing is a crush
of larks shivering without sound?

When lit by his touch in a public place
—an elevator with a metal face—shall I finger grief for luck
work stares into the "bride is never naked" stuff?[14]

NOTES

1. Susie Tharu and K. Lalit, eds., *Women Writing in India: 600 B.C. to the Present*, vol. 1 (New York: Feminist Press, City University of New York, 1993).

2. Meena Alexander, *Fault Lines: A Memoir* (New York: Feminist Press, City University of New York, 1993).

3. See "Theatre of Sense," in Meena Alexander, *The Shock of Arrival: Post-colonial Reflections* (Boston: South End Press, 1996).

4. Alexander, *Fault Lines*, 128.

5. Ernesto Laclau and Chantal Mouffe, *Hegemony and Socialist Strategy: Towards a Radical Democratic Politics*, trans. Winston Moore and Paul Cammack (London: Verso, 1985).

6. Meena Alexander, "Translating Violence: Reflections after Ayodhya," in *Blood into Ink: South Asian and Middle Eastern Women Writer War*, ed. Mariam Cooke and Roshni Rustomji-Kerns (Boulder, Colo.: Westview Press, 1994).

7. Meena Alexander, *The Storm: A Poem in Five Parts* (New York: Red Dust, 1989).

8. Meena Alexander, *Nampally Road* (San Francisco: Mercury House, 1991).

9. Alexander, *Fault Lines*, 73.

10. Meena Alexander, *Women in Romanticism: Mary Wollstonecraft, Dorothy Wordsworth, and Mary Shelly* (London: Macmillan, 1989).

11. "Dotbusters" are racist and violent gangs that target Indians, particularly women who wear the traditional dot (bindi) on their foreheads. New Jersey is home to a large immigrant Indian population and has been the site of several such attacks.

12. Meena Alexander, *Nampally Road* (New Delhi: Orient Longman, 1991).

13. Meena Alexander, *Manhattan Music* (San Francisco: Mercury House, 1996).

14. Meena Alexander, *River and Bridge* (Toronto: TSAR Press, in press).

CHAPTER 3

Pedagogical Alternatives:
Issues in Postcolonial Studies

Interview with Gauri Viswanathan

Deepika Bahri and Mary Vasudeva

This interview was conducted in segments, by mail and through telephone conversations in March and May 1994, between Viswanathan's busy schedule and repeated trips to India.

DB/MV: Given the current proliferation of work done in the name of the "postcolonial," it seems imperative that we work toward developing a definition. Much of the work done under this label seems to suggest very different notions of what "Postcolonial" Studies should entail. How would you define the term?

GV: "Postcolonial" is a misleading term because it assumes, first of all, a body of knowledge or a specifiable period of time *after* colonialism. It is sometimes used interchangeably with "decolonized": Ngugi's apt phrase "decolonising the mind" accurately describes the agenda of postcoloniality.[1] I might define Postcolonial Studies broadly as a study of the cultural interaction between colonizing powers and the societies they colonized, and the traces that this interaction left on the literature, arts, and human sciences of both societies. But in its more popular usage, I suppose, "postcolonial" has come to signify more or less an *attitude* or position from which the decentering of Eurocentrism may ensue.

DB/MV: Does nomenclature both enable certain narratives and their study and disable others?

GV: In this case, "postcolonial" has enabled the inclusion of modern literatures into the English curriculum, on the grounds of a global link between these literatures forged by colonial history. But at the same time I think it has disabled, to some extent, a serious study of the specific histories of these other societies: All postcolonial societies, whether of India, Africa, or the Caribbean, are assumed to have a parallel history. The term "postcolonial" sometimes tends to rob serious study of non-European literature of a contextual focus. Therefore, I would like to see a judicious balance of concentrated regional study with a broader theoretical emphasis.

Furthermore, the term has acquired the characteristics of an adjective that expresses attitudes rather than a field of study—like "radical" or "subaltern"—so that there is a self-selection even in what is taken up for discussion. The term "postcolonial" has not evoked the kind of resistance that Fredric Jameson's characterization of Third World literature as allegory certainly has, though one could make a strong argument that there are distinct allegorical overtones.[2]

DB/MV: Could you elaborate on the allegorical overtones in the use of the term "postcolonial"?

GV: I was contrasting the fierce resistance Jameson evoked in critics, when he spoke about Third World national allegory, to the ready acceptance of the term "postcolonial." I don't think people had too much difficulty in seeing how the term "Third World" homogenized multiply constituted histories and disparate territories into one unified whole, and people actively resisted this totalizing tendency; however, the same kind of resistance has not occurred with the use of "postcolonial." People have accepted the term as an accurate representation, whereas I think that the term has to be specialized, particularly in the context of Third World nationalism.

DB/MV: Do you think there has been much examination of the use and meaning of the term or its specificity?

GV: I don't think so, at least as far as I can see. It has not been subject to the kind of self-examination that "Third World" has; we say "the so-called Third World," but we don't say "the so-called postcolonial." People use the word as a descriptive term, and this is indicative of the tendency to approach Postcolonial Studies as a kind of self-positioning.

DB/MV: A kind of nonreflective self-positioning? You are saying people aren't seeing any necessary political or subversive charge in this term. Is this a term you see as emerging from the academy rather than a historical situation? There's obviously a certain historical grounding there—but do you see its use in the academy as separate, somewhat, from this grounding? What causes the acceptance of this term?

GV: I think the first part of your question provides the answer: You ask if it comes from the academy, and by and large it has come out of the academy. You do see it as a descriptive term in America, whereas in India and other countries with a colonial past it has a very specific meaning coming out of a history and a moment. Coming out of the academy, in journals for instance, it has quite a different political charge; it definitely conveys a set of attitudes to the study of culture.

DB/MV: You seem to be suggesting that Postcolonial Studies in the United States may actually be a way of reading culture, and that the postcolonial is not limited to certain texts or geographical spaces or temporal moments but may actually be a strategy.

GV: I believe so.

DB/MV: Obviously, the time is ripe for Postcolonial Studies—one need only glance through a university press catalogue to see all the work being done under this label. Why is this the right moment? Why is this "the" postcolonial moment? Why have the term and field gained so much currency in the last few years? ·

GV: It's probably not accurate to say it has come into its own now; the ground has been prepared over the last couple of decades. When the doors for immigration opened up in 1965, whole groups of South Asian professionals flooded into the country. Their presence and intellectual activity were bound to have some kind of impact on the restructuring of the curriculum. The ground was prepared much earlier by this immigration.

Now, you are suggesting that this is the postcolonial moment. I suspect that the timing of this moment has largely to do with some of the successes of feminist criticism, and with African American and Asian American Studies increasingly coming into their own. I think too that the new research being done in South Asia—and elsewhere, but we're focusing on South Asia here—is becoming more available as publishing agencies in Asia are expanding their markets. These factors are enabling Postcolonial Studies to gain ground; a kind of global interaction is occurring that has prepared the ground for them in the America academy.

DB/MV: How do English Studies continue to work as a neocolonizing force on once colonized countries?

GV: The debate still goes on in India, as in other formerly colonized societies, whether English should be retained or not. And it has led to a lot of linguistic chauvinism, a return to regionalism. The reaction to the hegemony of some other Indian language as a national language has, paradoxically, strengthened the status of English, and in South India in particular it is fairly commonplace to hear spirited defenses of English, partly to ward off the impending dominance of Hindi and North India. I read somewhere in one of the Madras newspapers that as a way of raising the standard of English—and thereby fighting Hindi—incentives of many kinds are offered in some schools to encourage students to speak English, incentives such as pronouncing some schooldays as "all-English" days when no other language is to be spoken. Things haven't worked as they should have, however, and the result has been that a deathly silence pervades the classrooms of these schools, because students still feel terribly diffident about speaking English, a language which to most students is as alien as Hindi. I raise this point because it is facile to describe English as simply a neocolonizing force, when there are far more complicated factors involved, such as regional nationalism, caste politics, intrasocietal antagonisms, and so forth. In some instances, on the other hand, where English has been challenged by cultural nationalism, it has been accompanied by a spurt of creative activity. One sees a new pride in learning the vernacular languages and literatures, where before (say, ten or twenty years ago), those who studied English studied no other language and had very little wish to do so. A very healthy trend in Indian universities is that many teachers and scholars of English literature feel less compelled to focus their scholarly and pedagogical attention solely on English writers and have produced significant work on such topics as Indian women's writing, Indian nationalism, vernacular literary writing. So I think the situation is changing, at least in India, and the excitement of poststructuralist criticism has encouraged many students of English to turn a more critical eye on what they study rather than merely celebrate the exalted virtues of English literature. By turning a critical eye, I mean placing the literature of England within a historical context of imperialism, class conflict, and gender issues. So while English literature continues to be studied, a younger generation of teachers has permitted, to some extent at least, alternative ways of presenting that literature to a generation that does not feel obliged to commemorate timebound values.

DB/MV: Today we see many English literature departments attempting to broaden their notion of the canon by including "ethnic" and "multicultural" literature. What are (or should be) the limits of the label "English Literature"? Given the danger of "defusing" the potential power of "radical" texts by co-opting them into English literature departments that you touch on in your final chapter of *Masks of Conquest*, how do we incorporate multicultural literature (do we?) without perpetuating the system we claim to be challenging?[3]

GV: Of course, the easiest way of diluting the radical force of a text is to co-opt it into the mainstream curriculum, and to some extent the steady inclusion of so-called minority literatures in the mainstream English literature curriculum has reduced their oppositional force. But I see no reason to be negative about the inclusion of multicultural literature if it has forced the field of "English" to rethink its accepted parameters. "English Literature" is increasingly being rewritten as "Literature in English," and the change is a healthy one. It deterritorializes the national implications of English literature, and it refocuses attention on language rather than nation as the creative principle of literature. I'm wary of having "postcolonial literature" in English departments without defining what postcolonial literature is in the first place. "Literature in English" is a much more satisfactory term for me, at least if such literature is studied across cultures and territorial boundaries.

DB/MV: What are the implications of including the discipline of "postcolonial literature" in English departments?

GV: There are a number of healthy implications, among them recognition that the history of English literature must include an account of the creative output of the countries colonized by England; that there are multiple versions of the colonial experience; that though the colonizer may have imposed his culture on the colonized, the colonized have developed their own imaginative and intellectual resources out of the material of cultural imposition and interaction; and that the right of the colonized not only to address but also be heard in the metropolitan centers is now acknowledged.

DB/MV: What might be some negative implications?

GV: I imagine that from the point of view of those who advocate postcolonial literature—I think this is implicit in your original question—there is a danger of defusing its radical charge by including it. I was aware of this possibility and in my book *Masks of Conquest* I alluded to the problem in the context of the Anglicist-Orientalist controversy in nineteenth-century India, having arrived at that conclusion from my own work in the area. The co-optation of certain literatures can in some ways defuse their oppositional nature. Another negative implication might be the recent spate of positions in postcolonial literature in the academy in the absence of discussion about what the term means—this could be a way of neutralizing the other presence by incorporating it. A bigger danger is that the term "postcolonial" becomes a kind of replacement for other literatures, such as Asian or African American, without really dealing with the political challenges imposed by the other constituencies or other literatures.

DB/MV: We were speculating that one of two things could happen: Either Postcolonial Studies would be maintained as an exotic, segregated field of study or it would be subsumed under the larger umbrella of English departments. The problems with the former are obvious, but in the case of the latter, in addition to the danger of losing the radical charge of such literatures, we are concerned with the danger that departments offering these courses (because it seems to be the thing to do) would, under budgetary constraints, use existing, untrained faculty who might not be able to provide the necessary context and background for these materials.

GV: Sure, then we would merely reproduce an earlier "world literature" program, very uncritical in its structuring. That's obviously dangerous.

DB/MV: Certainly your suggestion of foregrounding "postcolonial" as a method of reading would be a useful counter to this tendency.

GV: Yes, I do see it as a method, and I did indicate that one could teach very canonical texts, Jane Austen and so on—of course, Said has done that in *Culture and Imperialism*—using this method.[4] I would also add to what Said has done, to really try out something like a postcolonial reading of canonical texts so that what appear to be concerns exclusive to the postcolonial situation—fundamentalism, sectarianism, and so on—could be read in relation to nineteenth-century novels. Dickens's *Barnaby Rudge*, for instance, which is about mass mobilization and the horrific effects of militant Protestantism, shocks someone into the recognition that what seem to be exclusive problems of Third World society are, in fact, problems you could find within English society. That makes us rethink the problems of the Third World and consider that these difficulties have become part of an international, global history. We have forgotten this because of the way we have chosen to read these works. Postcolonial as a method of reading would be a healthy way to counterbalance the ahistorical functions that postcolonial literature has acquired over the past years.

DB/MV: Who is the audience for research in this field? Who *should* be the audience?

GV: One of the clearest indicators of the would-be compartmentalization of the field of Postcolonial Studies is the expectation that there is a specific—and specialized—audience carved out of the general audience of literary students. I think research in English and American literatures has manifestly shown that such distinctions are false, and that the cultural history of the Anglo-American world is inseparable from the history of Western colonialism. Edward Said's *Culture and Imperialism*, with its penetrating critique of the permeation of Western culture by colonialist assumptions, definitively dispels the myth of postcolonial work as specialized work done apart from so-called mainstream literary studies. Amy Kaplan and Donald Pease's *Cultures of United States Imperialism*, performs a similar service for the study of American literature.[5] To be really worth the name, research in postcolonial literatures should enable scholars and students to read canonical and noncanonical English works more critically and with greater attention to historical specificity. I think Edward Said's work in this area continues to be the model for such types of research in its effort to reach out to a broad audience and in cutting across disciplinary boundaries.

DB/MV: What kind of canon "reformation" (destruction?) would you like to see within English literature departments?

GV: The kinds of changes that English literature departments must undergo are obviously not restricted to including postcolonial literatures. And so I think it is an inadequate response simply to say that there ought to be more representation of literatures produced outside England. I should also emphasize that I don't think canon reformation is simply a matter of adding or subtracting a work or body of works. *Masks of Conquest* attempted to show that the curriculum is often the ground upon which competing historical forces get worked out, such as tensions between colonial officials and Indian elites. I see the contemporary debate about curriculum in the United States as being played out against a much wider background than a simple matter of selection and omission. The curriculum battle is less about what books to read than about how to reflect an increasingly complicated society with different class and ethnic compositions. The language of contemporary curricular restructuring has not changed all that much from the discourse of empire through which English literature was universalized. Robert Young's recent book *Colonial Desire* shows that Matthew Arnold's concept of culture was undergirded by nineteenth-century racialist assumptions and that Arnold rewrote culture as a history of racial antagonisms, thereby displacing the spirit of class antagonisms.[6] The way we talk about culture and the curriculum might bear a similar type of analysis.

DB/MV: What kind of material should be studied and taught under the umbrella of Postcolonial Studies?

GV: Material which indicates that the Eurocentric way of looking at the world is collapsing, especially in the formerly colonized world. Incidentally, I don't think only works written by non-Western writers qualify as Postcolonial Studies. For instance, as I mentioned earlier, I think it is perfectly possible to teach a work like Dickens's *Barnaby Rudge* from a postcolonial perspective and examine the sectarian conflict of the work as a counterpoint to the sectarian violence of the present world. Sectarianism and religious fundamentalism are viewed as essentially problems of the so-called Third World, but how often is English literature read in terms of the sectarianism that informs its own history? When you read *Barnaby Rudge* this way, it's impossible to take a stable, unchanging view of Eastern societies as characterized by religious tensions, violence, tribal warfare, when English society itself is seen to have been riven by religious intolerance and wild mob passions. By moving from this English literary text to colonial representations of sectarianism, we might see the extent to which there is a selective rewriting of a language of otherness out of the materials of tensions in English civil society.

DB/MV: In disciplinary terms, how do Postcolonial Studies in the Western academy differ from those in "geographically" postcolonial societies such as India?

GV: I think your question itself illuminates the mercurial quality of the word postcolonial. In the West it has acquired a density of meaning that incorporates African African and minority experiences, whereas in India it is still a time-bound concept, indicating a break with the colonial past. India is still trying to define itself as a postcolonial society, but it needs to be said that such critical, oppositional definitions currently emerge far more vehemently from intellectual elites than from, say, India's middle classes, which through their own consumerist fantasies are self-consciously fashioning themselves on a Western model to which oppositional concepts like "postcolonial" are irrelevant.

DB/MV: Could you say a little more about the Orientalizing of South Asia by South Asians in the United States?

GV: I think this is one of the most striking experiences that a lot of us have, living in the United States. There are so many South Asian communities. On the one hand, there is the academic world where we produce these critiques and where many of us, at the same time, maintain a strong interest in South Asia and are concerned about how South Asia figures in the West. And there are other communities that we know of through our cultural contacts that are so uncritical of their presentation of India to the West, they Orientalize themselves by celebrating the things that are part of a history of domination. Why is this happening? There is so little communication between these communities, one so critical and the others so complicit. The latter continue to represent themselves through film and journalistic media as the exotic East; one instance of this is in travel ads. To what extent does the failure of communication between these groups, in fact, nullify the critical activity South Asian academics are producing? Our own work is vitiated by our inability to engage with these other communities.

DB/MV: We can certainly see this in the popular marketing of India as exotic, in the invitations to come to the land of romance and mystery.

GV: I feel that there is a lot of room for South Asian intellectuals to enter the space that has been inhabited by popular marketers; we have to rethink our place by entering the area of the popular media.

DB/MV: How would we do that?

GV: There are a number of people in New York, for instance, who are dissatisfied with what has become the staple of South Asian television. I think this is a very fertile area for South Asian intellectuals, a very powerful though neglected area. Recently, a number of South Asians have gotten together to make documentaries of cultural figures and writers that might be of more interest to other groups of South Asians, not only those interested in Indian mass-produced films. We need to show that there is a vital, dynamic South Asian presence in America that is not felt strongly enough by the popular media. One way to do this is by mobilizing Indian business not only to support popular elements but also to sponsor cultural and intellectual activity. It will be a long process, of course, but this is the moment, in the academy, to enter the broadcasting media.

DB/MV: How would you say South Asians are Orientalizing themselves? Some Indian groups are very active in organizing cultural events, dance troupes, that sort of thing; would you say all of these activities are Orientalizing?

GV: I have in mind events like the India festival or department store India affairs. I know a couple of years ago there was a big exhibition called "India Affairs" at Bloomingdale's which served the Orientalization purpose. The dance troupes are much more limited because they are not going out to a wide American public. These events have wide appeal among the Indian population, but we are still not making other alternatives available to the Indian public. The other rethinking of India going on by painters, musicians, poets, and academics is not being presented; you don't really hear very much about that, and instead you keep seeing the romantic version of exotic India.

DB/MV: What particular role can or should South Asian scholars be playing in Postcolonial Studies? How do you see your own role?

GV: It's an undeniable fact that a great deal of what has now come to be called postcolonial criticism is the work of either South Asians themselves or South Asianists, as much in India as in the United States. But I think South Asian scholars need to remind themselves that their contributions don't lie simply in developing postcolonial theory but in turning literary criticism into a practice, into a viable tool for analyzing contemporary cultural trends in cinema, literature, the arts, and so on, that can speak to a broad audience.

DB/MV: Should we be trying to make postcolonial theory more accessible and relevant to those outside restricted discourse communities?

GV: Obviously. Much of what passes by the name of postcolonial theory is too esoteric and arcane to have much influence outside. The politics of identity, the constructions of difference and otherness, feed so necessarily into analyses of contemporary culture that postcolonial theory should inherently have a usability in even the journalistic sense. For instance, as I've said, here in the United States it is remarkable the extent to which the South Asian community is so evenly divided in the way its members perceive their own culture: While one part of the community in academia and the professions has produced marvelous critiques of Orientalism, another part continues to Orientalize itself in its avid promotion of an exotic version of India through films, television series, cultural events, and the like. The gap in perceptions is astounding, and it is truly dismaying to see the extent to which the Indian community participates in its own Orientalization. This is where I think postcolonial theory can be useful, in both the United States and India: to make audiences and readers aware of the nature of representation.

DB/MV: One last question. If you accept the notion that the colonizing impulse is common to humankind, what is so special about European colonization? Why do we date the postcolonial moment from the moment of European colonization?

GV: We don't. A common criticism is that if we are talking about colonialism, why not look at Brahmin exploitation and earlier colonization projects that were equally if not more insidious in their impact. I do think that we are talking about the moment now—it is very hard to say what colonialism or postcolonialism will mean in two or three centuries. We focus on European colonialism because we are accentuating the fact that European colonialism has left a very significant impact on non-European culture now. It is very hard right now to be able to describe the current trend in culture, architecture, film, without including the influence of the West. Contemporary India cannot be disconnected from its colonial past, even through one strand of Indian historiography, the Cambridge school, does contest the exceptionalism of British colonialism as a purely cultural phenomenon. We focus on European colonialism to find a reference point for the changes that have occurred, such as modernity—as the postmodern moment that has entered the South Asian cultural space. And I think that European colonization does provide that reference point.

NOTES

1. Ngugi wa Thiog'o, Decolonising the Mind: The Politics of Language in African Literature (Cambridge: J. Curry, 1986).

2. Fredric Jameson, "Third World Literature in the Era of Multinational Capitalism," Social Text 15 (1986): 65–88.

3. Gauri Viswanathan, Masks of Conquest: Literary Study and British Rule in India (New York: Columbia University Press, 1989).

4. Edward Said, Culture and Imperialism (New York: Knopf, 1993).

5. Amy Kaplan and Donald Pease, Cultures of United States Imperialism (Durham, N.C.: Duke University Press, 1993).

6. Robert Young, Colonial Desire (London: Routledge, 1995).

CHAPTER 4

Transnationality and Multiculturalist Ideology

Interview with Gayatri Chakravorty Spivak

Deepika Bahri and Mary Vasudeva

> This interview took place at Gayatri Chakravorty Spivak's office at Columbia University on 12 November 1993. We had caught Spivak at an obviously busy time, since she was preparing to leave the country in less than a month. Meanwhile, she had two days to complete her compilation of materials for a course on theorizing women. As we settled into her office, cluttered with the accumulations of a long academic career—including literally hundreds of books, neatly alphabetized—she told us about the enormous amounts of primary material she had gathered for the course and the task of sifting out the First World self-confessional stuff that might obscure larger and more important issues. This gave us the cue for our first question.

DB: In looking through your work we have found that if we intertextualize you, we might be able to come up with an approximate composite sketch of Spivak the theorist, the academician. Perhaps. You mention in an interview with Robert Young that people don't like your being anecdotal, that these are the same people who say that women should tell their stories—is there a narrative about you that you want to tell and that you think people should know?[1] You were referring just now to the use of confessional narrative in discussions of subject position. What purpose do personal narratives serve for you?

GS: I talk a lot about my life rather than my subject position: that is to say, how I, as a subject ("I"), may be positioned (historically? rhetorically? psychologically? politically?—you name it) in the sentences that I say, write, and do. (Your copy editor wants a definition of "subject position," but "doing a sentence" seems a bit enigmatic. Why did you use the phrase "subject position" in an interview? For me it is a tough Foucauldian concept-metaphor.[2] "Doing a sentence" might be unpacked as acting in such a way that when the interpreter or receiver of the action reduces it to the statement form of appearance [an *énoncé*], rather different from diagnosing an ideological presupposition, this particular proposition might emerge. Oh dear. If you just meant biographical details of race-sex-gender, then perhaps you *were* using a somewhat modish phrase unnecessarily, and your copy editor is right to rear.) Anyway, when I talk about my life I try to see it as representative of various kinds of historical lines, political lines, class lines, and so on. In fact, I say rather little about what life stories are like because it is not necessarily useful for us as feminists to decide that talking about lives is not intellectually okay. But at the same time I do feel, as does someone I admire very much, Assia Djebar, that it is useless to be really autobiographical when I'm trying to be didactic. Therefore, the tactic is to present myself and things that have happened to me as an example of certain representative cases. This is useful, it seems to me. Now this is not about subject positions. Subject position is something that we in fact cannot ourselves declare. It is something that should keep us careful because a subject position is assigned, and the word there is "sign"; it is that which makes itself visible through our textual productions in language and action. It is therefore given over to readers. There isn't *a* subject position.

MV: Is it valid to engage in this kind of "representation," however aware we might be of the provisionality of these produced identities? Is this a sort of strategic essentializing?

GS: I was quite interested to see, when I was reading with my class I, *Rigoberta Menchu*, which is of course classic testimonial, that what Rigoberta was doing was representing herself as representative even as she was pointing out quite openly that she was not representative.[3] Rigoberta Menchu is an organic intellectual. She is taken, of course—because people will not read her carefully—to be the subaltern as such. There is a difference between the two things. I was very pleased to see this. I felt that I had at last some kind of authority for the sort of thing that I have been doing, really, in the interest of using a life story as a life story, as representative of certain kinds of things. My own inclination in all these anecdotes has been to represent myself as less worthy of benevolence. I put myself a notch above my class position; I put myself a little less politically correct than I would deem myself to be. I think there is safety in those kinds of gestures. It's like keeping your watch fifteen minutes ahead of time so that you're not late. Although I'm a green-card holder, I regularly speak of my own group as the new immigrant. I identify myself as such, since identification is self-representation.

Only once did I self-consciously attempt to try something like just giving memory details, which is of course also not a life story, we know that, but nonetheless I tried it. In the context of Hindu fundamentalism, I wanted to show how I was brought up as a Hindu in a self-consciously ecumenical household, because I believe with scholars such as [historian] Gyanendra Pandey that we are complicitous with fundamentalism; it is not correct to say that it's only the others, the lumpen, the irrational, the gundas who are actually engaged in violence. We should see ourselves as complicitous. An Indian who was in my audience who was visiting the United States said quite correctly that I was being romantic. Because it is true that when one speaks one's memory in that way, especially on issues such as fundamentalism, racism, it does sound either romantic—if it is the way I was trying to do it, which is just simply like a home movie, standing at a lectern—or, I think, somewhat meretriciously inspirational, when people do it under the genre of "speaking personal pain" behind a podium.

DB: That's an interesting stand because we've just come away from doing an interview with Meena Alexander, and we were discussing the particular space of cultural narratives in the rapidly mounting discourse in Postcolonial Studies. She was talking about the personal and the public coalescing in what we call personal narrative. And you, of course, talk about the miraculating agency of the socius: that there's no such thing as really personal or really public because they are already defined.

GS: Now your copy editor wants a gloss on "the miraculating agency of the socius." It is interesting that the hard phrases are in your questions rather than my answers. Where on earth did I use that phrase? Surely not to mean there is nothing really personal or public? I think I picked up "miraculating" from Deleuze and Guattari over twenty years ago and used it to mean the unquestioned assumption that people from the same group (whatever *that* might mean, and the same person may have different "identities," some of which might clash) will behave, act—thus "agency"—similarly.[4] Thus I was perhaps talking about the representations of the collective (rather than the public) as or in the personal? There is something that we call personal and something that we call public, and to that extent they do exist. I wanted to say that we should not take them as final instances. No, I think it would be counterintuitive to say that there is nothing called personal. And it might be irresponsible to say that there's nothing called public, since there is a public sphere. Therefore, on a certain level of agency I think if we don't make these distinctions we will be irresponsible. But the word "is" is a tough word. So what one should think about is in what way one has ascertained the being of these things. I don't want to say there is nothing called personal and nothing called public. It would be on a very trivial level incorrect. Also, they emerge in oppositions, don't they? When in fact you are in what, in the history of the language, is the social situation clearly recognizable by you and others as public, then since it is clearly pushing away what is personal, something like the personal certainly emerges. And in the same way, when the personal is pushing away and differentiating itself from the public, it is certainly there. But it is the mode of their existence that we really have to think through when we use them.

Now Meena, of course, is a poet, and given the social and historical ways in which poetry and intellectual production have been differentiated, we should honor the differences. Exactly according to the way in which I'm asking you to think of the difference between personal and public. I'm not interested in making poetry enter once again into a firm relationship with the life world. I'm much more interested in making use of the fact that poetry, fiction, art have been in a certain way separated from the so-called life world, the Lebenswelt, because as such they now can, precisely by acceding to the personal, make visible the limits of the purely rational enterprise in controlling violence. I'm not interested in turning the clock back, because I very firmly believe that what is said to return is not the repressed but a version of it; the repressed is not a thing that we return intact. We really have no control over making the repressed return. And so, I use these differences because in a certain sense they do exist, but in a certain sense.

DB: At the same time, one needs to be aware that autobiography is also biography. One needs to keep the tensions alive. [Here we are interrupted by Spivak's assistant, who has been trying to track down a particular book for the course]

GS: Should I look at the description you sent me? [We had sent Spivak a description of the collection we were putting together, our own stakes in the project, and our motives and rationale for the undertaking]

DB: Certainly. In some ways, throughout your work you've tackled the issues we raised in our questions. Perhaps we should turn this over to what you might find interesting to talk about.

GS: It's not just what I find interesting to talk about so much as my reaction to your very careful description of the kind of book that you are putting together. First off, Mary, I presume from your last name that you're married to a South Asian.

MV: Yes, my being married to a South Asian and growing up in a household where I was always pushed to think critically are very much part of what I bring to this project, while Deepika brings her quite different background. If I might speak for her, her Anglophone and Anglophile education in Calcutta, her interest in local theater and politics, and a very Western-centered graduate education in the United States place her in a very different position. Recognizing the need for intercultural dialogue, we came together to talk about issues that we feel have an impact on both of us and society in general. The issue we wanted to raise with you was one of credentials and positionality.

GS: I think that the description of oneself as a white, Western academic feminist might be revised. Kumari Jayawardena's powerful book *Feminism and Nationalism in the Third World* shows us how much a marriage is a legal institution.[5] You are married to a Hindu who undoubtedly has some stake, conscious or unself-conscious, in the fact that we have not been able, and (I'm quoting Pandey again) the generation with the memory will never be able, to write the "history" of partition. Although Jayawardena cannot be held responsible for the point I am going to make, the story tells itself as you look at the figures she's describing. We see the way in which marriage is skewed in terms of the female and the male partners in the contract, in terms of cultural participation. It is comparable to the transplantation within migrancy, although it is not the same. One has to think through that the text of one's life is not separated from one's intellectual work, especially if one is working in cultural politics. The white woman married to an ex-colonial is vectored more toward the so-called national origin than the well-placed migrant woman who has come through an elite colonial education. That's not something one simply writes off as one describes oneself in an enterprise. I had thought about that. And then I had also wondered why you described yourselves as working in the Middle West. I was wondering particularly what kind of South Asian underclass there is in areas where you work.

DB: The population in our university town is largely composed of students and faculty.

GS: The Midwest for me is very significant. I taught as you know at Iowa for twelve years, and I think what I was most struck by in my students was their profound moral imagination. (How does one assign cause? But nonetheless one does.) I had thought of the fact that the migrancy patterns there came so much from Anabaptist, Scandinavian, proto-communist, Welsh nonconformist origins. And yet there wasn't, in that contemporary context, much awareness at all of what it was like to live in a place where there are plenty of African Americans or a very large Jewish population. At that time, of course, the waves of new migrancy had not really started quite as much as it is evident now. One of the most peculiar things about academics who want to claim marginality is that they seem always to find their examples in the underclass. Whereas in the Middle West this is not quite possible, it is possible in New York City. So I wondered if you had invoked the Middle West with any of that in mind. Then I wanted also to ask you—I know that you already have quite a few submissions and you are going to write an introduction soon—what kind of view you have now about the word postcolonial. What, then, is "postcolonial" for you now?

MV: That's a very good question. That's something Deepika and I have been struggling with throughout the entire project. We are aware of the usual connotations of the word, but we are uncomfortable with defining it in static terms.

DB: We believe that we need to predate that discussion and start with how one defines colonization in light of the fact that the history of humankind is the history of exploitation. We are also interested in why, in discussions of colonization, everyone focuses on the First World.

GS: You're saying that you don't have a very clear idea of what postcolonial is.

MV: On the one hand, yes we do. Of course we can formulate a definition in terms of the departure of colonizers from countries that had been colonized and then the resulting production of knowledge and power that has arisen from that. But I think you yourself say that that term is very hard to codify, even bogus.

DB: In academic discourse everyone seems to assume that we all share a common definition. We've seen a lot of work that just starts at that point—"Let's look at postcolonial literature"—and never problematizes postcolonialism or colonization. We've seen work on terminology and the role of the hyphen, what happens when you do away with the hyphen, that sort of stuff, but no real historicizing or investigation.

GS: Was that hyphen essay in *Australian Feminist Studies* or *Australian Cultural Studies?*

DB: I was thinking of a 1989 or 1990 article by Vijay Mishra and Bob Hodge. I believe it was called "What Is Post(-)Colonialism?"[6]

GS: Ah yes. And then also something from *Social Text*—you've seen it?

DB: That special issue?[7]

GS: Yes, right, where I think Madhava Prasad talks about that "without the hyphen."[8] I wish I could remember things well.

DB: Anne McClintock and Ella Shohat discuss terminology too in their pieces for that issue.[9]

GS: Yes, they talk about the usefulness of the term or the lack of usefulness of the term. Anne looks at an important issue. We were together at a conference where she and I were agitating together for a careful use of the term. I think I said it was bogus in an interview. I've learned how not to give interviews through giving those kinds of interviews. [*Laughter*] Unfortunately, since those interviews are easy, that book—best not to name it, perhaps—sells more than the other books, and I feel a little uncomfortable. It's taught me a lot about how to talk like a book rather than like a person. [*Laughter*] At any rate, we were both speaking very strongly about the uselessness of the term. But the collection that came out of that conference is still called *Colonial Discourse, Postcolonial Theory*.[10] But in the *Social Text* issue, Anne is talking about a case where I think perhaps, with some hesitation, the word bogus can be used. She's talking about the word postcolonialism. There I think there is a problem. And also she's talking about a very specific show, which I also went to, and I was also quite turned off and in quite the same ways. I just never wrote anything about it. I was very pleased that McClintock did do so. On the other hand, I think that one should have short definitions, which can help in some ways.

DB: So you can get the work done? You talk about inhabiting a position and then critiquing it. So one could sort of work with the definition almost as a homeopathic necessity?

GS: Something like that. And one can certainly describe, as you were saying, without asking all those "what is" questions. One can say that places used to be colonies and then there was independence—which is a legal change after all—and establishment of constitutions. These are very abstract things. Definitions, it seems to me, should concern themselves with abstractions. This is good. You can very easily know the difference between industrial capital and commercial capital, but this does not allow you to talk about the violence of capitalism. In that sense, there's a fact of independence, establishment of citizenship, passports, and so on. And then you can begin to see what sorts of problems arise that the abstractions cannot capture.

Now I would like to tell two stories in my way. I was at a large conference on deconstruction in New York last month. I was speaking at the roundtable; I was not one of the people presenting long papers. I had ten minutes. The conference topic was "deconstruction is/in America." I began by saying that from the start what interested me was that Derrida was Algerian, born in Algeria, with early education in Algeria, and lived during the Second World War in Algeria. Since I had ten minutes, I said I'm not going to talk about this, because our interest here is Europe and America—that's what we're talking about. I couldn't develop this point, and I was quite sure that it was taken simply as one of the regulation multiculturalist pieties; since I was the ethno-cultural agenda on that conference, I was the only one who was culturally different and so on. I think it was taken as one of those token gestures. What I really meant there, if I had had the time to go into it, was that when in 1967 I encountered *De la grammatologie* I didn't know who Jacques Derrida was. I bought the book from the catalogue. The 1966 structuralism conference had passed me by; I was a young assistant professor in Iowa. In those days postcoloniality was a secret, unlike now; it took one to know one, as it were. What I had liked in the book was that I had thought I was resonating with someone who was not quite not French in the way in which I was not quite not British. Such a person, as a sort of insider/outsider, knowing it in a very specific way, was exploring what he called Western metaphysics from that position, subject position if you like—that's the one that was assigned to him by me as I read. But the thing to remember is that it was then a secret of that sort; it resonated because you thought, hey, that's what's going on.

Now of course it's not only not a secret, but the word "postcolonial" is used to cover all kinds of bases. It is even used to avoid the question: Who decolonizes?

It is used to avoid the question—Ngugi's wonderful title "decolonising the mind" has also become a kind of grab title for sale—of what it is to decolonize anything other than the mind.[11] It is used to block investigation of the failure of decolonization, which we see all over the place, and also the fact that the relay has passed to neocolonialism, of which we are a part. These questions are not looked at. And, from the outside, as someone trying to avoid the epithet "postcolonial" applied to herself, according to that formula of subjection, and acknowledging and recognizing that chattel slavery and colonization are different—with all these qualifications, if you look at the sort of imposed power, continuity of insurgency and struggle, consolidation of something like an independence struggle by positing identity in the pan-Africanist and civil rights movement, then the winning of something like negotiated independence in the changes in the law and with emancipation in between, and then the beginning of neocolonialism as in a relay of internal colonization in the sense of an incredible and slow increase in racist rage and backlash; and if you also look at the failures of decolonization in various ways that have been pointed out by critics from within the African American society, then, considering all these factors, the only postcolonial society in terms of internal colonization in the United States, for all of us, the new immigrants, is the African American and not ourselves. So these are the two stories—one a story, the other a kind of hesitant speculation from the outside—these are the two things I'd like to say with regard to what it is we think postcolonial to be. [*Spivak's assistant enters with information*]

MV: It seems we caught you at a horribly busy time.

GS: The way we are doing this course is very hard work. The big famous anthologies do not pay any attention to the fact that in all of Europe, Italy is one of the strongest bastions of homeworking, sweated women's labor. They pay no attention to this at all, although there's stuff on unionization, and so on. Europe is for them, still, Europe. So that's why I'm getting as much of it done as I can this afternoon. And how do I know about Italian homeworking? I have to follow through in the way you just saw. That is why it is an advanced seminar. It is very irresponsible to work with beginning graduate students in a seminar, where the teacher is learning as she is teaching in the most elementary sense. You always learn as you teach, that's a different thing. The students in this class know that it is a class somewhat like a reading group, and what they are getting the "benefit" of, and the way I'm earning my salary, in other words, is the length of time over which I have been thinking about how to organize new material. That's all they're getting. It's a research seminar in that basic sense.

DB: What do you think our theory should have to do with the "Third World" woman?

GS: This is a problem of postcoloniality. We talk about academic women, as we are talking here, we make anthologies and so on, and yet, as Uma Chakravorty asks in her very interesting essay, although it's not fully developed (but how would one develop it?), in that rather useful volume called *Recasting Women:* What about the Vedic dasi?[12] There is all that talk about Gargi, Maitreyi, three thousand years of Indian women writing. But how about—and this is the question of subaltern studies—the fact of the ordinary woman? Ordinary in the sense of absolutely baseline. And in fact, that is why Djebar in her *L'Amour, la fantasia*, has talked about the unimportance of *her* writing *her* autobiography because it is not impossible to do it in any serious sense, given the international book trade.[13] What she's really more interested in is being able to get into a situation where the person who is ordinary in that sense (I hate the word grassroots, and the word subaltern is now absolutely useless because of the way it has become a buzzword, so I don't know what to say—just say right "down there") can speak an autobiography that is not a commodified testimony to fit our desire for evidence. The effort it requires to be able to be in a situation where *she* can use *me*—*that's* the book. In the overture to her *Women of Algiers* she speaks to other Arab women who have been able to obtain liberation, liberty, freedom, whatever, and she says that in a postcolonial situation our solidarity is not to speak for, not to speak about, but to speak *tout contre*—it's translated somewhat unsatisfactorily as "very close to" or something like that.[14] In the French of course it is "up against," it has the againstness within it as well. When you get that close, the point is not that you're really speaking for the right thing; it is always also against. The writing itself is an act of violation, in a certain sense. When I asked her to comment on this phrase, she said that we so often get fixed on the first one, and when we get fixed on the first one, she becomes commodified, monumentalized, in a certain way, which also stops us looking at the thing that Catharine MacKinnon, in quite another context, has called exceptionalism.[15] Then that too, in fact, becomes counterproductive. So in that sense, the notion of the feminist anthology, which is considering the elitism of some other kinds of feminist theory, overlooks completely this incredibly important issue of the most important example of gendering in neocolonialism: women in homeworking—the women in export processing zones and export-based foreign investment factories, subcontracting areas. These women are somewhat written about. But not the "homeworker" in post-Fordism. This is postcoloniality, much more than ourselves going on about us and our cultural backgrounds and so on. The homeworking phenomenon, women's sweated labor inside the house, with no control over indefinite lowering of wages, is so invisible and yet it is an international phenomenon. It is so difficult to organize. The word "invisible" is repeatedly used by concerned feminist sociologists; it is not just sort of a nice theoretical word used by deconstructivists. The sociologists themselves, women like Sheila Allen and Swasti Mitter, say that they are invisible. We're reading the Italian stuff because in the European context we have decided that the way we should divide it up is northwest Europe, southern Europe, and post-Soviet. If we didn't know about homeworking from outside documentation, then in fact what we would have missed is precisely the postcolonial element in the Italian context.

Where does one begin, where does one end? This too is a very serious issue of postcoloniality—that is to say, new patterns of gendering within neocolonialism. It is changing dynamically as huge abstract organizations like the World Bank and GATT (General Agreements On Tariffs and Trade) make policy. As they are deciding to change strategy, those patterns of gendering remain in place. If one really looks at it from that point of view, then, Assia Djebar's remarks become extremely important so that we look away from ourselves, look at the problem in order to see what is below us rather than how the top is not paying attention to us.

DB: Should we be trying to open up the discussion to make it more accessible and relevant to those outside restricted discourse communities?

GS: From that point of view, your self-description, Deepika, as growing up in Calcutta, is relevant. When I'm speaking to middle-class or upper-middle-class Calcuttans, I quite often look at the question of servants. And of course servants themselves have to be explained in terms of exploitation and domination. The fact of having servants as a visible marker has an oblique relationship to class superiority, because in an exploitative society the place taken up by labor-saving devices, which are implicitly and unrecognizably locatable as harming others, like radiation you don't see passing through you, has to be contrasted to visible domination, as of servants, which is more like a knife cutting in so that you see that you bleed. But nonetheless, in the context of Calcuttan middle-class or upper-middle-class backgrounds, I've heard young Calcuttan women, anthropologists, talking about how they should relate (which is basically a U.S. discourse), as advantaged people, let's say, for example, to the women in the tea gardens. And I asked the particular young woman the question, how do you deal with servants in your house in Calcutta? Why doesn't that question arise? What are the construction, constitution, political feeling, history, relationship to the female servants in our households? I think that's the most important question, autobiographical if you like, we can ask ourselves. Rather than looking at ourselves as colonial subjects and how people don't know enough about us. You see what I'm saying—that's a post-colonial topic. Simple, but completely undealt with. The sort of complaint that you hear all over the place, this is a very global thing, you hear it in South Africa but you also hear it in Calcutta from women who have very many fewer privileges than we have in the United States, "the servants are not as they used to be." We just dismiss it as "oh, that's the way mothers talk."

MV: What kind of historical background is necessary for those working in Postcolonial Studies?

GS: Think about the fact that Calcutta has, for what it's worth, a left-front government. If you look now at the way in which so-called economic restructuring happens, which is a huge global phenomenon, in the new world order after the dispersal of the Soviet Union, the barriers between fragile state economies and the international economy are falling one by one. Most of my feminist colleagues in the literature area don't know anything about what this means. They don't even think about the fact that this restructuring has changed the relationship between Calcutta and the central government in India. When people who don't know any of this hear Indian informants talk about how India is becoming better now, they take it as authentic information. Think about specific TV programs that you get out of Doordarshan, where a woman has actually designed and structured the whole program (so that's already a point for feminism) on the model of the new European multilingual TV, so that the program is both in Hindi and in English, at the same time. In the new Europe they use all of the EEC languages in a certain way so that it becomes one. Imagine someone who hasn't done the homework in terms of this restructuring, listening to this, how much it seems like it's the real thing. So there's the woman speaking Hindi; there's a man who really looks like your New Age man, young also, who is doing the English, very respectful, almost subservient to the woman. All the people who are interviewed are speaking some in Hindi, some in English, with proper Indian accents. This looks like absolutely authentic information. And yet what they're talking about—in phrases like "forty or forty-five or fifty years of retrogressive economic policy is now being completely overhauled so that there will be a new India, and so on"—in fact, what they're talking about is this so-called liberalization of the economy: economic restructuring. It is in the context of this enormously transnational, global, postcolonial phenomenon that our mothers and our aunts and our grandmothers are saying, "Oh, servants are not what they used to be anymore." And that's in fact a text in the most robust sense, not in the sense of verbal text, where "we" as upper-class or middle-class Calcuttan colonial subjects, women, should be focusing our attention. So that for me is a postcolonial task that is really rather different, if you see what I mean. It is only then that we can know that "women in development" are the worst victims of restructuring even in psychoanalytic terms.

DB: I'm thinking of Tendulkar's *Kamala* and some of Mahasveta Devi's work and wondering what place their work has in investigating some of the issues you have raised.[16]

GS: Well, but that's not academic intellectual work. You know what I mean. Fiction should indicate the limits of rational speculation. When we read fiction as information, it stops the other kind of work. That's why I say I really honor the differences. If we don't honor them and say there is no theoretical difference, that allows one to make specious claims. If I may quote Derrida here, he has talked about the absurdity of people claiming that their subject is decentered. He has spoken with contempt about this. When you invoke the decentered subject, you make small compromises every day and you allow the systems to remain intact. Acting in the name of the decentered subject is like saying "this is my subject position"; it's the same category of mistake. You make small compromises every day which lack all rigor, and you allow the system to remain what it is. They fixate on Rigoberta Menchu or Kamala or Mahasveta's heroines and, in fact, it's business as usual. Or you get benevolent information retrieval essays, whereas information retrieval work and learning how to read fiction should, in my view, supplement one another persistently and perhaps take the place of the constant complaint of "pay attention to us." Why should I make myself representative as a colonial subject rather than make myself representative as a female employer of female servants? Which one do you choose? Victim or agent?

DB: Does our use of the terms "postcolonial" and "Third World" allow us to be complicit in and profit from a corrupt system of politics?

GS: In the first pages of *Capital* and indeed all through the book, Marx is telling the worker, do not think of yourself as a victim of capitalism but think of yourself as someone who produces capitalism, the agent of production. That's his phrase. When he says the "agent of production" he means the worker. In that sense, he says, a good factory is more dangerous than a bad factory because in a bad factory we have all this empirical suffering—and you can say, "Oh well, it's suffering and domination." But in a good factory you say, "Oh how good this is, how well we are running it." And in fact what you are doing is *you* are constructing capitalism. This is not something people pay attention to. It's the same kind of thing that I'm saying. Why define ourselves as victims of First World knowledge factories and thus avoid making visible for all those very same knowledge factories—in a continuing stream of work, in the name of postcoloniality, not in the name of information retrieval—that they are also the place where *we* are agents of domination? Or even agents of exploitation, to which point I may come later. Fiction should not be a substitute for this work. Fiction makes visible the limits of this kind of work. The two should go together. In fact, the stream of "fiction" should come into these essays rather than let them continue as two completely different kinds of work, a primary and a secondary line. One is where you have all these facts and figures, and in the other literary critics continually write on fictional or testimonial characters, or on mechanics of representation.

MV: I'm very interested in what you're saying about choosing texts for a literature classroom and choosing texts that combine the fiction with material on, say, "Italian homeworkers." What might a pedagogy of the postcolonial look like?

GS: First of all, I'm not a good teacher. When anyone talks about teaching, you have to assume that person is just a wonderful teacher. This always leaves me a little cynical, frankly. One has to think about this in terms of how one teaches. One has to think first of one's own problems in reaching students. Students are not *tabulae rasae*. They come from a world. Of course, they are infantilized by our models of good teaching, so they fall into that. Their own model of good teaching becomes that kind of self-infantilization. So that's the first difficulty in how one teaches. Funnily enough, when you infantilize them, that is supposed to be nonhierarchical good teaching. This I find extremely troubling. On the other hand, what's the opposite? So one has to think through questions of teaching, it seems to me, not just always in terms of what *everybody* should do. That's the problem with theory too. You can say, "Well, we don't have enough theory about South Asians," but unfortunately, the assumption of all theory is that it is for everyone. And so these pedagogy books supposedly talk about everyone, whereas (a) it seems that one should begin from the fact that one is a teacher rather than what pedagogy should do, and (b) it depends not only on one's own abilities but also on the composition of students where one teaches. Even in New York City, the composition of a Columbia University classroom is so very different from the composition of, let's say, a classroom in Baruch College and, again, so very different from the composition of a classroom in Manhattan Community College. To an extent, it seems to me that we really have to be responsible to where the students are coming from and what education for them seems to be for. Teaching on the graduate level, one sees the constant eliding of the fact that they are there for certification, validation, competition, individualism—all this stuff. Not only certification and validation in the class but recommendation letters, competing for jobs, competing for tenure. I earlier used the word meretricious about inspirational prose. It seems to me that the problem of the end of a pedagogy is something that one has to think through: how exactly one should produce information about homeworkers to supplement Italian feminist anthologies. And Italian feminism is not the entire class either. We're not getting anything done because there are so many things we have to consider before we can answer what good it is to be doing this in this kind of classroom. Who are the students? What is this so-called education for? Education otherwise remains supposedly in the service of a dated notion of an essence of knowledge as knowledge about knowledge (Derrida's good phrase in "Mochlos").[17]

The other day one of my former students called me "Ms. Supplement" because she had taken a class (my point of view develops and changes) in 1991, and certainly that's what I was talking about, supplementing literary texts with social science texts. What I'm really doing with this Italian feminist anthology is I'm supplementing social science texts with primary material. In the fictive text there are holes which in fact are created by the limits of fiction. Part of the limit of fiction is what I was talking about earlier, the kind of space that has been cleared for fiction in the last two or three hundred years within the European tradition in which we all teach. We must first recognize the shape of the holes so that what we bring in from the social science text is the shape of that hole. As craftspeople we know very well that if we don't cut the block exactly like the hole, there will be no fit, and the damn thing won't work. Believe me this is not just an analogy. It is hard to teach this way. Especially if one is not a particularly adroit teacher. You have to share this with your students. I tell my students right at the beginning of the semester and throughout, I have certain problems with teaching, and I started full-time teaching in 1965. If I have not, with all my raised consciousness, been able to remedy these, with all these efforts, then there is little chance I'm going to be able to this semester. They have to be aware of this, and the nature of our contract depends a great deal upon a responsible handling of the problem.

I was listening to a talk by Gyanendra Pandey on Manto's famous short story which says that after partition the governments of India and Pakistan decided to exchange the inhabitants of insane asylums. This is a story that truly shows, makes visible, the limit of the rational historiography of the partition. Whether it happened or not is empirically still unverifiable. The only document that Pandey, who is a historian, has so far been able to unearth says that at this point it is not something we can take a decision on—which of course leaves the question open for further research. Now that's a hole in the fiction. If it's a group of students who are learning about other cultures by just reading the fiction, they are not brought into the supplementing of the nature of policy. Why was the exchange of insane citizens postponed, and so on? So the two begin to flesh each other out. And the primary material as such is something different again.

Part of our reading material one day was a book by Noeleen Heyzer on Southeast Asia, really a very good book.[18] I said, even though Heyzer's book was not the only one we were reading, it was almost the only text that mentioned anything about what I'm calling *gendering* in neocolonialism in Southeast Asia. One could miss that, with all the facts and figures in the book. In fact, you can easily dismiss this book as nontheoretical. We don't know how to recognize theory. It has to come dressed like theory, especially since most of the other fact-filled texts were doing other kinds of things. One could miss it very easily, but toward the end of the book Heyzer says that one of the most important things is care and concern. This is where we begin to supplement. We started talking about ethical singularity; that doesn't mean throw Heyzer away. Not at all. It is also not a question of adding or putting on reserve. After twenty-five years I stopped giving reserve lists because I saw that reserve lists were read with another kind of mind-set. Everything we read is right there on the table. This makes for bad teaching too—students don't know what we're going to discuss that day. But you take that risk. You ruin your classroom time because of the dangers of careless reading of the ethical moments in fact-filled texts. On the other side are the "radical" texts. You break down most of them and take away the radical language, and out comes old-fashioned liberal pluralism. From that point of view, adding is not the thing. It is to learn how to supplement and saying that there is more to be supplemented. Otherwise, people don't know how not to read Flaubert's *L'Education sentimentale* as an account of 1848. I'm really talking about a faculty development issue. The claim to interdisciplinarity is almost as useless as the claim to postcoloniality. It is something to be worked at in this way rather than something to be claimed.

MV: You talk about not being a "good" teacher. Is there something about the structure of the way we have to teach that prevents us from doing the kinds of things we would like to do in teaching? Maybe having our students for more than three hours a week or for only fifteen weeks? I'm wondering if it's possible to be a "good" teacher?

GS: I think a lot of my problems come from my temperament and personality, and that has to be taken into account. It's not always that we are being prevented. Unless one takes that into account, I think there is danger. We always put the blame on the structure. Also, when we talk about the problem of fifteen weeks and three hours, we have to think about what the alternative would be. In the interest of *what* were fifteen weeks and three hours put there? I don't think the issues are that clear-cut. On the other hand, I would hasten to say that when I say I'm not a good teacher, I am not comparing myself to people who teach in ways that cannot match the effort, sincerity, and concern for teaching that I bring to the classroom. I should not undermine myself by comparing myself with such teachers. I should also say that I have already won, over teachers who go in with the conviction that they can teach well. My standards are high because my standards are for myself and are focused toward the students. It is in terms of those standards that I see that I'm very far from being an able teacher. And there *are* able teachers. It's not just the structure. It is the structure

also—supported by and supporting the old-fashioned, really problematic notion of the Renaissance man, the notion of the canon, which is something we
haven't touched upon at all. Yet we've come too far to go on just faulting the
system. We should also look at ourselves as agents of teaching.

Now, I want to look at your second question, which reads: "If we can say that
identity and self are produced by a complex set of determinants, what produces
"postcolonial"? Does this naming and our reliance on language enable a dualistic, not to mention simplistic, fixing of identity that denies heterogeneity and/or
does this question itself reveal our preoccupation with linguistic binary oppositions? A related question: Is the identity politics card an *ethical* or useful one for
academics to play, or does it take the radical out of radical politics?"

Let me ask you, how do *you* see issues of identity? Remember I like simple
definitions to begin with. We take it for granted that one cannot have huge, ex-
haustive, correct definitions. On the other hand, if one is used to working on
TV, for example, one would be able to give a short answer. You cannot on TV
simply go on saying "Well, we don't really know." You can't construct yourself as a videographic agent if that's your answer. How do you see issues of
identity?

DB: We are looking at the ways in which people are presenting or representing themselves, what terms they are putting together, if you will, and what
profile is emerging.

GS: So do you see this as singular or collective?

DB: That question has troubled us. Partly we are trying to fill a gap that we
saw in other collections and anthologies, where we found that South Asians
were not represented together or, if people talked about Asian Americans, they
were not representing South Asians. But then we realized that this our project
might come off looking like a definitive representation of South Asian experience. That made us uncomfortable. We spent a lot of time wondering how this
collection will be read. In our introductory sections we issue a call for multi-
plying perspectives and representations. This would then be only one project
among many. In certain ways the South Asian experience, if you want to call it
that, will fit into larger narratives. That is something we can only touch on. At
this point, we'll just say that this is a representation within certain specified parameters. Let's multiply these stories. And that's something you called for. Your
message always seems to be diversify, don't generalize; go forth and multiply.
[*Laughter*]

GS: I'm a very untrustworthy person because I'm not very learned. Therefore I constantly change my mind. I learn more and I change my mind. I think
in a certain sense I should not write. But I can't be stopped from writing. I can't
stop myself from writing and speaking. I used to feel a certain degree of terror

of this. But now that I'm growing older I'm beginning to realize (I was always growing older, of course, but getting seriously older, hitting middle age solidly) that I'm not all that important. I should make it clear that I change constantly. Maybe one shouldn't congeal Spivak. [*Laughter*]

MV: What do you think of the issue of representation?

GS: Look at Asia. Of course Asian Americans are East Asians, and I say it is correct that it should be so. What the hell is Asia? On my desk there should be a book called *Asia before Europe* by Kirti Chaudhuri.[19] He makes the point that when you say "Asia," and of course when you say Africa, *mutatis mutandis*, you are assuming the prior set "Europe." And so in fact, he is trying to write a postcolonial history of simply the rim of the Indian Ocean, a precolonially defined region. That's not all of Asia. Asia becomes determined by the history of colonization, oppression, and the great lines of movement. As I said, I work with what history has given me. That Asian American is East Asian, to an extent, Southeast Asian; yet if you cross the Atlantic, in Britain, Asian is us. Why is that so? In Britain, one of the terms of opprobrium is "sari-wearing Asian." Why is that so? I haven't seen an East Asian wearing a sari there. In France, an Arab is generally North African, whereas, when we read a feminist anthology such as *Women, Islam, and the State* by Deniz Kandiyoti, North Africa is not in it at all.[20] There is Bangladesh and Indonesia but no North Africa there. These are not real names. When we say African, we don't think about North Africa; we think about central Africa. If we mean southern Africa, we say South Africa; we are not thinking about Zimbabwe, Botswana, and so on. These map names, we shouldn't try to correct them. We should, in fact, examine them in postcoloniality as what cartography has always been, phantasmatic. It seems to me that would be my input there. Are we going to do a numbers count for a falsely named "continent"?

Let me ask you: You say that the need for compilations of multicultural literature and theory has never been greater. Why do you think so? Why has that need never been greater?

DB: In a certain sense, we're talking about an academic need to reflect the diversity of our populations in the academy and to raise the issue of privilege.

GS: Is it just a kind of progress in knowledge, and therefore the issue of representation has become important? Do you think that's what it is?

DB: There is this need, manufactured or otherwise, for more, better, plural representations, particularly in the United States, because of the conflict politics that has arisen between the minority and majority races on the one hand, and among the minority races on the other.

MV: Maybe need isn't the right word. Maybe it's the time. The need has always been there. It's just that the time is right to talk about it as a need.

GS: Why? Remember I like videographic answers.

MV: Because we live in a world that is now global in terms of media, in terms of production. We now see India, Africa on our TV. People are ready to talk about multiculturalism. Whereas before, Africa and India were something "out there."

GS: Would this make sense to the mother of my friend Hiraman Tiwari, who's taking a doctorate at Oxford? His mother, from a peasant family, who has not in her life traveled the ten miles to Lucknow—would this statement of yours make sense to her?

MV: But we have been focusing on the academic dimensions, and we recognize that our audience is very specific.

GS: I know. Yet we live in a world that is not just academic. It's not just academics who see India on TV.

MV: Right. But the need we're addressing is something that's in the academy.

GS: I'm trying to go back to the statement you made that the time is right because we see everything on TV. Would this make sense to women and children who live in developing countries? There are villages where there are no books. I don't mean people can't buy books. There are no books. No newspapers. Of course there is a wonderful kind of last-ditch, totally indigenous effort at rural literacy. It is known that there is reading and writing, which can be learned. But the videographic image is not connected to that. There are many people to whom writing at speed is a thing to look at. So to an extent, it's not just that we're talking about an academic need but also that we're assuming a world which has been constructed for us, a need that closes other doors. I'm certainly not saying that your book should not exist; it absolutely should. I would not have agreed to talk to you if I didn't think that. I'm examining ourselves in a certain way, and I am wondering if you might speculate a little more about where the need comes from, what the need is for such collections?

DB: This book will serve an academic need, and the best I see myself doing is talking about the divide between the origin of the difference and the global, hybrid, migrant postcolonial. That has been privileged so far in what we are calling postcolonialism.

GS: Why do you think there is the academic need then?

DB: To fill out the layers. I look at the kinds of things that Salman Rushdie writes about, for instance. One of the things he talks about is the migrant transnational. This is a very strange way of trying to represent the people that Rushdie might have taken his materials from. There are all kinds of migrants. We're looking at the migrant, usually upper-class, middle-class intellectuals who have joined the academy and what they have to say. We're not even trying to speak for, to, or *tout contre* the people who might, for instance, be operating the sex shops in New York.

GS: I quite see that. I'm not really asking you what you're doing. This is an interesting project. The word "representation" is something I would fix on. I'm really asking you why there is a need in the academy for compilations of multicultural literature and theory. It's really not a question of your project, but it's a question about the reason for a need in the academy. What do you think is the reason for this need in the academy? Remember, I'm not asking you what the justification for your book is. I'm really asking you what the need for the compilation is? Why in general in the academy now is there a need for compilations of multicultural literature and theory?

MV: I would argue that there has always been a need, but there hasn't been the willingness, motivation, or climate to produce them that we now have in the academy. And that that need has always been a need to acknowledge, within the university, a world where there are people who don't have TVs and who aren't writing as we're writing, and that that is a need we're only now beginning to address. The academy has some responsibility to deal with those issues that it hasn't until now been willing to accept or been able to accept or even recognized that it should be accepting.

GS: My friend Rey Chow has written a rather interesting book, *Writing Diaspora: Tactics of Intervention.*[21] She begins by saying the sinologist Steven Owen wrote a controversially negative essay about world poetry not too long ago in the pages of the *New Republic*, while ostensibly reviewing the English translation of the collection *The August Sleepwalker* by a Chinese poet Bei Dao. Owen attacks "Third World poets" for pandering to the tastes of Western audiences seeking "a cozy ethnicity." Not a lot is written by non-Western poets that is distinguished by true national identity, he complains; it is instead "supremely translatable."[22] I'm really asking my question because I always take criticism seriously. I think the first step is to say "yes" to the critique—here, Owen's critique—and then to see where you just cannot say yes. It also seems to me that when one talks about cause and effect, one must keep asking the question in that mode, why, why, why? It is good to think about it in abstract terms. Rational abstractions are the only area where one can talk about cause and effect. And then one begins to see that the rationalizing of cause and effect has a limit. I feel convinced of Deleuze and Guattari's formulation twenty years ago, in the same book that gave us "miraculating," that capital is the abstract as such.

From my point of view now, the reason there is such a need for collections like yours is (and this is liberal multiculturalism) the financialization of the globe. Remember, this is a rational explanation, but that's what explanations are. Now, the people who are against political correctness are in fact fighting a losing battle. In *Eighteenth Brumaire*, one of the things Marx pointed out in his analysis of the French revolution on down was that whatever the conservatives and radicals were saying was not what was really going on. World history was working like *Hamlet's* father's ghost, the mole. The script was something else, and it was unrolling as they were doing this stuff. From that kind of viewpoint, the stage at which transnational trade is now, world trade one should say, it is necessary for people in the United States to "know other cultures." And again on a very rational plane, I would say, ideological apparatuses must bring this about. The way the transnationals are training people to know other cultures is infinitely more successful than the way we are. They're not pulling any punches.

I just read a review of my [translation of Devi's stories] *Imaginary Maps* by a woman who very authoritatively writes "Bengali" beside Mahasveta Devi and then brackets in "Bangladesh" [*laughs*]; her knowledge goes that far. So Indian West Bengal and Bangladesh are to her the same thing. Then she says that Spivak's introduction and afterword are not for beginners. I wrote back to my publisher saying that she's clearly thinking about an audience that is going to learn everything they need to know about that imaginary place called Bengal/Bangladesh from my introduction and my afterword. If I wrote that kind of silly thing in the introduction to yet another new translation of Dostoevsky, people would think I was crazy. But liberal multiculturalism—again, this is a very abstract focus analysis, because we are talking about causes and effects, so that we can begin to break this one up, but know this: Liberal multiculturalism is interested, basically, in bottom-line national origin validation. I was talking about the servants in Calcutta and that connection with financialization and restructuring rather than how *we* were produced. That's academic too, the servants in Calcutta. We, in fact, have had those servants, we academics who have come through. Opposed to that we have hybridity theories that always legitimize themselves in the name of the underclass. In fact, these often assume that the postcolonial, hybrid migrant in First World space has no other history and has not come from anywhere. They never look. I'm not faulting the migrant. I'm talking about our legitimation. They never look at the long visa lines in front of the British High Commission in New Delhi. They never look at the way the hybrid migrant, when he or she goes back, as they do (every summer I'm flying from Paris to Algeria and back, from London to Delhi to Dhaka and back)—these people, in their relationship to the underclass that did not, could not get away, don't look at the agency of the underclass; I'm talking about new and even second-generation immigrants. In fact, the privilege is given to the supremacists in the First World who are agents of racism. They are only interested in legitimizing themselves in the name of the hybrid victim. They do not see the whole scene. If one looks at national origin validation in terms of this need for liberal multiculturalism to produce the ideological basis for a financialized globe, and then if one looks at the hybridity theories, and in fact if one looks at the difference between labor export and U.S.-centric migration, one would lift the covering effects of words like exile and diaspora. In fact there is exile, there is diaspora. These are different kinds of things. I'm not faulting your subject, which is economic migration.

DB: In a performative material and local sense, how can postcolonialists negotiate the victim-agent position?

GS: I will in a minute come to how I think we can, like Marx's workers, become agents rather than self-represented victims, remembering of course that the worker never did, in the Marxian sense. So if one looks at the kind of hybridity theory I'm talking about, it is an abyssal conversation within Europe and between Europe and the United States. The claim for global hybridity does not often make the distinction that hybridity is a completely different phenomenon when it is on the other side of the North-South divide. Nonetheless, one can distinguish between someone who's losing weight because she's dieting and someone who's losing weight because she's starving, even though the phenomenon rationally is the same. Now in that situation, our claim to be included and the claim outside, "get off our backs," in the context of development and transnationality, are two different kinds of claims. It seems to me that if we are going to think of ourselves as agents in this situation, then in fact we must think of ourselves as Americans—in fact, acknowledge that we have come to be Americans. And that American is hyphenated. Just as Asia is not a cartographic "truth," to be American is not to be an "Anglo-clone." If we follow through on this argument, national origin validation legitimizes Anglo-cloning by reversal. The extraordinary racist argument comes through very clearly not only through the British National Party but even in the Ninety-sixth Street subway station, where I have heard, from an older minority, "Take your green card and go home." Now we legitimize by reversal when we talk about South Asia rather than Asia. We legitimize by reversal those kinds of arguments that come back from Enoch Powell on down to the Los Angeles riots. We can explode the assimilation argument if we look at ourselves as also American, hyphenated. But American is hyphenated. In that sense, we then begin to see that, having thrown in our lot with a northern economy—an exploitive economy, in fact—whether we like it or not, we are, in our every day, agents of exploitation. You turn on the faucet and you're agents of exploitation. We also are, at the same time, *wanting* to remain agents of exploitation. If all our social work, our community work is United States–focused, we can't get out of this argument. I'm certainly not speaking against working for the deprived, but if we are addressing an academic need, the academic's duty is to understand the big picture. The First World is not the world. I'm remembering now a Moroccan friend in Holland, a migrant activist who has just become the first nonwhite member of the Dutch parliament, who said to me once, not knowing me well enough, "Well, Gayatri, you know you have to understand that if in fact what I'm working for is successful, I'm not do- ing anything about the North-South divide." When academics make provisions for their old age by way of tax-shelter annuities, when they pay taxes, they are completely complicit with an exploitive economy. If we see ourselves, the Eu- rocentric economic migrants who came in hordes after Lyndon Johnson relaxed his quota in 1965, those are basically the South Asians. If we see ourselves as that, then in fact we can begin to look at real transnationality. If the U.S. academic has a multiculturalist need, it is to devise ways of undermining the current model of transnationality. The first step may be to discover how the nation of origin is suf- fering in a new world order where we are the agents. If we perceive that need, then we are a collective, like all our collectives, united by the fact that we are new Americans, not the old-style assimilated Americans. In fact, when we do our multiculturalism the other way, we are assimilated by the political position of liberal multiculturalism. Museumization. Commodification. I'm not saying that it's bad to have cultural accounts included in history courses, cultural studies, and so on, but what I'm saying is that it should relate here.

I would like to talk about something Cornel West has spoken of, easily and beautifully in a speech about his *Race Matters*.[23] (Given the way my time is go- ing this semester, I'll probably read that book when I go to India in Decem- ber.) West is married to an Ethiopian woman. And he was making the distinc- tion, "I'm a New World African, she's a new immigrant." The whole point is made in a flash. The New World African is American in one way. The new im- migrant is also American. Neither of these characters, the New World African and the new immigrant, will today go in for the old definition of everybody looking like some Anglo-clone, which is the assimilated American. But the only way in which to claim that position of agency is to say, quoting Derrida in *The Other Heading*, that we are also American, rather than put the focus on how we are Asian and not like the ones who are called Asian here.[24]

That brings me to your first question: "There are historians who argue that the history of colonialism is the history of humankind, that imperial expansion has never been a uniquely European experience. We are told, for instance, of Hindu colonies in the Far East dating back to pre-Christian times. Yet discus- sions on colonialism and postcolonialism are usually dated with regard to Eu- ropean imperialism. Bear with us as we splinter off into questions that rhi- zomatically seem to lead to further questions: First, how does one define colonization? Is colonization simply a necessary concomitant to human growth and development? What are the reasons why racism and exploitation within 'exploited' and 'disenfranchised' groups are not given the same attention as the occurrence of the same phenomena from without (a question you have raised yourself)? All these questions lead to a particularly potent issue for Postcolonial Studies: Is there anything particularly significant about European and Anglo-American colonization?"

What is significant about this last wave of colonization is that we're still in it because of the relay to neocolonialism. It's the one that fit; the word conjuncture is of course the heavy-duty word. "Fit" will do. The one that fit nascent capitalism. We also have the cusp examples: Chicana/Chicano, Latina/Latino. They are on the cusp of the end of conquest-based mercantile capitalism, when that cusp is hardly distinguishable from nascent industrial capitalism. There are old residual hatreds. How much do the Bosnian Serbs mobilize in the name of paying back for the Ottoman Empire, itself another cusp phenomenon? Contemporary imperialisms are more interesting, because there is a fit between the economic, the dominant, and the political. When we look at internecine racism within the so-called marginals, we must remember that imperialism is not identical with racism. Internecine racism is different from the Southern focus. For example, in the Indian context we are completely destroyed by not being able to theorize partition. We are completely taken up with structures of racism within India. Certainly no one is looking there to fault imperialism. It is the fundamentalists who are saying: We are the real anti-colonials. That is internecine. Assia Djebar, in *Women of Algiers in Their Apartment*, is looking to open up the picture of the same name by Ferdinand Delacroix. The black woman in that picture is the only dynamic figure; she has her feet placed in a movement and is turned around, holding the curtain. One of Djebar's major objectives is to see North Africa as African rather than only Arab, only Islamic. It seems to me that there are these movements—certainly class movements—within various social formations, all over the place. Whereas there is a strong hegemonic emphasis placed on the so-called theorizing done in the First World, which is then taken up by the elite universities in the former colonies. Although they're by no means small in number, one doesn't look at them. This whole business of the tribal movement in India, that is completely in terms of internal colonization. There is quite strongly a move—I'm thinking of Kumkum Sangari—to warn against romanticizing such people.[25] But that is a danger one must face, because the other side of romanticizing is censorship. They remain silent. It does seem to me that it's not that those kinds of movements are lacking but that imperialism is something other than racial prejudice or racial violence or religious violence. And the reason why the contemporary conjuncture of imperialism and its aftermath is so important is that we're still within it and because it fits the story of what again Marx would call the self-determination of capital. The real bind in studies such as ours is that we're within it in the strongest possible sense; we are also its agents. Therefore, we also question it in ways that leave our agency underreported. We manage its crises by our restricted radical activities.

DB: Could we ask one last question about your extra-institutional work? You say that the academy prevents us from asking questions of global import, that what is needed is a certain experience to teach for agency. What might that be?

GS: I think we really have to work that out ourselves. I don't really have a great reportable account of extra-institutional work. I go where I go, wherever I go. First of all, I'm only talking about my own way of finding a way of learning. And this is only an intellectual project, so how extra-institutional is it? I'm not interested in root-finding; therefore I don't just go to India. What is India anyway? When I go, I go in order to learn. I've talked about transnational literacy. Literacy is not knowing a language. When you're trying to become literate, you don't try to write a book in that language. It's as simple as that, my reason for not talking. I'm supposedly, by definition—and that's the representation that everyone wants me to choose—a marginal. If I chose that one, the fact that I'm not trained to do oral history, the fact that I'm not trained to do anthropology, the fact that I'm not trained to do any of these things, wouldn't matter. The book trade would pick me up. I have to watch out for those things; life is short. If I really want to learn, giving in to those demands I learn zero. I have nothing to transcode where I am learning to learn.

The one thing that I will not do (and I may be completely wrong) is join an international organization in that endeavor to learn, because I have learned enough about international organizations, even the most benevolent, how they work. Remember, in my book, one looks at causes and effects in terms of the abstract. I won't be institutional, since I'm not an anthropologist or oral historian looking for the primitive, nor will I join an international organization; in six or seven years I have never seen urban radicals in the kinds of places I'm talking about. There is nothing to transcode—it really is to learn. The way in which it affects me most noticeably is that I become increasingly amused by generalizations that are easily made and accepted. Is that a big effect? Are there other kinds of effects? I don't know what they are. I really sometimes think of Freud's idea of suspending yourself when you are analyzing. That is a model of responsibility. Transference is a model of responsibility. Responses coming from both sides. I really do try the hardest I can to suspend my analytical machinery. Even with indigenous NGOs [non-governmental organizations], I am careful. There are a few NGOs that actually conscientize, change the lives of women from the same stratum as the people who are "being helped." You have to see who becomes your patron, whatever it is you do. Those are not the kinds of places where you can just go and hang out. So you work, which also teaches you something. But for me it is really an alibi. And the last thing that, as an academic, one should do is to aggrandize herself by saying, "Ah, you see what I'm doing, isn't this just wonderful. See, I'm not just an elitist." I think that is the beginning of the end. There is a horrible, horrible thing in minority discourse—a competition for maximum victimization. You say there is a demand for multiculturalism. I have to find out who the hell is demanding this from me? Why the hell is there such a need? It's got nothing to do with who has suffered the most. It is absurd to claim authenticity by saying that the homeless in New York City or the rape victims in Pittsburgh have suffered much less than the people in the villages of Bangladesh. That is absolutely meretricious. I have no desire to make some kind of competitive list of who is the worst victim. I think that is where madness lies.

As Spivak delivers these final comments, she is tracing the outline of a key on an index card, making a few cuts with a blade, and showing us that this is a safe way to send keys by mail. She completes the task and ends by saying, "I can do practical stuff too. Never let it be said I'm only a theorist!"

NOTES

1. Gayatri Chakravorty Spivak, "Neocolonialism and the Secret Agent of Knowledge" (interview with Robert Young), *Oxford Literary Review* 12.1–2 (1991): 220–51.

2. Michel Foucault, *The Archeology of Knowledge*, trans. A. M. Sheridan Smith (New York: Harper, 1976), 91–92.

3. Rigoberta Menchu, *I, Rigoberta Menchu: An Indian Woman in Guatemala*, trans. Ann Wright (London: Verso, 1984).

4. Gilles Deleuze and Félix Guattari, *Anti-Oedipus: Capitalism and Schizophrenia*, trans. Robert Hurley et al. (Minneapolis: University of Minnesota Press, 1983), 10.

5. Kumari Jayawardena, *Feminism and Nationalism in the Third World in the Nineteenth and Early Twentieth Centuries* (London: Zed Books, 1986).

6. Vijay Mishra and Bob Hodge, "What Is Post(-)Colonialism?" *Textual Practice* 5.3 (1991): 399–414.

7. *Social Text* 31–32 (1992).

8. Madhava Prasad, "On the Question of a Theory of (Third World) Literature," *Social Text* 31–32 (1992): 57–83.

9. Anne McClintock, "The Angel of Progress: Pitfalls of the Term 'Post-Colonialism,'" and Ella Shohat, "Notes on the Post-Colonial," *Social Text* 31–32 (1992): 84–98, 99–113.

10. Francis Barker et al., eds., *Colonial Discourse, Postcolonial Theory* (Manchester: University of Manchester Press, 1994).

11. Ngugi wa Thiong'o, *Decolonising the Mind: The Politics of Language in African Literature* (London: J. Curry, 1986).

12. Uma Chakravorty, "Whatever Happened to the Vedic Dasi? Orientalism, National-ism, and a Script for the Past," in *Recasting Women: Essarys in Colonial History*, ed. Kumkum San-gari and Sudesh Vaid (New Delhi: Kali for Women, 1989), 27–87.

13. Assia Djebar, *Fantasia: An Algerian Cavalcade*, trans. Dorothy S. Blair (London: Quartet Books, 1985). One could compare this (with)holding with Derrida's "Circonfessions" (in Geoffrey Bennington and Jacques Derrida, *Jacques Derrida*, trans. Geoffrey Bennington [Chicago: University of Chicago Press, 1993]), I think, where the man allows himself to write inter-minably in order to catch at another sort of impossibility, below: the mother's way of liv-ing on rather than the Father's way of dying to the Law.

14. Assia Djebar, *Women of Algiers in Their Apartment*, trans. Marjolijn de Jager (Charlottesville: University of Virginia Press, 1992), 2.

15. Catharine A. MacKinnon, "On Exceptionality: Women as Women in Law," in *Femi-nism Unmodified: Discourses on Life and Law* (Cambridge, Mass.: Harvard University Press, 1987), 70–77.

16. See Vijay Tendulkar, *Kamala*, in *Five Plays* (Bombay: Oxford University Press, 1992), 1–52; Mahasweta Devi, *Imaginary Maps: Three Stories*, trans. and intro. Gayatri Chakravorty Spi-vak (New York: Routledge, 1995).

17. Jacques Derrida, "Mochlos; or, The Conflict of the Faculties," in *Logomachia: The Con-flict of the Faculties*, ed. Richard Rand (Lincoln: University of Nebraska Press, 1992), 1–34.

18. Noeleen Heyzer, *Working Women in South-East Asia: Development, Subordination, and Emancipa-tion* (Philadelphia: Open University Press, 1986).

19. K. N. Chaudhuri, *Asia before Europe: Economy and Civilisation of the Indian Ocean from the Rise of Islam to 1750* (Cambridge: Cambridge University Press, 1990).

20. Deniz Kandiyoti, ed., *Women, Islam and the State* (Philadelphia: Temple University Press, 1991).

21. Rey Chow, *Writing Diaspora: Tactics of Intervention in Contemporary Cultural Studies* (Blooming-ton: Indiana University Press, 1993).

22. Stephen Owen, "Books and the Arts: What Is World Poetry?" (review of *The August Sleepwalker* by Bei Dao), *New Republic* 203.21 (1990): 28–32.

23. Cornel West, *Race Matters* (Boston: Beacon Press, 1993).

24. Jacques Derrida, *The Other Heading: Reflections on Today's Europe*, trans. Pascal-Anne Brault and Michael B. Naas (Bloomington: Indiana University Press, 1992), 83.

25. Kumkum Sangari, "Figures for the 'Unconscious,'" *Journal of Arts and Ideas* 20–21 (1991): 67–84.

PART II

COMMENTARIES

CHAPTER 5

African Americans and the New Immigrants

Amritjit Singh

People of South Asian origin in the United States number about two million now and may be regarded as an "imagined community" within the broad framework of Benedict Anderson's definitions.[1] Although American conceptions of "race" play a significant role in how all immigrants of color are perceived (more on this later), their assimilation into American life parallels in many ways what earlier European immigrant groups have undergone. The replication in North America of homeland attitudes and hierarchies or even of subcontinental conflicts is not unique to our ethnic group, nor is the feeling of despair at the fragmented sense of community we frequently experience. Yet in some ways we are privileged today to have many significant new models of assimilation and hybridization beyond the "melting pot" metaphor that dominated the scene until the 1960s. These radically new approaches to immigration and ethnic diversity—suggested by the frequent use of such phrases as mosaic, descent and consent, kaleidoscope, salad bowl, double consciousness, and multiculturalism—have opened new spaces for self-definition for most new Americans.[2] Now that these approaches have become part of the public discourse in North America, it is no longer possible to insist on treating immigrants and the cultures they bring with them as inevitable sacrificial lambs on the altar of a real or illusory American Dream.

Ironically, these recent attempts to acknowledge or celebrate long-standing multicultural American realities have also inspired many prophets of doom—such as Patrick Buchanan, Alan Bloom, and our very own Dinesh D'Souza—to invoke the dangers of balkanization. The real perils of balkanization lie most probably not in these new conceptions of immigration or multiculturalism but

A short version of this essay appeared as an Op-Ed piece in the *Chicago Tribune*, 4 November 1992.

in the giant-size failure of all Americans—white, black, or brown—to make a difference in the way racism, poverty, unemployment and underemployment, drugs, and crime continue to plague the lives of our largest community of color: African Americans. There are more South Asians in this country now than the combined populations of Rhode Island, Wyoming, and Alaska. African Americans, however, outnumber the total population of Canada and form a large and diverse "nation within a nation."

South Asians have much to learn from African American history about being acculturated in North America, because of the myriad ways "race" complicates our real life experiences, including interethnic behavior. Recent demographic shifts such as the emergence of Asians as a visible large minority in some California locations (including, for example, the University of California, Berkeley, campus)—and white responses to such developments—are already persuading South Asian students and professionals to become more fully aware of their own history on this continent. I first came to the United States in 1968, and a major debate in the 1970s (evidenced in the early issues of *India Abroad*) was whether or not South Asians should seek or accept a minority status and give up the emotional and psychological advantages of being considered "Caucasians," as they were then classified by the Census Bureau. Today, some twenty-five years later, most of us would find the idea of empowering ourselves as Caucasoid not only laughable but even sinister. The ironies are further compounded when we learn the history of this concept in the struggle of South Asians to get acceptance as migrants or naturalized citizens in the early years of this century. The Naturalization Act of 1790 employed explicitly racial criteria, limiting citizenship to "free white persons." When this act was successfully challenged after the Civil War on behalf of blacks (notwithstanding the complicated history of African American citizenship between the notorious Compromise of 1877 and the Civil Rights Acts of 1964 and 1965), Asian Americans of all backgrounds became the most significant group excluded from citizenship. In 1922, in a case that denied naturalization to a person of Japanese birth, the Supreme Court circumvented the question of color by defining "white" as "Caucasian." In 1923 when a South Asian immigrant, Bhagat Singh Thind, tried to gain citizenship by arguing that he was a "Caucasian," the Supreme Court brushed aside anthropological and historical issues and invoked the popular meaning of the term "white." In turning down Thind's request, the Court applied the criterion of assimilability to separate undesirable from desirable immigrants: Asian Indians were distinguished from the European immigrants, who were deemed "*readily assimilated*" (italics in original) with the immigrants "already here." In 1924 the Johnson-Reed Act established immigration quotas based on the existing ethnic population of the United States, effectively excluding most Italians, Slavs, and Jews.[3] For South Asians, other similar painful lessons about "race" in North America are likely to emerge from a closer examination of the details surrounding the 1914 *Komagata Maru* incident in Vancouver, British Columbia.[4]

The assumption for ourselves of the label "South Asian" is a major challenge under any circumstances but would be even more difficult without adequate attention to the constantly shifting labels for other groups, including African Americans, Latino Americans, and Asian Americans in general. An attempt to forge a South Asian identity is sure to recall a history of similar attempts in the 1960s to reject the exoticizing label "Oriental" in favor of the term "Asian American," which, as Sau-ling Wong has noted, "expresses a political conviction and agenda," a recognition that (a) all Americans of Asian American descent "have been subjected to certain collective experiences that must be acknowledged and resisted," and that (b) if "Asian American subgroups are too small to effect changes in isolation, together they create a louder voice and greater political leverage." Further, this "larger pan-Asian identity has to be *voluntarily adopted* and highly *context-sensitive* in order to work." The process of realizing such political choices might also permit an understanding of the "legal contortions," outlined above, that have been used to achieve Asian Americans' exclusion from mainstream life, resulting in their historically functioning "as a peculiar kind of Other (among other Others) in the symbolic economy of America." Although as much voluntary immigrants as the Europeans, Wong continues, Asians "are alleged to be self-disqualified from full American membership by materialistic motives, questionable allegiance, and above all, outlandish, overripe, 'Oriental' cultures." And yet that does not exclude the possibility that they would occasionally be seen as adding "the spice of variety to American life" or being "held up as a 'model minority' to prove the viability of American egalitarian ideals."[5]

On lower frequencies, the label "South Asian" offers some of the same potential for valuable coalitions and political leverage as the term "Asian American." The label "South Asian" is based on an implicit recognition that new Americans of various national backgrounds in South Asia (India, Bangladesh, Pakistan, Sri Lanka, Nepal, Bhutan, and the Maldive Islands) and possibly others of South Asian ancestry from elsewhere in the diaspora (for instance, Fiji, East Africa, Guyana, Surinam, or Trinidad) have a common stake in how they come to terms with significant elements of homeland cultures as they grapple with their new situations in the United States. The adoption of a South Asian identity clearly calls for an acceptance of our shared culture (food, clothes, language, customs, cultural attitudes, and so on), despite subcontinental divides of religion, politics, and nationality, requiring a deliberate effort on our part to come to terms with experiences, needs, or agendas that bind us together as participants in American politics, culture, and economics. But any effort in that direction is retarded by our strong sense of marginalization and isolation in the United States, pushing us toward some kind of homeland activism. There is a tendency to see our lack of status in American society as a direct result of mainstream indifference or lack of respect toward a given national background, be it India or Pakistan or Bangladesh. Contributing to this fragmented consciousness are our own nostalgia for homeland and our genuine concerns about public issues affecting the lives of family and friends still living there. The diasporic South Asians have been heavily invested in projects that serve the needs of homeland nationalisms of one kind or another—political, religious, ethnic, or regional. The net effect of these tendencies is to reinforce "national" or religious or linguistic identities and impede any progress toward global citizenship or alert participation in American life, leaving us vulnerable to manipulation by several constituencies: self-styled leaders representing one cause or another on our behalf; our centers of worship (Hindu temples, Sikh *gurdwaras*, Muslim mosques, and Christian churches); homeland embassies and consulates; and "pro-India" or "pro-Pakistan" members of the American Congress.

Most South Asian student organizations on U.S. campuses, like our community organizations in general, project the image of being predominantly "Indian" or "Hindu" or "North Indian" or "Punjabi" or "Gujarati," which discourages free and full participation by South Asians of other backgrounds. At one level, many young South Asians have imbibed the attitudes and biases of their parents' generation—for the most part, immigrants who have arrived here since 1965 from the subcontinent or other diasporic communities. But the new generation also faces challenges as new Americans that the older generation has been able to avoid by means of a "sojourner" stance, or through the classical immigrant psychology of "paving the way for our children," or by seeking shelter in emotional ghettoes made up entirely of food and videos shared with South Asian friends.[6] Caught in their own confusions and struggles, South Asian immigrants of my generation, now in their forties and fifties, have not been very helpful in preparing their children for the cultural conflicts they face in their American lives. If anything, many of us have imposed our own ideas of pure identity upon them. For most of us, our idea of homeland is frozen in the moment we left our town or village or state or region. It is difficult for us to recognize that the "nation" we represent in North America is much too large and complex and constantly shifting, and that we are ourselves being challenged by the evolving new constructions of gender and family. Most of us continue to hoard real or imagined fond memories of homeland life, hoping they will serve as a bulwark for our children against the seductive and subliminal messages from the American media.

Having made an uneasy truce with "glass ceilings" but functioning other-wise in an officially egalitarian and open setting, we are often aware of serious difficulties with certain homeland values such as caste and other assumptions about life and duty that we like to call *samskaras,* but we keep our thoughts to ourselves—either because of our own ambivalence or because we are afraid of turning our kids away from homeland cultures and pushing them further into the lures of "American" values and life-styles. All this is complicated by the un-due pressure we place upon our children to become doctors or engineers and our general lack of respect for humanities and social sciences, disciplines that might allow us and our children to create spaces of understanding all of us des-perately need to negotiate our immigrant, diasporic lives. Few of us are ready to acknowledge that after two decades or more of our lives in the United States, we are neither purely Indian (or Pakistani) nor American. We have also failed to notice that despite the claims of some reactionary pundits, there has never been a fixed definition of being either Indian (or Bangladeshi) or American; for diasporic South Asians these ideas are constantly shifting. Yet our dialogic ex-istence represents a rich potential for perspective and action instead of the pow-erlessness we often identify with. Once we become aware of other ethnic his-tories in North America, not only can we learn from their sense of their past; we can also form mutually supportive coalitions with each ethnic or racial group caught in the same whirlwind of change and resistance.

Not long ago my wife, my teenage daughter, and I were in Maryland, near the Beltway, to attend the wedding of a friend's daughter. My friend, who mi-grated from India in 1985 at the age of fifty six, lives in a townhouse with his wife and four adult children—two sons and two daughters, one of them the bride-to-be and the other a single mother of a lively nine-year-old daughter, Asha. We admire the way my friend and his wife have found it possible to play supportive roles in the new lives of their four children. The wedding takes place at a local hotel which, I am told, caters ethnic foods of many varieties, some-thing unheard of only ten years ago. Money, it seems, is persuasive; local busi-nesses adjust quickly to accommodate new shades of population. Indian food is served at this wedding, which has gone very well indeed—with help from friends and neighbors. The "exotic" wedding ceremonies are explained in Eng-lish for the non-Indian guests, who appear to enjoy this multicultural setting.

After the wedding we stay on at our friend's house. By late afternoon several videotapes of the affair are available for viewing, and everyone is eager to ex-perience this instant transformation of the event into magnetic memory. Be-sides the three of us, there are two other visiting families in the living room: a scientist and his wife from upstate New York, and a real estate agent from Queens, New York, with his wife and two children—an eight-year-old girl named Roshni and a baby boy whose arrival three months earlier, we learn, had occasioned an extravaganza in honor of his maleness. My wife and I have feasted all day on rich, oily food and Indian sweets. We are ready for fresh air. My friend's granddaughter, Asha, and her young friend, Roshni, accompany us for a short walk around the neighborhood. The girls are eager to talk and show off. Asha, whose name means "hope" in Hindi, has promised to show us her school and the park she visits daily. As we walk away from the street my friend lives on, we leave his quiet suburban neighborhood behind. Several rows of well-kept townhouses give way to a busy metropolitan road.

Like the unexpected encounter with a stranger, this major road that runs through an otherwise sheltered neighborhood triggers in me other thoughts and memories. I think of a recent incident in Bellingham, Massachusetts, near us. A five-year-old Southeast Asian girl walking by herself on a busy road near her home was apparently lured by a driver into his car and then raped and murdered. All of a sudden I become protective of these two little girls who exude so much openness and trust. I ask them if they would walk all by themselves along a road such as the one we were now on. They assure me that they would not, that they have had strict instructions never to do so. But at this point, Roshni, whose name means "light" in Hindi, bursts out, "But Uncle, I have this friend in New York—she is twelve—and she goes all over, even to those streets where black people live. Her parents have told her many times that blacks would rob her and kill her, but she does not listen. She is a bad girl, very bad."

I am shocked more at the tenor than the content of her statement, as I have often heard similar sentiments mouthed by Asian Indian and Pakistani adults at social gatherings. In this very American view, broadly prevalent in Asian American communities, "black" is almost a synonym for violent crime and drugs. But at some of the same gatherings, I also find one or two younger people protesting this view. Unlike their parents, they have African American friends and have developed a better understanding of how racism and poverty operate in American society. Although their responses may not fit a sophisticated intellectual view of race and ethnicity, these young Asians appear to know at some level that the alienation they sometimes feel at work or school is experienced even more intensely by their black peers. They are also often in tune with rap and reggae; maybe the deep sense of "alienation" expressed in contemporary black music resonates with their own sense of rebellion against their parents' double standards: an insistence on seeing African Americans harshly through the prism of caste even as they cloak themselves in the highest American ideals of fairness and equal opportunity. Occasionally, the young people have also read The Autobiography of Malcolm X (1966), or Richard Wright's Black Boy (1945), or Toni Morrison's The Bluest Eye (1970), or seen a movie such as Do the Right Thing or Boyz N the Hood.

And though they may criticize the film *Mississippi Masala* for one representational flaw or another, most of them do not share their parents' discomfort at the love scenes between an Indian woman and a black American man.

But in Maryland that evening, when I think about Roshni's tender age, I am filled not with hope and light but with despair. So, when we return from our walk, I decide to talk with her father. At first, he appears a bit embarrassed; he even acknowledges his role in encouraging or shaping young Roshni's views. My daughter has perked up at this discussion; I know she likes political arguments, especially when she smells "racism" in the corner. When she makes the point—with the righteous idealism of youth—that we are all human, that we all have the same blood, and that a black person's blood might save his life in a hospital emergency, Roshni's father, joined soon by his wife, releases in mindless fury some of the worst stereotypes of African American life.

I ask him if he has any black friends; he pleads not guilty. But he asserts with confidence that Michael Jordan will soon go the way of Mike Tyson (rape conviction?) or Magic Johnson (HIV-AIDS?); that if middle-class people like us are paying unusually high taxes, it is only because of "all those blacks on welfare"; that blacks do not want to work or work hard; that blacks have contributed "brawn" but no "brain" to the development of this country. When I remind him about the need to understand the history of slavery and Jim Crowism, he informs us that he is not interested "in the past, only in the future." My daughter and I express our concerns about Roshni's future if she grows up with such negative attitudes toward any one group, but we soon realize that we are not getting anywhere.

Later on, our embarrassed silence is broken by the scientist from upstate New York who talks about how affirmative action has done little for blacks but given many whites a basis to complain about "reverse discrimination." He also wonders if Dinesh D'Souza is not right in condemning the academy as much too liberal. I often disagree with him, but we both enjoy the conversation and see in it an opportunity to learn from each other.

As Thomas Powell and others reminded us in the wake of the 1992 Los Angeles riots, many middle-class whites use their "feel-good" racism to try to rationalize the decline or stalemate in black American lives in terms of the "good choices," based on their character and determination, that they make but blacks do not.[7] But it is equally important for us to examine the process by which new immigrants have for over a century (mis)translated the black American presence into their often perplexed lives. In his 1929 essay "Our Greatest Gift to America," black journalist George S. Schuyler suggested, rather impishly, that the greatest contribution of American Negroes to the United States was not buildings and bridges, King Cotton, or Duke Ellington but the sense of superiority over blacks which new European immigrants were able to maintain in adjusting to the painful realities of their American existence. It is this false superiority, Schuyler told us, which inspired the "hope and pride of European immigrants," and spurred them on to "great heights of achievement."[8] Half a century later, in his 1981 introduction to *Invisible Man* (1952), Ralph Ellison noted that the African American's "darkness . . . glowed . . . within the American conscience with such intensity that most whites feigned moral blindness toward his predicament." Ellison went on to note that this "moral blindness" has been shared by "the waves of late arrivals who refused to recognize the vast extent to which they too benefited from [the African American's] second-class status while placing all of the blame on white Southerners." Cornel West and others have rightly directed attention to the need for the American discourse on "race" to move away from the "us/them" binarism in which the desire to blame seems to take precedence over finding ways of changing foundational structures that sustain racism, but we cannot move forward without grasping how the powerful mythology of "whiteness," a pervasive ethnocentrism, came into existence in the first place and how millions of poor and rich whites continue to benefit from it psychologically and materially.[9]

I do not think new Asian immigrants have disengaged themselves entirely from this pattern by which the old immigrants empowered themselves as "whites" instead of remaining ethnic Italian or Irish or what-have-you. The new Asian immigrants cannot become "white," so they seek overcompensation in real estate and material goods. Like Roshni's father, many Asian Americans make up for the lack of whiteness by acquiring a consciousness that is often as "white" and assimilationist and "mainstream" as that of most whites. Although it is understandable why most new immigrants would want to stay away from the underdog and identify aggressively with WASP culture instead, their continued failure to recognize the palimpsest richness of a multi-ethnic America only contributes to the terrible human consequences of racism and ethnocentrism.

For instance, although Asian parents are quite concerned about the power of peer pressure in their children's lives, they are unable to see the extremity of that pressure in, say, the life of little Pecola in Toni Morrison's *The Bluest Eye*. Pauline, Pecola's mother, has internalized mainstream images of "romantic love" and "physical beauty," which are described by Morrison's implied narrator as "probably the most destructive ideas in the history of human thought." Pauline "collected self-contempt by the heap" in having "equated physical beauty with virtue." Now, through the depth of generational self-hatred and parental abuse, Pecola has convinced herself that she will remain "ugly" unless she can acquire blue eyes. In an evocative brief scene, Morrison's protagonist walks into the neighborhood grocery store to buy Mary Jane penny candies whose wrappers picture "smiling white face. Blond hair in gentle disarray, blue eyes." While Mr. Yacobowski, the immigrant store owner, could not be held responsible for Pecola's feeling closer to dandelions and cracks in the pavement than to human beings, "nothing in his life" suggested that he might acknowledge Pecola's humanity. In a devastating critique of the "whiteness" mythology, Morrison's narrator raises the question, "How can a fifty-two-year-old white immigrant storekeeper with the taste of potatoes and beer in his mouth, his mind honed on the doe-eyed Virgin Mary, his sensibilities blunted by a permanent awareness of loss, *see* a little black girl?"[10] Can our Roshnis and Ashas really flourish as Americans until all of us can come together to break the cycle whereby countless Pecolas end up on heaps of rubbish every year?

Like Morrison's young narrators, Frieda and Claudia, many immigrant readers might feel beautiful beside Pecola's ugliness, eloquent beside her inarticulateness. In real life, most new immigrants are jolted into a shock of recognition only through their own first experience of subtle or open discrimination. Jewish immigrants have in some ways represented the insoluble aspects of this eternal dilemma. As a group of predominantly European stock, American Jews have had the real possibility of going the way most European ethnics have gone in acquiring a white American identity; but as a group with a resonant "re-memory" of their own past persecution—in Toni Morrison's sense of experiencing the affirmative possibilities of the past—they have had a tradition of resisting that temptation. Despite the widening black-Jewish rift in recent years, many Jewish Americans would acknowledge that there is no effective way of fighting anti-Semitism without making a similar commitment to oppose white racism and ethnocentrism.

In the 1960s and 1970s many Asian American writers, intellectuals, and artists were inspired by the civil rights movement and black consciousness. Ronald Takaki, for example, wrote several books and articles in Black Studies before publishing his major book on Asian American history, *Strangers from a Different Shore* (1989). Elaine Kim learned from African Americans "to reject the false choice between being treated as a perpetual foreigner and relinquishing my own identity for someone else's Anglo-American one." For her, "African Americans permanently defined the meaning of 'American.' "[11] The protest writings of Frank Chin and others were inspired by African American models, and some of their characters reflect an unusual awareness of black culture. For instance, the walls of Japanese American artist Kenji's apartment in Chin's *The Chickencoop Chinaman* (1974) are covered with posters of "black country, blues and jazz musicians which clash with the few Japanese prints and art objects."[12]

Today, as a community with a growing population and fragmented consciousness, Asian Americans are painfully aware of the variety of obstacles they face in their own pursuit of the American Dream but seem to have little direction or resolve to examine their new lives. Community newspapers and TV programs continue to inject homeland concerns and tensions into the lives of new Asian immigrants in unfocused and abortive attempts to create meaning. As mirrored in the multiplicity of internet news groups on regional and religious topics related to South Asia, these trends grow unchecked. Even though a sizable number of new Asian immigrants have arrived here better informed about American realities than were their counterparts earlier in the century, their participation in their new American lives is held back by patterns of nostalgia and parochial conflict. Some had been alert observers of the American scene long before they became landed immigrants. Many probably migrated less out of economic desperation than for purely professional reasons, or possibly because of a deeply felt attraction to the American ideology of "Life, Liberty, and the pursuit of Happiness" for all. Their awareness of choices and limits in this "nation of nations" has been much sharper than anything experienced by any earlier generation of immigrants. (Notice that some of this applies also to European immigrants arriving now but not to Southeast Asian refugees since the 1970s, who reflect the more classical pattern of immigration.) The expectations these new immigrants have of America are higher, and so are their disappointments when confronted with "glass ceilings" in corporate life or discriminatory quotas in university admissions.[13]

Perceptions based in "race" complicate the lives of all Asian ethnics, not just new immigrants. As David Mura has noted, the Sansei, third-generation Japanese Americans, find themselves visible targets in recurrent rituals of Japan-bashing, even though they haven't fully recovered yet from what the second-generation Nisei experienced during World War II.[14] Many fourth-generation Japanese Americans, over 90 percent of whom do not know the Japanese language, have also observed that a young new immigrant with a thick German or East European accent finds immediate and wide acceptance as an "American," whereas they are constantly asked to explain "where they had learned to speak English."[15] It is frustrating also to deal with "racial" attitudes affecting juries that have not returned strong convictions for the perpetrators of hate crimes directed at Asian American citizens in Michigan, New Jersey, and elsewhere.[16]

In the 1980s, however, the Reagan and Bush administrations and the media focused not on these problems but on presenting Asian Americans as a "model minority"—a burden in itself, which has in turn laid the groundwork for self-serving politicians of both parties to continue their divisive tactics on family values, deflecting attention from the urgent need for systemic change and collective responsibility.[17] Instead of addressing the root cause of the many problems all Americans of color face in some measure, the government agencies and the media have attempted to use the same stick to scratch the backs of Asian Americans that they have used to beat African Americans. Many educators have escaped their own responsibility by asking a simplistic question: if Asian Americans can make it, why can't blacks? It has become a common habit to assign individual responsibility without reference to the effects of harsh circumstance or long-term systemic exclusion. Our urban public schools—unable to meet the challenges of de facto segregation and the surrounding social chaos—have come to mirror the unfulfilled promises of a democracy. An expensive neighborhood in Nassau County, Long Island, where my cousin, a new immigrant, bought a house in 1965, is still forbidden territory for upwardly mobile black families. Such neighborhoods and their real estate agents have mastered the art of accommodating new immigrants as a way of deferring their struggle with their own deep-seated racism against blacks. Frequent attempts to treat "black" as just another color in the American rainbow are indicative of the widespread patterns of denial in American life with reference to its racial obsessions. No wonder, Gloria Naylor observed wryly in 1994, that Americans have learned new ways of talking about "racism" but not new ways of thinking about this painful reality. Even as we approach the twenty-first century, blacks are twice as likely to have a mortgage application turned down as others. Danny Glover and Bill Cosby still cannot successfully hail a cab in Manhattan without assistance from white bystanders. Meanwhile, affirmative action continues to deliver on its promises repeatedly to the same class of black individuals and families, even as it gropes in the dark for its truly intended targets amid the ever widening underclass.[18]

The heterogeneity of Asian American communities has compounded their general indifference to political participation and a marked absence of strong leadership. Many Asian American intellectuals and writers also seem to have bought into the divisive strategies that have dominated the political discourse in recent years. Possibilities of connection and coalition with other Americans of color are lost, for instance, in the vestigial colonial ventriloquism of Dinesh D'Souza and the celebratory assimilationism of Bharati Mukherjee. In the novel Jasmine and writerly statements such as "Immigrant Writing: Give Us Your Maximalists!" Mukherjee's cheerful, forward-looking attitude toward the possibilities of assimilation is achieved through a reductive and stereotypical representation of South Asian realities, a fantastic view of human psychology and individual consciousness, and dubious generalizations about immigrant and expatriate writing. Although one may make valid distinctions between expatriate and immigrant writers, some of Mukherjee's own work illustrates that the immigrant experience in literature can be as "dead and 'charming,'" or as exoticized as the re-created experience of an ancestral land.[19]

There is little desire among Asian Americans today to learn from the long experience of Native Americans, Latino Americans, and African Americans in
fighting discrimination. Yet the new Asian Americans, who often display a
"raw nerve"—a combination of naiveté and boldness—in attempting to sprint
their way to a colorblind America, may have much to learn from African Americans, who have been marathon runners against racism. There is much for all
"racialized" Americans to ponder in the extended lyrical meditations W.E.B. Du
Bois offers in his 1903 classic, *The Souls of Black Folk*—from his responses to the
failure of Booker T. Washington's ideology and practice as a "race" leader, to
his own journey toward self-definition as African American through his first
encounters with southern racial realities in Tennessee and Georgia. Among the
challenging lessons all new Americans of color could absorb is the coded message offered on his deathbed by the narrator's grandfather to his immediate
family in Ellison's *Invisible Man*: "Live with your head in the lion's mouth. I want
you to overcome 'em with yeses, undermine 'em with grins, agree 'em to death
and destruction, let 'em swoller you till they vomit or bust wide open." In facing such challenges of strategy and identity—as Ellison's young protagonist
does—we will open up the possibility of keeping our souls intact, of coming
to terms as individuals with our own backgrounds and situations without sur-
rendering easily to goals or labels supplied by others. The words of Woodridge,
the protagonist's English teacher, are likely to ring in our ears too, as we puzzle through the meanings of Ellison's textured novel in the context of our new
lives. "Stephen's problem, like ours," exclaims Woodridge with reference to
James Joyce's young protagonist, "was not actually of creating the uncreated
conscience of his race, but of creating the *uncreated features of his face*. Our task is
that of making ourselves individuals. The conscience of a race is the gift of its
individuals who see, evaluate, record." In the process, asserts Woodridge, we
would have create both a "race" and a "culture."[20]

Maybe Asian Americans bear no direct responsibility for what happened to
the blacks in the past, but can we afford to ignore what gets done now, if we are
to ensure a better tomorrow for all our Roshnis and Ashas? Asian Americans
cannot expect to escape the effects of racial neglect, benign or otherwise, and
as many of us know now from firsthand experience, the solution certainly does
not lie in focusing our energies on moving from one colorless suburb to another. As self-conscious citizens of the world, we are implicated not only in the
continuing patterns of violence and human rights violations in our ancestral
lands but also in the complicated national histories of our adoptive homelands.
Asian American denial of responsibility for the consequences of Native American, Latino American, and African American histories in the present American
moment is no less problematic than the self-professed innocence of many

young Euro-Americans—including some of my students at Rhode Island College—who prefer to think of racism against blacks either as something that happened in the past or as something that happens elsewhere (generally in the South), or both.

Unlike earlier European immigrants, some Asian Americans who have been here since 1965, when U.S. immigration laws were liberalized for Asians, have been able to move quickly into two-income suburbs without experiencing their Americanization in the crucible of the city. But most new immigrants still tend to hover around the metropolis, where they find a generous measure of acceptance and opportunity. In a 1992 speech, Governor Mario Cuomo noted that 370,000 native-born residents left New York City between 1980 and 1987 but were replaced by 575,000 immigrants, preventing a massive decline in population. Our cities provide the most significant arena for action if we want our precious diversity and "difference" to become assets for all of us instead of remaining disadvantages for some of us. The economic future of the United States is dependent upon how we educate, train, and integrate our growing underclass into the political mainstream. Although it would be a mistake to diagnose the despair of our cities purely in terms of existing patterns of misunderstanding between blacks and Asian Americans (because surely the sources of African American despair lie much deeper in U.S. history), the situation does call for a much wider role for organizations such as the National Urban League, the NAACP, and the Black-Korean Alliance in California.

According to historians Arnold Shankman and David J. Hellwig, even though black Americans do have a history of economic envy and ethnocentric contempt for immigrants, they have not generally shared the white nativist's need to scapegoat immigrants in times of recession. Blacks have "often indirectly acknowledged that the source of their bitterness was American racism rather than the lowly immigrant." Also, "with near unanimity and consistency Afro-Americans rejected schemes to limit or exclude Asian immigrants while the much larger flow from Europe continued virtually unchecked. . . . As with the Jews, blacks found comfort in the successes of Asians, especially in the Japanese, in the United States. If other visible minority groups could overcome racial barriers, so could they, many reasoned."[21]

At the same time, many in our poor, disenfranchised African American communities today do find satisfaction in scapegoating Asian Americans for the continued lack of opportunities that black youth face. For example, many blacks believe that Koreans have received favored treatment from American banks. They blame the absence of capital in black communities on the modest success of some Asian Americans (even though we know from researchers that the reasons for the absence of capital among African Americans are historically complicated and systemic).[22] Most Koreans and Hong Kong Chinese, however, deny such allegations, asserting that they have often invested in their new businesses the life savings they brought with them into this country. In fact, 1990 studies done by the Alexis de Tocqueville Institution, the American Immigration Institute, and the Hudson Institute show that new immigrants have always made strong contributions to U.S. economy and to the revitalization of cherished American values without taking jobs away from other Americans. And although most new immigrants, European or Asian, choose to have minimal interaction with blacks or their communities, Koreans have in recent years brought new capital and energy into "unsafe" black neighborhoods. As Korean Americans find ways of connecting more meaningfully with black youth and church groups around them, blacks might learn from the models of thrift and small business success that some of their Korean neighbors represent. We need to fight not one another but the redlining and other discriminatory practices that have hindered minorities, especially African Americans, in the first place.[23] To extend the words of warning issued by Elaine H. Kim after the Los Angeles riots of May 1992, "without an understanding of our histories," blacks and Latinos in one city, Asians and Latinos in another town, blacks and Asians in yet another neighborhood, would all be "ready to engage in a zero-sum game over the crumbs of a broken society, a war in which the advancement of one group means deterioration for the other."[24]

As a result of major changes at home and around the world in recent years, the American identity is under immense new pressures today, pressures comparable to those of the 1940s and the 1950s when American Studies as we know them now first came into being. There is a significant difference, however. Challenges to old and familiar definitions of America have come this time primarily from new immigrants of color and the continuing need to address the levels of discomfort that African Americans still experience about their Americanness. White ethnocentrism informs the many pessimistic predictions about the cracking-up of the American identity under an "incredible" pace of change and accommodation demanded by a growing acknowledgment of our multicultural realities. But surely the phoenix of a new American identity will rise out of the ashes of the old one, with constitutional structures serving once again as the wings. The visible tensions within and between American ethnic groups often mirror homeland realities or cultural differences, but they are more often symptoms of their shared economic powerlessness. Our lives in these United States as well as the futures of our Ashas and Roshnis are surely intertwined in the ways in which all of us, as Americans, learn to address issues of race and caste, gender and class, and find new solutions rooted firmly in our ideals of equal opportunity and equality, fairness and harmony.

NOTES

1. Following Benedict Anderson, *Imagined Communities* (New York: Verso, 1991), 6, one might view "South Asians" in North America as an "imagined political community [a kind of nation], . . . both inherently limited and sovereign. It is *imagined* because the members of even the smallest nation will never know most of their fellow-members, meet them, or even hear of them, yet in the minds of each lives the image of their communion."

2. The dyad "descent and consent" is derived from Werner Sollors, *Beyond Ethnicity* (New York: Oxford University Press, 1986). Suggesting that an emphasis on ethnic identity is not always helpful in understanding many key aspects of American culture, Sollors sees "the conflict between contractual and hereditary, self-made and ancestral, definitions of American identity—between *consent* and *descent*—as the central drama in American culture." He posits that "descent" is traced back to a non-American culture, whereas "consent" implies an embracing of all that is American. In viewing American diversity as "kaleidoscopic," Lawrence H. Fuchs, *The American Kaleidoscope: Race, Ethnicity, and the Civic Culture* (Hanover, N.H.: University Press of New England, 1990), asserts that the shared identity of Americans can no longer have exclusivity in the Judaeo-Christian tradition and observes that the United States is now home to a growing number of Hindus, Muslims, Buddhists, and Sikhs. The concept of "double consciousness" was formulated by W.E.B. Du Bois in 1897 and is enshrined in the opening chapter of *The Souls of Black Folk* (1903); for its origins in nineteenth-century thought and continuing influence, see Dickson H. Bruce Jr., "W.E.B. Du Bois and the Idea of Double Consciousness," *American Literature* 64. 2 (1992): 299–309; Bernard W. Bell, *The Afro-American Novel and Its Tradition* (Amherst: University of Massachusetts Press, 1987); and Gerald Early, ed., *Lure and Loathing: Essays on Race, Identity, and the Ambivalence of Assimilation* (New York: Allen Lane, Penguin Press, 1993).

3. The information in this paragraph and the one that follows is based on Sau-ling Cynthia Wong, *Reading Asian American Literature* (Princeton, N.J.: Princeton University Press, 1993), 1–17. Wong's discussion is based in turn on Sucheng Chan, *Asian Americans: An Interpretive History* (Boston: Twayne, 1991); Michael Omi and Howard Winant, *Racial Formation in the United States from the 1960s to the 1980s* (New York: Routledge, 1986); Jeff H. Lesser, "Always 'Outsiders': Asians, Naturalization, and the Supreme Court," *Amerasia Journal* 12.1 (1985–86): 83–100; Elaine H. Kim, *Asian American Literature: An Introduction to the Writings and Their Social Context* (Philadelphia: Temple University Press, 1982); and William Peterson, ed., *Concepts of Ethnicity* (Cambridge, Mass.: Harvard University Press, 1982).

4. In May 1914 a group of 376 South Asians—340 Sikhs, 24 Muslims, and 12 Hindus, mostly men, all from the Punjab—led by Gurdit Singh chartered the Japanese freighter *Komagata Maru* (renamed *Guru Nanak Jahaj*) for $66,000 to test the Canadian immigration laws as "British citizens." For two months the ship was anchored in the Vancouver harbor, and the passengers were not permitted to disembark. After a series of complicated maneuvers that involved the local Sikhs, undercover agent William Hopkinson, and the legal system in British Columbia, the ship was forced to leave Vancouver on 23 July 1914, arriving on 26 September in Calcutta, where a confrontation with the colonial police left twenty-six of the surviving passengers dead and most others in jail. For further details, see Joan Jensen, *Passage from India: Asian Indian Immigrants in North America* (New Haven, Conn.: Yale University Press, 1988); Hugh Johnston, *The Voyage of Komagata Maru: The Sikh Challenge to Canada's Colour Bar* (Delhi: Oxford University Press, 1979; rpt. Vancouver: University of British Columbia Press, 1988);

Sohan Singh Josh, *Tragedy of Komagata Maru* (New Delhi: People's Publishing, 1975); and Ted Ferguson, *A White Man's Country: An Exercise in Canadian Prejudice* (Toronto: Doubleday, 1975). The incident has inspired dozens of poems and at least two full-length plays: *The Komagata Maru Incident* (1976) by Sharon Pollock and *Komagata Maru* (1984), written in Punjabi by Vancouver-based writer Ajmer Rode. In 1989 the Canadian government supported several events in Vancouver and elsewhere to commemorate the seventy-fifth anniversary of the tragedy as part of its official diversity goals.

5. Wong, *Reading Asian American Literature*, 5–6.

6. For discussion of the complicated ways in which race, ethnicity, and immigration affect issues of American identity, see the introductions to Amritjit Singh, Joseph T. Skerrett Jr., and Robert E. Hogan, eds., *Memory, Narrative, and Identity: New Essays in American Ethnic Literatures* (Boston: Northeastern University Press, 1994) and Amritjit Singh et al., *Memory and Cultural Politics* (Boston: Northeastern University Press, 1996). For other views of generational styles and tensions within Asian communities, see R. Radhakrishnan, "Is the Ethnic 'Authentic' in the Diaspora?" (219–34) and Elaine Kim, "Between Black and White: An Interview with Bong Hwan Kim" (71–100), both in *The State of Asian America: Activism and Resistance in the 1990s*, ed. Karin Aguilar-San Juan (Boston: South End Press, 1994). Bong Hwan Kim talks eloquently about the pain and possibilities of his American upbringing, but even more significant are his reflections as a community activist on the challenges of forging an alliance between Korean Americans and African Americans in Oakland and Los Angeles.

7. Thomas Powell, "Feel-Good Racism," *New York Times*, 24 May 1992, Op-Ed page.

8. George S. Schuyler, "Our Greatest Gift to America," in *Anthology of American Negro Literature*, ed. V. F. Calverton (New York: Random House, 1929), 405–12.

9. Cornel West has made this point forcefully in *Race Matters* (Boston: Beacon Press, 1993) and elsewhere. In her keynote address, "The African-American Image in American Literature," at the Mark Twain House Symposium "The Power of Language" (Hartford, Conn., 1 October 1994), Gloria Naylor showed how the relationship between power and language might be illumined by our understanding of the process by which the American mythology of "whiteness" was created in the first place and how it continues to influence all Americans, including new immigrants. Naylor makes some of her points again in the introduction to *Children of the Night: The Best Short Stories by Black Writers, 1967 to the Present* (Boston: Little, Brown, 1995). See also Noel Ignatiev, "'Whiteness and American Culture: An Essay," *Konch* 1.1 (1990): 36–39; he argues that by "becoming whites, immigrants renounced the possibility of becoming truly American" (36). Studs Terkel, *Race: How Blacks and Whites Think and Feel about the American Obsession* (New York: New Press, 1992), corroborates the worst fears and realities about "the American obsession," and many of his respondents expose their guilt or ambivalence in having abetted or benefited from racist traditions and practices.

10. Toni Morrison, *The Bluest Eye* (1970; rpt. New York: Penguin, 1994), 122, 50, 48. Although some elements that shape Pecola's self-loathing are peculiar to her family situation, there are, as Morrison notes in her November 1993 afterword, other "aspects of [Pecola's] woundability [that are] lodged in all young girls." In narrating the story of how Pecola is destroyed by "the damaging internalization of assumptions of immutable inferiority originating in an outside gaze," Morrison says she tried hard to "avoid complicity in the demonization process Pecola was subjected to" by social rejections throughout her short life: "I did not want to dehumanize the characters who trashed Pecola and contributed to her collapse" (211–12).

11. Ronald Takaki, *Strangers from a Different Shore: A History of Asian Americans* (Boston: Little, Brown, 1989); Elaine Kim, "They Armed in Self-Defense," *Newsweek*, 18 May 1992, 10.

12. Frank Chin, "Act I of *The Chickencoop Chinaman*," in *Aiiieeeee! An Anthology of Asian-American Writers* ed. Frank Chin et al. (1974; rpt. Washington, D.C.: Howard University Press, 1983), 55.

13. For a discussion of "glass ceilings" in corporate life and informal quotas imposed by many Ivy League universities on the admission of Asian American students and the response of University of California to similar complaints on the Berkeley campus, see Chan, *Asian Americans*, 179–81; and Takaki, *Strangers*, 479–80.

14. David Mura, "Bashed in the U.S.A.," *New York Times*, 29 April 1992, Op-Ed page.

15. Takaki, *Strangers from a Different Shore*, 3.

16. In June 1982, Vincent Chin, a twenty-seven-year old Chinese American, was chased and beaten to death with a baseball bat in Detroit by two white men, who were apparently expressing their resentment over growing unemployment in the automobile industry because of stiff competition from Japan and mistook Chin for a Japanese. Asian Americans were outraged when Wayne County Circuit Court Judge Charles Kaufman sentenced both to three years' probation and a fine of $3,000 each plus $780 in fees. Despite appeals and retrials, neither man spent a single night in jail. Sucheng Chan (*Asian Americans*, 178) notes that the lesson learned in the Vincent Chin case was not lost, and Asian Americans immediately mobilized to monitor developments after another Chinese American, Ming Hai Loo, was killed in Raleigh, North Carolina, in July 1989. See also Takaki, *Strangers*, 481–84. The South Asian community in Jersey City was geared into action in autumn 1987 by the racist threats and assaults against them by "Dotbusters" (named after the ritualistic dot, *bindi*, worn on their foreheads by many Hindu women) and the heinous murder of Navroz Mody, a thirty-year-old Citicorp executive, by a gang of Latino youths, who did not touch Mody's white companion.

17. See Chan, *Asian Americans*, 167–71, and Wong, *Reading*, 37–39, 160–63, for the complex and conflicting ways in which the "model minority" idea is used in American discussions of race, class, and culture. Charles P. Henry, "Understanding the Underclass: The Role of Culture and Economic Progress," in *Race, Politics, and Economic Development: Community Perspectives*, ed. James Jennings (New York: Verso, 1992), notes that in presenting Asian Americans as a model of economic success to blacks, neoconservative scholars such as Thomas Sowell ignore the difficulties faced by many Asian communities (such as Filipino Americans) and the growing class cleavage within each Asian American community.

18. Naylor, "African-American Image." "Black underclass" is generally defined as "a growing number of Black persons who are uneducated, unemployed and often unemployable, . . . living in unrelieved poverty, and immersed in a culture conditioned by such abject circumstances, with only limited chances or no hope for upward mobility." This definition is provided by Mack Jones in "The Black Underclass as a Systemic Phenomenon," in Jennings, *Race, Politics, and Economic Development*. See also Henry Louis Gates Jr., "Two Nations, Both Black," *Forbes*, 14 September 1992, 132–38; William Julius Wilson, *The Truly Disadvantaged: The Inner City, the Underclass, and Public Policy* (Chicago: University of Chicago Press, 1987).

19. Bharati Mukherjee, *Jasmine* (New York: Fawcett, 1989); Mukherjee, "Immigrant Writing: Give Us Your Maximalists!" *New York Times Book Review*, 28 August 1988, 1, 28–29.

20. Ralph Ellison, *Invisible Man* (1952; rpt. New York: Random House, 1981), 16, 345–46.

21. David J. Hellwig, "Strangers in Their Own Land: Patterns of Black Nativism," in *American Studies Today: An Introduction to Methods and Perspectives,* ed. Amritjit Singh et al. (New Delhi: Creative Books; Providence: Off Campus Books, 1995), 329–30. See also Hellwig, "Afro-American Reactions to the Japanese and the Anti-Japanese Movement, 1906–1924," *Phylon* 38 (March 1977): 93–104; Arnold Shankman, "Black on Yellow: Afro-Americans View Chinese Americans, 1850–1935," *Phylon* 39 (March 1979): 1–17; Shankman, *Ambivalent Friends: Afro-Americans View the Immigrant* (Westport, Conn.: Greenwood Press, 1982).

22. Extensive commentary (including several essays in Jennings, *Race, Politics, and Economic Development*) on the problems of capital formation and the relative absence of savings in the black community highlights long-term poverty, unemployment, and exclusion; the lack of resources to transfer savings and assets from one generation to another; and the consequent low net worth of black families in comparison with white families having similar income. In 1984, according to the U.S. Census Bureau, black families with incomes between $24,000 and $47,000 had a net worth of $19,068, while the net worth of white families in the same income group was $60,304. Parallel figures for families with incomes over $48,000 were $70,125 for blacks and $150,045 for whites. Jacqueline Jones, *The Dispossessed: America's Underclass from the Civil War to the Present* (New York: Basic Books, 1992), ix–x, establishes that "in their commitment to formal education, to family, and to hard work, African-Americans have adhered to values shared by other Americans regardless of race, class, or regional identification." But by "emphasizing patterns of resourcefulness common to blacks and whites of a similarly low material condition," Jones also seeks to "illuminate the historic forces of marginalization that [have] engulfed the poor of both races."

23. There is considerable documentation of continuing discrimination against blacks in both housing and mortgages. A Boston Federal Bank study of 1991 mortgage applications found that blacks of all income levels are rejected for mortgages at twice the rate of whites; see "Eye of the Beholder," *National Review* 45.18 (1993): 18.

24. Kim, "They Armed in Self Defense," 10.

CHAPTER 6

Life at the Margins

In the Thick of Multiplicity

M. G. *Vassanji*

Global Tribalism: Small Is Hateful

The condition of the world today brings home to us—those of us who had forgotten—the pervasiveness of smaller ethnic, communal, or sectarian identities and the tenacity with which they survive. We have seen pluralism-based national identities—built on the idea that human equality and fraternity should ultimately override ethnic or other communal differences—disintegrate and these smaller components reasserting themselves, shaking off the old idealism and taking up apparently where they last left off. Neighbors turn against neighbors, communities that once joined forces to fight colonial domination and conquest take up arms against each other to settle scores and gain points in a new struggle for power, definition, and survival.

Bosnia, Rwanda, Sri Lanka are examples of the savagery that this sort of fracture leads to; there is also the communal tension in India with memories of the partition of the subcontinent still firmly etched in the minds of the communities most affected. And we have the reemergence of overt racism in Western Europe, of (ethnic) nationalism in parts of the former Soviet Union and Eastern Europe, and of tribal chauvinism in parts of Africa. Each of these cases, we are told, is unique, complex in its own way, with its own political and economic history and its more immediate causes for instability or breakup. Whatever those may be, ethnicity and communalism seem to have been the weakest fault lines, provided the easiest scapegoats and enemies, and stirred up the most deep-seated anger, suspicion, and insecurity.

In today's world one is left wondering pessimistically whether we are not simply just members of tribes after all. (I use the term "tribe" in a loose sense, of course. From the "South Asian"—a term I return to later—perspective, "community" is the more pervasive identity. For the most part I avoid the word "nation" in its European connotation and complexity, using it only in the sense in which it had meaning for us when I was growing up, to denote an independent country or state as in "United Nations.")

A View from the Margins

Those of us living in the relative security and comfort of North America are not immune to easy definitions of self and other, to the stereotypes and caricatures that go with them and the tensions and insecurities they evoke. The special case I want to consider is the marginal status of nonwhite immigrants in Canadian (and, with qualifications, American) society, which is primarily a development of European society, part of the present-day Western world. Here too there is struggle for space and definition; ideas of the purity of nationhood, though not encouraged, keep cropping up; and some of the phobias regarding "others" are deep-rooted and related to, if not the same as, those elsewhere in the world. We can take comfort in the absence of savagery and utter breakdown, but the 1992 outbreak of riots in Los Angeles, followed by disturbances the next evening in Toronto's Yonge Street, suggests grimmer possibilities for the future.

To be told that the most recent immigrants are always picked upon and discriminated against is clearly not a sufficient justification, and to be told that we are all immigrants is no comfort either; it is actually misleading, because the racism against Asians, Arabs, and Africans is part of a continuum that goes back to European and British racism and is related to the colonialism from which we have emerged. To be told that Canada (why not the United States too?) was also once a colony is fraudulent, in that it glosses over histories and memories—however painful and shameful—and shears one's language of its political and historical charge.

The marginalization of the non-European immigrant is concomitant to the marginalization of the world he or she comes from—a country and culture viewed as alien, backward, poor, and unhappy. Isolated incidents of racial violence or the activities of the neo-Nazis tell us one thing. It is, instructive, however, to observe the activities of the media, which reflect and sometimes even propagate the marginalization of the immigrant. The media achieve this under cover of respectability, responsibility, and objectivity, and because they are everywhere all the time, their influence is immense. My examples here are picked from the Canadian media, from coverage (during fall 1993 and spring 1994) that I happen to have watched on television or read in newspapers.

During an interview and viewer-call-back program on the Bosnia crisis on CBC *Newsworld* one evening, a caller with an accent started giving an opinion, whereupon the program host immediately interrupted him: "Are you a Moslem?" Very rightly he said, "That's beside the point." Indeed, for cannot one simply have an opinion on a world crisis? Not every caller is asked to give his or her religious, political, or ethnic identity. Similar relegation to the margin, away from mainstream debate and discussion, can be found on another talk show, a book program on TV Ontario, in which nonwhite "ethnics" are called upon to gripe about racism, multiculturalism, and the like, whereas white "establishment" figures come to vent their views on "literature."

Although it may not be deliberate that we don't hear of our home countries unless there is mass murder or famine there, it is not irrelevant. Europe and Britain are always in the news in Canada, as is the United States—not always because something goes wrong there but sometimes also for human interest. When an American hostage was released in Somalia, television news was understandably euphoric. Only later that night, on a foreign news broadcast, did one find out that a Nigerian soldier was also released, and yes, he had a name. How our home countries are perceived here is surely a measure of how we ourselves are perceived. And how we are perceived surely has a bearing on the acknowledged importance and need of our contribution to the image of our (or our parents') adopted countries.

A prominent cultural column in the Canadian national newspaper, the *Globe and Mail*, recently affirmed that despite the arrival of immigrants from warmer climates, "the heart of Canada is still true to the North."[1] The writer was alluding to the landscape and survival mythos described by Margaret Atwood and Northrop Frye, the Canada of cold winters and hearty spirit, skating and hockey. The position the article argues from is, to my mind, defensive though perhaps forgivable in a country that is perpetually insecure about its identity. The insecurity that the columnist reflected comes from the fact that the country is changing, has changed tremendously in the last twenty to thirty years; for example, about one-third of Torontonians come from non-English- or French-speaking homes. The reassurance given in the article was apparently for the "old" Canadians, for why would immigrants from various parts of the globe find comfort in Canada's identity remaining northern and traditional? Ascribing a single core or root essence to a diverse population in a changing country, positing an intact Canadian psyche derived from a view of nature and of history that many of the country's new citizens are not aware of, is not only naively simplistic and presumptuous but also dictatorial and threatening in disregarding diversity and disallowing change and choice. Although no one would scorn a coat, boots, or gloves in winter, and everyone from Edmonton

to Toronto to Minneapolis would decry a harsh winter, it is possible for people with different histories and origins to see themselves differently; surely in
the modern world, with its massive movements of people and tremendous facilities in communications, there is room for complexity and flexibility in how
one sees oneself or is seen.

Toronto is sometimes called the least Canadian city, as this same columnist
has reminded us.[2] But Toronto is, to a great degree, different because we immigrants have made it so. It is to us less provincial and less stifling, and gives
us space in which to develop. Hockey is an exciting game; our children watch
it on television and some play it, but it is not part of our mythos. We do not
take pride in, indeed gloat over, the hardships of winter and our own rugged-
ness. Even though blacks and Asians have been in North America for generations, I have never yet seen a professional hockey player from these groups.
That may yet happen, but it is obvious that the game is more attractive to the
"northern" folk; there *are* professional hockey stars playing in the North American leagues who were born and brought up in Russia and Eastern Europe. A
look at the names on a hockey lineup provides an important lesson on ethnicity (or race) and sport—as does a look at the names on a soccer lineup.

Immigrants are in large part urban. The size and diversity of the cities allow
them to maintain anonymity on one hand and strong communal ties on the
other. They also have an international presence. Gone are the days when distance ensured that immigrants had the barest or no contact with their homelands. Wasn't it a Canadian who said that the world is now a global village? The
urban immigrant *develops* an urban national identity, culture, being. For example, Manhattan-based Woody Allen is—to me—as American as Roy Rogers.
Isn't basketball, developed in the cities, an American (now international) game?
And aren't Broadway and its musicals—immigrant urban contributions—
American? Already Toronto is known internationally as a writers' city, largely
because of the presence and prolificness of immigrant writers there.

The recent flurry of discussions on immigration and multiculturalism have
taken heart, it would appear, from similar questioning in Europe. The political
climate is just right in a world returning to tribalism and intensely conscious
of nationhood, ethnicity, and culture. The debate in Canada asks the question,
what kind of country is this? Pointing a finger, it says, do we need more of them
in this, the best country in the world? Such questions are necessary from time
to time, but under such scrutiny immigrants are alienated; those who are nonwhite and non-Western, are triply alienated.

Sometimes these questions are considered in the crudest of terms. What is
the point of the gleeful (it appeared) CBC television news announcement that
a majority of Canadians are against multiculturalism when (a) a large percent-

age, if not a majority, are also racially biased, and (b) the country is so cleanly divided politically (Quebec, the Centre, the West)—as recent elections (1994) showed—that the term "majority" has to be qualified? That most people are vague about the term "multiculturalism" makes the survey results, as they were announced, even more meaningless (except to say that the majority do not like immigrants keeping to their strange ways). The same news item went on to show as an example of melting-pot integration a Chinese group reciting Christmas carols, followed by a scene of "multiculturalism" at work—a Sikh ceremony in a *gurudwara* (temple); thus the broadcast implicitly identified the country as Christian, oblivious to the fact that in a modern democracy people are free to practice any faith and that indeed there are non-immigrant white Sikh converts from Christianity.

As one of the views enunciated on a CBC program about immigration put it, "This country is slowly but surely being transformed from a nation of descendants of white Christian Europeans to a hodgepodge of European, African, Asian and South American cultures, languages, colours and religions. Speaking for myself, I am resentful of the fact, for example, that my children's teacher is no longer permitted to organize a Christmas concert. Instead it has become a 'Winterfest Celebration.' "[3] Such statements are presented as legitimate alternative views, and perhaps they should be so in a democracy. But the feeling an immigrant gets is that many people don't like my presence here and that that is a legitimate alternative.

One must not shy away from the fact that what is at stake for many people is the nature of the country: Is it going to be white, Christian, European—admitting a few Third Worlders out of charity—or is it going to change, to accommodate? To whom does the country really belong? These concerns reflect, to a degree, the same basic ethnic and racial conflicts for space and nationhood as those going on elsewhere in the world. For the immigrant, there is only one answer: For him or her to be anything but marginal, the country has to change, as Toronto, for example, has changed—much to the chagrin of its detractors.

The "South Asian": A Ghost Reawakened, or the Darkness That Never Was

Since the recent wave of migration from former British and other colonies to the United Kingdom, Canada, and the United States in the 1960s and 1970s, former postcolonial national identities have broken down and new configurations have emerged on the basis of race, culture, religion, and even sect. So, for example, the term "African" is used for anyone black, even though she is generations removed from that continent; likewise, a person of Indian origin whose family has lived in Africa for a hundred years is not "African," even though in his home country he would still be considered very much a "local." In response to the marginalization and racism suffered by immigrants, and partly also because of the presence of strongly identified groups such as "Blacks" and "Natives" and the racial politics and political advantages perceived for them, in Canada there have been attempts to formulate an entity called "South Asian." The term denotes any person of "Indian-subcontinental" origin, whether he or she comes from the subcontinent directly or over three or four generations via the Caribbean, Africa, Fiji, Mauritius, and so on. These attempts, mainly by political and literary activists, to identify and congeal a new minority group have so far been only partly successful. One reason is that the term "South Asian," imported from academia, is purely geographic, artificial, recent, and entirely devoid of any imaginative force in the way, for example, "Indian" and "South African" are, and tends to be both confused and confusing. Another reason is that the "South Asians" think of themselves and live as various communities. In fact, this is one of their characteristics as people originating in the Indian subcontinent. In the suburbs of Toronto, Vancouver, and Calgary, or in Queens, New York, the term "South Asian" would be quite alien; not so the labels "Bengali," "Punjabi," "Pakistani," and "Keralite," qualified by religion, sect, caste. Even some well-known Indian writers in the West don't forget to remind us of their castes on their book jackets.

There is, to me, something retrogressive about the loss of postcolonial national identities in favor of purely racial, ethnic, or religious ones. The national identities were broader. They had to do with the struggles for independence and freedom of such countries as Mozambique, Angola, Zimbabwe, and South Africa; they had to do with nonalignment and the problems of poverty and development. They asked for forgetting past differences and animosities and building something new in a community of nations. They came into being as symbols of pride, hope, and cooperation. Instead, in the new country to which we have come for a variety of reasons, we are labeled with a term that makes us a minority among minorities in a pluralistic or semipluralistic society, a term that qualifies one's creative output and even one's sexual preference. If accepted, this ethnic or racial marginal label is a letdown and even a betrayal of our previous ideals and home countries. The only politics associated with such an identity is *local*—for representation in government, for a share in arts grants, and so on. Although I would not deny the importance and rightness of such local goals, it seems to me that something is lost when the global dimension, where such inequities originate in the first place, are forgotten, and all we have are "visible minorities."

Still, I have recently come to acknowledge that however marginal it may have seemed twenty-five years ago, in the new world that was emerging with great idealism during my youth and marching forward with hope, "South Asian-ness" or "Indianness" is very much present in me, three generations removed as I am from the subcontinent.

Consider first a parallel example, that of V. S. Naipaul and the Caribbean Indian experience. It was thirty years ago that Naipaul first went to India; his family had left Uttar Pradesh in the northern part of the country something like a century before. He writes in his account of that visit that for the Indians of the Caribbean, India had become an area of darkness. It was distant, almost forgotten behind remnants of dimly remembered rituals. There is an element of truth to that statement, in the 1950s and early 1960s, Indians in the Caribbean or in Africa could think of themselves as going forward out of a British colonial experience into a new national and international identity that would come from it. But in Naipaul's observations on India and Indianness one senses also an element of denial. Naipaul did not like India; he could not identify with it. He observed it as an outsider, disliked being mistaken for an ordinary Indian. After he wrote *An Area of Darkness*, the Caribbean countries obtained their independence; there were problems between Indians and blacks; the countries deteriorated politically and economically; and there was large-scale emigration.

In Canada we now have people calling themselves "Indo-Caribbean" who are very much part of the projected new identity of "South Asian," seeking continuity with the mainstream Indian tradition and a bond with South Asians of other backgrounds. So, India: Was it truly an area of darkness or, rather, a dim, receding glow that was, under the circumstances, revitalized? To be sure, the Indianness of the Indo-Caribbean people was distant: caste, ancestral village, language had been all but forgotten; large numbers had become Christians. Yet the Indian identity, sorely bruised, persisted—different from the African identity. Indeed, it may be argued that these persistent and deeply felt differences are what gave rise to the racial instabilities in the region and contributed to the subsequent emigration of Indians to Canada and to the current "Indo-Caribbean" identity.

Not more than ten years after Naipaul went to India, I went to the United States from East Africa, to attend an American university. Our African experience was different from that of the Indians in the Caribbean. We had migrated to Africa as communities and kept our communal identities; we had preserved language, religion, sect, caste; India had been physically closer.

On my second day on campus in Cambridge, Massachusetts, a friend (of similar background to mine) and I were accosted by two Indians with very Indian accents, who asked, "Are you from India?" In those days this seemed to be a very common question. "No," my friend and I answered with full confidence, "from Tanzania." "Yes, yes," came the impatient reply, "but originally from where?" We had to concede that originally we came from Gujarat, India, way back when. Triumphantly, they walked away.

Arriving on the crest of African nationalism, ready to fight the "mbeberu" (racist) of South Africa and Rhodesia and Mozambique, and having imbibed a sense of social justice from Julius Nyerere (then president of Tanzania), we found something offensive about this reminder of an ancestral homeland we had left far behind. Our families had gone to Africa; we had come to America. Of what use now was India?

Gradually, however, roots became important. We had, after all, been raised as Indians or, to be precise, as an Indian community. And so a cultural acceptance of Indianness followed. If there was a longing to visit India, it was romantic and to some degree linked to the romantic affair of the American counterculture with the subcontinent. With the responsibilities of adulthood and career, this longing passed. When I was invited to go to India in January 1993, I accepted immediately; this would be my first visit, a momentous occasion. But as the time for departure drew closer, I felt hesitant: Why wake up old ghosts? Moreover, by Christmas the race riots following the destruction of the mosque at Ayodhya by Hindu fundamentalists were feeding all my worst stereotypes about India. I wondered if I would reach my hotel from the airport alive.

When I did go to India, having been reassured and encouraged, I was somewhat shocked to feel that a part of me was returning. I had thought I was going to an alien country—poor, violent, chaotic, backward. And yet when I arrived, I was hit by an eerie feeling of "sameness." There was a tremendous urge to make up for lost time, to see more and more of the place, to return again and again until this reawakened ghost was exorcised and dispatched where it belonged—in the past.

Living with Multiplicity: The Comforts of Contradiction

Because of my background in Africa and India, though historically more and more removed from my country (not having experienced its recent history), I have found myself in general terms forming an empathy with the larger "Third World." This is a term that a lot of academics spend time and energy disputing, finding it too general, pejorative, and so on. To me it simply means the part of the world that, despite its multifold diversity, shares a colonial past and with it a politics of anticolonialism and freedom struggles, a world that has been imaginatively constructed by the West in similar terms (non-Christian, backward, savage, and so on), a world with community structures and extended family patterns I find familiar and societies that are in some senses more easygoing and less rigidly disciplined than the Western ones. It is also the part of the world that is to a large degree poorer than the rest, though admittedly that configuration is changing.

Julius Nyerere, when I was growing up, said to us that a child who goes away for education is like a person who is given all the available food and water by a starving village and sent away to bring back supplies. I was a boy who went away from a poor country for higher studies, and so the Third World is the world I feel responsible to, feel guilty about.

In terms of self and identity, more and more I find myself coming to accept a condition that in fact I was brought up with. It is a condition of multiplicity and contradiction. The medieval Indian poet Kabir said that he bowed neither toward the Kaabah (in Mecca) nor toward any tirath (Hindu place of pilgrimage), that Rama and Rahim were the same to him. To a theologist or a purist there is an obvious contradiction here, but not to the poet. Although the fundamentalisms gripping the world were, because of the partition of India, beginning to arrive on our shores, we were still relatively free from them, and one of the hymns we sang also said that "Rama and Rehman" (another, related attribute of God) are the same. I was brought up in a community of Muslims who had been converted in medieval times but who quite unembarrassedly kept many of their "Hindu" beliefs and made sense of them. Thus Allah was a form of Vishnu, Muhammad simply Brahma, and weren't the Vedas nothing but the Quran? Ordinary middle-class Muslims and Hindus alike are aghast upon hearing this, but it was a creative response to conversion and to the schism between religions with purportedly humanistic and spiritual ideals. (In India still there are many commonalities with similar multifaceted beliefs; during my second visit there (in 1994) I went to a dargah (shrine) where, a caretaker told me, some Hindus were buried and some Muslims sent their ashes after cremation.) I grew up, moreover, an Indian-African of third generation on one side, fourth on the other, speaking—besides English—Swahili, Gujarati, and Cutchi. My family had lived in Kenya and Tanzania over these generations. Like schoolchildren of my age, I looked to England for "civilization"; I went to the United States for a university education, an experience in the early 1970s that profoundly affected and changed me; and I wound up in Canada pursuing a job and finally bringing up a family.

What is one's identity under these circumstances? What does it mean to be simply and only a "Canadian"? I live in Toronto; I find it one of the most livable cities anywhere. It is home, yet I sometimes feel I could not survive in Canada outside its city limits. It is a city I know, like, and enjoy, that I can write about comfortably; in fact, I have written a very "Toronto" sort of novel and am in the process of writing another. But I also write about Africa; the site of

Kilimanjaro is to me the most beautiful (as I recently confirmed when I visited Tanzania); when I hear the South African anthem "Nkosi Sikelele" during these days when the country is much in the news, my mind automatically says the identical words in Swahili: "Mungu Ibariki Afrika"—the Tanzanian anthem, sung to the identical tune.

And so I have come to accept a condition that my ancestors found quite natural: that of agglomerating all one's experiences, not denying anything in the interest of "purity" but always being wary of the purifiers—religious, national, or ethnic "fundamentalists."

Life at the margins has its comforts, and in multiplicity there is creativity and acceptance.

NOTES

1. Bronwyn Drainre, *Globe and Mail*, 15 January 1994.
2. Bronwyn Drainre, *Globe and Mail*. 1 January 1994.
3. *Prime Time News*, CBC, Toronto, 29 March 1994 (transcript).

CHAPTER 7

Mullahs, Sex, and Bureaucrats

Pakistan's Confrontations with the Modern World

Sohail Inayatullah

Identity or Identities

Pakistan's attempts to enter modernity on its own terms have been fraught with obstacles and contradictions. Caught between East and West by globalization, undone by leakages through the tenuous membrane of national sovereignty (the rise of ethnic nationalism and sectarianism), and yet vulnerable to the reemergence of Islamic and pre-Islamic myths long forgotten, Pakistan remains both traditional and modern.[1]

For Pakistanis there is an obvious dissonance between the claims of the West that civilization means Western civilization and Pakistani claims that Pakistan represents the land of the pure, the home of Muslims, with Islam representing the alternative to amoral capitalism and godless communism. The dissonance is even stronger when we Pakistanis confront our own behavior in light of official utterances as to who we are.[2]

In addition to a grand cynicism—the sense that all dreams will be betrayed—the dissonance between what is said and what is done has created a society where tolerance continues to decline and where the Other is less pure than oneself.[3] There is no middle ground; one is either sinner or saint. Inasmuch as most of us occupy space in a continuum, what results is civilizational neurosis. The univocal category "Pakistan" is itself constantly being undone by movements and ethnicities which, like the state, also lay claim to the mantle of One God, One People, One State—the Mohajirs and Pukhtoons, to mention but two such that have a vision different from the current Punjabi statist formulation.[4] Moreover, as in Iran, where the populace rejected Western technocratic elites and their claim for a secular Iran,[5] Pakistan's future hangs perilously between authoritarian mullahist nominations of social reality (only real Muslims should rule and live in Pakistan) and the accommodationist views of leaders such as Benazir Bhutto and Nawaz Shariff, who are far more concerned with bourgeois revolutions, even as they use the language of Islam to bolster themselves, to assure citizens that they are not selling their souls to the devils of the West or the militaristic polytheists of the East—the Other of Pakistan: India.

National sovereignty for Pakistanis is thus increasingly problematic in a world of CNN and Star TV, the diasporic Pakistani community, Pukhtoons traveling in and out of Afghanistan and Pakistan, Pakistan's own efforts to destabilize India through intervention in Kashmir, and India's similar efforts in Karachi. Only the "enemy" of India holds Pakistan together, with the worst-case scenario for the Pakistani that of friendship with India. Friendship with India would lead to the final battle of sectarianism, with each subgroup of Islam calling the other Kafir, nonbeliever. Already certain Sunni groups in Lahore have declared that they will not allow the Shia to worship Muharram (the ten days of mourning for the tragic events of Karbala, where in the seventh century the problem of the appropriate succession of the Prophet was violently "resolved").[6] The Pakistan police force can do nothing but watch the militarization and criminalization of various Muslim groups as well as political parties. This realpolitik frame stands in contrast to the original vision of Pakistan as the land of the pure, the homeland of Muslims.

Perfection and Despotism

Pakistan wants to escape traditional feudalistic society yet recover the utopia of original Islam. The search for perfection and its unattainability constitute, of course, the central problem of Islamic political theory. Classical Islamic theory is a search for the *khalifa*, the "righteous" representation of God; the Shia approach is the search for the perfect representative of God, the Mahdi. Western political theorists such as Hobbes and Montesquieu assumed that since we are all sinners, safeguards to the accumulation of power needed to be built into governance structures—the federalist political design. But Islamic civilization, Muslims believe, did have a perfect leader (a perfect representation of the laws of God) and a perfect constitution (the Medina constitution) and state. With the decline and breakdown of Islam, the structure of one-person rule remained even as rulers could no longer match the wisdom of the Prophet's successors. The community was no longer voluntary but based on coercion, on trying to restrain dynastic, ethnic, and personal histories. Faced with the breakdown of unity in the Islamic empire, Muslims opted for authoritarian and often brutal leaders. The choice was chaos or authoritarian leadership, with only the Medina state to look backward to. No social structures or institutions were created to tame power, lest the saint quickly become sinner. This remains the problem in Pakistan. Once a leader has been found to be impure, a new perfect leader is sought, who in turn disappoints, as we might expect in a search for an impossible morality.

This quest for idealism has been the betrayal of Islam. According to El-Affendi,

> by setting unattainable standards, it was easy to pass from the conclusion that perfection was impossible to the claim that all imperfect situations were equal. The present imperfect situation was therefore the best possible solution. . . . Classical theory then gave advice on how to tolerate tyranny. . . . Classical theory did not offer any recommendation on how to deal with such tyrants and dislodge them, which was the kind of guidance the pious needed, not advice about the limit to which they should tolerate tyranny.

The original state in Islam, then, became the representation of heaven and the original leader the representative of God. El-Affendi says the insistence on perfection "in the khalifa automatically removed from the community the right to criticize him, for everyone is by definition less pious, less learned and less wise than he is. In the end, the fate of the ummah [the larger global community] hung on the arrival of an individual who would unite in his personal charisma, saintliness and power. The waiting for this impossible arrival was bound to relegate Muslim thinking to the realm of mythology and passive ineptitude."[7]

Modernity has added to this paradox by making cynicism pervasive. Because of colonialism, the state cannot be trusted, yet all attempt to claim it. Politics has come to mean staying in power as opposed to meeting basic needs. Whatever the leader does is not enough; leaders who rise to greatness and attempt to transform social conditions become the victims of their own mythologies, each believing, as did Zulfikar Bhutto, that he or she is the perfect leader.

Furthermore, the conflation of Islam with a nation-state (as defined in Western secular terms) instead of with ummah forces individuals to fit into the straitjacket of One Nation and One People who are Muslims. Plurality is destroyed as the definition of "Muslim" becomes more and more restrictive. But defining Islam has always been in the hands of the few, the ulema, the keepers of the word. As Islam transformed from an oral tradition to a written to a mass written tradition, through the printing press, each step was opposed by the ulema and each new technology captured by them, keeping Islam a tradition committed to *ilm*, knowledge, controlled by the few. Perhaps when CD-ROM is widespread, the text of Islam will cease to be in the hands of a few and become more open to interpretation, with inner guidance and metaphorical spiritual understanding far more important than the fundament of the text, potentially returning Islam to the egalitarian revolution it once promised to be.[8] In the meantime, the Other is not allowed in Pakistani politics and social life, and the text remains both hegemonic and fractured.

The Politics of the Future

To survive the future, we need to move to a new equation of identity that balances localness and globalness, a theory of governance wherein the idea of Pakistan permits many Pakistans to exist in the context of a culture of tolerance. This is not the concern of policymakers, however. The great battle in Pakistan is over the question of national integration. Indeed, "writing the real" is associated with understanding both the successes and failures of national integration, some even arguing that Pakistan has always existed, eternally. The trauma of partition remains the defining moment in Pakistani history. It has created a knowledge discourse in which only nations and their functionaries are real. Those outside this discourse are considered unimportant; thus, social movements less concerned with state power are unable to function. The model of politics in Pakistan gives them little space. As nongovernmental organizations flourish, however, the state quickly creates its own NGOs as depositories of foreign funds. Neorealist or international relations focus on realpolitik, on the real as primarily statist and its goal, the accumulation of power and territory, far more real than unselfish acts of kindness, of generosity, of peace. Zulfikar Bhutto's vision that Pakistanis will even eat grass so as to attain nuclear status has made the region a spy novel, with the operators from the CIA, KGB, ISI, CBI all searching for the evasive Islamic bomb. Every action is blamed on a foreign element, on the grand plan to undo Pakistan being hatched in the board and war rooms of Delhi and Washington, or Moscow and Delhi. The net result has been the strengthening of the Pakistani state and the further erosion of human rights and social welfare programs. Recent news that a Christian boy was to be hanged for blasphemy against the Prophet merely finalizes the surveillance State.[9]

But more problematic than an interventionist state is the state that does not protect basic human rights. A man who recently converted to an illegal Muslim sect, for instance, was arrested, and the relatives who attempted to bail him out were beaten and one of them lynched.[10] This politics of suspicion results from a commitment to an abstract purity. And yet Pakistanis know when they are being misled. Even under former President Mohammed Zia-ul-Haq, the consciousness-raising of the masses had begun, a consciousness insisting that Pakistan is not so pure. One way to understand the critical edge citizens have is through popular humor. A joke told to me in the late 1980s best illustrates the political psyche of the nation at that time.

> The president is in Paris for a conference, where he sees a Pak-istani woman dressed in Parisian attire. He asks one of his men to tell her that the president wants to see her. At the hotel the president invites her to his room, where he chastises her for wearing foreign clothes. He tells her to take off her French coat. She does. "As a Muslim woman, how dare you wear a skirt? Take it off," he says. She does. "Don't you know about Islamiza-tion in Pakistan, how dare you wear such frilly underclothes? Take them off." She does and stands there naked in front of the president of the Islamic Republic of Pakistan. "Now come em-brace Islam," he says with his arms outstretched.[11]

This story reveals the frustration among many with Islamization in its sta-tist and mullahist forms, the obvious sense among the wealthy and the poor of the hypocrisy of Islam inside and outside the nation. But this is an under-standable situation in the face of many dilemmas: how to face the onrush of modernity; how to react to one's history when one's culture is being canni-balized by the ideas of Western materialism, technology, and history; how to bear the pain of traditional culture's being vanquished by the problems of heroin addiction; how to deal with one's sons and daughters who leave the homeland for London, and then come back but detest Pakistan except as a place to remember nostalgically the comfort of the family; and how to with-stand the threats to family of divorce, of feminism. The battle is one for moral space in a country where this space has shrunk, thus furthering tightening the definition of the moral.

An Islam built on social control ideology has been the mullah's answer. It hopes to alleviate uncertainty, to reduce future shock and culture shock, to make the world more predictable and less chaotic—to remind us Pakistanis of the rules and regulations of the agricultural and medieval era. Unfortunately, this kind of Islam has not sufficed, and Pakistan remains without a vision that would include the past yet develop a compelling image of the future.

The Past as Future

Pakistan does not have a vision of the future, only an imagined past either as the ideal Islamic polity or as the nostalgia of postpartition.[12] Zulfikar Bhutto's state socialism was a catastrophic failure, and Zia's Islamic Republic will be remembered for declining literacy and education under the guise of Islam, notwithstanding that Islam is the religion of literacy and knowledge accumulation, rather than being only about an essentialist identity construction.[13] Islam after all is an information system, its development a testament to the dissemination and classification of knowledge. This emphasis on information was necessary because it was crucial to define what the Prophet said, who heard it said, and what the criteria were for accepting the sayings of the Prophet. Visions of the future are difficult to engineer in colonized lands, where defiance of the state is considered a mark of honor because the state is always corrupt. The state is both to be gained, since it promises privilege and power, and to be resisted, since it represents official corrupt power.

At another level, in a world where there are few spaces for Muslims, where Muslims see themselves not though their own categories, their own myths, but as a defeated civilization, Pakistan as a revolution can but fail.[14] Witness Disney's *Aladdin*: In the opening scene we are told that this is a movie about culture and religion; "Aladdin" after all means the servant of God. But by the end of the movie he forsakes his history and says, "Just call me Al." In a world where only Als exist, Aladdin has no home. But the Islamic response in Pakistan has been not only to rid Islam of Al but to rid Pakistan of the plurality that was South Asia.

In Europe the search for purity comes out in the oppression of color; in Pakistan it comes out in the oppression of sexual behavior, since color is transparent. Understanding sexual relations in Pakistan, for example, has as much to do with the continuation of feudal relations as it does with the mythic significance of the battle between the men of Medina and the wives of the Prophet. While the women of Islam were pressing for revelation that would give women more rights, the men wanted to keep women as slaves, as in pre-Islamic Arabia. The growth of Islam hinged on how Muhammad and God would respond. The veil constituted the compromise between these two forces, argues Fatima Mernissi.[15] The veil gave women personhood: rights of inheritance, the right to engage in battles against the enemies of Islam, and the right to freedom from the male. Those women who wore the veil could not be leered at or treated as slaves, but those who didn't could be molested in the streets of Medina. This classic division remains. In modern Pakistan the *dapata* (a long scarf that covers the chest and, during prayer, the head) rather than the veil serves the function of signaling virtue. Foreign, non-Muslim women in this sense do not have personhood. They are outside the circle of Islamic purity.

Sex

Gender relations continue to define all cosmologies, as do human nature and human other. But in Pakistan where the streets are full of only men; men leer at any woman who can walk; members of the religious class use every legal effort to legitimize, rationalize, and legalize their deep fear of and distaste for women. Historically, it is legitimated by the story of Adam and Eve, for she ate the fruit that drove them out of the Kingdom of God. For the men of Islam, woman is the temptress, a weakness it is best to leave covered up. Her sole purpose is to produce more sons, sons who eventually will provide security, wealth, and status by becoming landlords, army officers, physicians, writers, politicians, and businessmen.

As the modern world electronically speeds into Pakistan's traditional culture—allowing for new types of choice—men have opted for legal remedies to resist change. President Zia-ul-Haq began the process of the brutalization of the Pakistani self by enacting the Hudood Ordinance, meant explicitly to punish those involved in extramarital affairs but implicitly to remind all of the will of the male state. Masud Ahmad's column "The Roving Eye" in Pakistan's national newspaper, The Nation, provides these examples. When asked if he would marry the woman with whom he had just consummated a relationship (and who was willing to do anything to be by his side), one man who was found having an affair said, "Never. She is a loose, immoral woman." Enter the state. If individual men are not strong enough not to be tempted by these "harlots," then the state must interfere; the collectivity of men is there to make certain that the apple is not bitten. Recently a young man shot his sister dead. What was her crime? She had been accused of having sexual relations with a man. Her brother in utter disgust decided that the family had been shamed enough. It was time to regain their honor.[16]

Sexual relations have also become big business. In the "City Diary" column of The Muslim, a daily newspaper, the writer advises couples to keep a fifty-rupee bill with them at all times. Police have been going to quiet corners of parks and asking for marriage licenses. Without a copy, the couple is whisked to the police station for some public embarrassment. If one has forgotten the license, however, a fifty-rupee bill avoids this journey. But one who is found with someone other than his or her own spouse is advised to be prepared for the worst.

Of course, at the same time as the moral majority attempt to police sexuality, the vast populace of youth remain sexually unsatisfied. Those who do not have a vocation—and thus no money and no social standing—are unable to marry: that is, to find sex. Their only standing comes from their family, who will not allow marriage until the young male has done something with his life—a something that is increasingly problematic as unemployment continues to soar.

Furthermore, for men and women, status is nearly impossible without wedding vows, for Pakistan is a societies of families, not individuals—hence the marriage of Benazir Bhutto and her dramatic entry into motherhood. Whatever her personal reasons, she knew that to be elected she had to become a mother. As a single woman, she would always be situated by critics in the land of Western whoredom. Although she had initially tried to locate herself at the other end of female archetypes, that of the Amazon or hero, and later as the daughter of a Great Man, her father Zulfikar Bhutto, it was as a mother that she finally found political success. This was because in a nation afraid of female sexuality, of sexuality as such, an Amazon could never last. The goddess image was unavailable to her, for she had lived outside the Muslim world. Moreover, she wanted political power, not eternal religious bliss.

Search for Home

Those of us who tire of such contradictions search for freedom in lands far from Pakistan. But home always calls, not only as an imagined nostalgia but as an attempt to return to culture, to that which has become fugitive in the capitalist relations of the West.[17] Within Third World theory, culture is believed to be the last unified discourse, the last remnant of the past not infiltrated by technocratic market relations.[18] But those living in such a culture, as my female relatives tell me, are not so convinced of its benefits. True, they want a world in which all of us read the Quran, but at the same time they would like to live in a world where their own status as women is not dependent on the nearest male relative or on the exhortations of the neighborhood mullah. Furthermore, culture (particularly the culture of the North within the South, of the elite in the periphery) has begun to unravel. Global television, travel, e-mail, and other encounters with those different from us—the Afghani freedom fighter; the daughter returning from London despondent that the overseas Pakistani she had just married still had a British girlfriend he had told no one about; or those who are not traditional *Goras* (the British), such as refugee Bosnian Muslims or industrialist Koreans—have all made problematic the idea of a Pakistani self. Of course, developing a postnational self or arguing for a South Asian confederation where the categories of Pakistan and India no longer exist is easier to do when one lives away from "home," someplace where the scars of partition have faded. Within Pakistan, the project of sovereignty takes on a desperate tone, suggesting that without national integration life would cease to exist. I have heard it argued that for Indians, giving up Kashmir is merely amputation; for Pakistanis it is death, since the conflict of Kashmir serves as a way to keep the nation integrated. Kashmir is the lifeblood, the heart and soul of the great Islamic republic. Nationalism is easy to deconstruct, but without the confidence of collective sovereignty, is a postnational, postethnic identity based on spiritual humanism even remotely possible?[19]

Thus, although local traditional culture has been strong at providing identity, it has not been able to compete with Westernization in providing capital and ideational mobility. Local culture has been based on land, on an imagined ethnicity, and a situated caste and class. Center culture can make inroads because it provides the entrance into modernity. Instead of the logos of Allah and ummah (the Islamic attempt to reconcile the local and global), it is now Coca-Cola and Marlboro that stand benevolently in the skies. By participating in these symbols the Pakistani middle class—those who cannot afford to send their sons to London or Iowa or Sydney—can enter the universalizing project of the moderns. This is pseudoculture, neither here nor there, commodifying, secularizing, and destroying traditional culture. Pseudoculture is also the ammunition of the mullahs in visioning an alternative Pakistan based on a idealized past (where they had space to stand, where they had power and respect, where all social configurations sprang from them). Is this what we yearn for? Or is it the new Pakistan that our bureaucrats promise us: bright city lights, big highways from Islamabad to Lahore, a protective military, and free education for our children? Or is there some other Pakistan? Clearly, we need an imagined self and community that answers our need for identity with respect to territory (land, not real estate) and also with respect to a transcendental community, a global community.[20] Unfortunately, modernity has created not the global village but in fact the alienated global city, as every Karachi-ite can well tell you. Modernity has also destroyed local immunity against mental illness. The Pakistani self is particularly susceptible, as it is caught between conflicting cultural demands (tradition, colonialism, nationalism, globalism), between rapid economic growth and rapid impoverishment, between the breakdown of the traditional Asian self and the lack of a new self.[21]

A postmodern self speaking to our need for mobility (whether physical or of labor and capital), identity, and well-being has yet to emerge. Modernity has provided the first and last (at least for the center) but not the second. Socialism and Third Worldism have made all three problematic. Creating a sovereign community that has space for many social configurations and allows mobility between them is not easy. The universal project of Islam at one time promised that sort of polity, but that is not how the story turned out. Instead, power has gone to either the mullahs or the modernizers. Those in search of other spaces—some metaphorical, some indigenous but universal, others eclectic—have not fared so well. Although social movements have begun to recover the social service dimensions of Islam—as borrowed from Christianity—it is the state that returns to monitor and appropriate social movements. There is not one Pakistan; there are many. Understanding our differences might be the first step in developing a postnational identity and economy aligned with neither mullah nor bureaucrat, neither modernity nor tradition, and especially not with the vacuity of postmodernity. But it is postmodernity that beckons. When all is said and done, though postmodernity recreates the Westerner into many persons—both consumer and producer, lover and loved—and can therapeutically rid the Westerner of the grand narratives of sin (central to Judaism, Christianity, and Marxism) as well as create mini-localisms, it holds little promise for those in the third space of Third World civilization.[22] Grand narratives are cosmological and historical, as in the case of Islam for Pakistan. Their removal promises only Western modernism or Western postmodernism. The alternative is clearly a search for diversity but in the context of an Islamic science or alternative modernity. This vision, possible perhaps because of the diaspora, has yet to become persuasive. Pakistan is either a caricature of the European West or the Arab West or the negation of India, a not-India; it has yet to come into its own. But can it make the jump into something else when it has not discovered its own sovereignty?

My own understanding of these Pakistans has been based on many voyages home.[23] Each one has been more than an airline schedule; it has been a flight of the self in search of some real or imagined or historical or yet-to-be space, a space where I hope to find a home that is neither commodified West nor feudal Pakistan; an alternative space that is interpretive, not literal, and negotiable, not fixed; a space that allows for an Islam that can coexist with Buddha's middle way or Shiva's Tantra; a place with 1,001 names of God (including the secular). But as we theorize from far away about what can be, it is still home that calls.

Home has yet to have the same level of identity as it does for Indians and Chinese; Pakistanis are not a primordial tribe.[24] Abroad, "Pakistani" is often conflated with "Indian"; conversely, South Asians in England are as a whole seen as "Paki," in the negative sense of the word. But the myth of Pakistan the pure land remains, at home and abroad. Political scientist Zeenia Satti divides "Westernized" Pakistanis into three categories: those who want to leave Pakistan at any cost; those who live outside but claim they will one day return; and those who live outside and make no pretense of desiring to return to inefficiency, poverty, and feudal social relations.[25] But the gaze of the nation does not just beckon home, it searches for fidelity outside. Does the expatriate drink, eat pork, have girlfriends? The answers to these questions become indicators of Pakistaniness. Those outside too internalize these values. Others return home seemingly not for themselves but for their children. Some friends sold their prosperous business in Texas once their two daughters reached a marriageable age. Back home in Pakistan, they quickly began their search for suitable grooms. In their desire to find a Pakistani who lived overseas but whose family lived in Islamabad, their older daughter was engaged to a Pakistani in London. Tragically, he turned out to be a wife beater. After her divorce, the family came back to try their luck in the United States.

At the right age, the mythic significance of the battle between the wives of Muhammad and the men of Medina continues. At a certain time all Pakistani families return home lest their daughters marry outside. For as with Mother India, the male can become foreign—that is, concerned with issues of statecraft, technology, accumulation of capital—but the woman represents tradition and thus must be moral, chaste, virginal, dutybound, respectful of vertical relations. [26] But modernity does not allow that distinction between male and female; both become commodified. Thus the contradiction: how to become modern and retain tradition. By dividing this conundrum between male and female, Pakistan hopes to have solved the problem. But women also desire wealth and individual freedom. The cost of these contradictions is cultural schizophrenia. For men, Westernization is about wealth and sex. For mullahs, Westernization is about losing identity and integrity; their only solution is to attack the modernizers. And when the West and modernity have evolved from an idea to a way of thinking, as Ashis Nandy has argued about Coca-Cola, then the only course is the politics of suspicion.[27] Tolerance gives way and signifiers of fidelity remain. For women, these signifiers are far more restrictive than for men, since it is women who must maintain culture, history, and morality.

One signifier that betrays my identity is my passport. Over the years, passport control officers diligently and repeatedly searched my passport, hoping to find something, touching each visa gently, then rapidly, hoping perhaps that a visa stamp would come off in their hands and I could be found guilty of fraud, of being the foreign spy I obviously was. This and other similar experiences finally forced me to relinquish my Pakistani passport, acceding to an instrumentalist view of national identity: that is, taking any passport that allowed one unrestricted travel. Traveling with an American passport has made journeys easier but identity far more problematic. Have I betrayed my Third World status by entering into a pact with the American government?[28] Or has my self become mobile, residing nowhere, seeing roots as nonsensical, even timid? Or is "nowhere" actually code for the rich West where one can afford rootlessness? An American passport thus begins the completion of a cultural route that starts with a T-shirt from the United States. That shirt or pair of jeans represents not tradition but identity as mobility. It represents a rejection of state power, of religious power, and of military power. That T-shirt represents the ability to choose life-style.

The modern then continues the long-term process of breaking down tradition. It is the breakdown of the community and the self, not a new arrangement, that characterizes Pakistani social space. My uncle speaks of a fifteen-mile walk to a friend's house to console him for the loss of his father, and of the friend's subsequent offer to shoot his enemies. The point of telling the story is to remember the sense of loyalty and friendship that is disappearing. He laments that in today's world of "mullacracy," though people speak of spiritual values, their actions are empty, utterly void of any moral strength.

We have thus not yet localized modernity, nor have we created an alternative modernity, one that breaks with feudal relations but retains ancient cultural myths that give selves coherence. Our reaction to modernity has been an attempt to escape its exchange-based political economy (through nationalizing industries) while all the time reproducing it in distorted forms, as in the case of the village child who insists on wearing Michael Jackson's white gloves. Majid Tehranian has referred to this fracture as identity and technology fetishism.[29] Just as the West has fabricated the East as the land of the fantastic, we have constructed the West as the great shopping center in the sky where everything is for sale and consumption. But when we are filled, we go back home and live the "moral" life.

Time and Technology

The car best exemplifies this fetishism. For Americans the car represents freedom; for Pakistanis it represents modernity. I am always surprised how calm we Pakistanis are at tea. Yet the minute we enter our cars, we drive urgently, honking madly if anyone slows down, even at a red light. Everyone is rushing somewhere, yet once we get there, we return to our agricultural roots and wait. We rest—forever, it seems. But in the car, Pakistan moves at the pace of the modern world, or even quicker. Miles-per-hour is the guiding metaphor, not as an indicator that one is going too fast but as a challenge to go even faster. This of course is the problematic relationship with technocracy. Going fast means catching up, entering the linear time of history. Going fast means playing the game of the West, of becoming technocratic like the West. Miles-per-hour equates with economic and cultural stages. Yet although individual cars may speed, the infrastructure as a whole causes them to slow down. Under Nawaz Shariff the plan was to build a superhighway throughout the country as one of the requisites of a modern nation-state; however, given that spatial travel remained plural—donkeys, tongas, bicycles, trucks, cars, individuals—that plan was abandoned, since it would serve only the needs of the rich, argued then out-of-power Benazir Bhutto.

The post office too has attempted to modernize and to enter different temporal spaces. Waiting in line at the stamp counter, I counted twenty of us jostling for the attention of two employees. There were other counters with modern titles—fax, electronic mail, and so forth—with an employee behind each one, but there were no takers for those services. Finally, after having mailed my postcards, I asked to see the manager. The assistant manager heard my analysis, but instead of making changes he immediately sent a clerk to help me purchase more stamps. It was a modern post office, and each counter had to have an attendant, even if the stamp counter had a mob of people waiting, clawing for attention. His sense clearly was that without fax and electronic mail, where would Pakistan be? Later I realized that I was the only person there who was not a lowly clerk. Time and power had been structured around class so that the rich and government officials never waited in line; they sent their bearers to do it. Thus, from the perspective of the postal service, it did not matter if there was mayhem to get to the counter; no real people, no sahibs, were waiting. If a sahib did come to the post office, it would be to use some of the modern conveniences, not purchase stamps.

Yet behind all attempts at modernity, tradition remains, strengthening the social bond, creating an authenticity that is almost Orientalist in description. While waiting in a line to have my ticket reconfirmed, I saw a man walk through the line and call out to the Pakistani International Airlines reservations officer. They embraced and began to tell stories about their relatives. At first I was angered and wanted to complain to the management, but then I saw that theirs was an implicit critique of modernity. The world of deadlines, of planes to catch, was far less important than the affection they felt. It did not matter that the line lengthened as they talked, they had entered an alternative time. Friendship, not efficiency, had become a way of knowing.

But this does not mean that linear time is fugitive. I once watched two men meet and embrace who obviously had not seen each other for a long time. After a few moments of conversation one asked the other to show him his watch. They compared watches for the next ten minutes. In a poor country where fashion for men is nonexistent, a watch becomes a symbol of status, a representation of difference. A watch becomes entry into modern space even as time remains embedded in the traditional social space of the family, of the seasons, of meetings with loved ones, of life and death.

In many ways, then, Pakistan exists out of time or, perhaps more appropriately, still uses the seasonal model of time: There is spring, fall, winter, and summer. The philosophy still is, relax and let God take care of everything. There is no rush. Everything is God's will (or God in the form of the state). And government functionaries use time for their own status, thus dividing Pakistan into those who have to wait and those who do not. Time becomes currency but not money.

Something Different?

Caught between the modern and the traditional, Zia's Pakistan attempted to close its mental borders to the threat of telecommunications and global travel.[30] When this effort was unsuccessful, the authoritarian past emerged, constituting the Western world as the site of accessible sex and degeneration. Privatization and the rise of a new, globally linked bourgeois have once again swung the pendulum closer to Western modern space, where the feudal lord and military officer will quickly adapt to changing times; the mullah may have a rougher transition period, as will the bureaucrat. But the lines of battle will continue to revolve around class, access to sex, and temporal location.

Our search is for pathways both out of modernist categories of understanding and away from traditionalist reaction to the modern. Modernity forces us to the secular, to the nation, to homogeneity, even as it breaks the feudal class and creates safe spaces for the bourgeois. Modernity's effort to transform time from seasonal (agricultural time) and biological (women's time) to fast, commodified, and scarce time has both succeeded and failed.[31] While new political and scientific technologies force us into the postmodern, the cyclical nature of history and culture return us to an unending present. We have not learned how to make social and physical technologies that are endogenous, based on the multiplicity of our histories. Our attempts to develop indigenous models of the modern have either been silly (using angels to levitate Pakistani astronauts to Mars) or reinforced feudal social relations, as in Islamic fundamentalism.[32] A way of moving to a space of understanding where we exist in many layers of social reality—and where ways of knowing include, for example, the empirical (literal), metaphorical (mythic and postmodern), and cultural (Islamic epistemology)—has remained elusive.

Through CNN and Star TV, PIA and global capital, Pakistan finds itself increasingly porous, even as many wish for a mythical sovereignty, whether national or Islamic. With Urdu music on Asian VTV—the counterpart of American MTV—recreating time and space (speeding time and making Pakistani cultural space appear attractively modern); with fair elections reigniting hope;

with genetic engineering, telecommunication, and virtual reality and CD-ROM on the horizon and their potential to transform Islam, perhaps we should be anticipating not more confrontations with the modern but the creation of a uniquely Pakistani postmodern. The epistemological richness, the cultural complexity, and a desire for a new vision are there, even if the betrayal of the dream of partition remains. Something different may indeed be possible. But if this seems too positive or Pollyannaish, we can focus on my friend Akbar, who was last seen driving around Islamabad chasing the few available Western women and the even fewer Westernized Pakistani women, with his mother swiftly chasing after him, hoping that he will find a job as a state bureaucrat and quickly get married before it is too late and a mullah finds him.

NOTES

1. For a general discussion of global culture, see Arjun Appadurai, "Disjuncture and Difference in the Global Economy," *Public Culture* 2.2 (1992): 441–29; Aijaz Ahmad, *In Theory: Classes, Nations, Literatures* (London: Verso, 1992).

2. The following story is all too typical: A businessman I met at a music party said to me, his eyes piercing mine, "We are rotten people. I am a very prosperous man. My business does well. But I have no peace of mind. I have to bribe everyone to get anything done. Peace of mind is everything." After hearing a bit of my history, he responded, "I too have lived overseas. But in a rotten country. Saudi Arabia. They are all uncivilized sorts there." He gave me his card and invited me to visit him, anytime.

3. See Zia Mian, "A Pakistan Pakistanis Won't Buy," *The News* (Islamabad/Rawalpindi), 16 April 1995, 6.

4. Mohajirs are an Urdu-speaking group that migrated from India at partition; much of the recent violence in Karachi is attributed to them. Pukhtoons are from the north of Pakistan (the North West Frontier Province); considered tribal and traditional, they move freely in and out of Pakistan and Afghanistan, and have frequently called for their own nation.

5. Majid Tehranian, "Communication and Revolution in Iran: The Passing of a Paradigm," *Iranian Studies* 13.104 (1980): 5–30.

6. Abuzer Abbas, "Sectarian Extremists Hold Punjab to Ransom," *Friday Times* (Lahore), 25 January 1995, 5.

7. Abdelwahab El-Affendi, *Who Needs an Islamic State?* (London: Grey Seal, 1991), 37, 39.

8. Zia Sardar, "Paper, Printing and Compact Disks: The Making and Unmaking of Islamic Culture," *Media, Culture and Society* 15 (1992): 43–59.

9. "A Christian in Islam," *The Economist*, 5 October 1994, 36. ISI stands for Inter Services Intelligence; it is Pakistan's intelligence agency. The CBI, Central Bureau of Investigation, is India's domestic intelligence agency.

10. Abdullah Jan, "Supporter of 'Infidel' Stoned to Death," *The News*, 10 April 1995, 5.

11. This joke was told to me by Syed Abidi, May 1987, in Honolulu. See also Syed Abidi, "Social Change and the Politics of Religion" (diss., University of Hawaii, 1988), esp. 218–21, in the section "Political Jokes and Sarcasm."

12. Sohail Inayatullah, "Images of Pakistan's Future," *Futures* 24.9 (1992): 867–78.

13. Zia Sardar, *How We Know: Ilm and the Revival of Knowledge* (London: Grey Seal, 1991).

14. Zia Sardar and Meryl Wyn Davies, *Distorted Imagination* (London: Grey Seal, 1990).

15. Fatima Mernissi, *Women and Islam* (Oxford: Basil Blackwell, 1991).

16. For a complete file of Masud Ahmad's weekly columns, one may write 25, St. 61, F.8/4, Islamabad, Pakistan.

17. See Arjun Appadurai, "Patriotism and Its Futures," *Public Culture* 5 (1993): 411–29.

18. Ashis Nandy, *Tradition, Tyranny, and Utopias: Essays in the Politics of Awareness* (Delhi: Oxford University Press, 1987).

19. P. R. Sarkar, *The Liberation of Intellect* (Calcutta: Ananda Marga, 1982).

20. I am indebted to Chitta Unni of Chaminade University in Honolulu, Hawaii, for this distinction. See his "It Is Only in a Present That There Is a Past" (paper presented at the Eleventh Annual Spring Symposium, Center for South Asian Studies, Honolulu, 14 March 1994).

21. See Sohail Inayatullah, "Frames of Reference, the Breakdown of the Self, and the Search for Reintegration," in *The Futures of Asian Cultures*, ed. Yogesh Atal and Eleonora Masini (Bangkok: Unesco, 1993), 95–130.

22. See Merryl Wyn Davies, Ashis Nandy, and Zia Sardar, *Barbaric Other: A Manifesto on Western Racism* (London: Pluto Press, 1993).

23. See Sohail Inayatullah, "Painfully beyond East and West: The Futures of Cultures," In Context 19 (1988): 50–53.

24. See Joel Kotkin, *Tribes: How Race, Religion, and Identity Determine Success in the New Global Economy* (New York: Random House, 1993).

25. Personal conversation with Zeena Satti, January 1990, Islamabad.

26. See Uma Narayan, "Eating Cultures: Incorporation, Identity, and Indian Food," *Social Identities* 1.1 (1995): 63–87.

27. Ashis Nandy, "The Philosophy of Coca-Cola," e-mail transmission, 24 January 1995.

28. Fortunately, I now have dual citizenship, Pakistani and American.

29. Majid Tehranian, "Dependency and Dialogue" (paper presented at the Twenty-fourth Annual Meeting of the International Studies Association, Mexico, April 5–9, 1983), 17. See also Majid Tehranian, *Technologies of Power* (Norwood, N.J.: Ablex, 1990).

30. This was also President Zia's political strategy, to use Islam to buttress the state by playing off different political parties against each other.

31. See Sohail Inayatullah, "From Who Am I to When Am I: Framing the Time and Shape of the Future," *Futures* 25.3 (1993): 235–53.

32. See Sohail Inayatullah, "Islamic Responses to Scientific, Technological, and Epistemological Transformations," *Islamic Thought and Scientific Creativity* 6.2 (1995): 47–68.

CHAPTER 8

Coming to Terms with the "Postcolonial"

Deepika Bahri

Some fifteen years after the term "postcolonial" began to circulate in the Western academy, the question "What is the postcolonial?"—raised by Vijay Mishra and Bob Hodge in 1991—continues to tax the imagination of academicians.[1] Essays interrogating the term, its use and abuse, its pitfalls and diffuseness, abound in journals and conference meetings. Discontent in and about the field has not, however, limited the scholarship in this area. Through an exploration of the term's history, usage, and definition in light of multiple criticisms and inadequacies, I attempt to evaluate what is lost and what might yet be gained by continuing to deploy it.

In a very literal sense, of course, the "postcolonial" is that which has been preceded by colonization. The second college edition of the *American Heritage Dictionary* defines it as "of, relating to, or being the time following the establishment of independence in a colony." In fact, however, the term is used much more loosely than this definition would suggest, sometimes yoking a very diverse range of experiences, cultures, and problems.[2] Thus is it used not merely to characterize that which succeeds the colonial but the chapter of history following World War II, whether or not such a period accommodates the still colonized, the neocolonized, or the always colonized. In their introduction to *Orientalism and the Postcolonial Predicament*, Carol Breckenridge and Peter van der Veer suggest that "'post' implies that which is behind us, and the past implies periodization. We can therefore speak of the *postcolonial period* as a framing device to characterize the second half of the twentieth century. The term 'postcolonial' displaces the focus on 'postwar' as a historical marker for the last fifty years."[3] Meanwhile, Gauri Viswanathan concedes that although "postcolonial" can be broadly defined as "a study of the cultural

An earlier version of this essay appeared in *Ariel: A Review of International English Literature* 26.1 (1995): 51–82.

interaction between colonizing powers and the societies they colonized, and the traces that this interaction left on the literature, arts, and human sciences of both societies," it is more popularly used "to signify more or less an *attitude* or position from which the decentering of Eurocentrism may ensue."[4] Additionally, some of the confusion stems from the use of the term both as "a literal description in formerly colonial societies" and as "a description of global condition after the period of colonialism," according to Arif Dirlik. In the latter sense, the notion of the "postcolonial" as a literary genre and an academic construct may have meaning(s) completely separate from historical moment(s). Dirlik in fact suggests that "one does not have to be *postcolonial* in any strict sense of the term to share" in the themes common in much postcolonial discourse.[5] Although the different connotations suggest that postcolonial discourse and theory can (and in fact do) serve many useful functions, several limitations seem to characterize much of the term's usage. Viewed as an attitude or framing device, the "postcolonial" becomes a surprisingly elusive and slippery configuration, laying itself open to the charge of ahistoricism.[6] The confusions inherent in its multiple deployments are significant because they point to its limitations in explaining contemporary global relations; moreover, even in its purely definitional sense the term can lead to cognitive erasures, displacements, and suppressions. It is tempting to concede that abstract shorthand definitions are needed as points of departure or we would discourse ourselves into stasis before we even begin, but a point of departure may ultimately determine not only *where* we might go but also *how far*. One might say that a little discomfiture is not entirely out of place when the term has gained acceptance and currency in the academy with altogether too suspicious ease.

Postcolonial theorists have attempted to remain sensitive to dissonances and problems in the field. A foundationally historical construct that grew out of the historical event of colonization, many argue, cannot be freed from its connections or obligations to history, both past and present. Nor, others would say, can it afford ethical blind spots in what was certainly meant to be an enterprise growing from a need for moral accountability. Despite scholarly efforts to contain inconsistencies and resist dichotomous constructions, however, certain slippages persist. The gap between enlightened high theory that grapples with inconsistencies, and academically material practices such as hiring, curricular design, and pedagogical method, for instance, is rarely addressed; nor does the theory emanating from metropolitan and Western centers pay sufficient attention to the material conditions of those who live in the postcolonies. Additionally, Dirlik has argued that it still remains for the postcolonial intelligentsia to "generate a thoroughgoing criticism of its own ideology" in "recognition of its own class-position in global capitalism."[7] Of greatest concern, perhaps, is a fundamental reliance on the seemingly essential and often inadequately nuanced binary colonizer/colonized, which can and does limit the field's potential for serious and useful critique.

Currently, definitional and terminological problems collude with this reliance on binary thinking even as the discipline argues vehemently against it, leading to both under- and overdeterminative claims. The currency and respectability of the category "postcolonial," despite the limitations repeatedly noted in much "postcolonial" discourse, must be addressed at a time when the field is becoming rapidly entrenched in the academy as a discipline, and postcolonial theory begins to assume, incrementally, larger proportions.[8] Those of us who are a part of the discipline of Postcolonial Studies would do well to continue to examine the limitations of the term "postcolonial," the mandate and scope of the field at large, and the slippages that must be confronted if the term and the field are to retain their promise of principled intervention. If we are now beginning to concede that "the United States is not outside the postcolonial globe," and that the term might be "prematurely celebratory," [9] let us consider the possibilities, first, that "postcolonial" can no longer be used in conventional ways if it is to be used responsibly, and second, that based on implicit definitional grounds, the term itself may obscure a more complete understanding of the issues attached to it.[10]

In an attempt to understand how the present usage of the term has developed, one might begin with the word, so to speak, and attempt to flesh out the complexity of postcolonialism by examining the key terms in the dictionary definition—time, establishment, independence, colony—and asking: But how long does this "condition" last? Is every experience that follows from the colonial encounter amenable to a characterization homogeneous enough to bear the label? (The latter, incidentally, is a crucial question for those studying the "texts" of the areas or spaces called postcolonial.) In a moment we will see how the definitional contributes to an understanding of colonialism as a primarily eighteenth- and nineteenth-century activity; for now, suffice it to say that the "colonial" of postcolonial discourse is more or less synonymous with "European" or "Western."[11] In a bid to situate it in more specific geopolitical terms, Anne McClintock has recently and justifiably accused postcolonialism of a "panoptic tendency to view the globe within generic abstractions voided of political nuance."[12] Certain "dominant" strains of postcolonialism create an abstract generalization, ignoring particularity among the colonized. In a recent essay Santiago Colás observes that "postcolonial critics and theorists have failed to examine the difference of Latin America. Scholars . . . ignore the particularity of Latin American culture as though it were irrelevant to their concerns." Complaining that inadequate attention to the relevance of Latin American experiences has led to the domination of a "false concept of postcoloniality," Colás argues for the use of geographical and historical qualifiers to "what has been presented as the general or universal concept of 'postcoloniality.'"[13]

But one might argue that if there is a tendency to universalize the notion of postcoloniality, there is also a concurrent failure to locate and understand colonialism within a more comprehensive historical framework that accounts for continuities along with ruptures. If postcolonialism did address itself to such a task, a different set of issues and questions would emerge. Within the larger conspectus of historical movements, one might then ask, given that the history of humankind is one of exploitation and colonization of various kinds, is not much of the inhabited world in one stage or another of postcoloniality? All over the world, people identifying with nations or communities have participated in some kind of colonialist maneuver. The ancient Akkadian civilization of 2800 B.C. is known to have conquered the Diyala region in the Near East, and there is ample evidence of Hindu colonization of far eastern Asia as early as the second century B.C.[14] If we accept John Tomlinson's definition of colonialism as "the invasion of an indigenous culture by a foreign one," India was colonized from as early as 2000 B.C., multiple times.[15] In short, it is customary but misleading to fix on colonization as a "Western" preserve, although the term itself may have its roots in Western language.[16]

To suggest that colonization is not unique to modern times is not, incidentally, to deny the importance of European imperialism: its scale and scope, its extraordinarily organized character, its ideological and cultural licensing of racist dominion, or, most significantly (since the previous features may characterize other empires of the past as well), its longevity and survival into the present. Rather, these observations are registered as a basis for speculation on the possible consequences of focusing on modern colonialism as if it were discrete instead of one in a series of colonialist moves, as if the most recent were the only visible one, as if this selective focus would allow us to explain contemporary situations satisfactorily.[17] An examination of premodern colonial activities may in fact give us a more complex understanding of structures of power and domination and illuminate the impact of older histories on both modern colonialism and contemporary global relations. Singular focus on dualistic characterizations of the Western colonizer and Eastern colonized, although providing a tidier configuration, effectively erases realities that lie, even if partially, outside the experience of modern colonization. One might include among them "native" breeds of colonization and oppression—a feature of "Third World" nations that feminists, in particular, have been quick to identify. To attribute a complex variety of problems to one teleological source is not only logically impaired but, more important, less useful. In conjuring up ancient history alongside the present, one is asking not for a reduction of disparate geopolitical experiences to one generic framework of human motivation and behavior stripped of historical and material contexts but a sensitivity to their interrelationship as a means of better understanding both in relation to the here and now. Human memory may be short and the list of immediate concerns long, yet one may wonder how those early experiences inform later historical phenomena such as religious fundamentalism and present-day discourse on colonialism and postcolonialism. That such explorations are rare if not completely absent in most postcolonial discourse is partly due to the limitations of our definition. The questions raised above may seem unnatural because the dictionary's phrase "establishment of independence" exerts a kind of force field, often obliging us to operate within a paradigm that dates our examination from the development of the modernist discourse of nationhood, blunting our ability to see the history that precedes it and promoting a study limited to the history that succeeds it.

Admittedly, as the term is defined and used at the moment, it is not possible to escape a conception of postcoloniality as integrally tied to European imperialism, because in two ways it does not easily allow us to transcend the temporal: First, it does not permit an understanding of colonialism outside the modern period, second, the "post" in "postcolonial," several critics recognize and contend, is a temporal fiction that obscures neocolonizing activities after the declaration of indepence in many countries. The phrase "establishment of independence," implicit in our general understanding of postcoloniality, is a description so embedded in the ideology of nationalism and nation-making that it leaves on the figurative gesture of independence the unmistakable and perhaps forever indelible trace of the imperial nation—a product, theorists argue, of decidedly European manufacture resulting from the industrial and capitalist movements of the eighteenth and nineteenth centuries.[18] Such a view occludes the possibility that "the idea of a nation is to be found as far back as the ancient world, although it is not clear that there was then what we understand as nation today," thus preventing us from conceiving of pre- or non-European "nations" as colonizers.[19] Further, it obscures the temporaneity of "nation" as construct,[20] and the prevalence of dual or even multiple loyalties based on ethnicity, language, and other factors.[21]

As a matter of fact, the characterization of "postcolonial" reliant on this vehemently national sense obscures both the nonnational character of many independence struggles in their early stages and the dangers that lurk in an insistence on national identity in the face of heterogeneous micronationalist and sectarian groups thrust into one national space.[22] In this way, not only can the European wave of colonialism be accused of suppressing local cultures—by finding them "peoples" but leaving them a "nation"—but the status of postcoloniality, dependent on nationhood for definition and recognition, itself implies rejection of both the people's prenational past and the proliferation of atavistic manifestations of these local cultures in the present. Narrower communal identities (Kikuyu in Kenya, Ibo in Nigeria, Sikhs in India, to name but a few) challenge the idea of nation based on citizenship and passports. Narratives of glorious nationalism, moreover, completely gloss over the fact that independent nations emerged not only because of heroic struggles but also because the empire was increasingly becoming an expensive proposition. Even more interesting, though "nation" is seen as a European construct, the erasure of the European ancestry of nationalism and the current explosion of discourse on "nationalism" in the context of Third World ethnic insurgence eliminates consideration of Partha Chatterjee's observation that "the two greatest wars of the twentieth century, engulfing as they did virtually every part of the globe, were brought about by Europe's failure to manage its own ethnic nationalisms."[23] Having furnished the formula for their existence, colonial scripts continue to inscribe the experiences of turbulent "postcolonial" states in vocabulary designed to match what can only be described as a neo-Orientalist narrative—a symptom, Chatterjee would say, of the persistent anxiety of the script writers. The connection between the globalization of world economy and the rise of local nationalisms is further obscured in master narratives of the nation that are integral to the achievement of postcolonial status.[24]

It could be argued, with reason, that the foregoing discussion suggests an elision of the distinction between nation and state—the nation-state more appropriately being the legacy of modern colonialism—but in fact, the rhetoric of nation is essential to the solvency of the political state, while the attainment of political sovereignty is premised on a "shared" sense of national identity.

Postcolonial discourse has addressed some of these issues better than others. It has been extraordinarily successful in shifting attention "from national origin to subject-position" in its relentless assaults on the narrative of the nation.[25] I would suggest, however, not only that this shift has contributed to a stripping of the requisite material and historical context of Third World situations but that these critiques are usually centered on dismantling the modernist ideology of nationhood rather than on exploring precolonial or contemporary manifestations of nationalisms that ought to be equally significant in any discussion of the crises of the moment. Transnationality and hybridity figure prominently in postcolonial discourse, but they tend to refer to postcolonial theorists in metropolitan locations more than to those in the Third World who are facing, with material consequences, the persistence of nationalist ideology that is informed by both colonial and atavistic notions of identity. In this sense, one might argue that attention to the European colonial moment and an aftermath defined almost exclusively by it (thus framing the Third World in neo-European or

Euro-American terms) continues to characterize a great deal of postcolonial discourse, a reflection perhaps of the presence of Third World intellectuals in Western academia and their obligation to continue writing back to the center to maintain a position of relevance to it.

However unsatisfactory the definitional and literal may be in explaining premodern, modern, and contemporary colonial global relations, they have continued to influence what can and cannot be included within the "postcolonial" frame. The danger in relying on static definitions is that the terms "colonial" and "postcolonial" then occlude all but a certain variety of exploitation dating from the marauding and appropriative enterprises of European mercantile expansion, since they lead to a nationalistic conception of colonial enterprise, and nation-making, as has been argued, is historically located in European movements. In much postcolonial discourse, colonialism is thus synonymous with "modern" colonialism, a totalizing term used for the most recent (although not the last) wave of imperial expansion.[26] Within this figuration of colonialism as European, however, several postcolonial critics have urged a more nuanced and reflective usage. Many would acknowledge that "postcolonialism," combining temporal selectivity with what might be seen as conceptual and moral binaries, almost exclusively connotes the oppression of indigenous peoples by European invaders, usually without acknowledgment of a series of qualifying factors: opposition within the mother country to owning colonies;[27] the need to refine the proposition that the European civilization was uniformly imperially racist;[28] the violence wrought by colonialism on and by both colonizer and colonized;[29] possible benefits resulting from the encounter; the very different role played by "memsahib" women in colonial situations and the challenge posed by their textual productions to a purely masculinist vision of imperialism; native complicity[30] and internal modes of colonization;[31] serious challenges to romanticized views of the colonized.[32]

Critics have been quick to note, moreover, that although "postcolonial" is customarily used to generalize a recent phenomenon that has now passed—usually indicating British and French departure from Africa, India, the Caribbean, and elsewhere over the last hundred years—the present moment in "postcolonial" nations is hardly "post" the colonial in any genuine or even cursory sense. That meaning of the term fails to account for the fact that mercantile neocolonialism, potent successor to modern colonialism, continues its virtually unchallenged march across the face of the earth, ensuring that the wretched will remain so and collude in (as they did before) but now also embrace the process of economic and cultural annexation, this time well disguised in the rhetoric of modernization and progress.[33] The continuing and in fact increasing economic and cultural dependence of these nations in the new world order makes a mockery of the assumption that independent status has been achieved on the basis of a signed document. That the economic and ideological characteristics of neocolonialism make it different from old-style colonialism is cause for more rather than less concern, since the enemy is now less visible and appears in the benevolent trimmings of "progress."[34] Anne McClintock objects that "metaphorically, the term 'post-colonialism' marks history as a series of stages along an epochal road from the 'pre-colonial,' to the 'colonial,' to the 'post-colonial'—an unbidden, if disavowed, commitment to linear time and the idea of 'development.'"[35] At the same time, "postcolonial" criticism is entirely committed to a repudiation of both Reason and Progress, the twin ideological mainstays of colonialism; effectively, as Homi Bhabha asserts, "postcolonial time questions the teleological traditions of past and present, and the polarized historicist sensibility of the archaic and the modern."[36] Yet the term "postcolonial" itself, we would be obliged to admit, is meaningless without its temporal resonance. Moreover, if it has not disabled the critique of neocolonialism, it has nevertheless, I argue, limited the kind of critique that may be offered, inhibiting proper articulation and apprehension of the dangers.

Many postcolonial critics applaud what they see as the dwindling of the split between colonizer and colonized, but it must be noted that this split continues to be the basis of Postcolonial Studies and to characterize many responses to postcolonial writers who venture to critique their own native cultures, challenging and thus violating the static principle "colonizer bad—colonized good." V. S. Naipaul's refusal to romanticize colonized peoples and exalt their values on this principle, for instance, has been ill received by many postcolonial critics. Although it may be useful to criticize his failure to depict the ongoing depredations of neocolonial mercantile maneuvers as he touts the importance of responsibility in the developing world,[37] far too little attention has been paid to the fact that decolonization has generally failed, and there has been no development of a genuinely decolonized discourse that might resonate at a more fundamentally material, even economic, level. So, for instance, one may read the recent Forbes magazine article "Now We Are Our Own Masters" as a classic example of India's capitulation to capitalist multinational neocolonial overtures—symptomized in one particular by the launching of a traditionally Indian item under the fast food model by "Dosa King" and announced in an accompanying banner by a figure bearing an uncanny resemblance to Abe Lincoln—but the same issue might also be fruitfully investigated in a general frame of collective responsibility and historical understanding.[38]

The critiques of globalization and economic transnationalism that abound in postcolonial discourse have served to initiate a very useful line of investigation into a contemporary phenomenon of some importance. But these critiques almost always target American or Euro-American multinationationals and/or suggest a vaguely "white male" malevolence in operation. Hardly if ever do we hear the question asked, what is the "diabolical" MNC (multinational corporation, often synonymous with American MNC) replacing, and how effective were those earlier economic models? Or who else, apart from the faceless MNC, celebrates the demise of the small producer—individual farmers and farm laborers (many of them women and children), indigenous and small industry—which is inevitable in this new model, and why? The sobering estimate that "for 95% of the population of underdeveloped countries, independence brings no immediate change," and very little thereafter,[39] and the reality of persistent class-based discrepancies tell us not only about the nature of multinational capitalism (now assuming a faceless, originless, denational aspect but primarily identified with contemporary Western colonial activities) but also about those who embrace it. In a divisive discourse of "us and them," the former is not an issue that can be usefully engaged, since it would implicate "us" in the undeniable plight of the people. These issues are for the most part selectively addressed, usually in the self-serving political narratives of fiery speeches by Third World opposition leaders, and very rarely in ethical ones.[40] To continue to hold the "colonizer" responsible for superior moral behavior without engaging the question of one's own ethical complicity is to deny one's own agency and admit to powerlessness, thus guaranteeing that no efforts to change the situation will occur. The metalepsis involved in anchoring the present moment (usually redolent in this context with suggestions of crises) to a selective past, and suturing the history of the present seamlessly with the experience of colonial imperialism, will only ensure that no genuine understanding of either will ever ensue. The dualism apart, this traffic in victimage can have serious consequences for any legitimate efforts at producing a discourse free from colonial reminiscing or, more important, developing an indigenous economic and political model that is able to address local concerns. One wonders, in fact, if much of the postcolonial discourse circulating in the Western academy would even consider the latter as its goal, given that its primary address is to the West, and a specific sector in the West at that.[41] Most egregiously, moreover, the failure to move beyond perpetrator/victim models seriously belittles the efforts of those who are effectively resisting transnational capitalism and maldevelopment projects in the Third World when they threaten the rights and survival of less empowered groups.[42]

Any developing hegemony of a postcolonial method that relies on the colonizer/colonized dichotomy should give us pause, if it casts the "postcolonial" as passive victim and encourages a culture of blame and self-pity (to celebrate self as victim is really to victimize the self anew) at a time when it may be a great deal more useful to examine the practices of the colonized more carefully. The ease with which European imperialism gained a hold in the colonies was certainly due to its superior resources, but it was also a function of the willingness of subjects to be colonized. The question here is not whether native complicity makes colonialism more or less right or wrong, but what it means for postcolonial societies today. Until this unpalatable question is examined, it may not be possible to recognize the ways in which previous subjects of empire are now willing to be neocolonized. In this context, the "neocolonized" might benefit from the reminder that the "multinational" is not only "them" but also "us." This observation is rendered more poignant if we consider that virulent critiques of MNCs come not only from erstwhile colonies such as India but also from "postcolonial" critics resident in the putative home countries of MNCs and fully implicated in their economies.[43]

A similar claim to immunity from complicity characterizes the claim to postcolonial status. The term can be and is used in reference to the United States and other settler colonies as well, often to the annoyance of those who see these as colonizing nations in their own right. One might note in passing that critiques of such appropriation of "postcolonial" status can be levied only under the comfortable umbrella of the essential binarism that characterizes much postcolonial discourse: Critics in Western metropolitan universities can thus pretend that they are outside the economic and political structures of the countries they reside in, while those in more "legitimate" postcolonial locales can ignore internal modes of colonialism in their own countries, or relegate them to a "different" system of exploitation, or even position them on a continuum with and as a result of European occupation. The implication of pre-European societal and production models in the colonial project, as I have attempted to argue earlier, or "precolonial" colonialism and internal colonialism as relevant and related phenomena, thus also remain largely untheorized.

As dissatisfaction with terminology and the limitations of the field grow, one might wonder why the field of Postcolonial Studies continues to flourish. How do we explain "the recent spate of positions in postcolonial literature in the academy"?[44] What does the politics of the moment have to do with the dramatic escalation of interest in postcoloniality? And what role does postcolonial literature play in issues we would normally describe as economic and political? The prior discussion, though related to "postcolonial" history and economics, may seem unrelated to a discussion of literary theory; however, postcolonial discourse, even when it focuses on literary texts from formerly colonized locales, is informed by principles similar to those of what we have come to know as "Cultural Studies." As Vincent B. Leitch argues in *Cultural Criticism, Literary Theory, Poststructuralism*, "Literary works are increasingly regarded as communal documents or as events with social, historical, and political dimensions rather than as autonomous artifacts within an aesthetic domain."[45] Whereas contemporary critical theory in general mobilizes sociological, historical, political, and institutional modes of inquiry, postcolonial discourse—given its nascence in specific historical events—is particularly given to an interdisciplinary method of analysis. Its connections with poststructuralism and postmodernism, discussed below, have reinforced this tendency. In quite another sense, economics and politics have much to do with the ascendancy of the term "postcolonial" over other contenders. A brief history of the various usages that precede and coexist with the term will help situate this claim in the context of prior and contemporary debates.

In the academy and the associated publishing industry the term "postcolonial," hyphenated or not, is used to describe the literatures and the theory of former, mostly British and French, colonies and diasporic writers and intellectuals from these spaces. Sometimes, but not commonly, the term also refers to Latin American cultural productions. Because so much of the support for the field comes from the English and Anglo-American academy, productions in English have been most prominent in the field, bolstered by attention from such award-granting institutions as the Booker in England or the Governor General's in Canada.[46] The cognate terms "commonwealth" and "Third World" have all but disappeared as prefixes from the body of literature that is now largely designated "postcolonial" but succumbs on occasion to the appellation "new literature in English": The "new" differentiates it from "old and established," while the Anglophonic character gives it continuity and position with the old and established. Needless to say, vernacular language literatures produced in these parts are either still vaguely subsumed and marginalized under the category "postcolonial" or designated by national origin or ethnic markers. "Postcolonial," clearly, would seem to be the term du jour. Let us also note that "minority," "resistance," and "multicultural" literature betray significant overlaps with, even as they evince differences from, the "postcolonial." Yet though they have been used to describe concerns and texts that share similarities, these various terms are hardly interchangeable.

The supercession of these terms—particularly "commonwealth" and "Third World," its close affiliates—by "postcolonial" is only partially comprehensible when we consider that none of them is immune from the criticism leveled against the earlier terms. Salman Rushdie, after confessing in his 1983 essay "Commonwealth Literature Does Not Exist" that the seductive environment provided by conferences and cultural forums on "commonwealth literature" might lead one to imagine that such a subject actually exists, roundly berated the "new and badly made umbrella" under which disparate non-British literatures were forced to huddle without any regard for their differences. He concluded that non-Western literature was being ghettoized, contained, and relegated to the margins in what might even be considered a racially segregationist move. The very name "commonwealth literature" would necessarily lead to its being read in nationalist terms, often exclusively so, and to a resurgence of exoticism in the guise of authenticity; moreover, even as the term erased the differences between the various "new" literatures, it would confine similarity to the experience of occupation by a foreign nation. Nevertheless, you could call this chimeric creature into existence, he warned, "if you set up enough faculties, if you [wrote] enough books and appoint[ed] enough research students."[47] Amen, we might say, as we observe the rapid development in the area of postcolonial studies.

Often uncannily reminiscent of Rushdie's objections to the category "commonwealth" are Aijaz Ahmad's remarks in his rejoinder to Fredric Jameson's much publicized 1986 essay, "Third World Literature in the Era of Multinational Capitalism." Jameson contends that inclusive heterogeneity should be the principle in organizing educational curricula in the West, and that an aesthetics of Third World literature must rest upon its being read as national allegory on the strength of this world's being defined by its experience of colonialism and imperialism.[48] Ahmad bemoans the "suppression of the multiplicity of significant differences among and within both the advanced capitalist countries on the one hand and the imperialized formations on the other," an objection registered against all such terms that deploy simplistic binary bifurcations between colonizer and colonized by a diverse array of critics, including Gayatri Chakravorty Spivak, Sara Suleri, Diana Brydon, Homi Bhabha, Abdul JanMohamed, and Kumkum Sangari.[49] Ahmad goes on to reject theories that achieve their tenuous coherence through obfuscatory and specious generalities. Ahmad's critique of the three worlds theory in general and Jameson in particular is a complex one and not amenable to hasty paraphrase; suffice it to say that he alerts us to the limitations of theoretically unified categories and exhorts us to fix our eyes on the need for "greater clarity about the theoretical methods and political purposes of our reading" rather than on the goal of more coherent narratives of textual production in this or that part of the world.[50] Similar charges of false universality and ahistoricism have, of course, been brought against "postcolonial."

Still, there are some who prefer the relatively more resistive connotations of the earlier terms. Diana Brydon confronts those so willing to dismiss "commonwealth" literature because of its seeming stereotyping and universalizing, arguing that these critics deny the writers who use this label the specifity they would hope to claim, while providing little evidence for their criticisms. Moreover, she adds, critics of commonwealth literature have ignored the "wealth" that such literature has to offer: "To recognise what we hold in common is not to underestimate our differences, but to provide us with a context for understanding them more clearly." Similarly, Trinh T. Minh-ha points to the power of a term such as "Third World" when used subversively by those it names. Ella Shohat, too, suggests that the term "does still retain heuristic value as a convenient label for the imperialized formations, including those within the First World."[51] Despite defenders, however, the use of "commonwealth" and "Third World" appears to be waning in part in response to the problems suggested by Rushdie and Ahmad but perhaps in greater part because "postcolonial" is more readily acceptable to the academy for reasons investigated below.

"Postcolonial," despite its obvious links to both "commonwealth" and "Third World," has been accorded considerably more respectability than either term. The growing currency within the academy of "postcolonial" was consolidated by the appearance in 1989 of *The Empire Writes Back: Theory and Practice in Post-Colonial Literatures*. The compound, which first appeared in the *Oxford English Dictionary* in 1959, is used in that title (like the unhyphenated word in the *American Heritage Dictionary*) to indicate a period that follows colonization. In their introduction to the book, Bill Ashcroft, Gareth Griffiths, and Helen Tiffin use it to "cover all the culture affected by the imperial process from the moment of colonization [modern European colonization] to the present day." The editors suggest that this term is to be preferred over others "because it points a way towards a possible study of the effects of colonialism in and between writing in english [sic] and writing in indigenous languages . . . as well as writing in other language diasporas." They reject "commonwealth" because it rests "purely on the fact of a shared history and the resulting political grouping"; "Third World literature" is seen as pejorative; and "new literatures in English" is considered Eurocentric and condescending toward the new in comparison with the old, even though its de-emphasis of the colonial past is a desirable feature for some. The term "Terranglia" is mentioned without comment, but it would seem to carry territorial and proprietary—not to mention Anglocentric—connotations.[52] Welcoming the term "post-colonial," Vijay Mishra and Bob Hodge advocate its use on the grounds that it "foregrounds a politics of opposition and struggle, and problematizes the key relationship between centre and periphery."[53] They also laud its challenge to the canon. Having said this, they call into question the catachrestic reduction by Ashcroft, Griffiths, and Tiffin of postcoloniality to no more than textuality and the further diminution of textual gestures to either/or categories: the appropriation or abrogation of English. The exclusivist focus on English and the insistence on reading culturally syncretic texts without attention to their culture-specific details are also criticized as features of a post- or neo-Orientalist version of critical exercise. It is useful to recall here Ahmad's caveat against unified theories that simply dismiss as inessential those parts that do not fit their schema. In the matrix provided by Ashcroft, Griffiths, and Tiffin, the relegation of non-Western textual productions to a realm not so much peripheral as invisible—because they are, barring some translations, unavailable to the majority of Western scholars—is an astute strategy if one is going about the business of attempting a coherent theory, but the fact that such texts exist poses the most potent threat to any theory from which they are absent. Ultimately, it is not simply that theory is gray, as Goethe puts it, but that if it does not work in practice, it does not work in theory. Mishra and Hodge suggest that we might talk about not one but several postcolonialisms. Dropping of the hyphen permits us to recognize one version as implicit in colonial discourse, thus emphasizing continuity rather than rupture. They also urge a greater distinction between settler and nonsettler countries and a celebration of many small narratives of postcolonialisms, themselves configurations susceptible to change. In subsequent years, however, Mishra and Hodge's idea of several postcolonialisms—a salutary effort to challenge what is often a totalizing tendency in the paradiscourses of postcolonialism—has failed, as preceding discussions demonstrate, to find the multivocal articulation they intended.

In the last decade or so, "postcolonial" has come through and won the purple by its deployment as an apposite adjective for "theory," "space," and "condition," a distinction not commonly accorded to "commonwealth" or "minority" discourse; it has also spawned such neologisms as "postcoloniality" and "postcolonialism." Its evolution into the status of theoretical apparatus and disciplinary entity from its humble beginnings as a descriptor for literature is a notable transmutation. I argue that among the many reasons for this are some that should give us pause because they raise questions about our own complicity, the dubious stakes and standards of the academy itself, and the imbrication of the two in our willingness to maintain a discourse system that is diffuse at times and conflicted at its worst.

The growth in the size and stature of Postcolonial Studies—its validation, in fact, as a disciplinary subject—has been coeval with the growing interest in multiculturalism and the not unrelated phenomenon of global economic and cultural transnationalism (more on this later). The changing ethnic and racial demographics of Anglo-America (already evident for some years in the United Kingdom); the increasing numbers and influence of immigrant South Asians in general and in the academy in particular (postcolonial theories have certainly been furthered more by this group than by any other); the development and reception of programs devoted to the study of other ethnic groups, chief among them African Americans, as well as associated political and economic gains;[54] and the increasing availability of texts in English by non-Western authors (often resident in the West) are all factors that have contributed to the development of Postcolonial Studies as a discipline. The concomitant growth of Women's Studies and the impetus to conceive of global feminisms should also be acknowledged as related and influential, as should the mounting theory in support of representation and identity affirmation. The twin bogies of essentialism and authenticity conjured by the latter continue to vex identitarian politics, but a certain strategic essentialism—a "generalizing" of the self to engage a question of some importance while knowing that "one is not just one thing"—is accepted by most postcolonial critics as a necessary stage in the developing discourse.[55] The tenuous relationship of this position (however qualified and mediated) with related movement of our times, postmodernism, bears examination.

Perhaps one of the most significant reasons for the exponential expansion in postcolonial discourse is the host climate generated by the development of postmodern theory and the postmodern critic's suspicion of an objective historical consciousness.[56] Ahmad suggests that the influence on Western thinkers of the colonial encounter and the disintegration of empire produced an examination of the West's "place in the world" and much of the mistrust of the text as a hermetic construct; an incidental result of this, Ahmad contends, was that "literature was pressed to disclose the strategic complicities whereby it had traditionally represented races—and genders—and empires."[57] The postmodern method that ensued allowed a reopening of closed and demarcated territories. Sara Suleri's disarticulation of the Third World woman and denaturalization of the category of woman—the claim, indeed, that "there are no women in the Third World"—is a gesture very much in keeping with postmodern disavowal of essentialist productions of meaning. So is Chandra Talpade Mohanty's rejection of Western feminism's treatment of women as an "already constituted, coherent group" and of Third World woman as stereotypical victim, which results in the "suppression—often violent—of the heterogeneity of the subject(s) in question."[58]

It would be entirely appropriate to contend that postcolonial discourse has profited enormously from "the politics of poststructuralism," which, says Robert Young, "forces the recognition that all knowledge may be variously contaminated."[59] Arif Dirlik has gone so far as to say that "crucial premises of postcolonial criticism, such as the repudiation of post-Enlightenment metanarratives, were enunciated first in post-structuralist thinking and the various postmodernisms it has informed."[60] Postcolonialism's truck with postmodernism, however, demonstrates a strategic mobilization of some of its principles and conscious abjuration of others: On the one hand, "post-colonial criticism's key beginning point . . . is that a 'parodic' repetition of imperial 'textuality' sets itself specifically in opposition to the interpellative power of colonialism" (using the notion of intertextual parody Linda Hutcheon defines for postmodernism);[61] on the other hand, the postcolonial wants to allow for the positive production of oppositional truth claims, says Stephen Slemon: This "referential assumption would appear to make . . . a postcolonial criticism radically fractured and contradictory, for such a criticism would draw on poststructuralism's suspension of the referent in order to read the social 'text' of colonial power and at the same time would reinstall the referent in the service of colonized and post-colonial societies."[62] Much of the postcolonial critique of postmodernism, in fact, quarrels with its denial of subjectivity, a luxury not available to cultures still contending for some modicum of expression.[63] Moreover, as Kumkum Sangari puts it, "the postmodern preoccupation with the crisis of meaning is not everyone's crisis," nor is postmodern skepticism conducive to culturally grounded modes of de-essentialization; worse yet, it "denies to all the truth of or the desire of totalizing narratives."[64] Nevertheless, metropolitan postcolonial theory is replete with poststructuralist methods and the writings of Michael Foucault, Jacques Derrida, Gilles Deleuze, and Félix Guattari, since deconstruction allows for the critique of what Spivak refers to as "founded political programs."[65] The serviceability of poststructuralism for postcolonial criticism aside, the connection between the two, one might speculate, is partly responsible for the latter's status in the academy, a completely indigenous "postcolonial" discourse being either considered or rendered an impossibility for various reasons: the lingering influence of colonial texts in Third World curricula and universities, the continuing need for legitimation of the marginal by the central, and the persistent disregard for any productions that might be delinked from the metropole or Western modular constructs of postcoloniality.[66]

The foregoing discussion details one symptomatic instance of two interrelated problems: first, that postcolonial discourse betrays its inability to avoid writing back to the center or passing through it in the same way that the postcolonial nation is unavoidably, and often counterproductively, tethered to its founding "parent"; second, that while an incipient discourse may be permitted some conceptual license and flexibility in using conflicting models, the failure to theorize scrupulously its own contradictions may sooner or later limit its potential for useful discussion.[67]

In light of that comment, one must observe that also significant in the march of "postcoloniality" through Western universities is the mobilization of the term "postcolonial" in the service of displacing, and perhaps erasing, various unmentionables. A series of critics have articulated their uneasiness about this misuse of the term and the field. Ella Shohat comments on the relief evidenced in a multicultural international studies committee, of which she was a member at City University of New York, at the sight of the term "postcolonial" in lieu of such threatening terms as "imperialism" and "neocolonialism."[68] It has thus become a "safer bet," one more word to name the margin and a way of managing and containing what might be too explosive and incendiary by another name; as Spivak explains, "When a cultural identity is thrust upon one because the center wants an identifiable margin, claims for marginality assure validation from the center."[69] This validation works as a surprisingly efficient clamp on the subversive potential of a marginal movement. Gauri Viswanathan suggests that "the co-optation of certain literatures can in some ways diffuse their oppositional nature. Another negative might be the recent spate of positions in postcolonial literature in the academy in the absence of discussion about what the term means—this could be a way of neutralizing the other presence by incorporating it. A bigger danger is that the term . . . becomes a kind of replacement for other literatures, such as Asian or African American, without really dealing with the political challenges imposed by the other constituencies."[70]

The suppression of these literatures and the recruitment in the name of affirmative hiring of metropolitan imports from the elite ranks of erstwhile colonies (intrinsically sanctioned and approved by their British education) should be matters of greater concern than they seem to be. The employment and promotion of these individuals in "Postcolonial Studies" as surrogates for real social change circumvents the need to acknowledge the marginalization and exploitation that continues unheeded while the academy produces "highly commodified distinguished professors" such as Spivak and racks up points on the scorecard of cultural diversity.[71] The erasure of considerations of class and the realities of the disenfranchisement of Native Americans or African Americans or second- and third-generation Asian Americans are masked by academic gestures of acceptance of the visible difference presented by displaced Third World postcolonial intellectuals.

Moreover, critics argue that the postcolonial increasingly functions as "sales tag" for "the international commodity culture of late (twentieth-century) capitalism."[72] In seeking to "reveal societies globally in their complex heterogeneity and contingency," as Dirlik phrases it, the term "postcolonial"—progressively more abstract and difficult to define—is accused of obscuring the particulars of oppression in specific interactions while relying on a diffuse legacy of a mostly distant colonial past that is receding from public memory in most postcolonial societies. Metropolitan postcolonial discourse, particularly of the "high" theoretical kind, is thought to reflect a species of discourse increasingly void of geographical or historical specificity. The very diffuseness of "postcolonial" makes it a welcome substitute for the "less tractable vocabulary that insists on keeping in the foreground contemporary problems of political division and oppression."[73]

Lest these characterizations of the reception of "postcoloniality" in the academy seem to smack of paranoia and to intimate sinister conspiracy, let us also acknowledge what might be more benevolent, if no less questionable, reasons for its acceptance. As Julia V. Emberley suggests, "Postcolonial is neither another stage in the development logic of colonial history nor part of an evolutionary model signaling the demise of the historical effects of colonialism. Postcolonial is a contemporary configuration which implies a new direction in the analysis of ideological relations which constitute the 'First World's' symbolic debt to the so-called Third World." In this context, one might say that "postcolonialism" has flowered under the pressure on the West to be understood and forgiven— thus assuaging, at least symbolically, the real or imagined guilt provoked by such texts as Said's *Orientalism*—and embraced within the framework of evolutionary and moral progress. Emberley reminds us that the readership for this work, which "circulates as a consuming virus, feeding off ills perpetuated by the epistemic violence . . . of imperialism in an effort to heal the dislocation and alienation that has ruptured the ties between a 'homeland' and academic privilege," is primarily if not exclusively North American and British.[74]

Effectively, then, we are faced with a *market* for postcolonial wares in this part of the world. I do not use the economic term lightly, for it may provide a potent clue to the ambiguous but deceptively welcome use of "postcolonial."[75] I have invoked earlier the connections between "Postcolonial" and "Multicultural" Studies. While it is true that the American education system is now serving an increasingly diverse student body, the promotion of these fields in an era of globalization must also be acknowledged and reported. The role of the "multicultural" or "postcolonial" text in this economy is not only ostensibly to instill tolerance and acceptance for diversity but also, one might speculate, to develop a student body mobilized for a global economy and comfortable or at least minimally "literate" in other cultures, the latter being entirely commensurate with a multinationalist corporate perspective.[76] Success in both areas is yet to be proved or demonstrated; in fact, these texts, although they may legitimately provoke interest in "marginal" cultures for some students, have the potential to reinforce stereotypical attitudes; solitary literary texts deployed in reductive and representative ways may function as rationalizations for a lack of genuine investigation into other cultures. If, as Spivak argues, "liberal multiculturalism is interested, basically, in bottom-line national origin validation,"[77] the persistent reading of culturally "Other" texts for their "difference" and distance from the dominant culture could foster rather than erase divisions.

A fuller account of the emergence and popularity of postcolonial discourse as a specific function of global capitalism is to be found in Arif Dirlik's "The Postcolonial Aura: Third World Criticism in the Age of Global Capitalism," which attempts to explain the currency of the postcolonial in an age of late capitalism characterized by simultaneous globalization and fragmentation. The nexus beween market considerations and the explosion of interest in matters postcolonial—which straddles global and local concerns while locating its address to and in the West—is not one that postcolonial scholars can choose to ignore. Dirlik's contention that metropolitan postcolonial discourse is oblivious of or unwilling to acknowlege the conditions of its existence, however, is belied by at least one postcolonial critic's clear sense of the implication of postcolonialism and multiculturalism in an era of transnationalism.[78] Although one must for the most part agree that these connections are not always recognized or announced, at the same time it is misleading to conflate the "postcolonial" with the "multicultural," as Dirlik does or as my own connecting of the two in the preceding paragraph might suggest. Within Anglo-America the multicultural (having to do with minority cultures, to read the term as it is really meant) may be and has been defined as a victim of "internal" colonialism in the West, but it matches the postcolonial only in the abstract sense of connoting or opposing oppression by Euro-American-centrism. A "postcolonial" text, as it turns out, can be used as a sanitized "multicultural" text: one located outside the immediate frame of conflict politics in the West and therefore posing a limited threat, if any, while still meeting the requirements of cultural diversity. Moreover, though postcolonial texts are used in multicultural courses, Postcolonial Studies—perhaps because the material is seen as more complex or demanding of interdisciplinary analysis—is largely promoted in graduate rather than undergraduate curricula. The prestige of postcolonialism may be attributed to a variety of sources: its links to and use of poststructuralism's language and methodology, the theoretical sophistication of many of its practitioners, and its increasing defusion of political charge.

It will be interesting to take stock of the respective losses and gains on the multicultural and postcolonial sides of the culture wars in Anglo-America. With the advent of the "angry white male" (a construct that conceals similar anger among many nonwhite groups) on the scene, one might speculate that the more abstract and less politically grounded metropolitan postcolonial discourse is the more likely to survive if one believes with Dirlik that "postcoloniality . . . is appealing because it disguises the power relations that shape a seemingly shapeless world and contributes to a conceptualization of that world that both consolidates and subverts possibilities of resistance."[79] In light of the assaults on political correctness and on multicultural education as one of its academic vehicles, the abstractions of postcolonial theory and discourse along with their absorption into an expanded English Studies curriculum might render it less vulnerable to attack in the public arena and therefore more appealing to university administrators.

Meanwhile, in programmatic terms, the selection and teaching of both multicultural and postcolonial texts are matters of some concern. When used in multicultural curricula, the postcolonial text—often the diasporic, transnational kind—is obliged to share the conflicted space of the multicultural. A central issue here is one not only of representation but of a *particular type of representation*. The contract is fairly simple: Minoritized subjects are encouraged to represent themselves and their communities, in art, literature, and so on; their productions are to be accepted and disseminated, usually by "multiculturals" and primarily through educational institutions, in a spirit of learning, tolerance, and respect. Neither side of the bargain is inherently damaging. The problem is that such subjects are to speak *as minorities*; they are to *represent* in individual voices their communities and the victimization suffered by them; and their texts are to be used, often solo, to "inform" students. In the postcolonial text the subject must be represented as one suffering from the consequences of European colonization; in the diasporic text located in the West (such as Bharati Mukherjee's *Jasmine*) the subject is to assume "minority" and "victim" position within the dominant culture. Moreover, regardless of the authors' socio-economic status, they are to assume the personae of victims in proxy for the truly silenced others who do not have access to the means of cultural production. The potential political charge of the postcolonial text is thus muffled by a local agenda that uses it to celebrate diversity and difference within a domestic context.[80]

Another pedagogic issue with regard to postcolonial courses is the selection of materials: the choice of metropolitan texts that capitalize on the status of postcoloniality and neglect other candidates ("postcolonial" as a label is too often used for the "highbrow" migrant who is the one most likely to be published), or "national" texts that match the composite profile necessary to maintain the self/other model.[81] On the one hand, one can only welcome the inclusion of "newer" literature, even if only in English. On the other, it might be well to remember the conditions under which such texts arrive. First, accessibility in the colonizer's language is often a prerequisite for inclusion in postcolonial curricula; thus any text picked is "marked" by the colonial encounter, even if only by language. Second, it is careless to describe and include texts written in English as *representatively* "postcolonial" at the expense of rich and perhaps more telling tales in the vernacular which may or may not deal with "colonialism" as such. Third, what is selected for "translation" into the metropolitan academy may be chosen for similarly limited considerations. One need not be particularly insightful to note that it is purposely blind to read experience in terms of selective stimuli and causes, and impossible (or it should be) to study the present without all of the past that precedes it.

Of perhaps even greater concern is the fact that such texts have been introduced into the curriculum on the basis of a forged link, a colonial past; this may certainly be a starting point, but little effort is then made to examine and problematize that link in the classroom. Such an approach, says Viswanathan, precludes "a serious study of the specific histories of these other societies: All postcolonial societies, whether of India, Africa, or the Caribbean, are assumed to have a parallel history." But even as difference is thus be reduced to sameness, commonalities with dominant cultural texts can be ignored in *favor* of difference by ghettoizing these texts and segregating them in their enclosed space. Both would appear to be deficient reading strategies. The opposite of reading only in terms of difference is not necessarily reading in terms of homogenization. Good reading should always be about noting the particular; problems arise only when difference is adduced as a totalizing framework. The quest for "sameness," in fact, might offer surprisingly rich yields. For instance, Viswanathan recommends applying a "postcolonial" method of reading to canonical texts "so that what appear to be concerns exclusive to the postcolonial situation—fundamentalism, sectarianism, and so on—could be read in relation to nineteenth-century novels [such as] *Barnaby Rudge*." This could make us "rethink the problems of the Third World and consider that these difficulties have become part of an international, global history. . . . Postcolonial as a method of reading would be a healthy way to counterbalance the ahistorical functions that postcolonial literature has acquired over the past years." Viswanathan's "Tao" of postcolonialism is a useful response to an already growing trend within the field to subsume other "minority" experiences or to analogize them. Another alternative is offered by Spivak: supplementing with extensive primary materials from the country of origin as a way to begin bridging the gap between literature and not-literature.[82] The adoption of these methods alone, however, will not obviate the messiness of terminology itself, or absolve us of the need to reconceptualize the bases of our discipline.

It remains to note that I have made free reference to "postcolonial discourse" as if some ghostly essence of it existed "out there" which this discussion has somehow been able to transcend. That essence will be impossible to locate in a field that takes many shapes and forms, even if they can all be said to share certain assumptions and limitations. Mine is one attempt among many to examine the ambiguities in the field (a project already initiated by Huggan, McClintock, Shohat, and Spivak, among other critics) and admittedly participates in, while seeking to critique, the nebulous ideology that permeates the discipline. It may be useful to recall Slavoj Zizek's notion of ideology as "a kind of reality whose very ontological consistency implies a certain non-knowledge of its participants . . . as to its essence."[83] That this discussion may be found to reproduce the assumptions and ambiguities it has attempted to identify should not, then, come as a surprise. My goal has been to heed the voices of dissent that seek to promote productive dissonance in order to maintain a sense of resistance in the field. Perhaps few have expressed this need more honestly and eloquently than Santiago Colás: "In whatever form the concept of postcoloniality is deployed, it must remain resolutely negative: in my view, it must mark failures, shortcomings, distances to be traversed, and pockets of domination in thought that remain critically unexamined, let alone eradicated in their practical form."[84] As he argues, postcolonialism's usefulness lies in its willingness to keep examining itself while it continues to produce itself.

In keeping with Colás's imperative, I close with what remain abiding and still useful questions: What is the impact, in popular and populist as well as material terms, of generating academic formations that rely on static binaries? How can we activate the continuum rather than the polarities between binaries? How can we teach our students the contradictions and conflicts inherent in our curricular programs? How can we discuss the marginalization and oppression that certainly exist without reducing these experiences to managed and misleading categories? How can we prevent discussions of oppression and colonization from absolving individuals and groups of responsibility? Can we acknowledge that academic "speaking for" minoritized subjects may often be not only an unethical usurpation but an effective smoke screen that diverts attention from more pertinent issues? that we are complicitous in the same exploitive modes of production we are privileged to criticize academically? that a certain sort of academic "postcolonial" has prospered by assuming, catachrestically, the identity of disenfranchised lower-class immigrants and those in our countries of origin who will never be able to escape their material conditions? Can we recognize that ultimately our concerns with terminology and theory might be but need not be idle indulgences if we are able to acknowledge and accommodate the materiality of the world in which they arise? If this list is as tedious as some others I have used, it is to give due credit to the enormous complexity of the tasks that await us. It is too early to be satisfied with the condition of Postcolonial Studies and too late to dismiss their impact.

NOTES

Acknowledgments: Special thanks are due to Mary Vasudeva, Joseph Petraglia-Bahri, and Mary Catherine Harper for their many comments and suggestions during the drafting of this piece.

1. Vijay Mishra and Bob Hodge, "What Is Post(-)Colonialism? *Textual Practice* 5.3 (1991): 399–414.

2. See Anne McClintock's eloquent critique in "The Angel of Progress: Pitfalls of the Term 'Post-Colonialism,'" *Social Text* 31–32 (1992): 84–98.

3. Carol A. Breckenridge and Peter van der Veer, "Orientalism and the Postcolonial Predicament," in *Orientalism and the Postcolonial Predicament: Perspectives on South Asia*, ed. Breckenridge and van der Veer (Philadelphia: University of Pennsylvania Press, 1993), 1.

4. See the interview with Gauri Viswanathan (Chapter 3 in this volume).

5. Arif Dirlik, "The Postcolonial Aura: Third World Criticism in the Age of Global Capitalism," *Critical Inquiry* 20 (Winter 1994): 332, 336.

6. According to Indrani Mitra (Chapter 16, this volume), "The absence of analytical precision in the term has allowed a shift in the focus of Postcolonial Studies from the resistance literatures produced in the imperialist and neoimperialist sites of struggle to a more domestic celebration of cultural diversity and difference."

7. Dirlik, "Postcolonial Aura," 356.

8. See Gayatri Chakravorty Spivak, "Neocolonialism and the Secret Agent of Knowledge" (interview with Robert Young), *Oxford Literary Review* 12.1–2 (1991): 224: "I find the word postcolonialism totally bogus." Ella Shohat, "Notes on the Post-Colonial," *Social Text* 31–32 (1992): 110, calls for a systematic interrogation of the term because of its susceptibility "to a blurring of perspectives." See also Graham Huggan, "Postcolonialism and Its Discontents," *Transition: An International Review* 62 (1993): 130–35; and Dipesh Chakrabarty, "Postcoloniality and the Artifice of History: Who Speaks for 'Indian' Pasts?" *Representations* 37 (Winter 1992): 128–38.

9. Gayatri Chakravorty Spivak, *Outside in the Teaching Machine* (New York: Routledge, 1993), 217; McClintock, "Angel of Progress," 87.

10. In "Notes on the Post-Colonial," 111–12, consider Shohat's injunctions: "The concept of the 'post-colonial' must be interrogated and contextualized historically, geographically, and culturally. My argument is not necessarily that one conceptual frame is 'wrong' and the other is 'right,' but that each frame illuminates only partial aspects of systemic modes of domination, of overlapping collective identities, and of contemporary global relations."

11. Even in a purely modern sense, the conflation of "colonizer" with "European" is a highly problematic one. See Ann Laura Stoler, "Rethinking Colonial Categories: European Communities and the Boundaries of Rule," in *Colonialism and Culture*, ed. Nicholas B. Dirks (Ann Arbor: University of Michigan Press, 1992), 319–52.

12. McClintock, "Angel of Progress," 86.

13. See Santiago Colás, "Of Creole Symptoms, Cuban Fantasies, and Other Latin American Postcolonial Ideologies," *PMLA* 110.3 (1995): 383, 393n.

14. R. C. Mazumdar, *Hindu Colonies in the Far East*, 2d ed. (Calcutta: Firma K. L. Mukhopadhyay, 1963).

15. John Tomlinson, *Cultural Imperialism : A Critical Introduction* (Baltimore, Md.: Johns Hopkins University Press, 1991), 23. For the purposes of this essay, "indigenous" refers to people who have developed a culture and tradition distinctly their own. Tomlinson's introduction addresses this issue in some depth.

16. The *Oxford English Dictionary* dates the term "colonize" in written English to 1622; "colonialize" to 1864; "colonizer" to 1781.

17. For a fuller discussion of the "radically different" nature of modern European imperialism compared with earlier forms of overseas domination, see Edward Said, "Yeats and Decolonization," in *Nationalism, Colonialism and Literature* by Terry Eagleton, Fredric Jameson, and Edward W. Said (Minneapolis: University of Minnesota Press, 1990), 69–95.

18. Though not Marxist, Ernest Gellner, in *Nations and Nationalism* (Oxford: Blackwell, 1983), proposes economic reasons for the rise of nationalism: i.e., the development of industrialist society which took place in certain parts of Europe in the eighteenth and nineteenth centuries and in the twentieth century in other parts of the world. Particular forms of polity and culture are necessary for industrial economic growth, he suggests, thus illustrating the nexus between nationalism and industrialization. With industrialization, old states had to change cultural life and social structure to maximize advantages and profits. Gellner believes that it happened not because European thinkers invented it but because it was appropriate to the needs of the time. In *Imagined Communities: Reflections on the Origin and Spread of Nationalism* (London: Verso, 1983), Benedict Anderson explores the psychic dimensions of nationalism in addition to economic ones. He cites print capitalism as the principal material condition which spreads the idea of nation and the ideology of nationalism, not only within one nation but throughout the world. Printing standardizes language and aids the development of capitalism and the centralized state. Scientific discoveries and exploration of the world contribute to this process, as well. Anderson also explores the emotional appeal of nationalism contained in the belief of some sort of perpetuity through membership of a continuing nation.

19. James Kellas, *The Politics of Nationalism and Ethnicity* (New York: St. Martin's, 1991), 22.

20. "A nation," says Rabindranath Tagore, "in the sense of the political and economic union of a people is that aspect which a whole population assumes when organized for a mechanical purpose" (*Nationalism* [New York: Macmillan, 1917], 19.

21. A 1986 survey in Scotland found that 53 percent of the people expressed a degree of dual nationality (Kellas, *Politics*, 19). The proliferation of such terms as Asian American and African American in the United States and factionalist moves in many other parts of the world indicate the crisis of the national construct.

22. According to Frantz Fanon, "History teaches us clearly that the battle against colonialism does not run straight away along the lines of nationalism." It is the abuses of colonizers and forced labor, he suggests, that allow for a temporary suspension of race and tribe loyalties in such struggles (*The Wretched of the Earth*, trans. Constance Farrington [New York: Grove, 1963], 148).

23. Partha Chatterjee, *The Nation and Its Fragments: Colonial and Postcolonial Histories* (Princeton, N.J.: Princeton University Press, 1993), 4.

24. In the Indian context, Vandana Shiva suggests, "fundamentalists fail to relate the current erosion of freedom and autonomy to the Indian state's subservience to global capitalism" ("Masculinization of the Motherland," in *Ecofeminism* by Maria Mies and Vandana Shiva [Halifax, Nova Scotia: Firewood, 1993], 110).

25. Dirlik, "Postcolonial Aura," 335.

26. The distinction between "ancient" and "modern" is seldom noted in discussion of "colonialism." And "last" would be seen by many postcolonial critics as a debatable adjective in the context of ongoing and new colonialism in many parts of the world.

27. See George H. Nadel and Perry Curtis, eds. *Imperialism and Colonialism* (New York: Macmillan, 1964), 3.

28. O. Mannoni suggests in *Prospero and Caliban: The Psychology of Colonization*, 2d ed., trans. Pamela Powesland (1950; New York: Praeger, 1964), 24, that "European civilization and its best representatives are not, for instance, responsible for colonial racialism; that is the work of petty officials, small traders, and colonials who have toiled much without great success."

29. Ashis Nandy argues in *The Intimate Enemy: Loss and Recovery of Self under Colonialism* (New Delhi: Oxford University Press, 1983) that colonization emphasized dehumanization of people; institutionalized violence and social Darwinism both in India and in England; created a false sense of homogeneity in Britain which froze any quest for social change; reinforced Britain's view of itself as benevolent Christian entity; and, finally, reinforced the misguided belief in its omnipotence.

30. "Imperialism after all is a cooperative venture. Both the master and the slave participate in it" (Said, "Yeats," 74).

31. As Spivak asks (Chapter 4 in this volume), why doesn't the question arise of how middle- and upper-middle-class women deal with servants in Calcutta? "What are the construction, constitution, political feelings, history, relationship to the female servants in our households?"

32. The failure of Indian and Pakistani critics to theorize the embarrassing events of the partition, for instance—pointed out by Gyanendra Pandey, "In Defense of the Fragment: Writing about Hindu-Muslim Riots in India Today," *Representations* 37 (Winter 1992): 27–55—might be cited as a symptom of such blindness.

33. As Spivak puts it, neocolonialism is "more economic and less territorial, . . . in fact neocolonialism is like radiation—you feel it less like you don't feel it—you feel like you're independent" ("Neocolonialism," 221).

34. M. E. Chamberlain suggests in *Decolonization: The Fall of the European Empires* (Oxford: Basil Blackwell, 1985), 77, that whereas the colonizers needed to keep the colonies reasonably prosperous for economic and moral reasons, "multinational companies have no such automatic check upon their operations. In some areas, at least, it would seem that neo-colonialism has proved worse than colonialism." More recently, Masao Miyoshi has argued that "colonialism is even more active now in the form of transnational corporatism" ("A Borderless World? From Colonialism to Transnationalism and the Decline of the Nation-State," *Critical Inquiry* 19.4 (Summer 1993): 728.

35. McClintock, "Angel of Progress," 85.

36. Homi Bhabha, "DissemiNation: Time, Narrative, and the Margins of the Modern Nation," in *Nation and Narration*, ed. Homi Bhabha (London: Routledge, 1990), 291–322.

37. See, e.g., Rob Nixon, *London Calling: V. S. Naipaul, Postcolonial Mandarin* (New York: Oxford University Press, 1992).

38. Peter Fuhrman and Michael Shuman, "Now We Are Our Own Masters," *Forbes*, March 23, 1994, 128–38.

39. Fanon, *Wretched of the Earth*, 75.

40. See Mies and Shiva's *Ecofeminism* for a serious discussion on the ethical and ecological impact of MNC-dominated economics.

41. Though I have not called much attention to the uncritical usage of such terms as "white" and "the West," I would point out that these constructions assume a manufactured, undifferentiated oppressor. My reference here, however, is to the Western academy, which comprises both white and nonwhite and indeed Third World intellectuals as well.

42. See, e.g., the catalogue of peasant, tribal, and other resistance movements in Claude Alvares, *Science, Development, and Violence: The Revolt against Modernity* (Delhi: Oxford University Press, 1992), or the discussion of powerful grassroots ecofeminism in Vandana Shiva, *Staying Alive: Women, Ecology, and Survival in India* (New Delhi: Kali for Women, 1988).

43. See Spivak's comments in her interview (Chapter 4, this volume).

44. Gauri Viswanathan's interview (Chapter 3, this volume).

45. Vincent B. Leitch, *Cultural Criticism, Literary Theory, Poststructuralism* (New York: Columbia University Press, 1992), ix.

46. Australia, New Zealand, and sometimes South Africa also occupy positions of varying degrees of importance as part of the Western intellectual center.

47. Salman Rushdie, "Commonwealth Literature Does Not Exist," in Rushdie *Imaginary Homelands: Essays and Criticism, 1981–1991* (New York: Penguin, 1991), 70.

48. Fredric Jameson, "Third World Literature in the Era of Multinational Capitalism," *Social Text* 15 (1986): 65–88.

49. Consider, e.g., Sara Suleri's observation that "the story of colonial encounter is in itself a radically decentering narrative that is impelled to realign with violence any static binarism between colonizer and colonized" (*The Rhetoric of English India* [Chicago: Chicago University Press, 1992], 1–2).

50. Aijaz Ahmad, *In Theory: Classes, Nations, Literatures* (London: Verso, 1992), 285. See also R. Radhakrishnan's response to Jameson's formulations: "Poststructuralist Politics: Toward a Theory of Coalition," in *Postmodernism/Jameson/Critique,* ed. Douglas Kellner (Washington, D.C.: Maisonneuve, 1989), 268–300.

51. Diana Brydon, "Commonwealth or Common Poverty? The New Literatures in English and the New Discourse of Marginality," *Kunapipi* 11.1 (1989): 1, 6; Trinh T. Minh-ha, *Woman, Native, Other* (Bloomington: Indiana University Press, 1989), 97; Shohat, "Notes on the Post-Colonial," 111.

52. Bill Ashcroft, Gareth Griffiths, and Helen Tiffin, eds., *The Empire Writes Back: Theory and Practice in Post-Colonial Literatures* (London: Routledge, 1989), 2, 24, 23. As Helen Tiffin notes in "Commonwealth Literature: Comparison and Judgement," in *The History and Historiography of Commonwealth Literature,* ed. Dieter Riemenschneider (Tübingen: Gunter Narr Verlag, 1983), 23, the term "connotes an English proprietorship over land and would make all post-colonial Commonwealth nations a little uncomfortable."

53. Mishra and Hodge, "What Is Post(-)Colonialism?" 399.

54. See Ahmad, *In Theory,* for an extensive discussion of the conditions in which Third World literature as a field has been shaped and the role of Black Studies in its inception and development.

55. See Gayatri Chakravorty Spivak, *The Postcolonial Critic: Interviews, Strategies, Dialogues,* ed. Sarah Harasym (New York: Routledge, 1990), 60.

56. Ashcroft, Griffiths, and Tiffin, *Empire Writes Back,* 162.

57. Ahmad, *In Theory,* 58.

58. Sara Suleri, *Meatless Days* (Chicago: University of Chicago Press, 1989), 20; Chandra Talpade Mohanty, "Under Western Eyes," in *Third World Women and the Politics of Feminism,* ed. Chandra Talpade Mohanty, Ann Russo, and Lourdes Torres (Bloomington: Indiana University Press, 1991), 333.

59. Robert Young, *White Mythologies: Writing History and the West* (London: Routledge, 1990), 11.

60. Dirlik, "Postcolonial Aura," 336.

61. Linda Hutcheon, *A Poetics of Postmodernism: History, Theory, Fiction* (New York: Routledge, 1988).

62. Stephen Slemon, "Modernism's Last Post," *Ariel: A Review of International English Literature* 20.4 (1989): 6, 9.

63. See also Simon During, "Postmodernism or Postcolonialism?" *Landfall* 39.3 (1985): 366–80; and Radhakrishnan, "Poststructuralist Politics."

64. Kumkum Sangari, "The Politics of the Possible," in *The Nature and Context of Minority Discourse*, ed. Abdul R. JanMohamed and David Lloyd (New York: Oxford University Press, 1990), 243.

65. Spivak, *Outside*, 121.

66. The last is pointed out and critiqued by Spivak: "The work that is being done on Indian linguistic theory, Indian ethical theory, that stuff is not given any acknowledgement because that is being done in the bosom of Sanskrit departments" ("Neocolonialism," 237).

67. Of course, it can be quickly, and accurately, noted that this essay is prone to many of the limitations it seeks to identify.

68. Shohat, "Notes on the Post-Colonial."

69. Spivak, *Outside*, 55.

70. Viswanathan, Chapter 3 (this volume).

71. In "Postmarked Calcutta, India," an interview with Angela Ingram (*The Post-Colonial Critic*, 86), Spivak refers to herself, with some irony, as a "Brahmin, upper-class, senior academic in the United States, [a] highly commodified distinguished professor."

72. Graham Huggan, "The Postcolonial Exotic: Salman Rushdie and the Booker of Bookers," *Transition: An International Review* 64 (1994): 24.

73. Dirlik, "Postcolonial Aura," 329, 344.

74. Julia V. Emberley, *Thresholds of Difference: Feminist Critique, Native Women's Writings, Postcolonial Theory* (Toronto: University of Toronto Press, 1993), 5.

75. I am indebted to Spivak for pointing out this connection in an interview in November 1994 and for thus stimulating the ensuing reflections. Dirlik's "Postcolonial Aura," which I encountered later, has also seemed an attempt to respond to the question, "Why is now the postcolonial moment?" which Mary Vasudeva and I had asked several of those we interviewed for this collection, and one that Spivak in turn had asked us.

76. See, e.g., Mary Connelly's "Ford Wants Work Force to Represent All Its Publics," *Automotive News*, 13 March 1995; or refer to National Public Radio's *Morning Edition* program no. 1548, 22 February 1995, "Shifting Demographics Make Diversity Training Boom."

77. Spivak's interview (Chapter 4, this volume).

78. See ibid.

79. Dirlik, "Postcolonial Aura," 356.

80. I am grateful to Mary Vasudeva for sharing her insights on the problems of teaching multicultural literature. To paraphrase her views: Often, it is believed that multicultural literature must be taught by "multicultural" people. This is not necessarily a bad thing, but it smacks of tokenism and suggests that only minorities can explain or teach minority literature—yet if this is the case, how can we expect nonminority students to learn it? Perhaps it is even more damaging, however, that minorities who have no interest whatsoever in teaching multicultural literature are "supposed" to do so anyway; after all, that is their experience. The obvious problem with this arrangment is that teachers who have prepared to teach Shakespeare or Joyce are "invited" to teach a subject they have not done any work in; the more insidious problem is that we begin to see minorities as people who know only about

minority issues, as persons expert in multicultural affairs but inadequate in any other area. Moreover, white students expect a minority teacher to unveil the true meaning behind the text, to tell them the answer because they are incapable of figuring it out: "I don't understand what the author is talking about," they complain. "I'm not black/Hispanic/Chinese/African/Indian!" By the same token, students often wonder with what authority a nonminority teacher is interpreting a postcolonial or multicultural text.

81. Literary criticism in the field is also likely to select its materials with the market in mind. As Huggan ("Postcolonial Exotic," 29) points out, "For every aspiring writer at the 'periphery,' there is a publisher at the 'centre,' eager to seize upon their work as a source of marketable 'otherness.'"

82. See Viswanathan's and Spivak's interviews (Chapters 3 and 4).

83. Slavoj Zizek, *The Sublime Object of Ideology* (London: Verso, 1989), 21.

84. Colás, "Of Creole Symptoms," 392.

PART III

STUDIES IN THE MEDIA AND POPULAR CULTURE

CHAPTER 9

An Explosion of Difference

The Margins of Perception in *Sammy and Rosie Get Laid*

Ranita Chatterjee

Framed with sound bites from Margaret Thatcher, Stephen Frears and Hanif Kureishi's second collaborative film, *Sammy and Rosie Get Laid* (1987, U.K.), firmly situates itself not only in the British but specifically in the London scene of race, class, and sexual politics. While focusing on the infidelities and complexities of the lives of Sammy, an accountant of South Asian descent, and his wife, Rosie, a white social worker, Frears and Kureishi also attempt to portray a landscape of exuberant intermingling between people from different ethnicities, sexualities and classes. Thus, we see Sammy's affair with Anna (a white American photojournalist) and Rosie's fetishized attraction for Danny (a black squatter) interspersed with the narrative of Sammy's father, Rafi (a former Pakistani dictator), negotiating a reconciliation with both his son Sammy, whom he abandoned, and his former beloved, Alice, whom he left behind. All these relationships are further framed by the ghostly apparition of one of Rafi's numerous tortured victims, who becomes visible at crucial junctures in the film, and by the insightful commentary of Rosie's friends Rani and Vivia, an interracial lesbian couple. Moreover, Danny appears in every significant moment in the film: He is both the first character we see and the one we are least likely to see in certain scenes. A summary of the film, then, is virtually impossible. To attempt one would collapse the several levels on which the film operates, especially since it centers on so-called "others," or those individuals generally marginalized in mainstream productions, such as women, people of color, and lesbians. Precisely because *Sammy and Rosie Get Laid* dramatizes the politics of the interracial relationships among these groups, I argue that the film implicitly explodes the notion of representation with regard to the traditionally hegemonic notion of the "other."

There has been little critical scholarship on films about Canadians, Americans, and Britishers of South Asian descent, but the films themselves (especially this one) have generated debate among reviewers and audiences alike, particularly within various South Asian communities. I am thinking of the recent crop of critically acclaimed North American and British feature films depicting the experiences of South Asians in the diaspora:[1] Stephen Frears's *My Beautiful Laundrette* (1985, U.K.), as well as *Sammy and Rosie Get Laid*; Barry Alexander Brown's *Lonely in America* (1990, U.S.A.); Mira Nair's *Mississippi Masala* (1991, U.S.A.); Srinivas Krishna's *Masala* (1991, Canada); Deepa Mehta's *Sam and Me* (1991, Canada); Gurinder Chadha's *Bhaji on the Beach* (1993, U.K.); and Harvey Crossland's *The Burning Season* (1993, Canada).[2] These English-language films from both sides of the Atlantic attempt to capture the complexities of a racial, and often sexual, experience that is marginal to what Pratibha Parmar, a British filmmaker of South Asian descent, defines as the "mainstream, the malestream, and the whitestream" of North American and British society.[3] Since these works create a narrative space that depicts and engages experiences other than those of the predominantly white, heterosexual mainstream audience, the reviews always "read" the films as narratives of race, specifically as narratives about South Asians. Reviewers who see such a film as a story about the racial community tend to react to the film's social critique with a racial anxiety that overlooks the dynamics of the sexual narrative. I am suggesting that we both read these films as racial narratives—in our attempts to bring the diasporic South Asian back into view in the dominant cultural marketplace—and look beyond race and ethnicity so as not to transform the racial marker into a tool of imprisonment for the minority culture. The marginalized content of these films is also mirrored in the lack of criticism analyzing them individually or as a group in current film scholarship. Given the voracious but productive response to these postcolonial films from the larger arena of activists, reviewers, and audiences both in and out of diverse South Asian communities, I want to reconsider the complex representation of postcolonial South Asian identity and its relationship to other minorities (whether racial, sexual, or class) in *Sammy and Rosie Get Laid*, created by the British-born Pakistani playwright Hanif Kureishi.

One of the first films to paint a manifold portrait of South Asian experiences in the diaspora, *Sammy and Rosie Get Laid* both encourages and resists a reading that seeks to understand a particular set of marginals, such as those that constitute the "essential" South Asian identity or the postcolonial one. On the one hand, the film's complex mapping and displacement of the sexual economy—specifically the heterosexual family romance plot—by the racial economy, located most powerfully in the central black character, Danny, complicates any attempt to situate this film solely within the arena of postcolonial representation. On the other hand, a closer look at how its predominantly heterosexual bias is criticized by the marginal interracial lesbian characters of Rani and Vivia suggests that a reading focused on the sexual dynamics will not be satisfactory either. It is this complexity of representation, I argue, that is ultimately achieved in the film, which resists easy readings of otherness and difference because of those characters in the film who occupy the margins of perception: Danny, Rani, and Vivia.

Edward Said's general remark about the "rather agitated and somewhat turbulent field" surrounding postcolonial representation aptly pertains to *Sammy and Rosie Get Laid*: It is as difficult to discuss this film without talking about a crisis in representation as it is to find a character in the film who is not having a crisis.[4] Although a box office success in North America and Britain, it has received surprisingly little critical attention since its release in 1987.[5] Rather, it has been relegated to the annals of films on diasporic South Asians. To date, there are only two critical articles on the film: bell hooks's "Stylish Nihilism: Race, Sex, and Class at the Movies" (from her 1990 book *Yearnings: Race, Gender, and Cultural Politics*); and Gayatri Chakravorty Spivak's "In Praise of *Sammy and Rosie Get Laid*," which appeared in *Critical Quarterly* in 1989. In response to this lack of both critical discussion and representation in film of South Asian and postcolonial subjectivity, Pratibha Parmar has noted:

> As diasporic Asians, we hunger for images which in some ways reflect our dreams and our desires and our realities. Media representations are a critical component of our identities, particularly for those of us who are perceived to be on the margins of the mainstream, the malestream, and the whitestream. Our need for reflections of ourselves, both on the big screen and on the small screen, are important in shaping our sense of self. For lesbians and gay men the ability to make oneself heard or seen, and the ability to alter what others hear and see, is also very necessary.[6]

Parmar's remarks demonstrate not only her recognition of the need for media images of diasporic South Asian identities but also her awareness of the differences within such images of ourselves, differences beyond the racial—in her case, sexual—that demand to be taken into account in both portraying and discussing these postcolonial "others." It may be self-affirming for minorities (sexual or racial) to find images of themselves in films, but the dominant culture appears to prefer a static portrayal of minorities. The box office success of *Sammy and Rosie Get Laid* both in Britain and in North America testifies to the mainstream audience's curiosity but also demand to see the other represented in film. Though the mainstream movie-goer may require its other, as I discuss below, this dominant cultural desire simultaneously prevents the marginalized other from entering the mainstream of critical work. In short, an invisible wall is left standing between the center and its margins.

Although *Sammy and Rosie Get Laid* predominantly focuses on the lives of fair-skinned brown men and their white women lovers, other interracial relationships, both straight and lesbian, appear at various crucial junctures in the filmic narrative. Before we consider these moments of marginal representation, it is important to acknowledge the theoretical complexities of *viewing the other*: that is, anyone outside the white/heterosexual/middle-class/masculine norm. Productive critical work has unraveled the complexities of representing the other both in film and in literature, but much of this discourse has been marked by a desire to crystallize the other. Indeed, from a metaphysical and also pragmatic perspective, alterity, or radical otherness, is necessary for self-definition. If one agrees with a poststructuralist notion that language in its broadest sense is not only referential, as Saussure indicates, but also self-referring, as Derrida argues, one can begin to see the exigency of creating an *other*. Gayatri Spivak has remarked that "a subject position is a hard place, and we cannot read it ourselves; we are given to others even as we make inevitable public attempts to read our subject position."[7] Alterity becomes the requisite for subjectivity, and the only medium through which our ontological status can be disclosed.[8]

Donna Haraway's statement on "situated knowledges" is useful in this context: "The knowing self is partial in all its guises, never finished, whole, simply there and original; it is always constructed and stitched together imperfectly, and *therefore* able to join with another, to see together without claiming to be another."[9] The self that is created is neither whole nor free from the other: each recreates itself in response to the other. And the other does not exist only because of the self. Edward Said reminds us that "to see Others not as ontologically given but as historically constituted would be to erode the exclusivist biases we so often ascribe to cultures, our own not least."[10] What is crucial here is the struggle to recognize the difference between the self and the other without either absorbing the other into the same—that is, not acknowledging the other as ontologically separate—or emphasizing the difference to the extent of disavowing the other's contribution to the self's identity. Put simply, to emphasize difference is to eliminate it by virtue of its difference; to recognize difference is to have already engaged with it. In film, this task involves the viewer and the object of her or his gaze (the other on the screen) in a coconstructive subject/object relationship that is continually changing, depending on the specific filmic representation. Once we acknowledge the necessary presence of the other within ourselves, however, we must also "see" the other in all its contradictions. Crystallizing the other for our own self-identificatory process denies the varied marginal sites of perception within our constructed monolithic "other."

Rey Chow in "'It's You, and Not Me': Domination and 'Othering' in Theorizing the 'Third World,'" has observed that "othering" means "making way for 'others' to come forth not as spectacles but in their contradictions."[11] For example, *Sammy and Rosie Get Laid* opens with a brutal shooting by London bobbies of a black woman in her kitchen, juxtaposed with a closeup of Anna's creamy white posterior tattooed with a "W." In a later scene, while the streets below are engulfed in a riot, Sammy is blissfully insulated in his apartment, his ears plugged with headphones blaring Shostakovich, his nose filled with coke, his mouth stuffed with a milkshake and a hamburger, his eyes on an open pornographic centerfold, and his pants down. In the background his father, Rafi, runs out of Rosie's study, now the guest room, in panic at the flames that are engulfing the streets as well as (in his delusion) the portrait of Virginia Woolf hung in his room. To all appearances, what we have here is mere spectacle: that is, a spectacle of Sammy's narcissistic attempts to satisfy his varied desires, against the backdrop of violence. As Chow suggests, however, in viewing these scenes as contradiction rather than as spectacle, we will be able to see the complexities of the other. Read as contradiction, the death of the unnamed black woman followed by the scenes of Sammy in bed with Anna and later alone in his apartment direct the viewer to consider the way in which Sammy's attempt to insulate himself from the surrounding chaos through his commodification of pleasure (we note that the hamburger he is eating bears the American Mcdonald's trademark) is his way of obliterating both the familial tensions in his relationships and the racial tensions in his surroundings. In other words, what we may view as spectacle can be read for its darker messages through contradiction. It is the very crisis of representation seen by the casual viewer as spectacle that it engulfs the marginalized other in such a way that to the dominant culture the problems of the minorities are "unreadable" except as entertainment value. Thus, the difference is between viewing the problems of the other as entertaining, and engaging with the other and thereby recognizing the contradictions. Trinh T. Minh-ha encapsulates the difficult task of doing what Chow asks in arguing that "it is, indeed, much easier to dismiss or eliminate on the pretext of difference (destroy the other in our minds, in our world) than to live fearlessly with and within difference(s)."[12]

Hanif Kureishi's portrayal of ethnic diversity and the interaction of races and sexes in *Sammy and Rosie Get Laid* cinematographically literalizes that call "to live fearlessly with and within difference(s)." Kureishi's sprawling canvas of diverse people, music (we hear Indy pop, Western classical, and American soul), languages, accents, classes, sexual orientations, ideologies, nationalities, and ethnicities not only deconstructs any form of classification but also resists the white as norm. The white heterosexual men who predominantly occupy center stage in North American and British mainstream cultural productions are noticeably absent in Kureishi's Britain. Furthermore, because of this absent white norm, none of the film's characters are easy to locate. Far from making the multiplicity of images a negativity and the white male a point of nostalgia for unity, the absence of the traditional white heterosexual male as implied center liberates the conceivable play of images on the screen, thus enabling a veritable explosion of difference. While the characters in *Sammy and Rosie Get Laid* may appear as caricatures in some moments (as in a scene with Rani, Vivia, and Rafi that I discuss later), they do not remain static with identifiable racial or sexual markers. In its maddening juxtapositions of scenes and incidents the film celebrates postmodern multiplicity and, in so doing, destabilizes the audience's need to identify a stable "other" on the screen (normally accomplished by enabling viewers to sympathize with and vilify different characters, often according to stereotypical expectations).

Prathiba Parmar in an interview with Kureishi concludes that the filmmaker not only refuses "the burden of being a speaker for his race and community" but also "mercifully . . . doesn't deal with the language of positive and negative stereotypes. . . . His characters refuse a singular categorization of themselves bound by a static sense of ethnicity."[13] Kureishi's refusal to locate the positive marginal experience has been a point of contestation in various South Asian communities. In "The Sound Barrier: Translating Ourselves in Language and Experience," Himani Bannerji discusses this self-conscious racial anxiety on the part of minority cultures—that is, the positive-image fetish—as a barrier to productive self-reflections: "The overwhelming preoccupation with what 'they say we are' and 'what we are not,' our 'otherization' by 'them' precludes much exploration or importance of who we actually are."[14] What Kureishi acknowledges by his indifference to this value-laden dichotomous form of representation is that the marginalized group's pressure to provide positive images is just as restrictive as the dominant group's desire to present negative or absent images. For a filmmaker to indulge either in positive images to rectify a racist practice of excluding marginalized groups or in negative images to reinforce current racist stereotypes is to deny the individual subjectivity of the marginalized character. Rather, what Kureishi does is play with the viewer's need to locate the diasporic South Asian experience by shifting the identities of his characters in different situations so that no one character is recognizably good or bad. For example, Rafi may appear as the old, neglected, traditional father striving for a reconciliation with his disrespectful "hip" son Sammy, whose sexual escapades with Anna he finds disturbing. Yet we also see Rafi as a lusty man eager to escape his past political crimes while renewing his previous acquaintance with Alice, a white British woman. Kureishi's refusal to provide positive representations of South Asians in Britain should be applauded, not condemned. Kureishi's own position of being an ethnic mix between a white British mother and a Pakistani father further reinforces the necessity of recognizing the limitations of labels, whether race- or value-laden, in the face of the lived reality of numerous diasporic South Asians of mixed ancestry and upbringing. Since positive portrayals often position the character as "a mouthpiece, a ventriloquist for an entire social category," which neglects the differences among those in the marginalized group, these portrayals insidiously or unwittingly reinstate the pernicious assumption that all marginalized people are the same.[15] In fact, if we briefly consider the heterosexual relationships that are foregrounded in the film, we see that in many ways, Rosie, Anna, and Alice along with their fair-skinned brown lovers Sammy and Rafi are far from being the marginalized other.

In a special issue of *Quarterly Review of Film and Video* titled "Discourse of the Other: Postcoloniality, Positionality, and Subjectivity," the editors Hamid Naficy and Teshome H. Gabriel state that "to examine the boundaries of difference is to acknowledge the relations of difference as the relations of power."[16] The heterosexual relationships of Sammy and Rosie, Sammy and Anna, Danny and Rosie, and Rafi and Alice (all between nonwhite men and white women), the lesbian relationship of Rani and Vivia (between a South Asian woman and a black Caribbean woman), and the friendship of Rafi and Danny (between a Pakistani man and a black British man) all graphically explore the negotiations of power over the representation of the other at the site of sexual and racial intersection. Though Alice may acknowledge the existence of a black British socioeconomic underclass, we do not see her actively doing anything about it. Though Anna, the American journalist, may take photographs of the riots, suggesting some concern with the racial tensions in Britain, what is emphasized in the film is her desire for Sammy—specifically, her desire to reconcile him with his father (in the middle of the riots she takes a picture of Rafi and Sammy). Rosie, too, mingles with lesbians, interracial couples, and blacks and is a concerned social worker who chooses to live in the lower socioeconomic area of London, yet for all her downward mobility she often participates in culturally imperialist attitudes. When Rosie accuses Rafi of various heinous crimes and afterward describes the tortures he allegedly inflicted on his victims, we get the sense that she is interested not so much in political activism as in exposing her father-in-law's evils to her husband, Sammy.

In another scene, Rosie comes to Rafi's defense when Rani and Vivia, the researchers of his crimes, confront the Pakistani politician. At this point the screen is dominated by a view of Rosie's white back, visually separating the two women of colour on either side in a perfect visual analogue of the imperialist divide-and-rule policy conducted on the pretext of maintaining the peace.

Sammy and Rafi are also more than racially marginalized men in Britain. Despite his brown skin, Sammy is a prospering accountant who has the luxury to be concerned with satisfying his own desires more than those of others more oppressed. Sammy's confession to his mistress, Anna, that "my prick keeps leading me into trouble. I'm like a little man being pulled around by a big dog," astutely captures his self-indulgent personality.[17] Rafi Rahman, who flees his native country because of his political crimes and throughout the film is pursued and terrorized by the ghost of one of his victims, also enjoys class power. Rosie discovers that Rafi has inflicted such torture and pain on various people in Pakistan that he is not any better than the British imperialists who colonized the country.

For bell hooks, all these straight characters are merely "politically aware, cool people . . . [who] hide in desire, in that narcissistic space of longing where difference—rather than becoming the new site for resistance and revolution, for ending domination—becomes the setting for high spectacle, the alternative playground."[18] Though Rosie, Anna, Alice, Sammy, and Rafi may ultimately represent the chic and politically correct, my objection to hooks's description is that her reading of the film absorbs contradiction into spectacle and imposes the expectation that the film should provide a political site of resistance for people of colour. This assumption that traditionally marginalized groups (and the difference they represent) cannot "hide in desire" but must be "the new site for resistance and revolution" is yet another stereotype. If the film portrays these characters as self-indulgent and ineffectual, I believe this is precisely the point Kureishi is trying to make: that sympathetic understanding cannot replace effective activism, no matter what the "difference" is (racial, sexual, class, or whatever). Being nonwhite or nonmale or nonheterosexual does not exempt one from replicating yet another hierarchy of privilege. Though some audiences might view the white women and postcolonial men in Kureishi's film as exotic objects invested with the responsibility of revolution or resistance, as hooks would prefer, we must recognize their freedom not to be burdened with this responsibility of representation. In other words, these so-called marginal characters should be entitled to the same contradictory impulses that motivate the viewer's subjectivity.

In contrast to hooks's political critique, Spivak's "In Praise of *Sammy and Rosie Get Laid*" celebrates this complexity of representation. Spivak comments that the film is enmeshed in "a whole chain of displacements in terms of which you are shown how a quick fix or a quick judgement or a quick read is productively resisted."[19] Although she does not elaborate on the mechanics of this resistance to a "quick read," I suggest that this difficulty in reading the film stems from the characters of Danny, Rani, and Vivia. The relationship of Rani and Vivia, through their sexually marginal positions as lesbians in an otherwise heterosexual narrative, functions to remind us of the centrality of the film's main couples, who may be regarded as disempowered "others" by virtue of their race but are privileged members of society because of their sexual preferences. Similarly, Danny's black body serves to expose the unspoken hierarchy of color, or chromatism, in a primarily nonwhite film that ostensibly allows all differences to emerge without restrictions. His overwhelming presence in so much of the film implies a type of criticism through race of the self-indulgent, perhaps privileged lives of the central, fairer-skinned characters. Thus, Kureishi presents not a spectacle of racial and sexual others merely to entertain the audience but rather an intricate web of differences which, like Trinh's call to "live fearlessly with and within difference(s)," requires from viewers an active engagement.

These three characters provide the much needed critique of bell hooks's "politically aware, cool people." Danny, the only major black character, and Rani and Vivia, the only interracial lesbian couple, are simultaneously marginal and central to the film's concern with heterosexual coupling between diasporic South Asian men and white women. In the sexual climax that marks the midpoint of *Sammy and Rosie Get Laid*, we see that Rani and Vivia are noticeably absent from Kureishi's triple-decker fucking scene in which the screen splits to show the three heterosexual couples who "get laid" that night: Sammy and Anna, Rosie and Danny, and Alice and Rafi. In this sequence an infusion of soft lights and an ironic cover of the Motown song "My Girl" heighten the already stylized portrayal of bodies on bodies, the lovers licking each other in frenzied orgiastic interplay, with the camera cutting rapidly from couple to couple. By excluding the only lesbian couple from the scene and choosing to portray only heterosexual sex, Kureishi appears to be marginalizing his own inclusion in the film of an interracial lesbian couple as another difference. Mark Finch, in "Business as Usual: Substitution and Sex in *Prick Up Your Ears* and Other Recent Gay-Themed Movies," argues that since "explicit straight sex may have become boring—that is, unmarketable—for Hollywood, . . . gayness is represented only to exhaust it, to see what it can be made to say about heterosexuality and gender."[20] One might argue that Kureishi does not portray Rani and Vivia in his copulating images because to do so would be to put the lesbian couple within a heterosexual frame: literally, in the camera angle; thematically, in the film's reigning concern with heterosexual relationships. Instead of using lesbian sex to comment on straight sex, I suggest, Kureishi demonstrates by exclusion his recognition of Rani and Vivia's sexual difference: He does not try to understand them through a heterosexual lens; rather, he recognizes his difference from lesbian experience.

Teresa de Lauretis states in "Sexual Indifference and Lesbian Representation" that the "conventions of seeing" (that is, what the characters see) are "partially anchored or contained by a frame of visibility that is still heterosexual . . . and just as persistently color blind."[21] Although Kureishi's film is far from being colorblind, *Sammy and Rosie Get Laid* is clearly a heterosexist film. What I am arguing, however, is that moments of sexual resistance are located at the site of Rani and Vivia. In acknowledging his distance from lesbianism, especially lesbian sex, Kureishi presents Rani and Vivia in bed together the following morning *through Rafi's eyes* as dirty "half-sexed lesbians cursed by God."[22] Also as seen by Rafi (the camera makes it clear that we are looking at Rani and Vivia through his eyes), the lovers seem to explode in reaction to Rafi's homophobia into murderous violence: The interracial lesbian women, especially Rani, *appear* as hysterical men-haters. It is the postcolonial characters Rafi and Rani, however, who are the hysterics, since the language of hysteria in this case is their native Urdu; the heated curses thrown back and forth between them require subtitles in English. This gesture highlights the linguistic commonality of the two brown characters, while marking the cultural boundary between Rani and her lover, Vivia, an Afro-Caribbean who presumably does not speak Urdu. Bonnie Zimmerman in "Lesbians Like This and That: Some Notes on Lesbian Criticism for the Nineties" reminds us that "while sexual difference may not exist between or among lesbians, all other forms of difference do, . . . race, class, origins, employment status, age, religion, physical abilities."[23] Difference both inside and outside the space of gender sameness is graphically emphasized in this hysterical scene in which neither Vivia nor the film's presumably monolingual English-speaking viewers understand the curses. The subtitles translate for the benefit of the English-language audience's comprehension, while pointing to Vivia's ethnic difference from Rani. In a film that is otherwise acted in English, the short, subtitled sequence marks this hysterical moment as a linguistically foreign one. We are led to assume that this moment is *incoherently ethnic* and needful of the relief of prompt English subtitles: single *straight lines of white* English print that provide tracks whereby the bewildered monolingual English viewer can cross this erupted fissure of multiplied difference (woman/lesbian/ethnic/hysteric). The moment represents, in the words of Trinh Minh-ha, "a difference that defies while not defying, . . . it is not even recognized as difference; it is simply no language to the dominant's ear."[24] My point, then, is that the linguistic difference marks the sexual difference of lesbianism as encompassing difference as well. This displacement of sexual difference by another difference challenges, in Audre Lorde's words, "the complacency of those . . . who view oppression only in terms of sex."[25] In other words, what begins as Rafi's desire to mark Rani and Vivia as different, if not deviant, because of their sexual difference gets displaced by Rafi's sameness with Rani and her difference from her lesbian lover, Vivia.

Although one might argue that the stereotyping of lesbianism is still prevalent throughout the film, I am concerned less with whether the portrayal of Rani and Vivia is lesbophobic (I don't think it is) than with how it functions within the film's predominant concern with straight couples. Parmar argues that this interracial couple ends up "merely providing sexual spice and titillation."[26] Yet Rani and Vivia present some of the film's most potent social criticism. We should recall that Rani is a political journalist who discovers the atrocities committed by Rafi as a highly placed politician in Pakistan. There is a scene in which we see Rani, Vivia, and a Chinese British woman searching for facts about Rafi's past— the atrocities he has committed in Pakistan. Significantly, these three women of color, far from being merely an exotic backdrop for the film, serve to criticize the ruling ideology of the heterosexual "cool" characters. In fact, it is Rani who criticizes Rosie's protection of Rafi as "liberalism gone mad," a phrase that haunts the viewers' psyche as we watch the self-indulgent practices of these main characters who, while they discuss the oppressive conditions surrounding them, are more concerned with their next sexual fix. Moreover, it is difficult to forget Rani's incisive description of heterosexual sex: "You know that stuff where the woman spends the whole time trying to come but can't, and the man spends the whole time trying to stop himself coming but can't."[27] This comment is made literally from the margins of the scene—the camera brings the marginal foreground into focus—as if to point out that the critique is coming from those who are excluded from the central heterosexual narrative.

As lesbians, Rani and Vivia also reflect in their sexuality the threat they pose politically as whistleblowers on Rafi's record of political repression. Rafi explicitly hates lesbians and attempts to confirm that Rosie, whatever she is, is not one of them. Whenever Rafi indulges in homophobic sentiments about lesbians, he is confronted with his guilty political past either by Rosie or in the form of the ghost of one of his political victims. Rafi's horror at seeing Rani and Vivia in bed together triggers both the appearance of the ghost and his racist repulsion toward Danny. In this sense, the prospect of seeing lesbian sex arouses Rafi not sexually but psychically in that the sexual explosion by the lesbian couple begins the process whereby his unconscious guilt about his political crimes is brought to the surface.[28] This process consumes Rafi, finally leading him to suicide.

Though not sexually marginalized, as are Rani and Vivia, Danny is racially marginalized in *Sammy and Rosie Get Laid*, a film devoted primarily to interracial white-brown relationships. As Rani and Vivia through their sexuality function to reveal the multifaceted components of racially marginal "others," the representation of Danny is also complicated by his active role in both the racial and sexual relationships. In the scene in which he makes love to Rosie, Rosie appears to be the one in control. She initiates the sexual encounter. She is the one who, fully dressed, delights in Danny's naked body, which, as it comes to fill the camera's gaze, reminds the viewer of Robert Mapplethorpe's sensuous black male bodies. Danny's role, however, is more than that of a sexual object for Rosie's pleasure. Like Rani and Vivia, his character is the vehicle for social criticism. When he asks Rafi about Gandhi's strategy of passive resistance, the screen is physically divided by a darkened pillar that stands between Rafi and Danny, between brown and black. Danny, the black man, makes numerous wrong assumptions about Rafi, the brown one. Spivak has noted that it is Danny to whom "the misreading of India is given"; she suggests that this is the case "because one can say that Martin Luther King misread Gandhi in that way too."[29] In his ignorance, Danny assumes that Rafi is Indian, not Pakistani, and attributes the nonviolence of Gandhi to what we as viewers know to be Rafi's violent military dictatorship. In other words, this scene brilliantly captures the way in which blacks in Britain fail to acknowledge or recognize either the difference of being brown or the many nationalities and ideologies of brown people. (It may also be Kureishi's response to the film industry's label of *black* for all nonwhite films.)[30] Further, the scene exposes Rafi's opportunistic mentality as an exiled imperialist willing to cash in on any positive traits in essentialist images of brownness, even if they are contrary to his own views and practices.

Danny is curiously present in most of the scenes of *Sammy and Rosie Get Laid*. As a crowd forms after the shooting of the black mother and her son in the opening scene, Danny mischievously cuts the police barrier and lets the crowd in. Later, he emerges from the riots to help Rafi, who has fallen in the midst of the chaos. When he accompanies Rafi to Alice's house, his presence as a black man in a white neighborhood is foregrounded by Rafi's question as to why the neighbours are staring at Danny. Danny responds that these people suspect he may steal their cars. Despite this conscious acknowledgment that Danny's skin color makes a difference in an upper-class white neighbourhood, in the next scene we see Danny strolling through Alice's back yard in an overtly feminine hat. The gardener does not even notice him, but Danny becomes the background that the viewer cannot ignore. In the surreal scene that follows, Alice notices him, and upon being told that he is Rafi's friend Victoria, she invites him to join them for tea. Yet surely a woman like Alice, living where she does, would be slightly surprised at a black man calling himself Victoria and wandering around her back yard wearing her sun hat. Furthermore, when Danny is invited by Rafi to Sammy and Rosie's apartment, Sammy barely notices Danny's presence (although we do see Sammy puzzled at finding his father so friendly with Danny). When Rosie arrives, she definitely notices Danny but only as a sexual object. All these incidents suggest that Danny is more than just another character in the film.

The portrayal of Danny as someone who slips in and out of the main action or the main frame of the scene gives him a choruslike quality. Danny's character is not fixed to any specific narrative plot line but is free-floating, much like the caravan he lives in; his character is both part of the film's narrative and outside of it, as Spivak has also noted: "In certain ways he's completely outside all of the historical argument, all of the problems, psychosexual, social, postcolonial."[31] Danny comments on the plot as it unfolds, though whereas most choral characters do this verbally, Danny's critique comes from his presence. Far from being just colorful background, Danny's very presence on the screen suggests that as viewers we must take notice of him. And since we are not given any other clue as to how to read Danny, for he rarely says much, we end up *seeing* Danny. In other words, all we see and all we must see when he appears is a black body. His identity, however, is much more than that of a black individual, for within the racial tensions that underlie the plot of *Sammy and Rosie Get Laid* is the politically loaded body of the black man. The presence of Danny's character at crucial junctures in the film serves to criticize the difficulties of interracial sexual relationships. He is in the apartment when Sammy and Rosie are arguing under the veil of discussing Rosie's project on the sociopolitical connotations of various forms of kissing; he is in the triple-decker fucking scene; he is with Rafi when Rafi reunites with Alice; he is at the party when Anna sees Sammy lose interest in her. In all these scenes Danny's body is the unnerving presence that critiques the self-indulgent central characters who are so immersed in their own family and sexual politics that they fail to acknowledge the crumbling social politics around them.

Kobena Mercer in "Engendered Species" argues for the overdetermination of black masculinity:

> Overrepresented in statistics on homicide and suicide, misrepresented in the media as the personification of drugs, disease, and crime, such invisible men, like their all-too-visible counterparts [black public figures such as Magic Johnson, Clarence Thomas, Rodney King, Mike Tyson, and, I might add, O. J. Simpson],

suggest that black masculinity is not merely a social identity in crisis. It is also a key site of ideological representation, a site upon which the nation's crisis comes to be dramatized, demonized, and dealt with.[32]

Danny's black body becomes the site not only of the racialized sexual tensions in *Sammy and Rosie Get Laid* but also of Britain's crisis: its racial tension, its inability to accept difference. As sometimes Victoria, sometimes Danny, his character comes to represent not so much an individual as difference itself, the racial difference that is part of British society—Queen Victoria's legacy. Kureishi's choice of the name Victoria for Danny in his friendship with Rafi is thus a comment on the new imperialism in contemporary Britain. This is a reverse imperialism practiced by the previously colonized (in this case Rafi with all his corrupt political power and money) on the new Britishers (in this case the black Britisher Danny). The irony is that Britain is powerful in symbol only, but the symbol of Britain's glory captured in the name Victoria—the reigning monarch during the height of British imperialistic activities in India—now inhabits a black body, a squatter also named Danny. Moreover, Danny's alternate identity as Victoria implies a crisis in the very fabric of society. Within the discourse of representation, this shifting identity marks a crisis in the symbolic order. Judith Butler reminds us that "the crisis in the symbolic, understood as a crisis over what constitutes the limits of intelligibility, will register as a crisis in the name and in the morphological stability that the name is said to confer."[33] Danny's shifting gender and his unacknowledged presence in various segments of the film are symptomatic of the general crisis of racial others in a crumbling Britain.

Sammy and Rosie Get Laid opens and closes with sequences depicting racial politics at the site of black bodies. The opening scene of the brutal death of a black mother and her son serves to contextualize the dominant narrative of Sammy and Rosie's domestic problems as trivial. The closing scene of the squatters driving their caravans off the deserted lot as the bulldozers roll by also serves to distance the viewer from the domestic problems of Sammy and Rosie. In this ironically epic scene, we see Danny atop a bus smiling at the camera while we hear the voice of Margaret Thatcher preaching racial harmony. Kureishi is ultimately criticizing Sammy and Rosie as liberal, heterosexual, bourgeois, downwardly mobile urbanites who think they can seamlessly or unproblematically occupy or inhabit the racial and sexual *other's* field of disintegrated social relations that they find so superficially fashionable.

Kureishi's attempt to "tell it like it is" without positive or negative images is in bell hooks's view a "politics of inclusion."[34] As if to demonstrate the inability to represent the other through the monolith of one medium, Kureishi released along with the movie the script and a constructed diary about the project itself, essentially providing multiple readings of the varied representations. In an interview with Marcia Pally in *Film Comment*, Kureishi makes it clear that he insists on breaking fixed categories of representation: "There's no such thing as a gay or black sensibility. I don't think being black or female so pervades a writer's mind that all experience is different from that of whites or men. Besides, the job of the writer is to invade his character's minds, and they can't all be exactly like him. In the end, categories become absurd. Each individual would end up in his own. What about celibate writers or tall writers or green-eyed ones?"[35] Simultaneously articulating a new sensibility while resisting the ghettoization of this position, Kureishi questions the political and ideological implications of the spectator's desire to fix a label on the object of the filmic gaze. The playing with labels in Frears and Kureishi's work notwithstanding, it is important for the critic to recognize a film such as *Sammy and Rosie Get Laid* as different from other films precisely because it focuses on diasporic South Asians in Britain. Too often the desire to praise a film for its universal qualities rather than for its insight into a specific experience disregards the significance of the film's representation of that marginal experience.

The *real* empowerment or liberation that Kureishi's film depicts is the ability of the marginalized other to be more than an object of interest, more than a representative *other*. Hence, audiences find themselves immersed in a particularly explosive site of racial and sexual interaction that contests a stable viewing of the marginal other: South Asians are portrayed as professionals both educated and corrupt, sexually liberated and conservative. Moreover, blacks and lesbians are represented as abjects both of the dominant culture and of the privileged minority culture, yet these characters are not portrayed as insignificant, powerless outsiders. On the contrary, Danny, Rani, and Vivia are given the crucial task of exposing the flaws and narrowmindedness of the main characters (Sammy, Rosie, Rafi, Alice, and Anna). Because Rani, Vivia, and Danny are both marginal and central to *Sammy and Rosie Get Laid*, labeling Kureishi's depiction of them as either lesbophobic or racist is reductive. In fact, Kureishi is using the margins to critique the center, instead of using the center to define the margins. Clearly, what he manages to accomplish with his proliferation of *other* representations is to portray the lives of the disenfranchised not to evoke sympathy but to shatter the false stereotypes. This means removing those groups traditionally associated with power—white, specifically heterosexual men—from their position in the arbitrarily constructed center of society. Ultimately, it is the singular perspective itself that explodes and allows for differences to emerge, turbulently and with much agitation, within a field of exuberant crisis. Thus, any reading of the film needs to confront both the spectacle of contradictions that it presents and the crisis in representation that this implies.

NOTES

Acknowledgments: I thank Carole Farber for encouraging me to consider both postcolonial theory and the films of Hanif Kureishi. I am also grateful to Tomo Hattori and Deepika Bahri for numerous discussions on this film. Preparation for this essay was assisted by funds from the Social Science and Humanities Research Council of Canada.

1. By "South Asians in the diaspora" I mean in particular those inhabitants of Canada, the United States, and the United Kingdom who originate from the Indian subcontinent: Pakistan, India, Sri Lanka, Myanmar (formerly Burma), Bangladesh, Nepal, and Bhutan.

2. *Bhaji on the Beach*, which has received rave reviews, is the first feature film to be directed by a woman of South Asian descent in Britain. Although a comedy about a group of diverse women on an outing to Blackpool, it addresses such serious issues as domestic violence, interracial relationships, unwanted pregnancy, arranged marriages, and racism and sexism within the South Asian community. *The Burning Season* is briefly mentioned in the Canadian popular movie magazine *Tribute* 10.6 (1993): 32. The film's lead actor and actress, Om Puri and Akesh Gill, are interviewed in a special film and video issue of the Canadian journal *Rungh: A South Asian Quarterly of Culture, Comment, and Criticism* 1.3 (1992): 23–29.

3. Many big-budget films about South Asians—such as *Gandhi, Octopussy, The Far Pavilions, A Passage to India, Jewel in the Crown,* and *Heat and Dust,*—all depict the colonial experience, not the diasporic one. In addition to the feature films I mention, numerous alternative and experimental films that also explode traditional representations of South Asians from the diaspora deserve critical attention; e.g., Pratibha Parmar's *Double the Trouble, Twice the Fun* (1992, U.K.) explores the realities of being disabled, homosexual, and of South Asian descent in contemporary Britain.

4. Edward W. Said, "Representing the Colonized: Anthropology's Interlocutors," *Critical Inquiry* 15.2 (1989): 205.

5. Several reviews that came out shortly after the film's release, though they have not created interest among cultural critics in North America and Britain, do offer provocative interpretations: Bert Cardullo, "Three Ways to Play House," *Hudson Review* 41.2 (1988): 348–56; Jill Forbes, "Underneath the Arches," *Sight and Sound* 57.1 (1987–88): 65–66; David Nicholson, "My Beautiful Britain," *Film and Filming,* January 1988, 9–10; Margaret Walters, "Laid in Britain," *Listener,* 21 January 1988, 30; and Judith Williamson, "Dirty Linen," *New Statesman and Society,* 29 January 1988, 26–27.

6. Pratibha Parmar, comment, "Womanvoice, Womanvision—South Asian Women and Film: Excerpts from Desh Pradesh Workshops," *Rungh: A South Asian Quarterly of Culture, Comment, and Criticism* 1.1–2 (1991): 18.

7. Gayatri Chakravorty Spivak, "A Response to 'The Difference Within: Feminism and Critical Theory,'" in *The Difference Within: Feminism and Critical Theory,* ed. Elizabeth Meese and Alice Parker (Amsterdam: John Benjamins, 1989), 210.

8. Both psychoanalytic and Hegelian philosophical articulations of self-identification provide powerful theoretical models for the concepts of self, subject, and other(s). Romantic thinkers such as Hegel and Schlegel and a post-Romantic tradition beginning with Freud and

Lacan stress that knowledge and therefore recognition of the self as self is attained only through an incorporation of an O/other. Though the *Other* has an ontological status prior to its incorporation, it loses its alterity or radical difference and becomes an *other* in the process of being recognized and desired by the self in question. In this way, the self *assumes* its subjectivity.

9. Donna Haraway, "Situated Knowledges: The Science Question in Feminism and the Privilege of Partial Perspective," *Feminist Studies* 14.3 (1988): 586.

10. Said, "Representing the Colonized," 225.

11. Rey Chow, " 'It's You, and Not Me': Domination and 'Othering' in Theorizing the 'Third World,' " in *Coming to Terms: Feminism, Theory, Politics,* ed. Elizabeth Weed (New York: Routledge, 1989), 161.

12. Trinh T. Minh-ha, *Woman, Native, Other: Writing Post-coloniality and Feminism* (Bloomington: Indiana University Press, 1989), 84.

13. Prathiba Parmar, "Sammy and Rosie," *Marxism Today,* February 1988, 39.

14. Himani Bannerji, "The Sound Barrier: Translating Ourselves in Language and Experience," in *Language in Her Eye: Views on Writing and Gender by Canadian Women Writing in English,* ed. Libby Scheier, Sarah Sheard, and Eleanor Wachtel (Toronto: Coach House Press, 1990), 40.

15. Isaac Julien and Kobena Mercer, "De Margin and De Centre," *Screen* 29.4 (1988): 5 (introduction to a special issue on race).

16. Hamid Naficy and Teshome H. Gabriel, "Consuming the Other," *Quarterly Review of Film and Video* 13.1–3 (1991): ii (introduction to special issue).

17. Hanif Kureishi, *Sammy and Rosie Get Laid: The Script and Diary* (London: Faber & Faber, 1988), 40.

18. bell hooks, *Yearnings: Race, Gender, and Cultural Politics* (Toronto: Between the Lines, 1990), 163.

19. Gayatri Chakravorty Spivak, "In Praise of *Sammy and Rosie Get Laid,*" *Critical Quarterly* 31.2 (1989): 87.

20. Mark Finch, "Business as Usual: Substitution and Sex in *Prick Up Your Ears* and Other Recent Gay-Themed Movies," in *Coming on Strong: Gay Politics and Culture,* ed. Simon Shepherd and Mick Wallis (London: Unwin Hyman, 1989), 77.

21. Teresa de Lauretis, "Sexual Indifference and Lesbian Representation," in *The Lesbian and Gay Studies Reader,* ed. Henry Abelove, Michele Aina Barale, and David M. Halperin (New York: Routledge, 1993), 153.

22. Kureishi, *Sammy and Rosie,* 46.

23. Bonnie Zimmerman, "Lesbians Like This and That: Some Notes on Lesbian Criticism for the Nineties," in *New Lesbian Criticism: Literary and Cultural Readings,* ed. Sally Munt (Hertfordshire, Eng.: Harvester Wheatsheaf, 1992), 12.

24. Trinh T. Minh-ha, "All-Owning Spectatorship," *Quarterly Review of Film and Video* 13.1–3 (1991): 199.

25. Audre Lorde, "Age, Race, Class, and Sex: Women Redefining Difference," in *Out There: Marginalization and the Contemporary Cultures,* ed. Russell Ferguson, Martha Gever, Trinh T. Minh-ha, and Cornell West (New York: New Museum of Contemporary Art; Cambridge, Mass.: MIT Press, 1990), 283.

26. Parmar, "Sammy and Rosie," 39.

27. *Sammy and Rosie Get Laid,* dir. Stephen Frears, with Shashi Kapoor, Frances Barber, Claire Bloom, and Ayub Khan Din; screenplay by Hanif Kureishi; Cinecom/Film Four, 1987.

28. I am grateful to Tomo Hattori for pointing out the significance of the ghost's appearance, and to Nancy Ring for helping me to refine this part of my argument.

29. Spivak, "In Praise," 86, 87.

30. In the British film industry the term "black" has been used to identify all films by and about non-white people. Julien and Mercer ("De Margin and De Centre," 3) indicate that *black* is a "political term of identification among diverse minority communities of Asian, African and Caribbean origin, rather than . . . a biological or 'racial' category." In "Locating the Asian Experience," *Screen* 29.4 (1988): 121, Perminder Dhillon-Kashyap criticizes the use of "black" to label films about Asians in Britain: "The narrow use of the term "black" in Britain to refer mainly to those of Afro-Caribbean origin, and the fact that much of the black independent film sector in Britain has engaged in debate with black writers and critics in the US, where black experience is very different, has meant that the Asian perspective in British film culture has tended to be excluded." Although there is an urgent need not to ghettoize works such as *Sammy and Rosie Get Laid* as films depicting "the Asian perspective," there is an equally strong need for a strategic essentialism. The tension is between asserting the uniqueness of the Asian experience and resisting the essentializing of this experience. In the words of Sunil Gupta, "There has to be a recognition that Indians are not the same as Blacks, although we share several factors in common, such as colonial history and an isolation from the mainstream in this country [England]. Culturally, however, we are standing on completely different ground. . . . The time has come to resist the pressure, from both whites and Blacks, to merge us together into one category of Black" ("Black, Brown, and White" in Shepherd and Wallis, *Coming on Strong*, 178). To read Kureishi's *Sammy and Rosie Get Laid* as a specifically brown film, then, is to locate its difference from both black and white films in Britain, even though the former term supposedly incorporates the diasporic Asian experience.

31. Spivak, "In Praise," 86.

32. Kobena Mercer, "Engendered Species," *Artforum* 30.10 (1992): 74.

33. Judith Butler, *Bodies That Matter: On the Discursive Limits of Sex* (New York: Routledge, 1993), 138.

34. hooks, *Yearnings*, 157.

35. Marcia Pally, "Kureishi like a Fox," *Film Comment* 22.5 (1986): 55.

CHAPTER 10

Emigrants Twice Displaced

Race, Color, and Identity in Mira Nair's *Mississippi Masala*

Binita Mehta

The relationship between nonwhite minority groups in the United States today is an issue that requires our immediate attention. To recognize the gravity of the situation, one has only to look at such disputes in Brooklyn as the 1990 black boycott of two Korean grocery stores, and the clashes between the Hasidic and African American communities in the Crown Heights neighborhood. The much publicized April 1992 riot in South Central Los Angeles following the Rodney King verdict was not simply a black versus white incident but one that involved members of African American, Korean American, and Latino communities. Peter Kwong explains the complex nature of the violence in "The First Multicultural Riots": "The fixation on black versus white is outdated and misleading—the Rodney King verdict was merely the match that lit the fuse of the first multiracial class riot in American history." Many Korean American stores located in Koreatown, north of South Central Los Angeles, were looted and burned down by Latino, mostly Central American, immigrants who lived in the area. The Korean American community was mobilized by the riots and "came to see themselves—for the first time—as victims of white racism" when neither the local nor state police came to their aid.[1]

With the influx of immigrants from Latin America, Asia, and the Caribbean to the United States, American society has become more complex. The black/white dichotomy no longer provides an analytical model for the problematics of race, color, and identity. Many historians and cultural critics recognize the need for new coalitions, especially among marginalized communities and peoples of color. Manning Marable speaks of a new stage of black freedom in the United States that no longer involves only blacks but includes all people of color: "We must find new room for our identity as people of color to include other oppressed national minorities—Chicanos, Puerto Ricans, Asian/ Pacific Americans, Native Americans, and other people of African descent."[2] Taking a broader perspective, philosopher and theologian Cornel West expresses the need for unity between different groups of people—regardless of race, class, gender, or sexuality—while maintaining individual identity. The new cultural politics of difference "affirms the perennial quest for the precious ideals of individuality and democracy by digging deep in the depths of human particularities and social specificities in order to construct new kinds of connections, affinities and communities across empire, nation, region, race, gender, age and sexual orientation."[3] Like Marable and West, Edward Said suggests that binary oppositions rooted in imperialism have disappeared and that "new alignments made across borders, types, nations, and essences" have challenged the notion of identity: "Just as human beings make their own history, they also make their cultures and ethnic identities."[4] Contemporary debates on race and color in the United States must necessarily include relations between nonwhite minorities.

In her 1991 film *Mississippi Masala*,[5] Mira Nair depicts the complex relations between two nonwhite minorities in the United States, the Indian and the African American, prompting a reflection on issues of race, color, and identity.[6] The Indian family depicted in *Mississippi Masala* has migrated via England from Uganda, East Africa, to Greenwood, Mississippi. Expelled from Uganda by General Idi Amin in 1972, they are twice displaced: Indians by culture and tradition, Ugandan by birth, they move to the United States to live in a motel owned by relatives, themselves immigrants from India. The narrative includes many vignettes about the family's social and cultural adjustments in a small southern town, but the main thrust of the film is the violent opposition of the parents, father Jay (Roshan Seth) and mother Kinnu (Sharmila Tagore), to the relationship of their daughter Mina (Sarita Choudhury) with Demetrius (Denzel Washington), an African American who owns a rug-cleaning business. Mina and Demetrius's relationship brings to the surface the prejudices of the extended Indian family toward African Americans, rendered particularly poignant by the fact that they are both minority communities in Greenwood, as well as by their peculiar status with respect to the white community.

Preceding a detailed analysis of the film, some background information about Ugandan Indians is in order.[7] Mercantile and commercial ties between the East African coast and India date back a thousand years, when Indian merchants lived in Zanzibar and traders from Karachi and Bombay did business regularly with Madagascar. Soon the Indians moved inland, and by 1900 they "controlled wholesale trade along a two-thousand-mile stretch of coastline."[8]

The British used Indians first as soldiers, then as labor to help build the Ugandan railway. The railway opened up remote areas of the country, paving the way for more Indian immigrants, who arrived in large numbers, opened shops, and soon controlled most of the retail trade in Uganda. Although the British encouraged the prosperity of the Indians, real power in Uganda remained in British hands. As the Indians prospered, however, the black African population was relegated to the bottom rung of society: "Indians created a second-class [stratum] for themselves, while the Africans were automatically relegated to the third, and lowest," according to G.S.K. Ibingira. As the business class in Uganda, Indians controlled most of the wealth, excluding Africans from the economic structure. Soon Indians were involved in every aspect of the country's economy, from laborers to the professional classes; they hired Africans as servants, making them work long hours and paying them low wages. Africans resented the Indians not only for their wealth but also because they "lived an isolated communal life, they never mixed with Africans, and their interracial dealing never went beyond business matters."[9] In addition, Indians were not concerned with social change, preoccupied as they were with making a living, educating their children, and planning suitable marriages for them. The relationship between Indians and Africans deteriorated further with the growth of African nationalism and worsened after Ugandan independence. These social and economic conflicts were among the reasons invoked by General Idi Amin when he decided to expel all Ugandan Asians during a ninety-day period in 1972.

The Indian community in Uganda comprised a mixed group of Hindus, Muslims, Christians, and Sikhs. Most came from the states of Gujarat, Kathiawad, and Kutch on the northwest coast of India, plus some from the Punjab. In their social structure the Hindus were divided into caste and subcastes (jati), and the Muslims into two principal sects, the Sunnis and the Shias (which were further divided into subsects). Although Indian immigrants wanted to prosper in Ugandan society and were willing to become Ugandan citizens, they were unwilling to give up caste and cultural differences. They were not able to transfer to Uganda the traditional hierarchy of the caste system as it existed in India, but "caste exclusiveness still remained."[10] For example, marriage within one's caste or subcaste was rigidly followed, and needless to say, marriage between black Africans and Indians was completely out of the question. (Members of the Muslim Ismaili sect, however, were encouraged by the Aga Khan, their religious leader, to become Ugandan citizens and to assimilate into Ugandan society.) Indians from Uganda and other African countries retained caste and kinship ties, maintaining customs such as endogamy, in the countries they migrated to after expulsion—England, Canada, and the United States.[11] In a study of East African Gujaratis in Britain, Maureen Michaelson observes: "Despite the double migration of Gujaratis from India to East Africa, and thence to Britain, Hindu Gujarati castes have retained remarkable resiliency and in many important aspects continue to operate according to traditional restraints."[12]

The historical and social context of the Ugandan Indian family is set up in the first frame of *Mississippi Masala* and continues by means of flashbacks throughout the film. Beginning and ending in Uganda, the film opens with an attempt to enunciate the rationale for Idi Amin's expulsion of Indians. The grim pre-credit sequence in Kampala, set in November 1972, shows Jay and his childhood friend Okelo (Konga Mbandu) in a car stopped at a roadblock where a policeman shines a flashlight in their faces. After a tense moment, the policeman allows them to leave. We later learn that Jay, a lawyer, had been jailed for denouncing Idi Amin as an evil man during a BBC interview, and that Okelo had bribed the police in order to obtain Jay's release. Reluctant to leave the land of their birth yet realizing that they have no choice, Jay, Kinnu, and Mina pack up whatever belongings they can carry, abandoning their home to their African servants. During the bus ride to the airport, Mina's mother Kinnu is forced out of the bus by Ugandan policemen who jeer at her and throw a photograph depicting her husband in lawyer's robes into the mud. In a final humiliating act, one policeman tears a gold chain from around her neck with a rifle. Mira Nair based this scene on one of the many reports of harassment and mistreatment by Ugandan officials related by Ugandan Indians who had left during the expulsion period.[13]

We meet Mina's family again in Greenwood, Mississippi, 1990. Moving from the lush landscape of the Kampala hills overlooking Lake Victoria, the camera scans the North American concrete jungle of motels, highways, supermarkets, and automobiles. From the drumbeats of Africa to the rhythm of Mississippi blues, the soundtrack reflects the change of scene.[14] The adult Mina fills her supermarket shopping cart with gallons of milk. The camera follows Mina outside and slowly pans from an Indian woman counting dollar bills to a black teenager loading groceries into the trunk. Suggested here are the class differences between a typical middle-class Indian immigrant who has attained material success in the United States and a black teenager who is relegated to menial labor. Mina's own nuclear family, however, does not fit neatly into the stereotype of the successful immigrant. In a major change from their comfortable upper-middle-class existence in Uganda, in the United States they are forced to live in a motel, the Monte Cristo, owned by relatives. Mina's father spends his time filing lawsuits against the new Ugandan regime for the restoration of his property and possessions. Her mother runs a liquor store, purchased with money borrowed from relatives and located in a black neighborhood, much to the horror of other Indian women in Greenwood. Mina works as a maid in the motel, cleaning bathrooms and helping out at the front desk.

The motif motif is significant in *Mississippi Masala*. Motels are quintessentially American: convenient, inexpensive, and linked to working-class life both as rest stops for traveling families and as sites of illicit sexual encounters. Driving through South Carolina and Mississippi during research for the film, Mira Nair found a number of Indian-owned motels. Many of the owners were sponsored and financed by relatives and, like Korean grocers, employed family members who needed only a limited knowledge of English to carry on their daily business.[15]

In this "no man's land" of "truck drivers or prostitutes or lovers having a tryst," says Nair, the Indians continue to preserve their way of life, their religion and food habits.[16] Moreover, because motel chains are standardized nationwide, many have no character, no style; by and large they look the same everywhere. It is precisely this lack of identity, this standardization, this neutrality, which acts as a symbolic backdrop of a paradoxical nature for the Indian family seeking to maintain its identity. The motel creates a natural community for immigrants like Jay and his family. Nuclear families have their own living quarters and share certain areas during social events such as weddings. Because the motel is self-contained, it is an ideal setting where the Indian family can practice social and religious customs without fear of interference from the outside world and maintain their exclusiveness, their separateness from other ethnic groups. History and tradition are preserved; family ties are strengthened. Yet at the same time the motel serves as a site of transition. For Jay, Kinnu, and Mina the chintzy environment of the Monte Cristo stands in stark contrast to their life of elegant comfort in Uganda.[17] The scenes of leave-taking from Uganda, as well as scenes of the extended family in the motel in Mississippi, symbolize the temporary and the transitional, emphasizing the binary structure of rootedness/rootlessness that operates throughout the film.

The "ghettoization" of immigrants suggested by the motel is not particular to Indian immigrants but typical of immigrant communities in general, for whom the ghetto becomes not only a space for maintaining their culture but also a space of empowerment in hostile surroundings. The motel in *Mississippi Masala* has allowed the Indians to maintain their cultural exclusiveness, but Mina's relationship with Demetrius forces them to leave that security and to confront not only questions of their own identity as Ugandan Indian immigrants in the United States but also their feelings towards other communities in Greenwood, especially the black community.

Despite the fact that Nair's treatment of representation, identity, and displacement is complex and nuanced and has the potential for suggesting productive coalitions between Indians, and African Americans, bell hooks and Anuradha Dingwaney are severe in their critique of the film, denouncing it as a stereotypical portrayal of blacks, Indians, and whites and lacking in political commitment.[18] Calling Nair's work "another shallow comment on interracial, inter-ethnic, transnational 'lust,'" hooks writes, "Nair's film compelled commentary because spectators in the United States have never had the opportunity to see a Hollywood narrative about Africa, India, and African-American cultures" (41). Dingwaney reports that fellow Indians found it "the only film that dared to represent working class Indian culture in the United States. They praised the film for conveying so much realism," but both hooks and Dingwaney question the portrayal of a "real" that is already a selection by the director: "Often stereotypes are used to embody the concept of the 'real,' or the everyday" (41). These critics admit that *Mississippi Masala* shows familiar images but assert that the familiar "need not embody the stereotypical," which only confirms "hegemonic Western notions of Indian traditionalism or the parochialism of both the black and white in the deep South" (41). They also claim that although black and Indian viewers were uncritical in their enjoyment of the film—because they felt that it did indeed explore Indo-black relationships— nevertheless, the film's exploration of that relationship was "shallow, dishonest, and ultimately mocking." (41).

Their critique, less valid in some cases than in others, nevertheless facilitates the introduction of critical questions for the film in particular and for interminority relations in the United States in general. The issue of filmic "truth" and "realism" in ethnic or racial representations is a highly contested one. It is obvious that Nair makes a choice in her depiction of the Indian family and offers her version of the "truth," based on interviews with Ugandan Indians who had settled in the United States and were mostly in the business of operating motels in South Carolina and Mississippi. To that extent it is real. Although representations can have a real effect on the world, Ella Shohat and Robert Stam observe that they can also lead "to an impasse in which diverse spectators or critics passionately defend their version of the 'real.'"[19] hooks and Dingwaney's complaint that the film "offers only stereotypical portraits of southern whites and blacks" (43) is, however, valid to a certain extent. It is true that the film has its share of black, brown, and white stereotypes. Demetrius's brother Dexter (Tico Wells) is depicted as a wastrel spending his time on the streets with his friends and listening to rap music. In keeping with images of the sexual prowess of black males, much is made of the unbridled sexuality of Demetrius's partner Tyrone (Charles S. Dutton). The white motel owners depicted in the film hate the Indians yet hate the blacks even more. Some Indians, such as motel owners Anil (Ranjit Chowdhry) and Kanti (Mohan Agashe), are portrayed as greedy vultures. Yet it must be acknowledged that the film has its share of nonstereotypical, multifaceted characters: Mina, Kinnu, and Jay among the Indians; Demetrius and his Aunt Rose (Yvette Hawkins), with her heightened sense of self, among the blacks.[20] hooks and Dingwaney do not allow sufficiently for the multiplicity and plurality of Indian immigrant experiences, or for the complexities and diversities of the African American experience presented in the film. In contrast, while Shohat and Stam understand the importance of "the study of stereotyping in popular culture," they are aware of its downfalls: "First, the exclusive preoccupation with images, whether positive or negative, can lead to a kind of *essentialism* . . . . This essentialism generates in its wake a certain *ahistoricism*; the analysis tends to be static, not allowing for mutations, metamorphoses, changes of valence, altered function."[21]

Nair is careful to present a family situated in a very particular historical context; the film portrays the experiences of one Indian family that emigrated from Uganda. The temptation to read this family as representative of all Indian immigrants in the United States may be understandable in light of the paucity of Indian images in the American media; it may be more useful, however, to attempt to understand the complexities in their lives and the important issues that surface with regard to race relations in representing that family.

When hooks and Dingwaney remark that "there is little interaction between the two cultures when the focus is the United States" (41), they point to a lack that is all too exemplary of the huge gap that exists between minorities in this country. Mina and Demetrius's attempt to bridge this gap emphasizes both the gap and the difficulties that attend their effort. Mina does have dinner with Demetrius's family for the birthday of his father, Williben (Joe Seneca), however, and Demetrius meets Mina's father on one occasion. Whereas Mina is very warmly received by Demetrius's family, and they, especially his brother Dexter, are intrigued by her African-Indian roots, Demetrius's meeting with Jay is confrontational. This encounter must be understood in light of Jay's experiences in Uganda as well as his observations about race relations in the United States; no less important to the confrontation are Demetrius's own experiences with racism among minorities and the long history of African American struggles for recognition and acceptance.

Jay's reaction to Demetrius, complicated by his love/hate feelings for Uganda, brings multiple and conflicting histories to the fore. In a conversation early in the film, Jay agonizes over being forced to leave the country of his birth: "I've always been Ugandan first and Indian second," he exclaims to Okelo. "I've been called a bootlicker and traitor by my fellow Indians." He asks, "Why should I go, Okelo? Uganda is my home." Okelo sadly replies, "Not any more, Jay. Africa is for Africans—black Africans." hooks and Dingwaney claim that Jay "never reflects on the power relations between Indians and blacks in Uganda, that the film so skillfully erases and denies" (43). On the contrary, Jay is fully aware of the exploitive relationship that existed between Indians and blacks in Uganda, and this understanding is depicted in one of flashbacks: On their last night in Uganda, Jay is in a bar drinking with some Indian friends and reminiscing about their lives. When one of them raises the toast "Uganda, you have been so good to us until this madman [Idi Amin] came," Jay responds that it was the Indians who had created the "madman." Noting the failure of the Indian community to make itself a meaningful part of Uganda, he says, "Most people are born with five senses. We are left with only one, sense of property." Unlike the prejudices of other members of his extended family, there is a good amount of self-reflection on Jay's part as to the unequal relationship between Indians and Africans in Uganda. Jay's character in the film is much more nuanced than it appears at first glance. Although he can easily be dismissed as prejudiced against blacks because of his rejection of Demetrius, he had, unlike other Indians in Uganda, established professional and social ties with blacks there, as his close ties with his childhood friend Okelo reveal.[22] There develops a definite strain in the relationship when he is forced to leave Uganda, perhaps because he unconsciously blames Okelo for Idi Amin's decision. Yet though his feelings toward blacks are definitely embittered after his expulsion and the loss of the social and economic status he had enjoyed, Jay still has mixed feelings about Ugandan blacks. When a fellow Indian in the United States comments that Jay was "a champion defender of blacks" in Uganda and that the "same blacks kicked him out," Jay insightfully remarks, "Cruelty has no color." Nevertheless, despite his liberal ideas (he also tells Demetrius that Mina is free to love whomever she wants to), he warns Mina that ultimately, "people stick to their own kind. You are forced to accept that when you grow older. I'm only trying to spare you the pain." It is precisely because the power relations between the races cannot be denied that Jay is sensitive both to exploitive relations between Indians and blacks in Uganda and to the struggle in store for those who abandon "their own kind."

Influenced by his own experience in Uganda ("After thirty-four years that's what it came down to, the color of my skin"), Jay expresses his misgivings about Demetrius's relationship with Mina, saying that he does not want his daughter to struggle as he did. Demetrius, in turn, is obliged to invoke the history of black men in the South. On hearing the word "struggle," he explodes: "Struggle, struggle, look, I'm a black man, born and raised in Mississippi, not a damn thing you can tell me about struggle." He continues, "You and your folks can come down here from God knows where and be about as black as the ace of spades, and as soon as you get here you start acting white and treating us like we're your doormats. I know that you and your daughter ain't but a few shades from this right here [points to his skin], that I know."

Demetrius's scathing critique reflects the Indian community's tendency to affiliate with the dominant rather than minority cultures in the United States.

Discussing Indian attitudes toward race and racism, Mira Nair says that when asked if he had experienced racism, an Indian motel owner is reported to have said, "'I'm just a white person who stayed in the sun too long,'" thus identifying with the whites and implying that he considered himself light enough to be accepted by white society.[23] Attitudes toward skin color in the film likewise show that the Indians identify with the whites rather than the blacks; the preference for light skin color is frequently stressed. Mina makes light of her dark skin in talking with her mother, who wants her to go out with the lighter-skinned Harry Patel, an eligible young Indian. Color also becomes the subject of gossip between two Indian women, who discuss the probable effect of Mina's skin color on her marriage prospects with Harry Patel. One of them sardonically remarks, "You can be dark and have money, or fair and have no money. But you can't be dark, have no money, and expect to get Harry Patel." The concern with gradations of skin color is something Indian culture shares with African American culture, but it serves to drive them apart rather than bring them closer.[24] Near the film's conclusion, as Mina and Demetrius try to reestablish their relationship after the scandal (which ensues when they are found in a motel room together), he asks Mina why she had not warned him that her family had "trouble with black folks." "You didn't ask," responds Mina, implying that her family was perhaps transferring its social segregation from blacks in Uganda to their American situation. But Shohat and Stam suggest that just as Spike Lee's *Do the Right Thing* (1989), which deals with the tensions and affinities between Italian American and African American communities, "calls attention to how some members of recent immigrant communities have used Blacks as a kind of 'welcome mat,' as a way of affirming, through anti-Black hostility, their own insecure sense of American identity," so also racist behavior toward blacks may have been learned by the Indian family in *Mississippi Masala* after arrival in the United States, or reinforced if already present.[25]

The Indians' relationship with the whites in Greenwood is also conflicted. They may wish to maintain physical and social distance from the blacks and to identify with the whites, but white attitudes toward Indians are founded on racism and ignorance. Neighboring working-class white motel owners confuse the Indian family with American Indians. When one of remarks, "Send them back to the reservations where they belong," the other responds, "How many times have I told you they are not that kind of Indian!" The very same white motel owners—who resent the Indians encroaching on their territory and complain to the police about the family making too much noise during wedding festivities—express a sense of solidarity with the Indians after learning of the Mina-Demetrius scandal; they call up Anil's father Jammubhai (Anjan Srivastava) and ask in a conspiratorial chuckle, "Are ya'll having nigger problems?" The whites in this incident are blatantly racist, and the "conspiracy" involves their assuming that the "brown" Indians share their virulent racist feelings against blacks. Another scene reinforces the stereotype of Indians as cow worshippers. As Mina is buying gallons of milk and buttermilk for Anil's wedding, the supermarket clerk jokes, "Holy cow! Are you opening a dairy?" Seeing that Mina is not amused, he apologizes for his flippant remark. White racist attitudes toward the black family are more overt, especially when the white bank manager threatens to repossess Demetrius's van. The discrimination suffered, albeit to varying degrees, by both Indians and blacks fails to create alliances between them and paradoxically widens the gulf that separates them.

That the community at large is unable to imagine the possibility of alliance with the African American community is underscored in a mock-coalitional scene—long before the confrontation between Demetrius and Jay—when members of the extended family fake a move to ally themselves with the blacks for selfish reasons. Mina first meets Demetrius when she accidentally runs into his van while driving a car that belongs to Anil, the relative who owns the motel her family lives in. Afraid of a lawsuit, Anil seeks the help of fellow motel owner Kanti, whose motel carpets are also cleaned by Demetrius and his partner Tyrone. In an attempt to find out if Demetrius is going to sue Anil, Kanti expresses solidarity with African Americans as members of nonwhite minorities: "Black, brown, yellow, Mexican, Puerto Rican, all the same. As long as you are not white, means you are colored." He concludes with "United we stand, divided we fall." Kanti's pat rhetoric is transparent in its slickness; we are not surprised to learn later that he was merely paying lip service to ethnic solidarity, using his color and minority status only to curry favor with Demetrius.

In fact, the gulf between the groups is only reinforced by Kanti's mouthing of a "line" that rings well but means nothing. Showing the Indians feigning friendship with the blacks, hooks and Dingwaney argue, only downplays "the significance of political bonding between people of color" and does not promote the coalition building among minorities "that subverts the status quo" (42).[26] On the one hand, they point out that the film does not emphasize enough that Indians in Uganda mediated between the oppressed blacks and the oppressing imperialist class; on the other hand, they criticize Nair's representation of Indians as conniving hustlers. But not all the Indians in the film are portrayed as conniving hustlers, any more than all the blacks or whites are. By placing minorities on the high ground, the critics can be faulted for reverse stereotyping. Should the Indians be judged by different standards because of their minority status? This critique in fact diverts attention from the possibility that Kanti's failure to internalize the values he so glibly musters might be read as a powerful comment on the larger failure of minorities to find common cause with one another. Later, when Mina and Demetrius are discovered in a Biloxi motel room by Anil and his friends, both African American and Indian communities defend their mutual isolation. Tyrone, when he bails Demetrius out of jail after that fiasco, observes bitterly, "Leave them fuckin' foreigners alone. They ain't nothing but trouble." He repeats with irony, "United we stand, divided we fall. Ain't that a bitch! Yeah, but fall in bed with one of their daughters, your ass gonna swing," referring both to the cultural value of female chastity in the Indian community and the false promise of unity that is destined to be belied.

If Jay is haunted by the ghosts of racial difference that constitute his betrayal by Uganda, and the Indian community is obsessed with maintaining its distance from blacks, Mina herself identifies more with the blacks than with the whites in Greenwood. In one incident, when Mina has a date with Harry Patel, they go to a club where she is perfectly at ease socializing with the predominantly black crowd, dancing with some black friends and later with Demetrius, but Harry becomes so uncomfortable that he angrily leaves the club without her. As an Indian who has never been to India, Mina also shares a common history with African Americans who, as Dexter explains, are Africans who have never been to Africa. Moreover, Mina also has fond memories of her childhood in Uganda and of her father's friend Okelo. She chastises Jay for his refusal to bid Okelo goodbye. "Okelo risked his life to save yours," she reminds him. "I don't know what more proof you need of his love. I remember his face when he came to say goodbye. You would not even look at him."

It may be true, as hooks and Dingwaney suggest, that Mina "is no civil rights activist in the making" (43), but she is acutely sensitive to the racism around her. She recounts to Demetrius the racism faced by Indian motel owners: "You know how many people come to the motel. They look at us and say, 'Not another goddam Indian.' Makes me so mad."[27] Moreover, though Mina is not given to making political speeches on racism and equality, her leaving Greenwood with a black man in a society where blackness has come to be feared and loathed is nothing less than radical. Breaking the social taboos of both her own community and the larger society around her, she is engaged in a revolutionary act for an Indian woman under any circumstances.

Although Mina's relationship with Demetrius is an attempt to transcend a devastating racial divide, after their actual sexual union the chasm between the two cultures gapes wider. Yet hooks and Dingwaney assert that the film's message is one of romantic love that breaks down racial barriers, a message that "deflects from the very real politics of domination that underlies our inability as individuals to bond and form sustained community while simultaneously embracing our difference" (41). They object to the use of romantic love as a means of bonding between the two groups. Mina and Demetrius are not blinded by the love that brings them together, however; they have a realistic idea of the problems they are likely to face. When Demetrius ironically asks Mina whether they will live on fresh air if they leave Greenwood, Mina responds, perhaps not so unrealistically, "I could be your partner. I know how to clean rooms." Demetrius is also fully aware of his financial responsibilities. The couple's departure demonstrates that they can be together despite their differences, thus rendering their bonding more challenging and circumspect.

Still more egregious to hooks and Dingwaney is the fact that whereas the film portrays the sexual frustrations of a newly wed Indian couple, it shows Mina and Demetrius's sexual encounter as so "intense and so fulfilling that it empowers them to abandon familial ties" (42). These critics exaggerate the impact of the one sexual encounter shown in the film; the narrative structure does not allow for more sexual trysts, or even for the development of the relationship, especially since Mina's relatives prevent her from meeting Demetrius after they are discovered together. Only when she finally slips away from her family's watchful eye to find him do they have a brief moment to connect emotionally and discuss their true feelings for each other. Admittedly, Nair may have forfeited the opportunity to represent a more complex and layered relationship between Mina and Demetrius; however, the sexual aspect of it is liberating for Mina, given her restrictive background and the repression of female sexuality within Indian society. The sexual difficulties experienced by the newly wed Indian couple may be perceived as an indictment of a certain Indian middle class, which treats sex as taboo and does not educate men and women, especially women, in sexual matters. Often Indian women (and on occasion, Indian men) are thrust into arranged marriages with little or no knowledge of sex, or of their future spouses.

Disapproval of Mina and Demetrius's sexual exuberance must be framed by another claim that appears in hooks and Dingwaney's review, that Nair mocks Indian traditions such as prayer and traditional weddings. They point to Jammubhai's speech during his son's wedding reception: "Even though we are ten thousand miles away from India, we should not forget our roots, our culture, our traditions, our gods." "By making these moments comedic," the critics remark, "Nair seems to stand with white Americans who insist that ethnic jokes and poking fun at non-white cultures is harmless and not meant to undermine respect for difference" (42). Yet they never question what aspects of Indian culture are being portrayed in the film. The social customs depicted are a potpourri of Hindu religious ritual and Indian pop culture: Family members gather for daily prayers, celebrate a traditional Hindu arranged marriage, listen to Indian music, watch commercial Hindi films on video, and wear Indian clothes. When hooks and Dingwaney speak about the film's lack of respect for "Indian" culture, they refer to Nair's depiction of a Hindu culture, thus conflating "Indian" and "Hindu" identity. They do not consider the religious, regional, caste, and class differences within Indian culture.

Indeed, Nair appears to ridicule not the customs themselves but the manner in which they are conducted, underscoring the pompous tone of Jammubhai's declaration, followed by his leading a Hindu bhajan or hymn in which many of the younger Indians participate only halfheartedly. The practice of rituals may help the older generation maintain a sense of identity, but the rites are perhaps meaningless to the younger generation. In fact, given that many of the Indians either left India a long time before or have never been there at all, the practice of certain customs may be anachronistic in a contemporary Indian context. For Mina, who has never been to India and who left Uganda as a child, these so-called traditions are merely symbols devoid of significance.

In their eagerness to present culture and tradition as sacrosanct institutions, hooks and Dingwaney do not acknowledge that Indian customs such as arranged marriages can be oppressive to Indian women. Anxious to see twenty-four-year-old Mina married, Kinnu encourages her to go out with Harry Patel. She admonishes Jay, who is less concerned about Mina's marriage prospects: "You want your daughter to be a thirty-year-old spinster, running a liquor store?" The sexual politics of propriety and shame are evident in Kinnu's remark. Both parents, although "Westernized" enough to encourage Mina to go out with eligible young Indian men, are shocked when she and Demetrius are discovered in bed together. Kinnu and Jay feel that she has brought dishonor to her family, though it is unclear whether they are upset because she has slept with a man before marriage, or because Demetrius is American, or because he is black. The film's allowing Mina a measure of sexual liberation constitutes less a glorification of sex at the expense of family than an arraignment of a sexual economy that uses the female body as currency for cultural survival.

Moreover, far from celebrating Mina and Demetrius's "self-chosen homelessness," as hooks and Dingwaney contend (43), the film shows that the decision is wrenching for the couple as well as their families. Mina and Demetrius call their parents before they leave; Demetrius receives his father's blessing, and Kinnu tearfully accepts Mina's decision, but Jay receives the news in stoic silence, refusing to speak to his daughter once he learns that she is with Demetrius.[28] Mina and Demetrius do not wish to leave their families. It is the families and the community that force their departure by refusing to accept their relationship. Moreover, they decide to leave Mississippi for a more practical reason: Ostracized by Greenwood society, Demetrius is unable to find work; moving to another state offers him more employment opportunities. It is important to emphasize here that it is not they who fail the family, but the family and community that fail them.

Nevertheless, hooks and Dingwaney see in *Mississippi Masala* the suggestion that "personal fulfillment cannot be found within the context of nation or family where one is able to reconcile the longing for personal autonomy with the desire to function within community" (43). Their comment echoes that of Demetrius's ex-girlfriend Alicia (Natalie Oliver); observing that there is no shortage of black women in Greenwood, she accuses him of letting down his family, his community, and his entire race. Dismissing the couple's decision as a manifestation of "bourgeois white western . . . individuality" (41), hooks and Dingwaney do not allow for the complexity of the role of immigration, whose very nature complicates notions of "identity," "family," "community," and "nation," which are nuanced and not monolithic concepts. Mina was born in Africa of Indian parents, and raised in the southern United States. She cannot deny her "Americanness" any more than she can deny her "Africanness" or her "Indianness"—if it were possible to identify an essential Indian, African, or American. Therefore Mina does not reject her identity but accepts her multiple identities. Because of her unique experience she is forced to create her own space, which does not necessarily imply rejection of tradition and family. Mina describes herself as a *masala* or mixture, a "bunch of hot spices." For Mina, *masala* is a social construction, a means of explaining her Indian/Ugandan/American identities, an amalgamation of her ethnic roots, as well as her immigrant past.

The term *masala*, literally a blend of spices, has various connotations in the film. At times it refers to the hybrid nature of the family, which is Indian, Ugandan, and now North American. Nair herself defines *masala* in a more postcolonial sense as a "polyglot culture of the Indians who were colonized in their own nation by the British and then forced by poverty to seek survival elsewhere."[29] Shohat and Stam comment that culinary terms like *masala* have a metaphorical meaning for filmmakers: " 'creating something new out of old ingredients'— as a key to their recipe for making films."[30] For several male characters in the film, however, *masala* is reduced to a description of Mina's sensuality and earthy good looks, a means of objectifying her as sexual object. Demetrius describes her as "hot and spicy." To Tyrone, Demetrius's oversexed business partner, Mina is "just ripe for plucking." He even mistakes her for a Mexican at first, reinforcing the Hollywood image of Latin American women as sex objects. When she corrects him and identifies herself as an Indian, he assumes she means a Native American (the only "Indian" he is familiar with) and refuses to believe her. Even the *New York Times* film critic Vincent Canby emphasizes Mina's sensual appeal as if it were the only thing that determines her relationship with Demetrius: "Her voluptuous presence defines the urgency of the love affair."[31]

hooks and Dingwaney's observations with regard to family and nation raise a number of important questions: Is the Ugandan Indian (Hindu) family in the film typical of all Indian immigrant families in the United States? What constitutes Mina's Indian identity, given the fact that she has never been to India? In their concluding paragraph, the critics write, "Exile is not homelessness, rather a deep engagement with 'home'" (43). The very question of "home" is central to the film, but what is "home" to the Indian family in the film—Uganda? India? the United States? What does Mina consider home?

There are no simple answers to these questions of identity and home. Cultural historians have discussed these very issues as they pertain to emigrant groups. Stuart Hall speaks about the notion of *migranthood* and the attitudes of migrants who know deep down that they are not going home, because "migration is a one way trip. There is no 'home' to go back to. There never was."[32] Ashis Nandy observes that South Asians in the diaspora "cling to the memories of [a] South Asia which no longer exists and to a myth of return to the homeland which is no longer shared by their children or grandchildren." Even Jay comes to realize that his home is now in North America, and that neither the India nor the Uganda of his memories exists any more. "Home is where the heart is, and my heart is with you," he writes to Kinnu from Uganda, using a well-worn cliché to attain perhaps a reasonable compromise in his own mind to his personal dilemma. Jay's resolve signals an important moment of commitment, to his wife and, by extension, to the "home" he must build with her in their new domicile, thereby recalling Nandy's suggestion that "the diaspora must work towards dismantling links with the mother-country and entering the political realm of their new country."[33] In this context one might say that whether or not Mina and Demetrius's departure is a celebration of individualism, more urgently it is a call for minority communities to recognize and begin to resolve their differences in their immediate surroundings. That the film ends not with the couple's departure but with Jay in a Kampala marketplace holding an African child in his arms and swaying to the beat of African drums suggests that despite the admittedly mawkish display, it points to a more hopeful future—or at least a longing for a better world in which such hopes need no longer be quixotic.

The film demonstrates how essential migration and displacement are to an understanding of the behavior of the twice-displaced Indians as Mina's family transfers its attitudes and behavior toward black Africans to black Americans. It ends on a note of uneasy reconciliation: All conflicts appear to have been resolved, at least temporarily. Mina and Demetrius have left Mississippi for an uncertain future but the "possibility" that the love relationship will work out. Both families have accepted the couple's decision, albeit with difficulty, and it becomes clear that the Ugandan Indian family must forge a new identity: a combination linking their Indian and Ugandan past with their present life in America.

Although *Mississippi Masala* does not have a radical political agenda, the film nonetheless makes a political statement by raising the necessary question of interminority politics, so rarely addressed in mass media. Given that minorities often seem preoccupied with making political statements of representation in opposition to the majority culture, the film creates a space where we can refine black/white issues in order to study the more subtle shades of relationships between minority groups in the United States. Indeed, the film urges that connections be made between different nonwhite minorities, old taboos broken, and new identities created. In a broader context, *Mississippi Masala* shows that binary oppositions such as black versus white, victim versus victimizer, are not necessarily the most significant oppositions in American society. The film declares that people of color must overcome mutual prejudice if they are to unite in a collective space of their own.

NOTES

Acknowledgments: I thank Deepika Bahri, George McClintock, Pia Mukherji, and Francesca Sautman for their helpful suggestions and patient reading of earlier drafts of this essay.

1. Peter Kwong, "The First Multicultural Riots," *Village Voice*, 9 June 1992, 29, 32. Edward T. Chang similarly titles his article tracing the historical roots of the riots "America's First Multiethnic 'Riots,'" in *The State of Asian America: Activism and Resistance in the 1990's*, ed. Karin Aguilar–San Juan (Boston: South End Press, 1994), 101–17.

2. Manning Marable, "Race, Identity and Political Culture," in *Black Popular Culture*, a project by Michele Wallace, ed. Gina Dent, Dia Center for the Arts, Discussions in Contemporary Culture 8 (Seattle: Bay Press, 1992), 302.

3. Cornel West, *Keeping Faith: Philosophy and Race in America* (New York: Routledge, 1993), 29.

4. Edward Said, *Culture and Imperialism* (New York: Knopf, 1993), xxiv–xxv, 336.

5. *Mississippi Masala*, dir. Mira Nair, with Denzel Washington, Sarita Choudhury, Roshan Seth, and Sharmila Tagore, Michael Nozik, and Mira Nair, Samuel Goldwyn Company, 1991.

6. I use "African American" and "black" almost interchangeably, but I specifically use "black" when I want to stress the issue of color.

7. This historical background of the Ugandan Indians derives from four principal sources: Grace Stuart K. Ibingira, *The Forging of an African Nation: The Political and Constitutional Evolution of Uganda from Colonial Rule to Independence, 1894–1962* (New York: Viking Press, 1973); Jane Kramer, "Profiles: The Ugandan Asians," *New Yorker*, 8 April 1974, 47–93; J. S. Mangat, *A History of the Asians in East Africa, 1886–1945* (Oxford: Clarendon Press, 1969); and H. S. Morris, *The Indians in Uganda* (Chicago: University of Chicago Press, 1968).

8. Kramer, "Profiles," 48.

9. Ibingira, *Forging*, 69, 107–8. It is important to note that Ibingira's stance is an official one. He played a major role in the independence movement of Uganda, was a founding

member of the Uganda People's Congress (UPC), and served as both minister of justice and minister of state after Uganda became independent.

10. Morris, *Indians in Uganda*, 27.

11. Within the United States, Suvarna Thaker's "The Quality of Life of Asian Indian Women in the Motel Industry," confirms that most of the Asian Indian women she interviewed (who had come to the United States from England and Africa) said they hoped to marry off their children within their "small caste," and some who said that their children might not marry in their own caste "would certainly appreciate it if the other partner were at least Indian" (*South Asia Bulletin* 2.1 [1982]: 72.

12. Maureen Michaelson, "The Relevance of Caste among East African Gujaratis in Britain," *New Community* 7.3 (1979): 350.

13. Bert N. Adams and Mike Bristow have written about Ugandan Asians' expulsion and later resettlement in their adopted countries; see, e.g., "Ugandan Asian Expulsion Experiences: Rumour and Reality," *Journal of Asian and African Studies* 14.3–4 (1979): 191–203, for the experiences of refugees they interviewed in 1973.

14. The move from Africa to the United States, part of the narrative of *Mississippi Masala*, is reminiscent of Indian commercial films where, in the course of a song sequence, for example, the protagonists change both costume and locale.

15. In her introduction to Suvarna Thaker's "Quality of Life," 68, Sucheta Mazumdar observes that a high percentage of Asian Indians in the United States invest in the motel industry. When asked why, some cite the security of investment in real estate; others, the fact that it provides jobs for newly arrived immigrants. For still others a motel provides a living area for the extended family, bringing in higher returns on investment than house ownership; in addition, the family also provides the labor to run the motel.

Michaelson "Relevance," 350–51, mentions similar settlement patterns of East African Gujaratis in Britain. Those who purchased homes in certain areas affected later settlement patterns: first, their homes served subsequent migrants from East Africa; second, they were "nuclei around which later immigrants clustered in specific suburbs or centres of Britain."

16. Quoted in Samuel G. Freedman, "One People in Two Worlds," *New York Times*, 2 February 1992, H14.

17. In contrast to the role of the motel in the film, helping to preserve a sense of history for the Indians, James Clifford ("Traveling Cultures," in *Cultural Studies*, ed. Lawrence Grossberg, Cary Nelson, and Paul A. Treichler [New York: Routledge, 1992], 106) quotes Meaghan Morris, "At Henry Parkes Motel," Cultural Studies 2.1 (1988): 1–47: "Motels, unlike hotels, demolish sense regimes of place, locale, and history."

18. bell hooks and Anuradha Dingwaney, "Mississippi Masala," *Z Magazine*, July–August 1992, 41–43. Quotations from this review are cited by page number in the text.

19. Ella Shohat and Robert Stam, *Unthinking Eurocentrism: Multiculturalism and the Media* (London: Routledge, 1994), 178. For further discussion, see the introductory section (78–82) to the chapter titled "Stereotype, Realism, and the Struggle over Representation."

20. Rose is quick to point out that her brother owes nothing to his white employers, given that they had only recommended Demetrius to the bank for a loan: "All you and the rest of them want is that he [Demetrius] know his place and stay in it. But the days of slavery, they're over, Williben."

21. Shohat and Stam, *Unthinking Eurocentrism*, 198, 199.

22. hooks and Dingwaney observe that Nair makes the relationship between Okelo and Jay ambiguous. At no point, however, does the film explicitly indicate, as they suggest, that Okelo is Jay's servant. Although one might concede that Nair perhaps waits too long to reveal that he is a schoolteacher, there are several instances in the film where we see the two men drinking and talking on equal terms.

23. Quoted in Freedman, "One People," 14.

24. Although color is not really presented as an issue for the black family in *Mississippi Masala*, it has played an important role in films by black Americans, such as Spike Lee's *School Daze* (1988), whose plot revolves around the tensions between the lighter and darker-skinned African Americans, as well as his *Jungle Fever* (1991).

25. Shohat and Stam, *Unthining Eurocentrism*, 237.

26. Mark A. Reid, "Rebirth of a Nation," *Southern Exposure*, Winter 1992, 27–28, disagrees. He says that three films, one of them being *Mississippi Masala* (the other two, *Daughters of the Dust* and *Fried Green Tomatoes*), "suggest that there is an alternative vision of Southern race relations gradually finding its way into mainstream media. . . . The community represented in each film represents the uneasiness of a society faced with emerging coalitions fighting the privileges of the status quo." These films "resist beliefs, socio-cultural customs, and detrimental ideas and practices which would inhibit the growth of their central characters." Mina and Demetrius, Reid argues, fight the forces that say love between people of different colors is unacceptable.

27. Sonia Shah, "Presenting the Blue Goddess: Toward a National Pan-Asian Feminist Agenda," in Aguilar–San Juan, *The State of Asian America*, 157, says that Mina is portrayed as "unconcerned with issues of race, history, culture and gender"—yet we have seen that Mina is aware of issues of race, history, and culture, although she may not be taking an obvious feminist position. I also disagree with Shah when she says that Nair hurts the South Asian American cause by portraying Mina as one of those "little more than exotic, browner versions of white women, who by virtue of a little color can bridge the gap between black and white." Nair, by virtue of her portrayal, is just presenting her own view on the subject and not protecting some South Asian American cause. Given the diversity among the South Asian Indian community, what "cause" is she hurting? Again, what would be an appropriate portrayal of an Indian character? Mina is considered "white" by Shah, because she is not political and socially conscious enough. In literal terms Mina is more "black" than "white" and feels closer emotionally to the blacks than to the whites in Greenwood.

28. R. Radhakrishan, "Is the Ethnic 'Authentic' in the Diaspora?" in Aguilar-San Juan, *The State of Asian America*, 225–26, sees in *Mississippi Masala* a "commodification of hybridity" as "the two young adults just walk out of their 'prehistories' into the innocence of physical, heterosexual love." He remarks that the term *masala* (see below) "trivializes histories" by allowing for "individualized escapes." "Just think of the racism awaiting the two lovers," cries Radhakrishnan. Yet the decision to leave their families is not an easy one for either Mina or Demetrius, and neither is blind to the problems ahead, racial or otherwise. Nor do I believe that the film trivializes the histories of any of the countries it discusses. On the contrary, both Mina and Demetrius are conscious of their roots and heterogeneous identities.

29. Quoted in Freedman, "One People," 13.

30. Shohat and Stam, *Unthinking Eurocentrism*, 314. There is a resemblance between *masala* and Gloria Anzaldua's definition of the "new mestiza" in her *Borderlands La Frontera: The New*

Mestiza (San Francisco: Aunt Lute, 1987). Anzaldua describes her Mexican American heritage as a hybrid mixture resulting from living on the "borderlands." Despite certain liabilities, the mestiza is seen as a positive, empowering force that strengthens rather than weakens: "This mixture of races, rather than resulting in an inferior being, provides hybrid progeny, a mutable, more malleable species with a rich gene pool" (77). The "new mestiza consciousness" is the creation of a new self, the amalgam of the different parts. It has political and feminist overtones, resulting in "a conscious rupture with all oppressive traditions of all cultures and traditions" (82). Implicit in *Mississippi Masala* is the notion of hybridity, but without the political and feminist agenda.

In Srinivas Krishna's film *Masala* (1991), the term has multiple meanings. It refers not only to the various story lines but, at another level, to the narrative structure, which borrows from video, television, and popular Hindi film. *Masala* is also used literally to mean the spices ground by the grandmother for a curry. Finally, it describes the hybrid quality of the Indian Canadian families portrayed in the film, who live their lives in a hodgepodge of Indian kitsch (Hindu Gods and idols, Indian food, arranged marriages) and the reality of a racist Canada (the protagonist, Krishna, is stabbed to death by a white teenager at the end of the film).

31. Vincent Canby, "Indian Immigrants in a Black and White Milieu," *New York Times*, 5 February 1992, 19.

32. Stuart Hall, "Minimal Selves," *ICA Document* 6 (1987): 44.

33. Nandy quoted in Nikos Papastergiadis, "Ashis Nandy: Dialogue and Diaspora—A Conversation," *Third Text: Third World Perspectives in Contemporary Art and Culture* (special issue: "Beyond the Rushdie Affair") 11 (1990): 103, 105.

CHAPTER 11

From Ritual Drama to National Prime Time

Mahabharata, India's Televisual Obsession

Sanjoy Majumder

The Mahabharata I grew up with in India is a vital source of nourishment, a measure of one's thoughts and deeds. It is not mere epic constrained by literary and narrative strategies, but a revelatory injunction, ethical and theological in purpose, that determines and defines the social and personal interaction of millions of Indians.

Gautam Dasgupta, in Peter Brook and the Mahabharata

We are telling a story which, on the one hand, is universal, but, on the other, would never have existed without India. To tell this story, we had to avoid allowing the suggestion of India to be so strong as to inhibit human identification to too great an extent, while at the same time telling it as a story with its roots in the earth of India. If it were to be placed uniquely in the realm of the imaginary, it would both betray and diminish its vitality to some degree.

Peter Brook, in Peter Brook and the Mahabharata

The Mahabharata has recently been introduced to Western audiences via Peter Brook's elaborate, international, and multiethnic theatrical production. Between 1987 and 1988 the English-language version, produced by Brook's International Center of Theatre Research (CIRT), traveled around the world, opening in Zurich and moving on to Los Angeles, New York, Perth, Adelaide, Copenhagen, Glasgow, and Tokyo.[1] Brook attempts to present the epic as a cultural text that is able to stand independent of any one history or social reality, as a universal tale of "all humanity."[2] This is significant when we examine the *Mahabharata* as a cultural text, for in his use of a multicultural cast Brook demonstrates two facets of the epic: its ability to be read as multiple texts (authorially as well as contextually), and its ability to be essentialized into a singular and hegemonic vision. This cultural appropriation also underwrites the process by which both the West, through colonialism, and nationalist Indians attempt to construct and define the notion of "Indianness" in its historic specificity.

In India, audiences can witness performances of the *Mahabharata* in an array of styles that range from a two-hour recitation by a single performer and informal women's singing groups, to all-night shadow puppet plays, to professional theatrical productions performed for thirty consecutive nights.[3] Numerous aesthetic forms are used to perform and narrate the epic, from folk styles such as the Chhau dance of Purulia, Burrakatha of Andhra Pradesh, and Therukoothu of Tamil Nadu to Sanskritic stylized forms such as Jatra, Kathakali, and Yakshagana.[4] These performances frequently celebrate ritual passages— births, deaths, and weddings as well as religious ceremonies.

This essay examines the popular adaptation of the *Mahabharata* made for Indian television by commercial Indian film producers and broadcast between 1988 and 1990. I argue that an analysis of the popularity of the television series needs to consider the *Mahabharata* as a multivalent text. If cultural practices can be recognized as consisting of various signifying practices, then as Tejaswini Niranjana, P. Sudhir, and V. Dhareshwar argue, the cultural critic needs to consider the discourses of class, caste, and religion which invariably intersect the site of cultural presentation. In this way one can delineate "the contestation of both 'Indian' and the very notion of 'culture' itself, [as] clearly the need today is to understand 'Indian culture' not as some kind of organic unified whole or as 'a way of life,' but as 'ways of struggle.'"[5]

Appearing again and again in multiple contexts and in diverse forms, the *Mahabharata* provides the basis for many of the textual strategies and moral codes employed in subsequent plays, performances, and even commercial films. Through its continual recurrence in different contexts, the epic can be seen as a "national" text, yet different "readings" applied to it make it a localized text as well.

The *Mahabharata* is one of the longest single poems that exists in a textual form. It comprises almost 100,000 stanzas of narratives dealing with conflicts, theology, morality, ethics, statecraft, and Hindu philosophy.[6] While it has been periodized by some historians between 1000 and 700 B.C. and others between 400 B.C. and 200 A.D., most historians tend to agree that it was originally a secular tale of war and strife to which sections have been added by a succession of Brahman priests. Romila Thapar presents it as possibly describing a local feud which may have caught the imagination of bards and which, subsequently, acquired a variety of episodes and interpolations.[7]

The televised version, which went on the air in the winter of 1988–89, is considered one of the biggest series ever made for state-run television in India. Made by Indian commercial film producer B. R. Chopra, it followed another renowned Hindu epic television series, the *Ramayana*, produced by Chopra's film industry rival, Ramanand Sagar.[8] The screenplay of the *Mahabharata*, which lacked the religious intensity of the *Ramayana*, was written by Muslim screenwriter Rahi Masoom Raza.[9] Both series were based on vernacular written texts rather than the rigidly structured Sanskrit versions. Stretched over seventy-eight and ninety-three Sunday morning hour-long episodes, the serials brought the nation to a standstill. Movies were canceled for lack of audiences; weddings and funerals were delayed; streets and markets were deserted, and traffic on many of the nation's highways came to a halt.[10] "Villagers clubbed together to hire televisions. People who had no set converged on the homes of neighbours and relatives, or in shops, to watch. . . . When a power failure blacked out screens in one district at a crucial moment, the substation was burned down by an indignant crowd."[11] The two series attracted a vast national audience with estimates varying from 70 to 600 million regular viewers.[12] In many instances television screens were draped with flower garlands in a gesture of ritual celebration. In the 1989 and 1991 parliamentary elections three of the major stars of the *Ramayana* won parliamentary seats as members of a right-wing Hindu revivalist party, the Indian People's Party, identified nationally as the Bharatiya Janata Party or BJP (see Chapter 12).[13]

Studies of both television adaptations emphasize the appropriation of the texts by nationalist forces and their "Hinduization." That is, their central discourses and conflicts are merged into discourses of Hindu nationalism and a reconstruction of history. Ananda Mitra argues that "the representation of Ram, Krishna and the Pandavas . . . reproduced the residual Hindu practices in India's cultural stock and memory."[14] This reading, however, overlooks the ambiguous presentation of such reproductions and the contestation of such practices. As Niranjana, Sudhir, and Dhareshwar emphasize, only through analyses of such cultural practices as a struggle over meaning can the seemingly disparate nature of these presentations of culture be located in an understanding of ideological formations.

In postcolonial India, one is confronted with a multiplicity of contradictory readings of what it means to be Indian. Different voices claim authentic readings of the past and the present.[15] The religious, class, and ethnic differences that were exploited by the British in the nineteenth and early twentieth centuries continue to be used by politicians and other power groups today in the competition for limited economic resources. Theorists such as Benedict Anderson, Eric Hobsbawm, and Homi Bhabha have consistently stressed that the nation is an imagined construction, maintained by entrenched power groups. Hobsbawm and Anderson both introduce the idea that a shared heritage is often invoked mythically by nationalists, to construct a cultural and historical past in which the legitimacy of the modern nation can be found. Bhabha too, in analyzing the presentation of national identity in fiction and other cultural forms, talks about the narration of the present in terms of the past; he argues that nationalist discourses persistently produce the nation as a continuous narrative of national progress.[16] In Hobsbawm's words: "It is clear that plenty of political institutions, ideological movements and groups . . . were so unprecedented that even historic continuity has to be invented. . . . It is also clear that entirely new symbols and devices come into existence . . . such as the national anthem, . . . the national flag, . . . or the personification of 'the nation' in symbol or image."[17]

Referring to the adoption of nationalism as a discourse in freedom struggles, Partha Chatterjee demonstrates that the invention of the nation as an ideology and discourse of power was a distinctly European concept. Although adopted and utilized to fight colonialism, it also affirms and reifies the "bourgeois-rationalist" ideology of the colonial masters: "Nationalism . . . asserted that a backward nation could 'modernize' itself while retaining its cultural identity. It thus produced a discourse in which, even as it challenged the colonial claim to political domination, it also accepted the very intellectual premises of 'modernity' on which colonial domination was based."[18]

These ideas are important in the consideration of the *Mahabharata* as a national text. The cultural and historical legitimacy of India has been invoked in presentations of pre-Islamic India, originating from the "pure" Aryan race. The indigenous name for India is "Bharat," which means "pure race" or the land of the descendants of the sage Bharata, himself a descendant of the Lunar kings of ancient Aryan India.[19] The *Mahabharata* is therefore very much a text about race, or racial origins. The appropriation of this discourse by nationalists is symbolically rendered in the closing sequence of each television episode: a narrative synopsis that summarizes the preceding action, followed by a song whose lyrics invoke the *Mahabharata* as a tale of Aryan India and as a salute to the brave warriors of the nation. The song emphasizes the idea that this is a narrative belonging to a unified India, overlooking the fact that it is a story of Hindu or pre-Islamic India. It becomes both a reference to the struggle of the independence movement—by mentioning the nation-state and alluding to those who fought for its freedom—and at the same time a clever suggestion that the foundations of the present nation were laid in its mythic past. This theme is used politically by right-wing Hindu nationalists as well as by cultural imperialists who suggest that pan-Indian notions of kinship and morality are universal. Militant Hindu nationalists insist that the essence of being an Indian is being Hindu, which they call "Hindutva," a term coined politically in 1923 to construct an identification of the Hindu community with the Indian nation.[20] Yet the heterogeneous traditions that constitute Hindu culture have no single foundation text or even a canonical body of texts. Instead, a mass of oral and written literature composed in more than twenty languages stretches back in time. Amid the diversity, the epic stories of the *Ramayana* and the *Mahabharata* have been fundamental. Both were transmitted orally for centuries and later translated into regional languages.

The medium of television itself becomes an important consideration in discussing questions of national identities and cultures. Charlotte Brunsdon and David Morley have demonstrated that the notion of simultaneity in viewership allows for a shared construction of time and space, and Benedict Anderson extends this observation in his argument of the nation as an "imagined community" where the national subject carries an "image" of his or her fellow national subject, allowing for a shared point of reference.[21] It is clear that the *Mahabharata* television series fulfills the aspirations of the Indian state as well as the middle-class elite, with its reliance on nationalist and Hindu religious imagery. The producer's idea of compressing the epic into dramatic episodes was not exactly new; local performers and traveling acting troupes have brought the narrative alive for audiences in village and towns for centuries. This series, however, was the first instance in which the entire epic was transmitted to mass audiences— a single version shown to an audience of unprecedented size.

Given the nature of the political economy of Indian television, this project acquires a unique resonance. Indian television, which began with experimental telecasts in 1959, is state-controlled.[22] Following the launch of a multipurpose satellite in October 1983, television grew on a very large scale all over India until a majority of the population had access to at least a community set.[23] India joined Marshall McLuhan's global village in late 1991 with the introduction of the Hong Kong–based Satellite Television Asia Region (STAR TV), carrying BBC, CNN, and outdated American soap operas. The response of the Indian state was to use its own satellites to increase programming by setting up five new channels as of 15 August 1993 (Indian independence day). Ironically, Western cultural imperialism is countered by the state's own hegemonic designs, in a hyperreal affirmation of Partha Chatterjee's observations on the nature of the nation-state in the post-colonial world.

Thus, through the reiteration of the nationalist overtones of the *Mahabharata* as well as its presentation on national television, the appropriation of the central discourses and codes of the text into a hegemonic nationalist vision is seemingly complete and irrefutable. Yet the nature of cultural production as the site of contested meanings and contested identities, as Stuart Hall has documented,[24] as well as the history of the *Mahabharata* as a polysemic text, conflate all such readings. Subjectivity, examined below, is better realized in its interpellations and formations as a multiple force, consisting of intersecting discourses of identity.

James Clifford and Trinh Minh-ha examine the notion of subjectivity and argue that the singular, unified subject (position) is a myth, for it denies the existence of multiple selves or identities that might even be contradictory. Both Minh-ha's notion of the subjective identity of the Third World woman and Clifford's notion of cultural identity in ethnic subjects are attempts to link history to cultural analysis. Authenticity, therefore, as these authors examine it, has less to do with discovering original histories than with the power to represent the subjectivity of the other.[25] This is a useful notion to consider while examining the *Mahabharata* as a polysemic text. No single text or discourse makes up the *Mahabharata*, even if it is presented as such. Thus the cultural project of those who wish to utilize it as an all-consuming hegemonic text is self-defeating. The epic already exists in multiple contexts; different communities across India have different versions and readings of it. Joyce Flueckiger and Laurie Sears have argued that the epic text in India is fluid, since it is written and performed in a variety of genres that may be either rigid or flexible. In the oral tradition, information about the epics is reported along with summaries of the stories, related cultural data, and hagiographies of authors and composers—all passed down from parent to child, or performer to apprentice. In this method of transmission the focus is on the context of the presentation rather than the presentation itself. Performances, on the other hand, consist of verbal and artistic enactments of oral and written texts.[26] The text, therefore, becomes a part of the communal experience, like a ritual. "Textualization," says Clifford, "is understood as a prerequisite to interpretation. . . . It is the process through which unwritten behavior, speech, beliefs, oral tradition and ritual come to be marked as a corpus, a potentially meaningful ensemble separated out from an immediate discursive or performative situation."[27]

Recurrences of the epic texts across different contexts is also a critical cognitive process. A bard or minstrel may recite a myth in a certain way, only to be interrupted by members of the audience with the argument that it differs from their version of the text. The subsequent explanation is that both versions are true but occur in different world eras. An event becomes important precisely because it has multiplied; hence, the spoken word is eternal, not the written word. There exists, therefore, a multiple interpretive frame through which the epic text is transmitted. This consists of the cultural perceptions and expectations of various traditions, particularly folk tradition, local legends, the ritual and performative frames, and finally the commentary that accompanies the performance.

Multiple readings of a text such as the *Mahabharata* are particularly helped by the ambiguous nature of the narrative itself, which both praises and condemns all its characters. There is no moral retribution for any single character, nor is there any one hero. This ambiguity is best represented in the section titled "The Game of Dice." In this episode Duryodhana, the crown prince of Hastinapur, invites his cousin Yudhisthira, the king of Indraprashtha—along with his four brothers and their "shared" queen—to a game of dice, in an effort to cheat him of his kingdom and possessions. The climax of the episode is reached when Yudhisthira, shorn not only of all his possessions but of his brothers, whom he has sold as slaves, is forced to stake his queen, Draupadi. After he loses her too, there is a dramatic scene in which she is dragged and humiliated in front of the entire assembly. In short, both sides are morally flawed; indeed, all the male characters in the royal chamber are morally condemned. Duryodhana plays the antihero, condemned for his avarice and lust for power, and ultimately for his treatment of Draupadi. His brothers and uncle are condemned for being unable to intervene or to answer Draupadi's questioning of the construction of kinship relations.

In a sense the *Mahabharata* is fatalistic, since the outcome is known to the audience in advance, and the focus is on the dilemmas and the discourses of power, kinship relations, the role and nature of the state, and conceptions of divinity. And it is clear that different sections have been appropriated for different agendas. Thus, the *Bhagvad Gita* section, which is a lengthy discourse on morality, duty, and divine retribution, is also produced separately as a religious text in Hinduism, often canonically represented as corresponding to the Bible or the Koran. As Romila Thapar points out, this is one of the instances of bardic poetry being given the sanctity of divine revelation. The folk text is converted by the Brahman into a religious text.[28] Central to the philosophy of the *Gita* is the doctrine of karma and transmigration: One's actions in the present life set the conditions for one's subsequent rebirth.

It is the central discourses of the epic that make it such an engaging and popular text relevant to different people in different parts of the country. The *Mahabharata* deals with the fundamentals of genealogy, politics, and power. Its social and political significance extends therefore to both the ruling class and the marginalized, for it does not resolve any of the dilemmas it sets up. This open-endedness allows the epic, I believe, to be read in different ways with different conclusions. An example of a possible subverted reading can be seen in the treatment of genealogy, which is central to the *Mahabharata*, for it begins as a tale related to a young boy to reconstruct his ancestry. This can be metaphorically used by nationalists to symbolize the genealogy of the Indian nation by invoking a mythic cultural tradition. The epic offers a vision of matrilineal genealogy, however (as opposed to patrilineage), which is inconsistent with normative patriarchal constructions of the nation-state. The line of the Kauravas, of whom Duryodhana is crown prince, comes to an end with the last generation, for they are all killed in the war that marks the final conflict of the *Mahabharata*. Yudhisthira and his Pandava brothers are born of divine unions between the gods and their mother Kunti, since their father is cursed and unable to sire children. Their birth outside the royal union can be either constructed as something sacred, since they have divine parentage, or deconstructed as destroying notions of patrilineage and replacing it with matrilineage.

Similarly, in "The Game of Dice," Draupadi questions the nature of the marital relationship. If, she argues, relations between a couple are equal, then a man cannot stake his wife on the gambling board. If, on the other hand, a woman is the property of a man, then Yudhisthira had forfeited his ownership right over her, since he had staked himself first and lost. The nature of the quibble aside, this is one of many central arguments that structure the *Mahabharata*.[29]

Since the epic was presented over the formal apparatus of state television, questions of form are crucial to determining the nature of this cultural presentation. As Brundson and Morley, followed by Anderson, show, the framework of television and broadcasting can shape and refract the discourse of the nation. At the same time, as we have seen, the *Mahabharata* follows a tradition of folk reenactment, with its attendant formal implications. How do these disparate forms of presentation combine in the serial version?

In its formal aesthetic, Chopra's *Mahabharata* can be mapped as spectacle, ritual drama, and realist narrative as well as in the aesthetic styles of commercial Indian cinema. The transition from folk text to national television text is a transition from folk traditions of oral storytelling, traveling theater, mime, and dance drama to the discursive space of national television. Although commodified for the national audience, elements of folk dramaturgy can still be found in the formal style of the television series.

As argued above, in the oral tradition it is not the tale that is significant but the process of relating it. The content therefore is less privileged, since its treatment is used as a process of confronting core problematics or issues. Since the *Mahabharata* includes narratives that are already known and privileged, it is the treatment that is significant here, or the version of the text that is presented. Narration has been formalized by the presence of a narrator (*sutradhar*) who introduces and concludes each television episode. The *sutradhar* is a dramatic device "borrowed" from classical Sanskrit drama as well as vernacular folk forms; the *sutradhar* is often a wise man such as Vyasa himself (the mythological author of the *Mahabharata*), or even a buffoon.[30] There is also, however, a "narrator" or narrative process internal to the medium itself: that is, the television as narrator.[31]

Other formal elements exist as well, borrowed from both folk traditions and the more recent cinematic tradition. The action is rigidly stylized rather than produced through the conventional aesthetic of realism. The focus is on the dialogue and the delivery. Each episode relies not so much on dramatic action (since the conclusions are known in advance) as on the presentation of arguments or conflicts. The stiff, stylized mode of presentation derives from folk dramaturgy, formally aestheticized in the classical Sanskrit dramaturgy of the medieval period. The most evident folk influences are boisterousness and simplicity of expression. The televisual narrative has to be less rigid and less sophisticated in an unselfconscious manner, for it must be able to reach the broadest possible audience. Privileged knowledge must, therefore, be kept to a minimum.

At the same time, there are elements of the aesthetics of Indian commercial films and a functional realism. The realist element comes from the attempt at periodization via costumes and sets, in the tradition of such film genres as the historical and the mythological.[32] Thus, considerable effort has gone into creating elaborate locations and properties. The cinematic element is more evident in the cinematography and the use of music and sound effects. The aesthetic of commercial Indian cinema is well summarized by Satish Bahadur: "charming stars, songs, dances, fights, chase, spectacle, lavish sets, big locations, melodrama and humor, a bit of everything all strung together."[33]

In "The Game of Dice" sequence the cinematic presentation alternates between preserving the sense of spectacle and presenting a sense of drama. The gambling mat is the focal point, but attention has also been paid to the sense of spectatorship, with the adversaries arranged on either side of the mat, and the council of elders placed against one side of the great hall. The camera movements are slow with a consistent use of deep focus in which the intent is to foreground the action. As in many commercial Indian films, songs are used to present elements of the narrative and, more important, elements of theme. Orchestrated sound effects are conventionally used to highlight dramatic tension.

The language of the series is a mix of the idiomatic Hindi popularized by commercial cinema and a common North Indian vernacular version, Hindustani. It is neither regional dialect nor the high-flown Sanskritic version used in most conventional theatrical productions or religious rites.[34] It thus emphasizes the neutral spectator and the universal national subject.

The immense success of the television serial is particularly remarkable, since the central narrative is familiar to every Indian viewer. Clearly then, the act of watching the series was more than just the consumption of a televisual text. Consequently, the following questions are necessarily foregrounded: What did the Indian spectator bring to the television screen every Sunday morning? How were conflicts of interpretation resolved? And how did the various subject positions of the viewers, created both by the text and by their own ideological moorings, enhance their reading of the text as well as mediate their experience of its production?

This essay is not a study of audiences and how they read texts. Nor is it a mere textual reading of the *Mahabharata*, examining form, content, and narrative modes. I reject linear causal theoretical approaches to the study of media texts which seek to explain action and events on the basis of the structural and interpretive impact of televisual discourse. Rather, I have tried to create space between constricting projections of the viewing experience and the media text. This allows for the setting up of multiple interpretive frames through which the analyst can examine negotiated readings of texts by viewers. A useful study of such an approach can be found in Purnima Mankekar's exploration of the "viewer's active negotiation of hegemonic discourse" in her study of women viewers of the *Mahabharata*.[35] She examines the ways viewers use their experiences and subject positions as interpretive frames through which they view texts, showing that the woman viewer is able to bring to the screen her own complex notion of her subject position and history.

As Niranjana and others argue, "The field of culture is . . . a constant battlefield where there are no victories to be gained, only strategic positions to be won and lost. Cultural practice then becomes a realm where one engages with and elaborates a politics."[36] The nature of this particular text is ambiguous, given its tremendous ties to popular memories and personal histories. I believe that the popularity of the *Mahabharata* derives from its intertextual characteristics as well as its functional impact on different audiences in different contexts. It presents a situation whereby it can be appropriated for both hegemonic and subversive purposes.

NOTES

Acknowledgment: I am grateful to Gita Rajan for reading and commenting on an earlier draft of this essay.

1. Production notes in *Peter Brook and the Mahabharata*, ed. David Williams (London: Routledge, 1991), 283–311.

2. David Williams, introduction to *Peter Brook and the Mahabharata*, 3–28.

3. Joyce Flueckiger and Laurie J. Sears, eds., *Boundaries of the Text: Epic Performances in South and Southeast Asia*, Michigan Papers on South and Southeast Asia 35 (Ann Arbor: University of Michigan Press, 1991), 1.

4. Balwant Gargi, Folk Theater of India (Seattle: University of Washington Press, 1966).

5. Tejaswini Niranjana, P. Sudhir, V. Dhareshwar, eds., Interrogating Modernity: Culture and Colonialism in India (Calcutta: Seagull, 1993), 1, 2.

6. It has been argued that much of the central philosophy of the Mahabharata consists of Brahmanic pondering. See Gautam Dasgupta, "Peter Brook's Orientalism," in Peter Brook and the Mahabharata, 262–67. Others such as Rustom Bharucha, "A View from India," in Peter Brook and the Mahabharata, 232, argue that it "provides a Hindu perspective of action in the larger cosmic context."

7. Romila Thapar, A History of India, vol. 1 (Harmondsworth: Penguin, 1966), 31–32.

8. Jagdish Bhatia, "War by Another Means: Two TV Soap Operas Vie in Popularity," Far Eastern Economic Review 143.9 (1989): 75.

9. Although this has been highlighted by the Indian state as demonstrative of its secular nature, it is more reflective of the surprisingly secular and progressive nature of the commercial Indian film. Raza is also a former member of the Communist Party of India.

10. Bhatia, "War"; Philip Lutgendorf, "Ramayana: The Video," Drama Review 34.2 (1990): 127–76.

11. Brian Cathcart, "Faith versus Reason: Lord Ram," The Independent, 13 December 1992, 25.

12. Manjunath Pendakur, "Indian Television Comes of Age: Liberalization and the Rise of Consumer Culture," Communication 11 (1989): 177–97; Arvind Rajagopal, "The Rise of National Programming: The Case of Indian Television," Media Culture and Society 15.1 (1993): 91–111; Cathcart, "Faith versus Reason."

13. One of the victors was Arvind Trivedi, who played Ravana, the antagonist of the Ramayana; he won from Sabarkantha in the west Indian state of Gujarat. Significantly, he defeated Rajmohan Gandhi, who is the nephew of Mahatma Gandhi and was standing for election from a constituency closely identified with the politics of the Indian freedom struggle and its vision of the Indian nation. The other notable winner was Deepika Chikhalia, who played Ram's consort Sita; she won from the city of Baroda in the same state (see Chapter 12).

14. Ananda Mitra, "TV & Nation: Doordarshan's India," Media Asia 20.1 (1993): 41.

15. Barbara S. Miller, "Contending Narratives: The Political Life of the Indian Epics," Journal of Asian Studies 50.4 (1991): 783–92.

16. Eric Hobsbawm, The Invention of Tradition (Cambridge: Cambridge University Press, 1983); Benedict Anderson, Imagined Communities: Reflections on the Origin and Spread of Nationalism (London: Verso, 1983); Homi Bhabha ed., Nation and Narration (London: Routledge, 1990), 1.

17. Hobsbawm, Invention of Tradition, 7.

18. Partha Chatterjee, Nationalist Thought and the Colonial World: A Derivative Discourse? (London: Zed, 1986), 18–19, 30.

19. According to the legendary history of India, two dynasties were originally dominant in the north—called Solar and Lunar—under whom numerous petty princes held authority and to whom they acknowledged fealty. The most celebrated of the Solar line was Rama of the Ramayana. Under this dynasty the Brahmanical system gained ascendancy more rapidly and completely than under the Lunar kings in the more northern districts, where fresh arrivals of martial tribes preserved an independent spirit among the population already settled in those parts. The most famous of the Lunar race, who reigned in Hastinapura, or ancient Delhi, was Bharata, whose authority is said to have extended over a great part of India, and from whom sprang the name Bharata-varsha, the country or domain of Bharata.

20. Miller, "Contending Narratives," 786. The term "Hindutva" was introduced politically in 1923 by V. D. Savarkar, an ideologue of the anti-Muslim, right-wing Hindu Mahasabha (Hindu Grand Council). In the 1980s and 1990s it has become a slogan used by militant groups to assert Hindu pride and target the minority Muslim community. It is also used to invoke the idea of Ramrajya, which Partha Chatterjee describes as "a utopia . . . a patriarchy in which the ruler, by his moral quality and habitual adherence to truth, always expresses the collective will" (Nationalist Thought, 92).

21. Charlotte Brunsdon and David Morley, Everyday Television: Nationwide (London: British Film Institute, 1978); Anderson, Imagined Communities.

22. Manjunath Pendakur, "Political Economy and Ethnography," in Illuminating the Blindspots: Essays Honoring Dallas Smythe, ed. Janet Wasko, Vincent Mosco, and Manjunath Pendakur (New Jersey: Ablex,1991), 82–108.

23. Author's field research notes from winter 1992–93. The Indian National Multipurpose Satellite (INSAT-1B) was the second of a series of satellites launched by the Indian Space Research Organization (ISRO). Pendakur, "Indian Television Comes of Age," and Rajagopal, "Rise of National Programming," are both excellent and comprehensive accounts of the development of Indian television.

24. See Stuart Hall, Culture, Media, Language: Working Papers in Cultural Studies, 1972–79 (Birmingham: University of Birmingham, 1980).

25. James Clifford, The Predicament of Culture: Twentieth Century Ethnography, Literature and Art (Cambridge, Mass.: Harvard University Press, 1988); Trinh Minh-ha, Woman Native Other: Writing Postcoloniality and Feminism (Bloomington: Indiana University Press, 1989).

26. Flueckiger and Sears, Boundaries of the Text, 1, 6.

27. Clifford, Predicament of Culture, 38.

28. Thapar, History of India, 133–34.

29. Purnima Mankekar, "Television Tales and a Woman's Rage: A Nationalist Recasting of Draupadi's Disrobing," Public Culture 11.93 (1995): 469–92, analyzes how a female audience "reads" the televisual text of the Mahabharata, subverting the dominant patriarchal construction of the narrative.

30. Gargi, Folk Theater of India, 4–5.

31. The structure of television viewership situates viewers in time and space and "frames" their reception of the television image. This dimension of a technological form acting upon cultural production of meaning is best examined by British Marxist scholar Raymond Williams in Television: Technology and Cultural Form (New York: Schocken Books, 1975).

32. While the historical as a genre is familiar to western filmmaking from the German expressionism films of the 1920s to the Hollywood recreations of, e.g., Ben Hur and Lawrence of Arabia, the mythological film has been particular to Indian commercial cinema since the days of Dada Phalke, producing films such as Raja Harishchandra (1913).

33. Satish Bahadur, "Aesthetics: From Traditional Iconography to Contemporary Kitsch," in Indian Cinema Superbazaar, ed. Aruna Vasudeva and Phillipe Langlett (New Delhi: Vikas), 110.

34. Eric Barnouw and S. Krishnaswamy in Indian Film (New York: Columbia University Press, 1963), describe Hindustani as the simplest form of Hindi, a "bazaar language" derived from a heteroglossic mix of simplified Sanskrit, Prakrit, and a bit of Urdu.

35. Mankekar, "Television Tales."

36. Niranjana, Sudhir, and Dhareshwar, Interrogating Modernity, 7.

CHAPTER 12

Television, Politics, and the Epic Heroine

Case Study, Sita

Mahasveta Barua

On a Sunday morning in January 1987 Indians all across the nation sat down, or stood around, to participate in yet another telling of the two-millennia-old *Ramayana*.[1] The epic, the primary text of which has been attributed to the poet Valmiki, has been retold hundreds of time in major and minor regional languages, through folk tales, ritualized readings, pageantry, and even film.[2] The telling referred to here took the *Ramayana* into yet another genre—the television series. Produced and directed by Ramanand Sagar, a Bombay filmmaker, the serial continued for a year and a half amid devotional frenzy on the part of lay viewers, and a certain amount of criticism on the part of social and literary critics.

The popularity of the *Ramayana* TV series was unmatched (until, of course, the serialization of another Indian epic, the *Mahabharata*, less than a year later; see Chapter 11).[3] It is difficult to calculate the size of the audience, since entire village populations stood around single TV sets, urban groups gathered at the windows of stores that sold TVs, and trains were said to "screech to unscheduled halts at stations that boast[ed] TV sets."[4] As Philip Lutgendorf, estimating 100 million viewers, points out, "While this figure—approaching one-eighth of India's population—may seem modest by Western standards, . . . it must be appreciated in terms of the limited number and distribution of television sets and the restricted availability of electricity in India." It must also be appreciated in terms of a consistent viewing audience every week from January 1987 through July 1988, which propelled the *Ramayana* beyond mere popularity. As Lutgendorf puts it, "Long before the airing of the main story concluded . . . , the *Ramayan* serial had become the most popular program ever shown on Indian television—and something more: an event, a phenomenon of such proportions that intellectuals and policymakers struggled to come to terms with its significance and long-range import."[5]

One particular long-range impact may have evolved in June 1991. More than three years after the conclusion of the series, Deepika Chikhalia, the young actress who had portrayed Sita, Rama's wife, was elected to the Indian parliament. What is most significant about her election is that she became a member of parliament from Baroda, in the state of Gujarat, without any political experience whatsoever and without being able to speak Gujarati, the local language. Her campaign strategy, *India Today* reported, was to introduce her public speeches with the statement that she would be speaking in the same language that she used as Sita—that is, in Hindi.[6] Since Indians generally have a highly developed sense of linguistic and regional loyalties and phobias, Chikhalia's victory is all the more astonishing.

The television phenomenon and Chikhalia's election, however, are related in a way that the epics have always been related to India's religious, cultural, social, and political life. Not only have various versions of the *Ramayana* (and the *Mahabharata*) drawn upon topical concerns and historical developments to aid interpretation, but various groups have drawn upon the *Ramayana*, utilizing selective readings to focus attention on their concerns, as Paula Richman points out: "The cultural uses of the Ramayana are manifold and ever changing. Particular groups at particular times in history develop an elective affinity for specific characters. . . . Sita has traditionally elicited the empathy of long-suffering wives. . . . Clearly, the significance of the *Ramayana* goes beyond specific texts to encompass twin processes that lie at the heart of culture. Thus some tellings of the *Ramayana* affirm the hierarchy found in social, political, and religious relations, while other tellings contest that hierarchy."[7]

Priya Adarkar observed that the TV version "has come at a particular time in our history which is why it is so successful. We must see it in the context of the ethnic revival and the success of the festivals of India abroad." However valid Adarkar's analysis, the effect of the continuing, age-old perception of the epic is more significant than the effect of contemporary history, as Prabha Krishnan and Anita Dighe argue: "The impact of these serials on female and male spectatorship can best be theorized if it is recalled that both the *Ramayana* and the *Mahabharata* are regarded as *dharma shastras*, that is, sources of tradition and guides to right conduct. Unlike Christian and Jewish traditions or, for that matter, Sikhism, the Hindus have no central sacred book. The sacralisation of the *Ramayana* and the *Mahabharata* . . . was an attempt to withstand political pressures in medieval times.[8]

Modern politics utilized this very sacralization to manipulate the voting public. By relating the popularity of the TV series to the election of Sita/Deepika, this essay examines broadly the political usage of the serial's and the character's popularity, and specifically the use of feminine symbols by contemporary Indian women. The political usage is dichotomous: While national politics gains by perpetuating the traditional image of Sita as goddess and good wife, feminist politics seeks to revise that image. I see Sita, the role model, as a site for contrary assertions in present-day India as she has been in earlier times. In the past she has been victim-heroine: Attitudes toward women led to her self-sacrifice; at the same time she was elevated to the status of divinity and role model to condone and justify these very same attitudes. In the present circumstance, on the one hand the role of Sita is being exploited by a patriarchal political system; on the other hand, the idea of a woman rising to power through Sita ostensibly recasts her as heroine, though this recasting is generally transitory. The political appropriation of mythic role models such as Sita to serve as symbols through whom female politicians are projected has remained unchanged since the nationalist era. Yet late twentieth-century India has seen the emergence of quite a changed woman.

Rajeswari Sunder Rajan describes this new Indian woman as one who has evolved and arrived in response to the times, and is modern and liberated: "She is 'Indian' in the sense of possessing a pan-Indian identity that escapes regional, communal, or linguistic specificities, but does not thereby become 'westernized.' The primary site of this construction is commercial advertisements in the media, both in print and on television." Sunder Rajan points out that this image of the new woman is derived from the "urban educated middle-class career woman"—in fact, a woman much like Deepika Chikhalia herself.[9] Outside the urban sphere and below the middle class, Indian women still function within an extremely restrictive society. Women's social movements in India seek to lessen this gap between women through legal, social, and educational changes. But when one of the new women such as Chikhalia uses a centuries-old female image such as Sita to further her own political career, she relies on and reinforces the differences between women.

In my three-part discussion I first look at the serial's popularity within the context of the *Ramayana*'s importance in Indian cultural and religious history and at its specific significance in recent political developments; next, I assess the significance of Sita to Indian patriarchal as well as feminist ideology; finally, I examine the problematics of a female politician's use of this role model to achieve independent status and power in relation to the women's movement in India.

Indian Culture, Politics, and the *Ramayana*

The recent usage of the epic, whether political or feminist, was made possible by the high-tech narrative device TV can be. Television can mesmerize audiences into a stupor with the most inane of soap operas; when its power combines with that of an epic that has always appealed to the masses, the resulting hysteria is hardly surprising.

In brief, the *Ramayana* is the tale of King Rama, an incarnation of the supreme god Vishnu, whose specific mission is to rid the earth of an immensely powerful demon-king, Ravana of Lanka. Rama is born the eldest son of King Dasaratha of Ayodhya. After his marriage to Sita and his anointment as crown prince, he is banished for fourteen years, thanks to the manipulations of his stepmother, Kaikeyi. Sita and his brother Lakshmana accompany him in his forest exile. There Sita is abducted by Ravana. Rama, with the help of a simian race and his greatest devotee, Hanuman, defeats and kills Ravana. Sita goes through a trial by fire to prove her fidelity while in captivity, and they return to rule in Ayodhya. In most versions, Rama then banishes a pregnant Sita when his subjects doubt her fidelity and question his acceptance of her. Sita takes refuge in Valmiki's hermitage, where she gives birth to her two sons, Luva and Kusha. Years later, when Rama asks her to stand trial again so that he will be able to take her back, she calls upon her Mother Earth to prove her fidelity by gathering her to the earth's bosom, and she is swallowed by the earth.[10] Rama returns to his kingdom with his sons and later ascends to the heavens with his followers. The epic has all the elements of heroism, the conflict of virtue against vice, and scenes of martial glory that guarantee popular attention. More than that, the identity of Rama as incarnate god raises the epic's tellings from popular entertainment to devotional experience.

One of the basic forms of the *Ramayana* as devotional experience is through *katha*—literally, narration. In this form it is read, or more often chanted, in a highly ritualized setting—emulating Valmiki, who himself tells the *Ramayana* to Luva and Kusha, the twins, who in some versions are said to enchant Rama's court with their telling, before Rama is aware that they are his sons.[11] In addition to narration, the *Ramayana* has reached even wider audiences through dramatization. In many North Indian states it is acted out in a form called Ramlilas through the ten days of Dussera, an annual autumn festival honoring Rama. At these performances, Lutgendorf shows, "the emphasis shifts from hearing to seeing as oral exegesis is replaced by visual and iconographic realization of the narrative." Unlike audiences at secular dramatic performances, those attending the Ramlilas are concerned not with the level of acting or plot movement but with watching their gods and heroes come to life and sharing the same time frame of existence with them. It was a similar devotional sense of participation that the audiences brought to the televised *Ramayana*. Urbane critics often found the episodes tedious and slow to unfold, especially in comparison with other shows utilizing modern techniques, but as Lutgendorf quite rightly says, "The emphasis in 'Ramayan' was squarely on 'seeing' its characters. Not 'seeing' in the quick-cut, distracted fashion in which modern Western audiences take in their heroes and heroines, but drinking in and entering into visual communication with epic characters. To most viewers, 'Ramayan' was a feast of *darsan* (or *darshan*, meaning an audience with or revelation from a higher authority).[12] Thus it was received not just as another popular TV series but as a legitimate version of the *Ramayana*, the latest telling in a line that is traced back to Valmiki. The producer, Ramanand Sagar, claimed, "I have put the scriptures on celluloid. You could say that there is Valmiki's Ramayan, Tulsiji ki Ramayan and now Ramanand Sagar ki Ramayan."[13] He is quite justified in his boast. Audiences treated their TV sets as altars, and the actors playing Rama and Sita as manifestations of their god and goddess. Many people would fold palms in prayer whenever Rama appeared on the screen.

With all objectivity suspended and the people approaching the screening as the unfolding of their gospel, the deep-seated beliefs of numerous sections of the population were offended by any revision or omission in the tale. As they made their opinions known, Sagar himself began appearing at the end of segments to justify or explain controversial revisions. Taking protest a step further, when the series was concluded with Rama's return to Ayodhya and his ascension, the All India Safai-Mazdoor Union (sanitation workers) launched a brooms-down strike and filed suit against Sagar and Doordarshan (the TV network) for discontinuing the serial without showing the role played by Valmiki, the original "scriptwriter," from whom many members of this union claim descent. As a result, the serial was extended as *Uttar Ramayan* to include the last book of the epic.[14]

The level of audience participation and response, audience-teller communication, alterations in the mode and extent of the telling itself were made possible only by the advancement of technology. According to Raymond Williams, "a technology, when it has been achieved, can be seen as a general human property, an extension of general human capacity. But all technologies have been developed and improved to help with known human practices or with foreseen and desired practices." He goes on to make the point that broadcasting, particularly television, can easily bring people within the sphere of influence of a particular group that desires to use this technology for its own purpose: Just as people can watch and listen to and be influenced by others in their immediate circle, they can watch and listen to television.[15] Thus, the age-old, slow communication of the epic could now be transformed by technology into immediate and unmediated access.

The particular financial and viewership concerns that govern televisual communication in the modern world were present here too; for example, the importance of viewer input. Joseph Turow, discussing pressure groups and tele-

vision entertainment in the American context, notes that the broadcast industry spends much money to cultivate the backing of politicians and advertisers
as well as viewers, but "circumstances clearly exist where the interests of these
three sectors do not coincide, and response to organized public demand for
changes in television material might sometimes be one of them"; television
networks generally try to cope with the demands to prevent a drain on their
normal operations and resources.[16] In India in the 1980s, politicians rather
than advertisers were of concern to the TV network, which is a government-
owned agency. In its catering to the public demand for explanation of perceived changes in the epic, and for an extension of the serial to include the last
book, we can detect political motivation on the network's part. Ensuring continued viewership, however, was monetarily sound as well. In his analysis of
television as a commodity, David Morley suggests that there is a point at which
the process of consumption of television itself is being commodified, the purchase of the set and the selection of programs taking parallel forms.[17] Though
Morley's discussion includes issues such as pay-per-view and subscription programming that are not applicable in this case, this point about the commercial
factor is still valid: The choice to watch the *Ramayana*, made by the viewers, was
certainly commodified by the producers. Viewing guaranteed further and extended episodes of the epic. And though the process of syndication was absent,
something better awaited—videocassette production and sale. Thus the cultural
ritual of storytelling itself was commodified by television culture.

This *Ramayana*, then, was unlike any other. One report aptly said, "The story
is old and the tellers many. But never before has the epic mesmerized a nation
into mass stupor: it needed the power of television to do that." The power of
television can similarly imprint the images of actors so thoroughly upon the
viewers that identification of actors with roles can be quite complete. When audiences prostrated in front of the TV, they did so before Arun Govil and Deepika
Chikhalia, Rama and Sita. When questioned about this phenomenon, Deepika
Chikhalia replied that people behave the way they feel, and the actors had not
asked anyone to do what they were doing. The reporter disdainfully remarked,
"Well, evidently people aren't too sure where the goddess ends and the actress
begins." Lutgendorf perceptively points out the obvious that has been missed by
certain cynics, that the confusion "of actors with roles they play is an essential
premise of all theatre, though its intensity varies along the spectrum of performance genres and media."[18] With a medium as immediate as television, a genre
as consistent and continuous as a series, and a cast of beloved gods, the identification of actors with roles is hardly surprising. Still, if the audience was not
sure where Sita ended and Deepika began, it must be noted that not all decisions
banking on the complete identification of actors with roles proved fruitful.

In the 1988 elections, Rama/Arun Govil and Hanuman/Dara Singh failed to sway voters when they campaigned for Rajiv Gandhi's Congress (I) Party. *India Today* reported that the party's "clumsy attempt to influence religious sentiments as an electoral hook, did its image—or its performance—no good." Yet in 1991, Sita/Deepika Chikhalia was elected to the parliament as a candidate for the Bharatiya Janata Party (BJP). Apparently the Indian masses are willing to place Sita (and probably even Rama) in power as living symbols of their ideals but are not willing to take the actor's word on another person's ability or fitness to rule. Like Arun Govil's, Chikhalia's campaign was an attempt to move voters through religious sentiment. The difference in 1991 was that the political maneuver was played out in a transformed India; the three years between the two elections had seen the extreme religious polarization of Indian society. Ramanand Sagar laid claim to having transformed "the cultural landscape of the nation by 'transporting everybody to that golden age. I have brought the college boy from the disco culture to the Ramayan. College boys don't say hi any more, they say Jai Sri Ram ki.' . . . And what Gandhi and Nehru and a host of others could not do, Sagar claims he has achieved with an Ali Baba–like magic mantra. *Ramayan* has 'achieved national integration.' "[19]

This is too far-fetched to be given serious consideration, yet the airing of the *Ramayana* and the *Mahabharata* and intense epic-watching have certainly heightened awareness of Hinduism and its tenets and revived latent pride in being Indian and Hindu. This heightened awareness coincided with the unfolding of a real-life religio-political issue: the Babri Masjid–Ram Janambhoomi controversy concerning Rama's birthplace, Ayodhya, which concluded violently with the 1992 destruction of the Masjid by Hindu fanatics, followed by countrywide communal riots in which hundreds died. The dispute over the land in Ayodhya on which stands a thirteenth-century mosque, built during the reign of the Mogul king Babar, dates back to 1885, when a Hindu priest asked permission to build a temple outside the mosque.[20] Dragging through a hundred years, the issue gained momentum in 1984 when the Vishwa Hindu Parishad (World Hindu Organization) launched a movement to liberate the site. Over the next few years certain political parties joined forces with the VHP, most notable among them was the BJP. By the time of the 1991 elections, the BJP was identified as Rama's party. This identification was encouraged, for being Rama's party was related to political ability, specifically the ability to achieve *Ramrajya*, Rama's rule, which has always been synonymous with ideal rule. Though this ideal was never based on an assumption of Hindu rule but rather on a just rule, the BJP did not hesitate to use the terms "ideal" and "Hindu" metonymically.

In discussing history as a source of nationhood, Partha Chatterjee shows how spurious and how politically motivated these claims to ancient models of true nationalism really are: "The idea that 'Indian nationalism' is synonymous with 'Hindu nationalism' is not the vestige of some premodern religious conception. It is an entirely modern, rationalist, historicist idea. Like other modern ideologies, it allows for a central role of the state in the modernization of society and strongly defends the state's unity and sovereignty. Its appeal is not religious but political."[21] In fact, one primary agenda of the BJP, according to a report, was to "wean away the moderate Hindu voter from Congress (I) with the cry of Hindu nationalism and project itself as a unifying alternative to 'pseudo-secularism.'" The report continued: "Ramming home one single religious programme—the Ram Mandir issue—will suffice. The party even proposes to give tickets to some sants (holy men)."[22] In accordance with this campaign strategy the BJP gave Sita/Deepika a ticket on which she rode to victory.

The Heroine as Victim

The obvious implication of this result is that the Indian public was paying instinctive homage to Sita, the ideal woman, who has served as a role model for centuries. But what qualities has she embodied? As Joanna Liddle and Rama Joshi put it, Sita "patiently endured all privations, resisted all attempts at seduction and later undertook without complaint the ordeal by fire to prove her innocence and fidelity." Sita gives up life itself to prove her fidelity to her husband, making the ultimate sacrifice: "The concept of sacrifice, then, is a powerful concept for women in orthodox Hinduism. It embodies the ideal of what women should be in a male-dominated society—silent, subservient, self-effacing."[23] Such an ideal woman is a *pativrata* (husband-worshipper) and the ideology that governs her is *pativratya*.

Vanaja Dhruvarajan points out that "this androcentric ideology has effectively sustained the patriarchal social structure which gave rise to it in the first place. . . . It is based on certain assumptions and beliefs regarding the nature of men and women and their proper interrelationship. People have a strong opinion that there is a basic difference in the natures of men and women. Men are ritually pure, physically strong, and emotionally mature; women, on the other hand are ritually pollutable, physically weak, and lack strong willpower."[24] It then becomes clear why the ideal woman should be conceptualized through her relationship to a man. Prabhati Mukherjee explains: "The orthodox Hindus remember the *pancakanyas* (five maidens) in their daily prayer. These maidens are Ahalya, Draupadi, Tara, Kunti and Mandodari," over whom rule the trio of Sita, Savitri, and Radha. It should be noted that none of these women are "maidens" at all; they are all wives. As Mukherjee puts it, "An ideal woman is she who is an ideal wife."[25] Krishnan and Dighe show that the ideology of the

Ramayana and the *Mahabharata* function as universalizing mechanisms to reinforce this conception of women: "Both celebrate male-bonding and female chastity, or the expression of female sexuality under male control. The values of these epics pervade the fabric of our society and, by extension, of media as well."[26] The stories of the five maidens are in fact derived from the two epics, and their "ideal" natures are validated throughout the texts and through every telling.

The irony of this conception is that while Indian men worship mythological ideal women/wives, considering them sacred and thus superior, their own wives in emulating these women must essentially accept a position of inferiority. In fact, this has been one of the contradictions of Indian culture: Although goddesses often hold the positions of governing deities in our religion, women occupy the most menial of positions in our society. I suggest, however, that the qualities drawn to women's attention are chosen selectively, while a host of other qualities are ignored or suppressed. Sita's status is based on her constancy to her husband and her sharing in his trials, but her rising to the challenge of life in the woods and her stubborn courage against her powerful male abductor are acts not defined by her role as wife. Her final act of sacrifice too is one that she decides upon herself. This independent, defiant act of the woman has been transformed into the ritualistic sacrifice of the *sati*. Sita's refusal to undergo a second trial by fire is given less attention than her having undergone a successful one earlier in the tale; through centuries, Indian *satis* have echoed this act of self-sacrifice by immolating themselves in their husbands' funeral pyres.

That Sita's ritual by fire had far-flung repercussions for Indian women was acknowledged by the TV series. The final episode focuses on the time following Ravana's death, when Rama must return to Ayodhya with Sita. The popular version of the epic recounts Sita's going through her *agnipariksha*, successfully proving her chastity while in captivity and thus her fitness to return to Rama, but the series puts a twist in this version. In the television adaptation, when Rama mentions the fire to his brother Lakshmana, Lakshmana flies into a rage and takes up the case of Sita in particular and women in general. Through him we hear of the injustices of such a trial. Lakshmana berates his brother for even calling Sita's innocence into question. Furthermore, he condemns a system that would consider a captive woman culpable even when she had no means of preventing sexual violation. Lakshmana's speech neatly summarizes contemporary views of this act. That such views are contemporary is pointed out by Sagar when he appears at the end of the show to justify the revisions and to say that regardless of precedent and tradition in the epic, one must consider the times. But the revision that Sagar seeks to justify is not so much Lakshmana's argument as Rama's reasons for requiring a trial by fire from Sita. Rama halts Lakshmana's tirade by gently reminding him that to question Sita's character would be to question his own, since they were both parts of one being. Instead, he tells Lakshmana that he had placed Sita in the care of the god of fire, Agni, before her abduction, knowing of the events to come. Thus the Sita who had been kidnapped was only a facade, and the real Sita had to be reclaimed from Agni. Regardless of the reasons for it, Sita cannot be separated from the trial by fire she has undergone, which enhances her stature as a heroine to be idolized and emulated.

We can briefly examine the two acts of sacrifice, the original and the mimetic, by applying René Girard's views on rituals and sacrifice. Speaking from an anthropological perspective, Girard states:

> If rituals conclude with sacrifice, it must be that to religious so-cieties the sacrifice seems like the conclusion of the mimetic cri-sis enacted by the ritual. In many rituals everyone assembled is required to participate in an immolation that might easily be mistaken for a sort of lynching. Even when the sacrifice is per-formed by a single person, that person usually acts in the name of everyone involved. The community affirms its unity in the sacrifice . . . . Suddenly the opposition of everyone against everyone else is replaced by the opposition of all against one. Where previously there had been a chaotic ensemble of particu-lar conflicts, there is now the simplicity of a single conflict: the entire community on one side, and on the other, the victim.[27]

Sita's self-sacrifice is just such an act, one in which she, the victim, faces an entire community. It must be remembered that Rama banishes her upon hear-ing the grumblings of his subjects. He must maintain his role as good king, and despite the fact that she is very dear to him, she must be discarded. Yet Sita car-ries on with her duties by bearing him not one but two sons, and the continu-ation of Rama's line is assured when he and his twin sons are united. At this point Sita becomes superfluous. Rama cannot accept and claim his sons without bringing Sita back to the kingdom, and he cannot do that without upsetting his subjects. When Rama asks Sita to agree once more to a ritualistic trial by fire to prove her fidelity, he moves toward accepting her, an acceptance that would have caused division within the community of ruler and subjects. Sita solves this problem and restores the equilibrium by removing herself. She asks her Mother Earth to gather her up if she has been a true wife. Though conditionally phrased, to Sita the outcome is a foregone conclusion. Her truth is proved, the commu-nity is united, and her absence makes her even more admired. As Girard puts it, "The community thinks of itself as entirely passive vis-à-vis its own victim, whereas the latter appears, by contrast, to be the only active and responsible agent in the matter. Once it is understood that the inversion of the real relation between victim and community occurs in the resolution of the crisis, it is possible to see why the victim is believed to be *sacred*.[28]

In the mimetic ritual of self-sacrifice by the *sati*, we see this same victimization. In a society where a woman's identity was realized through her husband's, his death ideally resulted in her nonexistence. If her children were grown, the woman became truly superfluous. The lot of widows was so dire that death was an acceptable alternative. As Girard says, "The sacrifice is simply another act of violence, one that is added to a succession of others, but it is the final act of violence, its last word."[29] The widow symbolized misfortune, and the community would be forced to contend with this unfortunate entity. Her self-immolation restored the balance, and the dead woman was thereafter glorified as a *sati*.

The woman immolating herself in fire chooses death much as early lynching victims chose to jump off the cliff to which they were chased. In primitive myths, victims are often driven to cause their own deaths. Girard mentions the Tikopian myth of Tikarau, who was chased to the edge of a cliff and, rather than letting the pursuers cause him to fall, was believed to have launched himself into the sky. Speaking of other modes of ritual execution such as collective stoning and abandonment in the middle of a desert, Girard goes on to say, "All these methods permit a community to get rid of an anathematized individual with little or none of the direct physical contact that might be dangerous in view of the contagiousness of violence. Participation is minimal and at the same time it is collective. The responsibility for the death of the victim rests upon no one in particular and this is an added advantage: the chances of further division in the community are diminished."[30]

Although the victimization and sacralization of Sita are not as dramatic as the Tikopian legend, and the mythology of the *Ramayana* is still part of Indian religion, the process of sacralizing her and, later, the victims of *sati* appears to be the same. The very act of ceasing to exist elevates them. Through time, the essential quality of stoic submissiveness, of women's minimizing their own existence, has been so glorified as to make it a desirable quality. Even today, the shamefully frequent occurrences of widow immolation are accompanied by communal rituals and fanfare, and, adding a twentieth-century twist, covered by the press.[31]

A Modern-Day Sita

We see the same glorification and exploitation of Sita in the association of her name with Deepika Chikhalia's and the BJP's quest for a seat in parliament. The nomination was obviously inspired by the public's identification of an actress with the role she played, and the political agenda was once again rooted in violence and patriarchal power. The nomination of this specific woman has no real significance for women in general, and the woman herself has only symbolic value. Further, in the modern Indian democratic process the symbolic value of the woman is relevant only to particular classes. If we consider Indian politics to be what Ernest Gellner calls an "agro-literate polity," his definition is particularly applicable: "In the characteristic agro-literate polity, the ruling class forms a small minority of the population, rigidly separate from the great majority of direct agricultural producers, or peasants. Generally speaking, its ideology exaggerates rather than underplays the inequality of classes and the degree of separation of the ruling stratum."[32] That an urbane, educated, aggressive woman can represent a traditional, self-effacing epic heroine is a concept that can be accepted only by those who are neither urbane nor educated. In their manipulation of public sentiment regarding the traditional woman, however, the BJP was simply following political tradition.

The political use of mythic female role models has quite a long history in Indian national politics. In "Recasting Women," Kumkum Sangari and Sudesh Vaid speak of the appropriation of the traditional female role model by the nationalist movement of the late nineteenth and early twentieth centuries: "The recovery of tradition throughout the proto-nationalist and nationalist period was always the recovery of the 'traditional' woman—her various shapes continuously readapt the 'eternal' past to the needs of the contingent present. Religion is the medium first for middle class and then for nationalist reform in the deepest sense." Sangari and Vaid point specifically to the conceptualization of a "Vedic woman" based on selective criteria that maintain the inegalitarian class system: "The Vedic woman, both in her own time, and after her appropriation by upper castes and classes in the nineteenth century, is built upon the labour of lower social groups and is also a mark of distinction from them."[33]

Partha Chatterjee too shows that the continuing perception of the heroine/goddess of Indian mythology has its basis in class structures. In "The Nationalist Resolution of the Women's Question" he contends that the specific ideological form in which we know the Sati-Savitri-Sita construct today is a product of the development of a dominant middle-class culture during the nationalist era. This construct emphasized the dominant characteristics of femininity in the new woman—the spiritual qualities of self-sacrifice, devotion, religion, among others—and Chatterjee goes on to say, "This spirituality did not . . . impede the chances of a woman moving out of the physical confines of the home; on the contrary, it facilitated it, making it possible for her to go out into the world under conditions that would not threaten her femininity."[34]

Though the "new woman" referred to by Chatterjee is one who lived more than a half-century ago, today's woman has continued to use mythic feminine symbols in much the same way politically. Modern Indian women who seek political power do so on patriarchal terms, balancing the masculine desire for power with feminine symbols. This use of symbols, while furthering a specific woman's career, continues to perpetuate a restrictive ideal for Indian women. It can safely be concluded that the Indian public reacts favorably to mythic symbols, male or female, but the woman to whom they respond does not herself symbolize women in general to them. Though the voting public may place one woman in power because she is believed to represent a symbolic woman, the status of women is not elevated through her.

In postcolonial India, Indira Gandhi is the most notable example of a woman utilizing numerous symbols and wielding power within a male-dominated political structure. Except for a period between 1977 and 1980, Indira Gandhi held immense power as prime minister of India from 1966 till her assassination in 1984. Yet whatever improvement was made in women's social and legal status during these two decades was not a result of any legislative efforts on her part. Having a woman in power did not alleviate the task of organizing women, nor did it lead to a changed social perspective regarding women's capabilities. As Sunder Rajan says, "In general, historical women leaders have been regarded—rightly—as individual figures and isolated examples not sufficiently or significantly representative of the status of the women of their society and in their times." Sunder Rajan sees two ways in which women achieve power—through birth and circumstances as in Indira Gandhi's case, and through merit as in Margaret Thatcher's case—and suggests that the role of gender is largely negated in both. Yet despite the minimal role played by gender in Gandhi's exercise of power, gender was highlighted in her pursuit of power during every election and in her representation as leader of the nation:

> One kind of identity that Indira Gandhi sought and was accorded
> was identification with the nation: India is Indira. In such an
> identification the female subject is no longer perceived in
> metonymic relationship to the nation, as its leader, but as an ac-
> tual metaphor for it, its equal and its visible embodiment. This
> transposes a familiar equation of the nation with the mother, al-
> ready a trope of nineteenth-century nationalist discourse
> ("Bharatmata"). Represented as the "mother," the woman leader
> is well able to reconcile aspects of nurturing and service in oppo-
> sition to the authority of the father, as well as to subsume both
> parental figures into a single complex authority figure.[35]

Apart from the specific Mother India image, the woman as nation or Indira as India appropriates the larger concept of the motherland. Acceptance of this particular woman's authority becomes synonymous with acceptance of one's patriotic duty to the motherland. Interestingly enough, Sunder Rajan shows that this Mother India image was celebrated and reinforced by the 1957 movie *Mother India*, allowing parallels to be drawn to Gandhi's representation: "Such a representation, with its mythic appeal and proportions, is readily accepted by the film's viewers. The apotheosis of motherhood, the elevation of it to its largest dimensions, results in a suprapatriotism. . . . There was no need for Indira Gandhi to draw conscious attention to the parallels—the mythic resources of such symbolic transformation already existed. Subaltern peasant and elite leader are united by class-transcendent patriotism and motherhood." The other existing representation of woman as a source of power that Indira Gandhi utilized was that of the goddess. In Indian religion and mythology, female power is vested in Shakti and her various embodiments, such as Durga or Kali. Drawing parallels to such goddesses achieved the same results as did equating herself with the nation. Furthermore, this kind of representation allowed female authority to display certain "male" aggressive characteristics, and "this meant that the recourse to military force did not have to be occluded in Indira's projection of her personality."[36]

Just as Indira Gandhi's representation was readily accepted by an audience that had watched *Mother India*, Deepika Chikhalia's representation as Sita was accepted by the millions of TV viewers who had actually watched the actress represent the goddess. Nevertheless, their ways of using images were not entirely similar. Gandhi used Durga and Kali, goddesses who in their own right symbolize power, to represent the forceful side of her personality. Chikhalia used Sita, a god's wife who symbolizes virtue and acquiescence, to disguise the concept of woman seeking power. Sita represents not the ruler but the ruled, the underclass women who must be won over in the elections. It was Sita's function as role model and as symbol of virtue that enabled Chikhalia's representation to be accepted, regardless of the dissimilarity between the symbol and the politician behind it. But in the need for symbols to represent the specific woman, both Gandhi's and Chikhalia's cases show how different these specific women are from the women they seek to represent. Sunder Rajan puts it well: "Women leaders' sharp disjunction from the collectivity of the women of their nation, in terms of both status and solidarity, highlights their unrepresentativeness. The divorce must be viewed, further, in the context of the overall inconspicuousness of women in political activity precisely in those countries that have been led by women."[37]

Where political activity by women in general has been inconspicuous in India, social movements and activity have been quite consistent. Leslie Calman in

Toward Empowerment: Women and Movement Politics in India has identified the women's movement in India as one that may have political goals—trying to empower women economically and socially to participate in a democracy—but has not sought to achieve these goals through political parties or government. I draw upon this when I identify the advances made by the women's movement as the result of a social rather than a political agenda. The present-day women's movement has been built upon and expanded its origins in the nationalist era. Calman describes the movement as extremely inclusive: "Its structure is highly decentralized. The movement is composed of uncountable organizations in both cities and rural areas; it claims participants who are wealthy, who are middle class, who are poor; who are communist, socialist, or resolutely non-ideological; who are members of parties or who hold political parties in contempt as elitist, opportunist or corrupt."[38] In other words, in opposition to women in political authority who often draw upon differences in class, the women's movement seeks to erase class as well as gender differences.

Since the representation of the traditional Indian woman is continually reinforced on the basis of class differences, gender and class inequities become a single issue. Calman divides the movement into two wings based on their ideological and organizational differences. "One, which is largely urban-based, focuses on issues of rights and equality; the other, with both urban and rural components, emphasizes empowerment and liberation." More important is their common goal: "The two wings of the movement share a desire to transform the consciousness of women and men, first to understand that women in contemporary India occupy an inferior position relative to men economically, socially and politically, and then to realize that this position is unjust, unacceptable, and alterable."[39] Thus, despite the political expediency of symbols that women leaders use, there is the inherent danger that these symbolic representations will undermine the status of modern Indian women and counteract the efforts of the women's movement. Displayed through media such as film and TV and carried over to political campaigning, they simply continue to legitimize age-old perceptions of women.

The women's movement too, however, has had quite a substantial effect on women in society, and in turn on film and TV. The independent young woman, gaining respect as an individual without being an appendage, is no longer an oddity, and in popular media we see reflections of that change. Earlier film heroines were generally modeled after the *pativrata* ideal: However strong the character, her identity gained validity through submission to her husband, family, and community. Women who sought pleasure and fulfillment for themselves were usually the vamps. But over the years films have gradually begun to show self-determined, individualistic heroines who are not vamps. In *Seeta Aur Geeta*, a movie from the 1970s about twins separated in childhood, Seeta is a Sita-type character, whereas Geeta, who is full of high jinks and ambition, is shown to be much more interesting. Nevertheless, as Geeta falls in love, she becomes more like Seeta, changing from pants to saris and maturing into the ideal. In numerous movies of the 1980s, however, this other kind of woman does not necessarily change into something else; she gets to keep her own identity. "Suddenly, though not altogether unexpectedly, a new formula has emerged from the fantasy lab of the Hindi film industry: the strong, self-willed, often revengeful Indian woman who knows her mind and won't tolerate injustice."[40] In recent movies such as *Zakhmi Aurat* (Wounded woman) and *Khoon Bhari Maang* (literally, forehead full of blood, referring to the vermilion that married women wear in the parting of their hair), among others, the women are often on the wrong side of the law (though apparently for the right, justifiable reasons). Moral questions aside, this change allows women to be presented as multifaceted; they can be reactionary, vocal, and still "good." One of the best known of Indian actresses, Rekha, says, "Times have changed, thank God. For the first time the heroine has emerged as a strong, tough woman willing to fight back, reflecting the Indian woman of today."[41] Even so, times have not changed so much that the heroines of the current movies are acceptable as representative of the ideal Indian woman. Regardless of what the "real" Indian woman of today may be, the symbolic representation of the ideal remains the traditional one, which still emerges in a good number of films and TV programs.

The effect of the women's movement shows, however, in the debate that often takes place regarding the value and the implication of the symbol itself. A 1988 film, *Pati Parameshwar* (Husband the supreme god), had a ban placed on it by the Central Board of Film Certification (CBFC) for glorifying submissiveness in women. The Bombay High Court revoked the ban, but the CBFC obtained a stay in order to take its case to the Supreme Court. The issue here is as much the depiction of women as *pativratas* as it is censorship and freedom of expression. The film is about the devoted wife of an adulterous husband; when he is hurt, she takes him to his mistress and panders to them until he finally repents and returns to her welcoming arms. The story runs afoul of a CBFC guideline that "empowers the censors to ensure that visuals or words depicting women in ignoble servility to man or glorifying such servility as a praiseworthy quality, are not presented."[42] Whereas proponents of the movie's message see it as glorifying Indian women, others condemn it for perpetuating undesirable ideas.

What is apparent from this debate, and the issues I have discussed, is that a role model such as Sita cannot be dethroned. Even if the class structure that enables a few women to achieve power and position and masses of others to be dominated were to become nonexistent, the power of myth would continue to exert its hold on the Indian consciousness. The mythology of the good wife tells us that domestic and social harmony has always been possible through this ideal woman, and even that Indian culture and tradition have been preserved through her. Who would dare displace such a figure? Deepika Chikhalia's usage of Sita is understandable when we consider the harsh consequences modern Indian women often face in rejecting the Sita-Savitri construct. A woman's achievements outside the domestic sphere are often minimized, and even considered failures, if she falls short in her role as wife, daughter-in-law, homemaker. Aware of this criticism, modern Indian women quite often overcompensate in the attempt to fulfill both their expected and their chosen roles. This sensitivity to social expectations results in the perpetuation of the traditional role model.

No simple answers or solutions can be offered here. If the symbol cannot be removed, however, perhaps the symbolic woman needs to be recast. Apart from their efforts to change public perception of what women should be as based on ancient texts, the women's movement may need to reinterpret the texts themselves. If the Sita-Savitri construct is based on these fabled women's association and relationship with their husbands, their history needs to be told from a feminine perspective, as independent characters in their own lives. The Indian epics and texts have always been remarkable for the fact that a single text can be a source of two vastly oppositional points of view, depending on what one wishes to believe and quote. Sita and Savitri have reached us as *pativratas* because their stories have been selectively told. Histories of Savitri's life have attempted to show the unconventionality of her choice of husband, and her remarkable courage in persisting in her discourse with the god of death to reclaim her husband from the dead. Her story shows a woman rescuing a man not from danger but from death itself, yet she is more extraordinary for the control she has of her own life. A history of Sita's life will show us a woman who walked out of a safe home to face the dangers of the world, a woman who had to overcome sexual harassment, and a woman who was a single mother—all conditions familiar to many women today. Though Sita is a member of the upper class, she, like women today, realizes that class does not afford women much protection. Even as a queen, she is powerless to prevent her own exile as a result of social speculation regarding her chastity. Nevertheless, she has enough strength to bring up her sons without her husband. In short, Sita is a wonderful ideal not because of who she is married to but because of who she is.

The problem that women today have had with Sita as traditional role model has always been that she is cast as a goddess, a heroine-victim, or a *pativrata*. In these symbolic forms she has served male rather than female history. It is not she but her representation in Indian literary, oral, and now audio-visual and political tradition that has been counterproductive to the women's movement and the achievements of contemporary Indian women. If Sita were recast as woman, perhaps the ideal Indian woman and the modern one would not need to be at such odds.

NOTES

1. I have used the Sanskritized spelling instead of the Hindi "Ramayan," though the TV series title is spelled both ways by different writers.

2. For a discussion on the variety of tellings throughout India, see Paula Richman's "Introduction: The Diversity of the Ramayana Tradition," in *Many Ramayanas* (Berkeley: University of California Press, 1991) 3–21.

3. Viewership polls and surveys show the *Mahabharata* and the *Ramayana* to be first and second among the ten most watched shows on Indian television, according to Prabha Krishnan and Anita Dighe, *Affirmation and Denial: Construction of Femininity on Indian Television* (New Delhi: Sage, 1990), 120.

4. Priya Adarkar, "Epic Spin-offs," *India Today* 13 (15 July 1988): 72–73.

5. Philip Lutgendorf, "Ramayan: The Video," *Drama Review* 34.2 (1990): 136, 128.

6. "Election Newsbriefs," *India Today* 16 (31 May 1991): 77.

7. Richman, "Introduction," 14–15.

8. Adarkar, "Epic Spin-offs," 73; Krishnan and Dighe, *Affirmation and Denial*, 121.

9. Rajeswari Sunder Rajan, *Real and Imagined Women: Gender, Culture, and Postcolonialism* (London: Routledge, 1993), 130.

10. Sita was supposed to be literally the child of the earth, as she was said to have been found by King Janaka while he was plowing.

11. The twins are not aware that Rama and Sita are their parents; they know their mother by one of her other names—Vaidehi (daughter of the king of Videha).

12. Lutgendorf, "Ramayan," 143, 145.

13. Quoted in "Heavenly Harvest," *India Today* 13 (15 September 1988): 88. Tulsi Das was a sixteenth-century saint-poet whose *Ramcharitmanas*, written in Hindi, with its combination of scripture and philosophy became a definitive and accessible retelling of the *Ramayana*.

14. "The Second Coming," *India Today* 13 (31 August 1988): 81.

15. Raymond Williams, *Television: Technology and Cultural Form* (New York: Schocken, 1975), 129, 131.

16. Joseph Turow, "Pressure Groups and Television Entertainment," in *Interpreting Television: Current Research Perspectives*, ed. Willard D. Rowland Jr. and Bruce Watkins (Beverly Hills, Calif.: Sage, 1984), 151.

17. David Morley, *Television Audiences and Cultural Studies* (London: Routledge, 1992), 213.

18. "Heavenly Harvest," 88: Lutgendorf, "Ramayan," 161–62.

19. "A Clear Shift," *India Today* 13 (15 July 1988): 16–20; "Heavenly Harvest," 89.

20. "Communal Time-Bomb," *India Today* 14 (15 December 1989): 81.

21. Partha Chatterjee, *The Nation and Its Fragments: Colonial and Postcolonial Histories* (Princeton, N.J.: Princeton University Press, 1993).

22. "A Militant Platform," India Today 16 (31 March 1991): 19–20.

23. Joanna Liddle and Rama Joshi, Daughters of Independence (New Delhi: Zed, 1986), 200.

24. Vanaja Dhruvarajan, Hindu Women and the Power of Ideology (Granby, Mass.: Bergin & Garvey, 1989), 26–27.

25. Prabhati Mukherjee, Hindu Women Normative Models (New Delhi: Orient Longman, 1978), 57, 17. Ahalya is the wife of the sage Gautama. Indra, the king of the gods, comes to her in the guise of her husband and turns her to stone. She is released by Rama's touch. Draupadi is the common wife of the five Pandavas of the epic Mahabharata. Tara is the wife of Sugreeva, the king of the simian race in the Ramayana. Kunti is the mother of the five Pandavas. Mandodari is Ravana's wife. Savitri is the wife of Satyabaan, whom she marries knowing he is destined to die in a year. She follows the god of death and persuades him to return her husband. Radha is Lord Krishna's consort.

26. Krishnan and Dighe, Affirmation and Denial, 104.

27. René Girard, Things Hidden since the Foundation of the World, trans. Stephen Bann and Michael Metteer (Stanford, Calif.: Stanford University Press, 1987), 24.

28. Ibid., 27.

29. Ibid., 24.

30. René Girard, "To Double Business Bound": Essays on Literature, Mimesis, and Anthropology (Baltimore, Md.: Johns Hopkins University Press, 1978), 182–83.

31. Sunder Rajan does an in-depth analysis of public discussion and representation of recent satis in her chapters "The Subject of Sati" and "Representing Sati," in Real and Imagined Women, 15–39, 40–63.

32. Ernest Gellner, Nations and Nationalism (Oxford: Basil Blackwell, 1983), 9–10.

33. Kumkum Sangari and Sudesh Vaid, "Recasting Women: An Introduction," in Recasting Women: Essays in Indian Colonial History, ed. Sangari and Vaid (New Brunswick, N.J.: Rutgers University Press, 1990), 10.

34. Partha Chatterjee, "The Nationalist Resolution of the Women's Question," in Sangari and Vaid, Recasting Women, 248–49.

35. Sunder Rajan, Real and Imagined Women, 105, 109. Bharat is the Indian name for India (from the legendary King Bharat); hence, Bharatmata literally means "Mother India."

36. Ibid., 110, 114.

37. Ibid., 116.

38. Leslie J. Calman, Toward Empowerment: Women and Movement Politics in India (Boulder, Colo.: Westview, 1992), 11.

39. Ibid., 12.

40. "Women Strike Back," India Today 13 (15 July 1988): 80.

41. Quoted in ibid.

42. "The Image of Women," India Today 13 (15 August 1988): 108.

PART IV

LITERARY CRITICISM

CHAPTER 13

Replacing the Colonial Gaze

Gender as Strategy in Salman Rushdie's Fiction

Sukeshi Kamra

The fictional author in *Shame*, in one of the many metatextual moments in the novel, asserts somewhat disingenuously that his "fairy tale" has escaped his control, that the women have taken over what was, he believed, a story primarily about males:

> I had thought, before I began, that what I had on my hands was an almost excessively masculine tale, a saga of sexual rivalry, ambition, power, patronage, betrayal, death, revenge. But the women seem to have taken over; they marched in from the peripheries of the story to demand the inclusion of their own tragedies, histories and comedies, obliging me to couch my narrative in all manner of sinuous complexities, to see my plot refracted, so to speak, through the prisms of its reverse and "female" side. It occurs to me that the women knew precisely what they were up to—that their stories explain, and even subsume the men's.[1]

This crafted "unconscious slippage" into the female realm in an equally crafted metatextual moment is a metonymic expression of Rushdie's almost obsessive concern with the enclosed feminine space so eloquently troped in the *zenana* (harem) of subcontinental Muslim culture. The obsession, more specifically, is with giving voice to the suppressed history of women of the sub-continent and hence with dramatizing the challenge such recuperation poses to an entrenched, male symbolic order. Good intentions and isolated feminist passages aside,

Rushdie's fiction is problematically riddled with familiar patriarchal modes of containment such as fetishism, signaling more clearly than ever the absence of the very subject the texts are largely about, as the fictional author of Shame makes a point of pointing out. One might very well ask of Midnight's Children, Shame, and Haroun and the Sea of Stories, "Is there a female in these texts?"[2]

Arun Mukherjee is one of the few readers of Rushdie's novels to have raised the issue of his seemingly unselfconscious reflection of patriarchal attitudes toward the female. Responding to Midnight's Children, she says: "Although I enjoyed and agreed with much of Rushdie's presentation and assessment, the narrative, despite its subversive intent, remains mired in patriarchy. Why, for example, use female genitalia to describe Sanjay? I didn't find it funny. Nor did I find Saleem's inability to have sexual intercourse with Padma funny because of the derogatory terms that are used to describe female genitalia."[3] Unfortunately, Mukherjee chooses to gloss the matter rather than make it a mainstay of her reading of the text. For there is much more to be said about the matter—the matter, broadly defined, being the politics of gendered space and, more narrowly defined, the tactical splitting of the female and the feminine in Rushdie's novels. Much has been written about the difference, or identity, of the terms "feminine" and "female." For the purposes of this essay, I am adopting the most received understanding of these terms, as described by Toril Moi: "'feminine' (and 'masculine') . . . represent social constructs [patterns of sexuality and behaviour imposed by cultural and social norms]"; "female" and "male" are reserved for "the purely biological aspects of sexual difference."[4]

Since I believe, along with many others, that Rushdie's writings owe much to his obsession with colonial paradigms and practices, I place his inscription of the female specifically within the context of his project of recuperation, which, as Rushdie himself points out, involves reiteration and parody of colonial tropes, among other practices.[5] Even a cursory glance at Orientalist practices, as described by Edward Said, Homi Bhabha, and Lisa Lowe, suffices to provide a rationale for Rushdie's very specific use of the categories of feminine and female, a use that otherwise (as attested by Mukerjee's article) evades comprehension except as a slippage.[6] Approaching the Rushdie novel as a postcolonial response to colonial practices requires that we ask certain questions of his texts: Do they locate the postcolonial world in gender, as do colonial texts, identifying political with sexual? Does Rushdie engender the self as exiled writer, as was the practice of Orientalist texts? Is his splitting of the feminine and female related to the propensity of Orientalists to locate subjectivity in the male and the neutral space associated with the male? And finally, is his reiterative and parodic practice conducive to a reclaiming of the highly fetishistic construction of the Oriental female/nation in colonial writing, particularly that of the eighteenth, nineteenth, and early twentieth centuries? or does it simply replace one kind of colonialism with another, as Feroze Jussawalla appears to believe?[7]

Midnight's Children, Shame, and *Haroun and the Sea of Stories* can be read as texts that inherently challenge the colonial paradigms of sexual and political control by locating the inscribing self in the feminine. That is to say, although the narratives repeat the trope of desire, they require both a transformation of the relations between the inscriber and the inscribed (which is also the object of desire) and a different inscription of the self. The fictional writer/storyteller in these texts appropriates and deliberately signals his appropriation of the structural space traditionally associated with the female. Typically, it is through this appropriated space and discourse that the textualized writer locates his relation with his fictional audience and with the world of which he writes (the "Orient"). While the feminine but biologically male writer takes center stage, the female, although placed in a historical, political, and cultural milieu, is often emblematized far beyond the requirements of the narrative. She is thus readable as a significant expression of the author's essentialist tendencies, who appears through his fictional authors to be identifying, and sometimes condemning, the female (and nation) as the space of castration, violence, shame. Emptied of one set of constructs, the female of a previously colonized and now postcolonial nation is, then, imbued with other sets. In sum, the representation of women remains a problematic one.

In discussing *Midnight's Children, Shame,* and *Haroun and the Sea of Stories,* I look at the narrator's creation of a gendered space for himself and for character in *Haroun;*[8] at the ramifications of such a deliberate adoption of what amounts to feminine *ecriture;* and briefly at the somewhat fetishistic inscription of the female by the narrators. I hope, in the process, to discover the rationale behind the tactical splitting of the feminine from the female that seems to occur in these texts.

Discussions of the nature of British colonial discourse by Edward Said, Homi Bhabha, and Lisa Lowe (who also speaks of French colonial discourse) suggest agreement on one crucial aspect of it: the association of the political with gender—the Occident with the male and the Orient with the female. Of all three, it is Lowe who addresses the issue most directly. Of the intersection of gender and the geopolitical in the textualizing of the East in Flaubert's *Salammbo,* for instance, Lowe writes in ways that underline the identification of gender with political entity, the fetishistic construction of the Oriental female and hence, by extension, of the Orient itself. The figure of Salammbo, she writes, "is a complicated representation of intersecting inscriptions: she is a forbidden object of desire as well as a material object of exchange . . . the infinite beauty of *la nature,* and the sacred, violent oriental world. She is a fiction of European man's

Other, represented as the seducer and recipient of . . . desire." The construction of subjectivity through a reification of a gendered difference that builds on geography thus places the Occident/male in the position of power, the centrality that is unaware of its own nonneutrality. Not surprisingly, English literary texts staging "encounters" between the Occident and Orient (such as Percy Bysshe Shelley's *Prometheus Unbound* and Lady Morgan's *Missionary*) engender the two in terms that lend themselves all too easily to Lowe's analysis. The Occident's engendered gaze is best expressed, however, in the travelogues, histories, archeological treatises, and cultural and religious accounts of English Orientalists such as Thomas Maurice and William Jones, since they are, textually speaking, the most immediate examples of the Occident as inscribing self.[9]

Rushdie's novels make the inscribing self (always Occidental in Orientalist texts) the subject to a lesser or greater extent, but with a difference: The inscribing self is only partially Occidental in *Midnight's Children*.[10] The fictional male writers in these texts position themselves or are positioned by the author in the ideological space of the feminine. The effect this has is one of parody of the inscribing male/Occidental self, particularly in its assumption of neutrality and centrality. For the feminine is associated with marginality, self-reflexivity, and especially a knowledge of the ideological nature of positions. Perhaps even more important is the fact that the feminine adopted is culturally specific to the Middle East. The Orientalist paradigm is thus doubly inverted: Not only is the feminine used to place the self, but the feminine is already an alterity (from the Occidental point of view).

The double alterity of the inscribing self is best expressed in *Midnight's Children*, where the fictional author, Saleem Sinai, sets the tone of his narrative by defining himself in terms of Scheherazade: "I must work fast, faster than Scherezade, if I am to end up meaning—yes, meaning—something" (4). Identifying himself with Scheherazade specifically in terms of activity masks a much more serious identification taking place, one that draws on the politics of gender implied in the frame narrative of *The Thousand and One Nights*. In brief, Scheherazade's act of storytelling and her offering herself as the next victim of the sultan's misogyny speak of the victimization of the female in and by the male symbolic order, her political disempowerment and dependence on the patriarchal identity of female with sexual/textual power for survival.[11] Thus, by drawing on the activity of Scheherazade to speak of his own activity, Saleem not only underlines his own alterity but points to his occupation of the marginalized world of the feminine, a world in which power is gained only through sexual/textual performance. (By the way, Saleem is employed as a chutney maker, an activity traditionally associated with the female world, the *zenana*, in the Hindustan Rushdie writes of.)

It is as a category of disenfranchisement, then, that Saleem Sinai evokes Scheherazade, throughout his utterance claiming disenfranchisement despite his politically enfranchised position as the inscribing male. His insistence on victimization, marginalization, alterity, all of which do indeed find a parallel in the frame narrative of *The Thousand and One Nights*, acts to locate the feminine as a space that best expresses his, the postcolonial writer's, subjectivity.

If it is true, however, that the feminine, specifically in the instance of Scheherazade, does express an indirect access to power, then the feminine as it is used by Saleem expresses a disenfranchisement (deliberately so) even more severe. In other words, Saleem robs the feminine, as it is expressed in Scheherazade's situation, of its indirect access to power through sexual/textual cunning by problematizing the issue of textual/sexual power. Hence, much of his utterance focuses on his inability to keep Padma, his sexual/textual audience, enthralled. Her response to the textual event she has been waiting impatiently to hear of—Saleem's birth—and its conflation with the sexual consummation she awaits equally eagerly is recorded by Saleem in terms that underline this failure at a closet empowerment: "Distressed, perhaps, by the futility of her midnight attempts at resuscitating my 'other pencil,' the useless cucumber hidden in my pants, she has been waxing grouchy. And then there was her ill-tempered reaction, last night, to my revelation of the secrets of my birth" (*Midnight's Children*, 141). Thus, whereas Scheherazade succeeds in gaining a measure of enfranchisement through a clever use of sexual/textual power—she becomes the sultan's wife—Saleem does not gain through these means or any other. He disappears into the closet, hinting at an untimely demise and the "threat" of marriage to the illiterate, working-class Padma. In sum, the feminine is evoked as a place insufficient to express the castration that Saleem wishes to convey, and Scheherazade serves the dual function of locating the male inscriber in the marginal position of the feminine in a patriarchal society and impressing on us his occupation of an even more marginalized space than that occupied by her in *The Thousand and One Nights*.

This impotent, postcolonial male writer who occupies the space of feminine, without agency except partially in his closet storytelling, can be read as an authorial attempt at parodying lionized Orientalists such as William Jones and Thomas Maurice. According to Said, to them can be traced the English claim of knowing the Orient better than anyone else, including the Orientals themselves.[12] Far from displaying their confidence, "knowledge," and hence mastery in writing of the Orient, Saleem Sinai mainfests an overwhelming sense of victimization.

Haroun and the Sea of Stories expresses a similar appropriation of the feminine, and to the same end. Once again, Scheherazade seems to be the category evoked to describe the political and personal state of Rashid, the storyteller of a post-colonial India. Rashid claims the kind of compulsion to narrate that Scheherazade is under: "[It's] the only work I know," he says "piteously" to Haroun after Soraya leaves, citing his occupation as the root cause of her dissatisfaction. Like her, his life and livelihood are dependent on keeping a fickle audience, the Indian public, fascinated. The political/textual disempowerment is similarly paralleled by a sexual/personal one. Rashid's manhood is questioned in Soraya's only utterance in the text, the letter she leaves behind. "You are only interested in pleasure," she writes, "but a *proper* man would know that life is a serious business" (*Haroun*, 22; emphasis added).

Thus, if the problem posed by the modern Orientalist is the fact that he remained "for so long unmarked" and refused to become a "racialized category," then through Saleem and Rashid, the postcolonial inscribers, Rushdie marks the hitherto neutral in terms of both gender and race.[13] Perhaps one could say, somewhat tongue in cheek, that his has been a castration of his predecessors, the Orientalists, in texts concerned either with the shift from the colonial to the postcolonial phase of the subcontinent's history or with the postcolonial phase itself. What is worth noting here, then, is not so much Rushdie's (conscious) participation in the recognized ritual of speaking/writing back to the center or the means he chooses—parody—but the specific inversions (of masculine Orientalist into subcontinental feminized male inscriber) and the tactical splitting he employs to accomplish it.[14]

Figuring the inscribing self as an alterity—feminine and Oriental—not only serves the purpose of reflecting ironically on the specific politics of the formation of subjectivity in Orientalist texts; it also serves another, equally significant purpose that emerges in the different textualizing of the relations between the inscriber and inscribed. In both *Midnight's Children* and *Haroun*, the heterosexual paradigm is replaced with a female homosexual one, with the postcolonial writer representing himself as the victim/lover of the postcolonial nation, embodied and engendered as the victimizing, tyrannical, female object of desire. Hence, Saleem Sinai, disingenuous yet again, records when he is about three-quarters of the way through his autobiography that the predominant motif of his life is his victimization at the hands of women he identifies with the postcolonial nation: "From ayah to Widow. I've been the sort of person *to whom things have been done*" (*Midnight's Children*, 285). "Women have made me," he says to Padma, "and also unmade me. From Reverend Mother to the Widow, and even beyond. I have been at the mercy of the so-called (erroneously, in my opinion!) gentler sex. It is, perhaps, a matter of connection: is not Mother India, Bharat-Mata, commonly thought of as female? And, as you know, there's no escape from her" (*Midnight's Children*, 483).

The continuity expressed by *Haroun and the Sea of Stories* in its use of the feminine is remarkable. The narrator suggests that the storyteller, Rashid, is the victim of three female forces, all of whom he desires and all of whom castrate him. These forces are the moon Kahani (which is not overtly identified as a female space), his wife, Soraya, and (a thinly disguised) Mother India. Not surprisingly, the three female forces combined are responsible for the disaster with which the mythic text opens: The nation is inhospitable, forcing the storyteller to tell lies so that corrupt Indian politicians may be elected; the wife leaves; and Kahani compels the storyteller to tell stories in a hostile environment.

The writing or speaking of one's story, of the kind described in *Midnight's Children* and written in *Haroun*, is in effect the kind of feminine *ecriture* that has literary echoes in the stories of Scheherazade and Philomel: the inscribing of one's violation in story or tapestry. It is a story of castration at the hands of an inimical female/nation. The Joycean echoes are almost too loud. The same sadomasochism defines the fledgling attempts of the national writer in his attempts to formulate his and his nation's subjectivity. The story is written in *Haroun and the Sea of Stories* not by the author himself but by an omniscient narrator whose identification with and sympathy for the storyteller is writ large in the text. The story told is of the victimization of the male storyteller (whose name is ironic, considering that Haroun al Rashid is associated inextricably with enfranchisement) and his reenfranchisement through the agency of his son.

This kind of story—one that acts as a testimonial to one's victimization—is also remarkably in the vein of feminine *ecriture* associated specifically with postcolonial and Third World nations. Chandra Mohanty speaks of the predominance of the testimonial and its replacing of the autobiography as the genre within which the formation of national and individual subjectivities can occur in the writings of women from or of such nations. Mohanty writes that testimonials "do not focus on the unfolding of a singular woman's consciousness (in the hegemonic tradition of European modernist autobiography); rather, their strategy is to speak from within a collective, as participants in revolutionary struggles, and to speak with the express purpose of bringing about social and political change."[15] I find it interesting that this is the kind of writing Saleem claims for his oral narrative. Early in the narrative he provides us with the raison d'être of his utterance:

> Please believe that I am falling apart. I am not speaking
> metaphorically; nor is this the opening gambit of some melo-
> dramatic, riddling, grubby appeal for pity. I mean quite simply
> that I have begun to crack all over like an old jug—that my poor
> body, singular, unlovely, buffeted by too much history, subject

> to drainage above and drainage below, mutilated by doors,
> brained by spittoons, has started coming apart at the seams. In
> short, I am literally disintegrating, slowly for the moment, al-
> though there are signs of an acceleration. I ask you only to ac-
> cept (as I have accepted) that I shall eventually crumble into
> (approximately) six hundred and thirty million particles of
> anonymous and, necessarily, oblivious dust. This is why I have
> resolved to confide in paper, before I forget. (We are a nation of
> forgetters). (*Midnight's Children*, 37)

In addition to locating an utterance of the formation of subjectivity, individual and collective, in the discourse of the testimonial, this statement speaks
of the identity of the individual and the collective (locating the latter in the former rather than vice versa). The history told is, as Saleem indicates elsewhere,
one of a concerted attempt to bring about change—change here being literally
the attempt to evade the destiny of repeating colonial practices.

The other function that the adoption of the feminine, and feminine *ecriture* in
particular, serves, then, is to signal the nationalist's writer's adoption of a space
and discourse already an alterity as a mode of inscribing subjectivity, of nation
and self. Thus, all the assumptions expressed by autobiography (a mode preferred by a number of the Occidental accounts of encounter with the Orient)
are rejected in favor of a discourse that expresses nation as a collection of discourses, a polyphony of voices. The refusal is not only of the history of the formation of subjectivity in the Occident in and through the creation of the space
of neutrality and centrality but of patriarchal modes of construction and containment, not to mention control of political and personal realms.

Rushdie's identification of the feminine, and feminine *ecriture*, with the space
of polyphony, and his serious exploration of both as the discursive context in
which the nationalist writer can begin the process of reconfiguring identity, is
most clearly expressed in *Shame*. In this novel the fictional nationalist writer is
not as obviously the subject as he is in *Midnight's Children*, and hence his "fairy
tale" (as he refers to it) is more clearly a testimonial than is Saleem's story. The
appropriation of the feminine is also more subtle. There is no Scheherazade informing a prominent storyteller, but a feminine trope informing a voice
merged with the collective sensibility: Shame, the trope evoked by political and
moral shamelessness in the newly formed postcolonial nation of Pakistan, is,
the narrative informs us, predominantly a female experience. Shamelessness,
the masculine prerogative, is the world of "sexual rivalry, ambition, power, pa-
tronage, betrayal, death, revenge" (*Shame*, 173). Shame, on the other hand, is
the female discourse that "explains" the stories of the male world. Although

the fictional author signals his participation in both—that is, in the schizo-phrenic reality that he divides along gender lines—his allegiance and identifi-cation with the female world of the *zenana* is clear.[16] For his response to a cul-ture whose identifying characteristics are its shameful, atavistic rites of pride, oppressive patriarchy, and postcolonial legacy is perforce a fairy tale that is, as he confesses, encircled by the walls of the *zenana*, a female space, and obsessed with "revealing" the shame at the heart of this culture.

Not surprisingly, the fictional storyteller's activity most closely parallels those of his female characters, all these activities being definable as attempts to leave testimonials behind. Rani, one of the central emblematic females, weaves her shame—linked with her husband's shameful sexual and political atroc-ities—into a series of shawls. Bilquis weaves hers into shrouds that double as *burkhas* (veils) and Sufiya assuages her shame in and through a ritual killing and eating of her human victims. And our fictional author weaves the oscillations of shame and shamelessness into a discursive violence that he labels, ironically enough, a "fairy tale."

When compared with that of *Midnight's Children*, feminine *ecriture* in *Shame* emerges as a more severely fragmented and violent act. Together with the ac-tivities of the emblematic female characters, it functions in a way diametrically opposed to Saleem's narrative. Whereas the latter is written or uttered in a spirit of fatigue and resignation at the pernicious hold of history (of colonialism) on the newly formed nation, this testimonial speaks of the perversion of the na-tion's psyche by its patriarchal, brown-skinned white men and dramatizes the moment of revenge: shame turning into its opposite, so violently dramatized in the figure of Sufiya Zenobia, who metamorphoses into a beast and adopts cannibalism as an act most befitting the shameless nation.

What then, it might be asked, is the role played by the female in the Rushdie novel? If, as I have attempted to argue, Rushdie's narrators appropriate the fem-inine to construct a female space out of which the masculine writer can speak, then the female is of necessity as marginalized and perhaps even fetishized, al-beit differently, in his texts as she is in the Orientalist text. As in the Original-ist text, the female is still an other, but the nature of the relations between self/writer and other/female are deliberately reconfigured: If heteroeroticism and male homoeroticism express the colonial paradigm, then lesbianism is the mode favored in these texts, with feminized male narrators speaking obses-sively of the insistently female world (in *Shame*, the *zenana*) and thereby under-mining the male symbolic order so much in evidence in Orientalist texts. Woman remains, that is, the object of desire—of Rushdie's narrators' liter-ary/sexual desires. The evidence lies in the predominantly emblematic nature of the women in the novels, including the ghostly figure of Scheherazade. Thus, while it is true that they are invested with historical and cultural dimensions, it is also true that they are overdetermined in a way the males are not.

Probably the most startlingly overdetermined female figures are to be found in *Shame*, where the narrator creates the symbolic subtext of shame through weaving female, violence, and shame together. Concluding the autobiographical statement on the predominantly female nature of his story,[17] the fictional author speaks in general terms of this intersection of tropes: "I hope that it goes without saying that not all women are crushed by any system, no matter how oppressive. It is commonly and, I believe, accurately said of Pakistan that her women are much more impressive than her men . . . their chains, nevertheless, are no fictions. They exist. And they are getting heavier. *If you hold down one thing you hold down the adjoining.* In the end, though, it all blows up into your face" (*Shame*, 173). The three major female figures in the text are an expression of the culture of shame and are reduced to metaphor, weaving their shawls and shrouds, turning cannibalistic, or choosing suicide as an option to participating in a culture of shamelessness as they do. To put it in Gayatri Spivak's terms, the women in *Shame* "seem powerful only as monsters, of one sort or another."[18] (One could also speak of their sexual overdetermination, a fact that leads Aijaz Ahmad to conclude, rightly, that "the typologies within which Rushdie encloses the whole range of woman's experience" in *Shame* are misogynist in nature.)[19]

Padma, in *Midnight's Children*, is similarly emblematized by Saleem Sinai. The metaphoric link that exists between Padma and the political state, the nation, has been pointed out by Nancy Batty.[20] Padma is explicitly linked with the Widow, herself the embodiment of the political state, which Saleem Sinai insists has reduced him to the textual/sexual ineffectiveness that defines him at the moment of his utterance. She is also represented almost always in terms other than herself, by references to the goddess Durga, by etymological talk of her name, which makes her the "dung goddess" and so on.[21] And in the final analysis, her story is virtually absent. Once again, woman is represented as the object of contemplation rather than of action. She is the receptacle of male paranoia and impotence (which she settles for over a life without Saleem Sinai) and is yet again the listener, not the speaker. The political state/female thus becomes an extended metaphor within which the author can locate his symbolic utterance.

Finally, the marginalization of the female is expressed in its most pristine form in *Haroun and the Sea of Stories*. The structurally central figure, Soraya, is denied voice, and her story—very briefly hinted at in the note she leaves her husband—remains untold. She returns only at the very end, labeling her active pursuit to find a more satisfying relationship a mistake—"I know that I made a mistake. I went; I don't deny. I went, but now, if you want, then I am back" (*Haroun*, 210)—and ready to participate once again in a never ending deferral of desire. This ending of restored harmony in reality only validates the feminized male storyteller's refusal to admit the validity of female desire. Similarly, the moon, Kahani, is the passive space over which the almost entirely male cities of Gup and Chup fight for control.

In the final analysis, then, Rushdie's texts, like Orientalist texts before them, prove the assertion of many feminists that woman does not exist except by negation and resistance of patriarchal naming. For if the feminine, already a patriarchal construct, is appropriated to express the male postcolonial writer's subjectivity, and if the body of the female is more expressive of the male gaze than of her own reality and acts as the positive repository of the author's sexual and political anxieties as well as of his own horrific sensibility, how are Rushdie's texts different from the scores of texts that violated both nation/Orient and Oriental female?

NOTES

1. Salman Rushdie, *Shame* (London: Picador, 1984), 173 (hereafter cited in the text by page number).

2. Salman Rushdie, *Midnight's Children* (New York: Avon, 1981), and *Haroun and the Sea of Stories* (London: Granta, 1990); page numbers in the text cite these editions. David Brooks's 1984 conversation with Salman Rushdie is important to a study of the representation of the female in the latter's novels. Rushdie, without irony, categorizes himself as a writer who can identify with woman as a dispossessed and victimized category: "You see, one of the things I have discovered is that migration has a kind of suppressed history, somewhat like the way in which women have been erased from history" (Brooks, "An Interview with Salman Rushdie," *Helix* 19 [1984]: 67). I argue, however, that his novels are problematic in their representation of women, a fact many readers seem to have missed. See Uma Parameswaran, "Salman Rushdie's *Shame*: An Overview of a Labyrinth," and Makarand R. Paranjape, "Inside and Outside the Whale: Politics and the New Indian English Novel," both in *The New Indian Novel in English: A Study of the 1980s*, ed. Viney Kirpal (New Delhi: Allied, 1990), 121–30 and 213–26 respectively.

3. Arun Mukherjee, "Characterization in Salman Rushdie's *Midnight's Children*: Breaking out of the Hold of Realism and Seeking the Alienation Effect," in Kirpal, *The New Indian Novel in English*, 117–18.

4. Toril Moi, *Sexual/Textual Politics: Feminist Literary Theory* (London: Methuen, 1985), 65.

5. Salman Rushdie, *Imaginary Homelands* (London: Granta, 1991), 403.

6. Homi Bhabha, "The Other Question: Difference, Discrimination, and the Discourse of Colonialism," in *Literature, Politics, and Theory*, ed. Francis Barker, Peter Hulme, Margaret Iversen, and Diana Loxley (London: Methuen, 1986), 148–72; Lisa Lowe, *Critical Terrains: French and British Romanticisms* (Ithaca, N.Y.: Cornell University Press, 1991); Edward Said, *Orientalism* (New York: Random House, 1979). I have placed these three critics in the same cat-

egory for reasons that become clear in the next section, but there are fundamental differences between their accounts of the discourse of imperialism in the French and British contexts. Bhabha and Lowe, for instance, take issue with Said's positing of the Occident and Orient, and the discursive representation of the latter by the former, in monolithic terms. Lowe writes that her project of tracing "orientalisms" is an attempt to "[resist] totalizing orientalism as a monolithic, developmental discourse that uniformly constructs the Orient as the Other of the Occident" (Critical Terrains, 4). Bhabha objects similarly to Said's locating of power exclusively in the hands of the colonizing powers: "There is always, in Said, the suggestion that colonial power and discourse [are] possessed entirely by the colonizer, which is a historical and theoretical simplification." Bhabha offers, instead, a belief that ambivalence is more than apparent in such discourse—in the form of the stereotype; ambivalence, he writes, is "one of the most significant discursive and psychical strategies of discriminatory power" ("Other Question," 25, 18).

7. Feroze Jussawalla, "Post-Joycean Sub-Joycean: The Reverses of Mr. Rushdie's Tricks in The Satanic Verses," in Kirpal, The New Indian Novel in English, 235.

8. The character Rashid, the storyteller, occupies the same space in this text, as a third-person, omniscient narrator, as do the fictional authors in the other two.

9. Lowe, Critical Terrains, 81. Sir William Jones wrote extensively on India, its mythology, laws, culture, literature, and religion and even translated a few ancient Indian texts into English. He is most remembered for his interpretation of Hindu law in a book titled Institutes of Hindu Law, or the Ordinances of Menu, according to the Gloss of Culluca, Comprising the Indian System of Duties, Religious and Civil (London, 1796). He is recorded as having said that it was his ambition "to know India better than any other European ever knew it" (Said, Orientalism 78). This statement locates India as the passive object of desire (which Lowe says is typical of the Orient in Flaubert's novels) and the Orientalist as the knower. Thomas Maurice also wrote a very influential text, The History of Hindostan, Its Arts and Its Sciences as Connected with the History of the Other Great Empires of Asia during the Most Ancient Periods of the World with Numerous Illustrative Engravings. 2d ed., 2 vols. (London, 1820).

10. Saleem (see Midnight's Children, 117–18) is genetically linked with the Angrez, being the illegitimate son of Wee Willie Winkie, whose wife, Vanita, was seduced by the Britisher, Mr. Methwold.

11. Scheherazade must keep the king satisfied both textually and sexually: in the epilogue we are told that "during this time Scheherazade had borne King Shahriyar three sons" (Tales from the Thousand and One Nights, trans. N. J. Dawood [London: Penguin, 1973], 405).

12. Said, Orientalism, 78.

13. Elizabeth Weed, introduction to Coming To Terms: Feminism, Theory, Politics, ed. Weed (New York: Routledge, 1989), xxxi, describing the problems posed by the patriarchal West to the feminist movement and feminist interests, writes, "The problem with Man is that it remained for so long an unmarked term; the problem with whiteness, as Hazel Carby has said, is that it still refuses to become a racialized category." I am of course applying these terms in a different context to the nature of the modern Orientalist who claims the space of the neutral and universal in his interaction with and writing of the Other.

14. Diana Brydon and Helen Tiffin, in Decolonizing Fictions (Sydney: Dangaroo Press, 1993), 89, point out that "the relation of the postcolonial text to its thematic ancestors is often parodic." They are speaking of novels such as Jean Rhys's Wide Sargasso Sea. I have not come across

articles suggesting that parody is employed in postcolonial texts to undermine the figures crucial to the process of Orientalism (understood here as a set of discursive practices): the Orientalists.

15. Chandra T. Mohanty, "Cartographies of Struggle," in *Third World Women and the Politics of Feminism*, ed. Chandra T. Mohanty and Lourdes Torres (Bloomington: Indiana University Press, 1991) 37.

16. So, for instance, he responds to the moral outrages within the Pakistani community in London, documented in newspapers, with a sympathy for the victimizers that arises from a sense of a shared sensibility: "The story appalled me when I heard it, appalled me in a fairly obvious way. . . . But even more appalling was my realization that, like the interviewed friends etc., I, too, found myself understanding the killer. The news did not seem alien to me." The story he is referring to, he says earlier in the paragraph, is of the murder of a Pakistani girl by her father "because by making love to a white boy she had brought such dishonour upon her family that only her blood could wash away the stain" (*Shame*, 115).

17. In his conversation with David Brooks ("Interviews," 58), Rushdie reveals that his intention was indeed to enter the text as himself—to "present the author in the work at the same level as the fictional material"—as a way of indicating his implication and participation in the processes of which he speaks in *Shame*: "To put yourself into the story, or myself into the story, was a way of saying that I was only a part of the thing that I was discussing, and to explain where it was that I was coming from, where it was that my point of view emerged from, and to make myself part of the dispute, part of the debate. Because then, it seemed to me, it was legitimate to use that material in the way that everybody else would in a discussion."

18. Gayatri C. Spivak, *Outside in the Teaching Machine* (New York: Routledge, 1993), 223.

19. Aijaz Ahmad, *In Theory: Classes, Nations, Literatures* (New York: Verso, 1992), 150.

20. Nancy Batty, "The Art of Suspense: Rushdie's 1001(Mid-)Nights," *Ariel* 18.3 (1987): 49–65.

21. To provide only one example of Saleem's incantatory fetishizing of Padma: "Padma, who along with the yaksa genii, who represent the sacred treasure of the earth, and the sacred rivers, Ganga Yamuna Sarasvati, and the tree goddesses, is one of the Guardians of Life, beguiling and comforting mortal men while they pass through the dream-web of Maya; . . . Padma, the Lotus calyx, which grew out of Vishnu's navel, and from which Brahma himself was born; Padma the Source, the mother of Time!" (*Midnight's Children*, 233).

CHAPTER 14

Style Is (Not) the Woman

Sara Suleri's *Meatless Days*

Samir Dayal

There are no women in the third world.

Then, when my father's back was turned, I found myself engaged in rapid theft—for the sake of Ifat and Shahid and Tillat and all of us, I stole away a portion of that body. It was a piece of her foot I found . . . which I quickly hid inside my mouth, under my tongue. Then I and the dream dissolved, into an extremity of tenderness.

I've lived many years as an otherness machine, had more than my share of being other.
　　　　　Sara Suleri, *Meatless Days*

In an interview, Gayatri Chakravorty Spivak has replaced an old question about female identity (particularly Third World female identity)— namely "What is woman?"— with another question: "What is man that the itinerary of his desire creates such a text?" In rehabilitating the position of the questioning subject she intends to call attention to the context of phallocentrism. The question she posed originally was "Who am I as a woman?"—a question that was also about "man in terms of the text produced." But now, she says, she "thinks about the arena of practice in a somewhat broader way. It also seems to me, now, that the women who can in fact begin to engage in this particular 'winning back' of the position of the questioning subject, are in very privileged positions in the geopolis today."[1]

Sara Suleri, as a professor of English at Yale, is in such a privileged position. Her memoir's articulation of Third World subjectivity explores alternatives to both contemporary Western feminist and postcolonialist conceptualizations of the feminine subject. Suleri elaborates a phenomenological space that is a parergon, departing on the one side from metropolitan narratives of feminine subjectivity and on the other hand from Third World narratives of that subjectivity. Her emphasis on the negativity of the subject conforms to what Naomi Schor describes as the contemporary ascendancy of the detail in the context of a "larger semantic network, bounded on the one side by the *ornamental*, with its traditional connotations of effeminacy and decadence, and on the other, by the *everyday*, whose 'prosiness' is rooted in the domestic sphere presided over by women."[2] Suleri's archly elevated poetic rhetoric situates itself in the persistently prosaic detail of the everyday of women's lives in Pakistan, although perhaps things are not quite as simple as this description suggests.

Suleri's exploration of the problematics of agency gains significance by contrast with various antiessentialist approaches to the theory of identity, not only French theory of (particularly feminine) subjectivity but also North American feminist theory, including the influential work of Cherrie Moraga and Gloria Anzaldúa (who, although they work and live in the United States, would not identify themselves with mainstream American academic theory).[3] Then again, there is a "positive" approach in perspectives such as Elizabeth Fox Genovese's: She argues that in capitalist contexts, the plenum of full individuality is the (ideal) telos of feminism.[4] There are also Third World, particularly subcontinental, antiessentialist approaches to the problematic of identity. Among the most notable is the antiessentialism of the Subaltern Studies group, which, as Lisa Lowe points out, "suggests that it is possible to posit specific signifiers such as Indianness, for the purpose of disrupting discourses that exclude Indians as Other while simultaneously revealing the internal contradictions and slippages of 'Indianness' so as to ensure that the signifier *Indianness* will not be reappropriated by the very efforts to criticize its use."[5]

Of course, there are other approaches within Third World postcolonial theory, just as there are other varieties of French and North American theory. Kumkum Sangari writes of "different modes of de-essentialization which are socially and politically grounded and mediated by separate perspectives, goals, and strategies for change in other countries."[6] One can say, at any rate, that Suleri's book does not meaningfully answer to the description of "North American feminist," although she studied and now teaches and writes in the most privileged sector of the U.S. academic universe. Her perspective cannot be unproblematically assimilated to a neatly defined Third World woman's minority perspective, at least not without acknowledging the privileges accruing to such a diasporic intellectual. Her situation within the academy is a factor in Suleri's self-articulation in the book, not to mention important in understanding how her exploration suggests some possibilities for articulating for Third World and particularly postcolonial literature a poetics of agency critically aware of the problematics of class, gender, nation, race, and ethnicity.

In Suleri's *Meatless Days*, "woman" is (dis)articulated as "meatless." It is the phenomenology of this meatlessness, this silence or absence, that the "autobiographical" novel teases out primarily in the author's relationship with her mother, a white woman in Pakistan. Everything she tells us about Mair Jones is also an oblique reference to Suleri's own postcolonial and diasporic situation in the West, an inversion and displacement of her mother's own situation. In describing this pivotal relationship Suleri stages a variety of antiessentialism as a way of resisting the perpetual risk of being turned into an "otherness machine."[7] But antiessentialism itself, if it is no more than an evacuation of the subject, may run the risk precisely of constructing the postcolonial as other. Anthony Appiah's comment on the general relevance of Suleri's resistance to being turned into "an otherness-machine" for the postcolonial intellectual puts into relief the novel's significance for Postcolonial Studies, even if only by virtue of its refusal of a homogenized definition of the "Third World" text. Appiah points out that "*as* [postcolonial] intellectuals . . . we are always at risk of becoming Otherness-machines. It risks becoming our principal role. Our only distinction in the world of texts to which we are latecomers is that we can mediate it to our fellows."[8]

The enigmatic quality of Suleri's text derives from a deliberate aestheticizing and abstraction of the subject as simulacrum, even as it insists on the particularity of the quotidian. The subject's abstraction from the immediacy of the everyday is customarily marked as masculine, just as the specificity of the quotidian is marked as feminine: for instance, intellectual labor and abstract and philosophical thinking come to be defined as the upper reaches of the masculine sphere, whereas domestic labor, mothering and rearing children, keeping the home fires burning are seen as woman's work, the feminine sphere. What is more, in much nationalist discourse, Woman becomes the very custodian of the National Thing, the motherland as patriarchal construction; she is the safe repository of the future or the essence of the people, the custodian of virtue, the center and keeper of home and hearth, and the object of masculine protection. There is a crucial imbrication of discourses of gender and nation, of gendered Imaginary, with the imagining of the National Thing.

But here the autobiographer confounds simple algorithms of (imagi)nation. She luxuriates in secreting the self into indeterminacy, and into a figure of speech—into language—even as she appears to reveal it in the homely detail.

Suleri flourishes her studied rhetoric as if to mock guileless self-disclosure. It is not a desire for self-discovery that energizes the work but rather an appetite for brinkmanship and an interest in the liminal positionality that she wants to adopt as a (postcolonial or Third World) woman. Furthermore, insofar as it is a totalizing concept, the "individual" is put into question by Suleri.

Through the aestheticization of the subject, Suleri's book moves toward a re-cognition that, as Carole Pateman argues in *The Sexual Contract*, the notion of the modern individual may itself be a patriarchal category of thought.[9] Suleri's journalist father is persistently (and rather too predictably) identified with the grand patriarchal narrative upon which the national Imaginary is built, and her mother's precarious situatedness as an unwilling trace of the colonizer in post-colonial space-time becomes a displacement of that discourse of nation. Suleri refracts her own becoming within the patriarchal context of Pakistan by re-tracing her mother's self-articulation, testing the limits of autobiography not only as a writer but as a woman. Her prose style constantly strives to accommodate content and consciousness, which alone allow one to speak of the subject. But, as such, subjectivity is also attenuated. Ultimately, content and consciousness are at once familiar and other, otherness here being a function of gender, class, nationality, sensibility: Style is (not) the woman.

Suleri refuses to settle either for depersonalization (as a woman) or for monolithic and therefore limited identity, given that the limitations are artificial, manmade. The subject position is not simply to be left unoccupied but to be filled again by a woman who reconceives herself in that position through the act of self-understanding and self-exploration. The novel can be autobiographical only by staging its suspicion of its own essentialisms about identity. In this sense, at least, Suleri seems to gesture toward French (and particularly Derridean) antiessentialism, a gesture she shares with Spivak, who proposes an essentialism under erasure as doing "scrupulously" what "in the long run is not OK." Even "awareness" is not enough; for the deconstructive critic, as Spivak goes on to say, "being aware is produced as a kind of symptom, in defence against all kinds of other things."[10] If anything, Suleri's tentative indirections are less pat than Spivak's.

The autobiographical text ought not to obscure the subtext of the Muslim ritual that lends the book its title. But *Meatless Days* must also be seen as a secularist counterpoint to a masculinist narrative of the nation. In the section tellingly titled "Papa and Pakistan," Suleri writes of the coincidence that during the era in which her father, Ziauddin Ahmed, employee of the imperial government in India, "decided to become Z. A. Suleri the writer . . . some Indian Muslims in England . . . invented that new coinage, Pakistan" (110). Her journalist father puts the stamp of his influence on his newspaper. By contrast, Suleri's narrativization of her Welsh mother, transplanted to Pakistan and thus translated to a condition of migrancy, is almost recherché in its ineffabilities, which prefigure Sara's own arabesques of selfhood: "She let history seep, so that, miraculously, she had no language in which to locate its functioning but held it rather as a distracted manner sheathed about her face, a scarf" (168). Mair Jones is well aware that her Pakistani passport can never cure or obviate suspicion about her allegiances. She is more political than Sara's father, even if she does not feel it necessary to advertise the fact, like her journalistic husband.

Sara seeks an alternative to her father's masculinist rhetoric in her mother's oblique style. In attempting to disavow the masculinist narrative of nation, Suleri also distances herself from her father. Thus, she can say, "We were coming to a parting, Pakistan and I." And although this separation is less a matter of political awakening than an aesthete's escape from being closeted in her patriarchal Pakistan to diaspora in an "unreal little town" in the American Midwest, she is aware of the politics of such a migration. She recognizes that her desire to leave Pakistan will exact a price: She fears she will not be "a nation any more," that she will become a minority (123).

Suleri genders "nation" and racializes gender; but in other ways, too, she complicates the category of identity. Hers is a prose in which the autobiographical impulse is refracted through a hyperconsciousness of the migrant's dispersal, of the need for eternal self-suspicion, of the perpetual self-distancing of the subject of the autobiography, of the interrogation of the epistemology of woman. If the category of woman is constructed by a rhetoric often serving masculinist interests, Luce Irigaray observes that in the "masquerade of femininity, the woman loses herself . . . by playing upon her femininity." How then should woman pose the question of her own positionality? Irigary recommends a rejection of the discursive subordination of women and counsels that "a *disruptive excess* is possible on the feminine side."[11]

Achieving such a disruptive excess not in a carnival of possibilities but in the ascesis of identity is among Suleri's chief concerns in Meatless Days. The disarticulated woman must shed the desiccated shells she traditionally has had to inhabit. But it is never just a matter of having multiple identity possibilities; what counts is whether the possible identities are satisfactory to the person who occupies them and, moreover, in Suleri's case, whether any reification of selfhood is necessary. Suleri's book calculatedly opens with a problematization of "speaking as"—speaking as a woman, as a Pakistani, as a woman of a certain class, and now as a diasporic. The denaturalization of the category woman is everywhere explicit. This too, then, is a possible meaning of her notion that "there are no women in the third world" (20).

Pakistan is identified at the outset as a place where women are confined to the domestic sphere (also the sphere of the quotidian) and differentially (depending on ethnicity, class, proximity to the metropolis, and so on) excluded from power in the public sphere.[12] In the public sphere female subjectivity is an empty category, but in the private sphere women are enabled to enter into community *among themselves*, as a vital collectivity. As Suleri writes with fine irony, "Leaving Pakistan was . . . tantamount to giving up the company of women. . . . The concept of woman was not really part of an available vocabulary: we were too busy for that, just living, and conducting precise negotiations with what it meant to be a sister or a child or a wife or a mother or a servant" (1).

It should be clear (and the fact that Suleri makes so little of it is telling) that class, gender, nation, race, and ethnicity are crucial factors in how "busy" these women really are "just living." Most women in Pakistan clearly do not have the relative luxury implied by the freedom the Suleri women have, even in the dailiness that the author emphasizes. Most women of the lower classes are "busy" struggling on a much more basic level, trying to hold body and soul together. The Suleri women, by contrast, seem to be concerned here chiefly with the luxury of seeking intellectual self-fulfillment: "what it *meant* to be a sister or a child or a wife or a mother or a servant "(emphasis added). We note the disingenuous placement of "servant" last; the problematic sign of class is raised only to be whisked away from under our noses by sleight of hand. This is not incidental. Suleri does not actively engage the question of what socioeconomic locations allow one to contemplate the *meaning* of these categories of female positionality in a Third World, Muslim household. Attention to class, then, should be central to an understanding of the mode or style of Suleri's prose, to the very construction of *her* Third World woman. In this light, Suleri's careful insistence that there are no women in the Third World itself needs to be approached cautiously, perhaps even suspiciously. In particular, the question must be asked: Does Suleri mean this term differently with respect to Third World women of different classes, or not? Although important questions of gender, the subject's epistemological status, and the discourse of the nation, are deliberately raised in Suleri's description, the question of class is conspicuous in its underemphasis or erasure.

In the passage quoted above, Suleri notes the displacement of the concept "woman" by other concepts such as "sister," "child," "wife," "mother," and "servant." These concepts, denoting social, sexual, and familial functions, as well as (if only sotto voce) class and ethnicity, are predicated on the subordination of woman to man. As Irigaray explains, such concepts lock women in "a system of meaning which serves the auto-affection of the (masculine) subject." To interrogate femininity as a given is to see that in "a woman('s) language, the concept as such would have no place."[13] Woman has no place; the self leaves no moraine behind it. But the absence or obviation of woman as a concept is apparently what made it possible for the Suleri women to ex-ist (to occupy the category "woman" and at the same time to stand outside it) in the patriarchal community of which they were (and are) a frequently unacknowledged part.

But the question of gender is not so easily obliterated as this account may suggest. Indeed it is possible that the very insistence on the subversion of the economy of gender through the problematization of "woman" may fetishize the category. Teresa de Lauretis observes that if the subversive woman's "skepticism" (as Nietzsche suggests) "comes from her disregard for truth," it is also paradoxically the case that "woman becomes the symbol of Truth, of that which constantly eludes man and must be won, which lures and resists, mocks and seduces, and will not be captured." The place occupied by this "affirmative woman" is a "constantly shifting" locus of enunciation, a "rhetorical function and construct which—call it différance, displacement, negativity, internal exclusion or marginality—has become perhaps the foremost rhetorical trope of recent philosophical speculation."[14]

Woman as signifier has been convenient for a masculinist theoretical appropriation. Katherine Cummings notes that "theory makers as far removed as Socrates and Derrida have toyed with becoming woman and played with 'her' castration, thereby complicating their position as gendered subjects." The strategy is a matter of style; the male theorist masquerades as a woman writing, in order to appropriate some of the advantages that the cross-texture or cross-dressing allows: "To seduce like a woman while preserving one's masculinity and mastery makes explicit 'the biographical desire' that inscribes itself in dominant theory texts."[15]

Suleri's tactic as a woman is to reappropriate the gesture of this masculinist mastery and transform it by a redoubled complication of gendered positionality. She explores the problem of the female subject as a function of *style* as well as gender. If her initial given, a commonplace of cultural theory, is that the subject is historically produced and culture-specific, Suleri also dramatically articulates her tacit premise that selfhood, so far as it is a useful category, is a matter of style and rhetoric, even if it is a style that obfuscates the questions of ethnicity, class, and social power. Although she never quite loses sight of the subject's situatedness in history and culture, Suleri seems untouched by the anxiety of some diasporics to deny that they are victims of *anomie* and deracination by tracing their roots across two cultures. Suleri constitutes her subject, herself, as "stylish" excess but also as an alterity that relinquishes none of its negativity. "Style" is a figure of difference, a simulacrum or trace. Suleri's impulse is to redescribe woman as discontinuous with the received images of (Third World) woman— the meaning of her hyperbolic declaration that there are no women in the Third World. Style is the woman—but only insofar as there is one.[16]

Beginning by problematizing the concept "woman" is strategically appropriate. Suleri's overture sets up the thematics of the book's exploration of subjectivity, but it is also appropriate to a wider theoretical calculus. This "autobiography" can be seen as an attempt to work beyond some of the constitutive illusions of "femininity." Her strategy is, then, different from that of the male (Nietzschean) theorist who masquerades as female for his own advantage. Suleri neither seeks nor seeks to hide a woman—herself—behind the illusion. Nor is she interested in the feminine reappropriated as self-identity or sameness-with-self. Her interest is to explore the pragmatic, dangerous, and *jouissant* (in the Lacanian, "excessive" sense) surrender of self to style, to a semiosis within which her woman remains or, better, *becomes*—in a kind of transubstantiation—"meatless."

If Suleri is fully conscious of her disarticulation as a woman in Pakistani society, she is also wryly aware of both the potential for woman's entrapment in the prisonhouse of language and the potency of her empowerment within the tropology of style. Woman may be constrained by a patriarchal discourse: "Admittedly I am damned by my own discourse, and doubly damned when I add yes, once in a while, we naturally thought of ourselves as women, but only in some perfunctory biological way that we happened on perchance. Or else it was a hugely practical joke, we thought, hidden somewhere among our clothes" (1). But she may also be enabled, by a control of metaphor and style, to deconstruct the weave of the text that figures woman *as* woman. Everywhere, Suleri's effort is to find an enabling style. As a consequence, her prose can occasionally seem overwrought. More often, Suleri's interest in language, in *ecriture* (feminine or otherwise), reminds the reader of her concern with the very mode of being, for a woman. Yet a reading of Suleri's text must for *this very reason* be troubled by a foregrounding of her aestheticization of female postcolonial subjectivity.

She presents herself as already engaged in the process of self-articulation even as a young girl, although that engagement is recuperated retrospectively through her mother's memory of Sara as a linguisitically precocious child: "I was absorbed with grammar before I had fully learned the names of things . . . [which] caused a single slippage in my nouns: I would call a marmalade a squirrel, and I'd call a squirrel a marmalade." Her willed self-seduction by grammar is both exhilarating and threatening, a delicious and dizzying relinquishing of control: "To be engulfed by grammar is after all a tricky prospect, and a voice deserves to declare its own control in any way it can, asserting that in the end it is an inventive thing" (155). In this struggle, her mother is her prototype and teacher, and in more ways than one; for instance, Mair Jones taught English, as Suleri does today. But Mair Jones's example is not an easy one to follow: "Sometimes, when I feel . . . tyrannized by the structure of a simple sentence, it does me good to recollect how quietly my mother measured out her dealings with impossible edges. What can I do but tell the same story again and yet again, as my acknowledgment of how dangerous it is to live in plot?" (154).

Plot threatens to jeopardize style, which has in this instance been elevated to the very apparatus of self-articulation: "Think how much a voice gives way to plot when it learns to utter the names of the people it loves. . . . How can syntax hold around a name?" (155). But this giving way is more a question of self-absenting and not so much abnegation. For "abnegating power is a powerful thing to do, as my mother must have learned to admit: in the eyes of Pakistan, her repudiation of race gave her a disembodied Englishness that was perhaps more threatening than if she had come with a desire to possess" (163). In declining to avail herself of the power of abnegation, and in her pointed occlusion of racial difference, Mair Jones offers her daughter a perplexing lesson about an imperative for postcolonial narrative: "In the necessary amnesia of that era, colonial history had to be immediately annulled, put firmly in the past; remembrance was now contraband in a world still learning to feel unenslaved" (163–64). She erases in herself the vestiges of empire even as she decenters her own subjecthood. As in Michael Ondaatje's *Running in the Family*, the narrative disarms the inertia of mere plot by decentering and rarefying the subject's voice: Autobiography in these texts is not merely a matter of recording and representing the empirical givens of a life but what I have called a kind of transubstantiation of the subject of autobiography into the semiosis of textual web.[17] So there is no priority of the "real."

I have suggested that the rarefaction of the lyrical voice seems an escapist disavowal of positionality, a problematic attempt to finesse questions of racial, class, and ethnic difference, in both Suleri and Ondaatje. But that rarefaction may pose an alternative to models of metropolitan postmodern antiessentialism at the same time as it resists the relegation of the non-Western postcolonial to mere otherness—to comparatively simple narratives of identity that are assumed to be the destiny of a Third World voice tied to local territorial tradition (as opposed to a deterritorialized modernity), to the material conditions of the Third World, and to generic orality. Like her Welsh mother, who sought to formulate in her private space an alternative to an imperialism she was suspected of representing, Suleri seeks an alternative both to the Western postmodernist dominant and to an easy postcolonialism.

Mair Jones's counsel, "Daughter, unplot yourself; let be," was difficult for young Sara: "I could not help the manner in which my day was narrative" (156). Only as an adult can Sara strategically choose the catachrestic pleasures of oblique syntax over sequentiality, narrativization over narrative. Adulthood is coeval with a stylistic liberation enabling her to engage fully and naturally with language. Sara's mother's grammar of self-liberation seems to entail the election of a language so rarefied that it is inviolable by thought. Mair Jones was comfortable, even as a young girl in Wales, with the notion that "familiarity isn't important," that it really doesn't matter. So it is not just that she later finds it necessary to become "more used to feeling unfamiliar in Lahore" (12). She steadfastly refuses to "grip" life (164), preferring in that refusal to find fulfillment in a kind of ascesis.

This is what Sara, too, finds necessary to learn in her own self-exile in America. From her translated and migrant perspective, Mair Jones's advice to her daughter is to affirm in herself the Nietzschean woman, to seek ascesis, to appropriate a self-conscious alterity, a nomadism as well as a deterritorialization that is not intended as a prelude to simple reterritorialization. As Jean Baudrillard puts it, "It is said that femininity has no substance (no nature, or specific jouissance, or libido—as Freud would say)." In this view, empowerment for a woman may come from a recognition that "as opposed to a type of feminine authenticity, here it is said that woman is nothing and that this is her power."[18]

Style, then, is not only a matter of grammar, syntax, and semantics. It is also a modus vivendi, the grammar of always becoming and never being; there is no "proper" self. David Shapiro offers a helpful definition of style as "a form or mode of functioning—the way or manner of a given area of behavior—that is identifiable, in an individual, through a range of his specific acts."[19] To put it differently, style is to be construed as performativity, not as essence. In this sense, style is (not) the woman.

As a young woman, Sara was perhaps unable to accede to style in this sense, but she already knew somehow that her mother had discovered her own womanhood as "inessential" and that that was her power. Her mother "moved in observation to a degree that caught my breath, made it draw back to create more space and murmur, 'I am observing what it means to be in observation.' During the years of her existence, I did not altogether understand this gravity, this weightlessness, she carried with her" (154). It was style that defined Suleri's mother. She had achieved, in her own way, a weightlessness and negativity that de Lauretis's Nietzsche might have envied, "liv[ing] increasingly outside the limits of her own body, until I felt I had no means of holding her, lost instead in the reticence of touch." But her mother's absence as style, as idiolect, left the young Sara nonplussed, "baffled by her lesson: if I am to break out of the structure of affection, I asked her silently, then what is the idiom in which I should live?" And now, as a grown woman, able to reflect on her own "struggle with the quaintness of the task I've set myself, the obsolescence of these quirky little tales," the author imagines seeing her mother's "spirit shake its head and tell me, 'Daughter, unplot yourself; let be'" (156).

Sara's mother is an example to her of how to remain elsewhere, discontinuous with the social fabric of a foreign culture into which she has married and which appears to envelop her. More generally, Sara learns from her mother how a woman must signify her disruptive excess and alterity. It is her mother's deconstructive and disillusioning force that Sara realizes she has absorbed into herself, albeit without full understanding: She was "quite happy to let Mamma be that haunting word at which narrative falls apart" (156–57). This is the disarticulation signified by the titular word "meatlessness."

In portraying her mother as an ideal to be emulated, the author/daughter subordinates herself to her teacher/mother. But in doing so the daughter also subordinates her father to her mother as exemplum.[20] Her father's authority is reduced to a rather crude authoritarianism, in contrast to her subtle mother: "My father . . . seemed to notice only beauty, whereas my mother seemed subdued with awe at the commingling of color that with our bodies we flung into her, comminglings in which she had colluded to produce" (161). In retaining the deconstructive word ("Mamma") at the center of her narrative, Suleri constructs a paranarrative or parable in which a daughter is able finally to set the deterritorialized mother against the nationalistic, phallocratic, patriarchal Pakistani father. Admittedly, this description of him does not suggest the great warmth and affection of Suleri's portrayal; far less does it adequately problematize the question of nationalism. The father's nationalism is rather too blithely deprecated; here, the reader might well feel, Suleri takes too much the metropolitan, Western perspective on the Third World. From that perspective, Third World nationalism has only too often, and sometimes too hastily, been ridiculed.[21]

That having been said, it remains true that Suleri proffers an important model of Third World woman as represented by absence, alterity, and incoherence. She decenters and subverts the phallocratic motifs of presence, identity or self-identity, and coherence (both narratological and familial). As she struggles to conceive of the union of this mother and this father, she writes that her plot "feels most dangerous to me." Her father's "powerful discourse would surround her [mother] night and day," and it remained to the children to "marry" the father's "mode of fearsome inquiry" to "Mamma's expression of secret thought" (157). Her mother maintained a distance, an absence, "a ghostly stretch of neither here nor there between her sea and our shore," despite Sara's expostulation "You are too retrograde, you have no right to recede so far!" (159). It is this self-erasure, the strength of her mother, that Sara invokes in her own story: "Today it saddens me to think that I could be laying hands upon the body of her water as though it were reducible to fragrance, as though I intensified her vanished ways into some expensive salt." But in the sadness is admixed a celebration: "Flavor of my infancy, my mother, still be food: I want my hunger as it always was, neither flesh nor fowl!" (159–60).

It is Ifat, Sara's elder sister (killed in an accident), who best apprehends or (dis)embodies their mother's lesson, if less consciously; did she not once say "ruefully" to Sara that "men live in homes, and women live in bodies" (143)? But Sara remembers her mother saying, as though with awful foresight, "I know how the human body is made" (166); and when Ifat dies, their father, too, refuses to allow an autopsy, for even he realizes that the true Ifat, the true woman, is not identical with the material body. Sara endorses her father's decision: "For Ifat's gold was in her speech, in language that reflected like a radiance from her: *they would find nothing at her interior*" (174; emphasis added). For Sara, then, it is a kind of poetic justice that Ifat is reabsorbed into language, and this time not into just an idiolect such as their mother's but into the at once impudently intrusive and relievingly impersonal discourse of "the news": "It was as though I did not have even the idea of a sister any more, for Ifat became the news. Her name was everywhere, a public domain, blotting out her face and its finesse into the terrible texture of newsprint" (125).

Ifat's disappearance is of course personally devastating. But the narratological purpose of rendering Ifat as so central to the novel is to enable remembrance fully reconciled to the impossibility of re-membering: an impossibility already prefigured in the dream of her mother where, "when my father's back was turned, I found myself engaged in rapid theft . . . I stole away a portion of that body. It was a piece of her foot I found . . . which I quickly hid inside my mouth, under my tongue"—but at this dramatic moment the dream "dissolved, into an extremity of tenderness" (44). Suleri cannot save, re-member Ifat, but can only mourn her beautiful sister by re-marking the evanescence of beauty and the ephemerality of the individual. The body is dust. This is the complementary aspect of the negativity of the subject, and Ifat's death requires for Sara an effort at reconciling it with the theoretical imperative to deconstruct the subject: "I could not conceive her body, then, nor tolerate the tales of that body's death, . . . such a moving body, one that, like water, moved most generously in light" (147–48).

In reflecting on the mother's lesson of the negativity of woman, or on the tragedy of her beautiful dead sister, Sara seems to acknowledge that it is not entirely a comfort to acquiesce to the insolidity of personhood: "Faces slip, become third persons in their bearing of themselves, a disheartening trick to observe" (176). In social terms, it is also an act of courage and anxious brinksmanship to inhabit language only, to surrender to style, because in this context of mourning

it is as if there were no other anchor for the self: "Living in language is tantamount to living with other people. Both are postures in equilibrium that attend
upon gravity's capacity for flotation" (177).

But it is at the personal and therefore ethical, rather than social, level that the
question of the negativity of woman—the inaugural question for the work—is
most piquant. Suleri recalls that once, as a young girl about to fall asleep, she had
watched her mother smoke a cigarette absently: "It was startling to me, piercing,
. . . making me repeat, 'She is not where she is; she has gone somewhere different.' It took me years to conceive of distraction as a mode of possible attentive-
ness" (179). The last word of the book, quite appropriately, is "disembodiment,"
and—to return to what I said at the outset—it is this unmaking to which the
maker of this tale aspires. What is remarkable finally is the autobiography's negative capability. Suleri does not at the end seem disconcerted to find that she is
not found but still and perpetually elsewhere—ghostly, meatless: "In the pale and
liquid morning I hold the Adam in me, the one who had attempted to break
loose. It is a rib that floats in longing for some other cage. . . . I join its buoyancy
and hide my head as though it were an infant's cranium still unknit, complicit in
an Adam's way of claiming, in me, disembodiment" (186).

Suleri mère's deliberate peace with disembodiment, or ghostliness, is a way
of coming to terms with the "mystery of being."[22] Sara's mother disappears
into language, and Sara's own autobiographical subject is in a sense "all talk,"
a rhetorical construct, stylized to the point of vanishing, so that style is and is
not the woman. But this should not be misconstrued as a mere language game.
Her displacement of the category "woman" is echoed by Trin T. Minh-ha's
suggestion that the point is "not to carve one's space in 'identity theories that
ignore women' and describe some of the faces of female identity . . . but patiently to dismantle the very notion of core (be it static or not) and identity."[23]

The tenuousness of "identity" in Suleri's text is a deconstruction of what Edward Said has described as the production of the Orient as static and even "eternal," within the "latent Orientalism" that he says has informed notions of the
East both in and out of the academy for hundreds of years.[24] Suleri's Pakistan
is not the tamely primitive, backward, and infantilized East of the Orientalist.
The deliberate offhandedness and lightness of her touch mock the cliché of the
deep or "profound" mystic character of the East, but it is also different from
the easy carnivalization of the fashionably postmodern narrative, the blithe celebration of multiple identifications, of hybridity, of ambivalence. Her novel has
a baroque ornateness that tempts—dares?—one to label it old-fashioned, passé.
One cannot fail to recognize at any rate that some of its stylistic antecedents belong to an *haute culture* of what is in literary terms nothing less than a bygone
era. Yet the bloodless abstractions of her prose defy the stereotypes of the East

as irrational, muddled, and inscrutable. Suleri mocks the notion that the Eastern woman is unthinkingly sensual; the Suleri women are formidably intellectual, though hardly incapable of passion. Suleri's voice suggests, precisely by its ellipticality and stylistic dislocations, the heteroglottal capabilities of literature of the subcontinental diaspora.

Suleri's baroque antiessentialisms would frustrate the Orientalist (or neo-colonialist) notion that the East needs a Western redescription or an "explanation," and thus a redemption from the depths of its obscurity and unreason, not to mention from its allegedly failed or false self-understanding. The world the Suleri women inhabit by no means conforms to the Orientalist construct of the East as characterized by "unimaginable antiquity, inhuman beauty, boundless distance."[25] But then again, they are not "modern" in any sense clearly articulated in Western discourse, and it is precisely in the everyday details she dwells on that Suleri emphasises the difference, the lag or gap. In this sense, Meatless Days poses an unusual sort of challenge to notions about writing by people of Third World origin.

Suleri's challenge to Western stereotypes, both positive and negative, about the non-Western woman can be understood in terms of Valerie Amos and Pratibha Parmar's observation that "historically white women's sexuality has been constructed in oppositional terms to that of Black women. . . . But [that has been done] in an uncritical way—the engagement with it is essentially selective." Because they adopt white male academic discourse, even feminist intellectuals buy into the premises imbricated within such a discourse and thus "repeat their racial chauvinism."[26] In Suleri's Pakistan, at least among women of her class, the overly simple stock narrative of the suppression of woman pales in the face of the elaborate and refined brinkmanship of the Suleri women's own disappearance and emergence within—their sophisticated inhabitation of—language, even though Suleri herself is silent on the issue of class in the text, and even though her deprecation of nationalism is inadequately theorized.

Suleri is not writing just for Western readers; she also troubles and complicates the perceptions of nation, family, gender, and power *from and for a subcontinental perspective*. Her portrait of the complex power relations between her father and her mother defies the simpler Western feminist critiques of hegemonic structures within the patriarchal family, but it problematizes that family within its own Third World context and for Third World observers. Family is one of the three areas (the others being sexuality and the women's peace movement) Amos and Parmar select to illustrate their thesis that "patriarchy cannot be viewed only in terms of its relationship to capital and capitalist relations but neither is it merely an analytical tool which explains the oppression of women by men within a range of different economic systems."[27] Clearly, Suleri's father in no way wields final and unambiguous control over his wife. The portrait of the father raises the question of the distribution of power within the traditional Pakistani family and within the patriarchal discourse of the nation. Suleri's women characters defy the tired stereotypes of gender roles within the Third World family. Those stereotypes are, as we know, sometimes promulgated by feminists with the noble intention of describing a situation from which women bereft of Western emancipation may finally be redeemed by it.

In Suleri's family the real power resides in the insubstantial (ghostly) figure of the mother, but what must on no account be forgotten is that the mother is white. How exactly does this complicate the question of ethnicity for postcolonial literature and literary theory in particular? Suleri, admittedly, does not explore this question as fully as one might have wished; however, her "autobiography" calls attention to the "trap" into which, say Amos and Parmar, white feminists have fallen: namely theorizing black women's experience as other (and inevitably inferior) in order to reappropriate it and thereby also reaffirm their own experience. Their harshest criticism seems reserved for the "hysteria in the western women's movement surrounding issues like arranged marriages, purdah, female headed households, [which] is often beyond the Black woman's comprehension—being tied to so called feminist notions of what constitutes good or bad practice in our communities in Britain or the third world." Amos and Parmar emphasize the need to articulate a new feminism "creating our own forms and content." In other words, they too emphasize the importance of a rhetoric, a style.[28] There is nothing frivolous about this, and I do not mean to suggest that it is only a question of being stylish. For Suleri, style is inextricable from (an implicit) politics, from an intensely particular view of the world that, for any particular person, is itself a product of a unique nexus of class, race, gender, and other sociocultural accidents.

Suleri achieves a certain freedom from anxiety about "authenticity"; her urbane narrative is not just the literary production of a Third World aspirant to a Western idiom. This is one sense of her fastidious insistence, when pressed by one of her students, that "there are no women in the third world" (20). Her internationalist style resists easy categorization and thereby resists the danger identified by Abdul R. JanMohamed: namely, the danger of the incorporation of the "third world intellectual" so as "to ensure the elimination of any oppositional or alien attitudes and tendencies."[29] Insofar as it seeks to represent the Third World experience, the "difficulty" of Suleri's style insistently reminds the reader of her attempt to make her cultural production unpalatable to the insatiable maw of the postmodern.

Suleri's elaborate and studied rejection of homogenizations of subcontinental subjectivity constitute an important move in the text of the diasporic narrative, but the move is, as I have been suggesting, not unproblematic. Regarded in its immediate United States context, Suleri's text thematizes the problem of a certain complex tokenization, which "goes with ghettoization," as Spivak notes. "When you are perceived as a token, you are also silenced in a certain way." The subcontinental, and particularly the diasporic, must resist being "used as an alibi, since we don't share the same history of oppression with the local Blacks, the east Asians, and the Hispanics."[30] Suleri seems acutely aware of this imminent danger in her implicit challenge to received construction of the subcontinental subject. The "stylishness" of her narrative amounts to a kind of refusal to be subsumed under certain stereotypes of subcontinental *narrative*, just as it challenges notions of womanhood in the Third World. Her text approximates what Gilles Deleuze and Félix Guattari identify as the deterritorialization of English, *at the very moment* when her narrative achieves an interminable displacement of subjectivity.[31] Indeed, the deterritorialization of language is coextensive with the displacement of subjectivity, for Suleri has taken great pains to establish that subjectivity resides in language and that individuality is a matter of "style."

Her father tacitly questioned Sara about the cost of becoming a "minority" in America, and she tries to understand what it means to inhabit a minority position as a diasporic subcontinental writer teaching at a major American university. Deleuze and Guattari argue that a minor literature is characterized in the first place by a "strong co-efficient of deterritorialization" of the "major language" in which a minority figure writes, in place of his or her own "minor" language. The second characteristic they point to is that in minor literatures, "everything" is political. Finally, everything has "a collective value" precisely because "talents do not abound in a minor literature," so that "the conditions are not given for an *individuated utterance* which would be that of some 'master' and could be separated from *collective utterance*" (original emphasis).[32]

Deleuze and Guattari's third characteristic seems remarkably inadequate for describing what is achieved in a minority text such as Suleri's. I have argued above that the opening scene of her book is a crucial moment because it suggests that "individuated utterance" is not at a premium: Suleri's Pakistani women do not see the need to distinguish themselves from one another or to insist upon individual identity. Yet surely it is too crude to describe her (minority) literary production as having "a collective value," even though it is true that she resists any ossification of subjectivity and thus also avoids the illusion of a bottom-line "authority" or authorship, in Deleuze and Guattari's sense. At the same time there is something disturbingly elitist about Suleri's work: It flies in the teeth of stereotypes of the Third World woman but ultimately leaves open the question whether its refusal to be fashionable or predictable springs from a reactionary politics and aesthetics. Similarly, the work is intensely personal without reifying the individual, but there is something curiously inturned and even insular about this autobiography, as though navel gazing were being elevated to high art. In this sense, the work's self-distancing from other modes of Third World writing is redolent of a kind of elitism.

If JanMohamed is right to insist on adding a fourth fundamental characteristic of minority literature, "its representation of marginality," surely a discussion of Suleri's variety of marginality needs to be complicated, at some level, by an examination of its privilege (recall Spivak's point that women who have the luxury of problematizing the "questioning subject" are in "privileged positions in the geopolis"). Although women in Suleri's text are not "ruthlessly subjugated," in JanMohamed's phrase, they are of course marginal figures. JanMohamed argues, I think rightly, that "the struggle against the hegemonic system can take many different forms that may not be overtly recognizable as political or economic. If, as Deleuze argues, the struggle must be carried on through literature before it becomes explicitly political or economic, then clearly criticism must also be involved in this struggle."[33]

But criticism—or theory—must be wary of simple and overgeneralized pronouncements about the character of minority discourse. Of course, descriptive generalizations are useful, but as Chandra Talpade Mohanty observes, it is when a group such as "women of Africa" becomes a "homogeneous sociological grouping characterized by common dependencies or powerlessness (or even strengths) that problems arise—we say too little and too much at the same time." Insofar as Suleri's work is taken to be the product of a feminist consciousness, representative of "third world feminisms," any discussion of it must, as Mohanty insists, "address itself to two simultaneous projects: the internal critique of hegemonic 'Western' feminisms, and the formulation of autonomous, geographically, historically, and culturally grounded feminist concerns and strategies. The first project is one of deconstructing and dismantling; the second, one of building and constructing."[34]

Suleri's *Meatless Days* resists assimilation under some generalized notion of minority or Third World feminist or even diasporic literature and is thus suggestive of alternatives for Third World writing, or at least for postcolonial writing from the subcontinent. Its stylistic difference, predicated though it may be on an infinite displacement of the "individual," requires us to consider whether it is advisable for Third World writing to locate itself firmly in the historical, political, economic, and social specifics of such minor literature, since in that materiality lies its constitutive "difference," whatever the accent in which that "difference" is articulated. A minority literature grounded in the material conditions of the Third World cannot be protected from scrutiny as a problematic alternative to "stock" Third World writing, for its treatment of gender, class, race, and nationhood raises as many questions as does its style. Nor can it afford to be blind to the implications of relegating Third World writing to a realm where it remains inferior to that of "developed" cultures of the metropolitan centers. Suleri's prose does nothing if it does not confound such simplified categorizations. It is not only an exemplary text for diasporic subcontinental postcolonialism; it is also a highly individualized (and thus it does not help to classify it as "modernist" or even "postmodernist") example of an exploration of subjectivity not through the mimetic modes often assigned to Third World cultural production by metropolitan discourse but via an antiessentialism, a meatlessness, inhabiting as it were the bare essentials of everyday life.

There is a danger that Suleri's "meatlessness" might be construed as mere amorphousness, and therefore as a flaccid negativity and once more a silencing of the Third World subject/woman. (This is, as Suleri notes elsewhere, a threat that postcolonialism constantly confronts: "The current metaphorization of postcolonialism [in Homi Bhabha's work, for instance] threatens to become so amorphous as to repudiate any locality for cultural thickness.")[35] On the contrary, it is important to recognize, as Suleri insists in The Rhetoric of English India, that "if colonial cultural studies is to avoid a binarism that could cause it to atrophy in its own apprehension of difference, it needs to locate an idiom for alterity that can circumnavigate the more monolithic interpretations of cultural empowerment that tend to dominate current discourse."[36]

NOTES

1. Gayatri Chakravorty Spivak, "Strategy, Identity, Writing," Journal of Politics 18 (1986–87); rpt. in Spivak, The Post-Colonial Critic: Interviews, Strategies, Dialogues, ed. Sarah Harasym (New York: Routledge, 1990), 42.

2. Naomi Schor, Reading in Detail: Aesthetics and the Feminine (New York: Methuen, 1987), 4.

3. Cherrie Moraga and Gloria Anzaldúa, This Bridge Called My Back: Writings by Radical Women of Color (Watertown, Mass.: Persephone Press, 1981), 205.

4. Elizabeth Fox Genovese, "Placing Women's History in History," New Left Review 133 (1982): 26.

5. Lisa Lowe, Critical Terrains: French and British Orientalisms (Ithaca, N.Y.: Cornell University Press, 1991), 198.

6. Kumkum Sangari, "The Politics of the Possible" Cultural Critique 6 (Fall 1987): 183–84.

7. Sara Suleri, Meatless Days (Chicago: University of Chicago Press, 1989), 105 (hereafter cited by page number).

8. Anthony Appiah, In My Father's House: Africa in the Philosophy of Culture (New York: Oxford University Press, 1992), 157.

9. Carole Pateman, The Sexual Contract (Stanford: Stanford University Press, 1988), 21, 38.

10. Spivak, "Strategy," 45.

11. Luce Irigaray, *This Sex Which Is Not One*, trans. Catherine Porter with Carolyn Burke (Ithaca, N.Y.: Cornell University Press, 1985), 84, 78. This book was originally published in French as *Ce Sexe qui n'est pas un* (Paris: Editions de Minuit, 1977).

12. Prominent Pakistani exceptions to this rule, as exceptions, underscore the fact that in traditional Muslim settings—from the middle-class or underclass religiously observant family to the law courts adjudicating rare rape allegations—the woman's place is severely circumscribed within a male-dominant code. Thus, although Benazir Bhutto may be head of state, she has learned that she must underplay her "Westernization" as a cosmopolitan, Harvard- and Oxford-educated modern woman and sign her deference to traditional codes of feminine behavior and dress, not to mention Islamic law.

13. Irigaray, *This Sex*, 122–23.

14. Teresa de Lauretis, "The Violence of Rhetoric: Considerations on Representation and Gender," *Semiotica* 54.1–2 (1985): 11–12. The explanation for this phenomenon, according to de Lauretis (13), is simple: "If Nietzsche and Derrida can occupy and speak from the position of woman, it is because that position is vacant and, what is more, cannot be claimed by women. . . . While the question of woman for the male philosophers is a question of style (of discourse, language, writing—of philosophy), for Salome, as in most present-day feminist thinking, it is a question of gender—of the social construction of 'woman' and 'man', and the semiotic production of subjectivity."

15. Katherine Cummings, "A Spurious Set (Up): 'Fetching Females' and 'Seductive' Theories in *Phaedrus*, 'Plato's Pharmacy,' and *Spurs*," *Genders* 8 (Summer 1990): 38.

16. Here too, Irigaray's comments on a woman's relation to language seem germane: "Women's social inferiority is reinforced and complicated by the fact that woman does not have access to language, except through recourse to 'masculine' systems of representation which disappropriate her from her relation to herself and to other women. The 'feminine' is never to be identified except by and for the masculine, the reciprocal proposition not being 'true'" (*This Sex*, 85).

17. Michael Ondaatje, *Running in the Family* (Middlesex, Eng.: Penguin, 1982).

18. Jean Baudrillard, *De la seduction* (Paris: Galilee, 1980), 149, quoted in Betty R. McGraw, "Splitting Subject/Splitting Seduction," *Boundary* 2 12. 2 (1984), 143.

19. David Shapiro, *Neurotic Styles* (New York: Basic Books, 1965), 1, quoted in Michael Shapiro, "Style as Figuration" *Stanford Literature Review* 3.2 (1986): 196.

20. Michael Shapiro puts forward a thesis that he claims is "novel, not having been made before by any student of style." The thesis is this: "The domination relation—that is, the relation of subordination and superordination—is, so to speak, the quiddity of style." He explains: "The clearest example of the centrality of dominance relations to the ontology of style is provided by imitation. To imitate is to reproduce not just substantive features but their hierarchy. . . . to imitate is to subordinate the imitator to the matter imitated and/or the original's creator" ("Style as Figurations" 200).

21. See Alok Yadav, "Nationalism and Contemporaneity: Political Economy of a Discourse," *Cultural Critique* 26 (Winter 1993–94): 191–229.

22. Marjorie Perloff, *The Poetics of Indeterminacy: Rimbaud to Cage* (Princeton, N.J.: Princeton University Press, 1981), 208.

23. Trin T. Minh-ha, "Difference: 'A Special Third World Women's Issue,'" in *Discourse* 8 (Fall–Winter 1986–87): 30.

24. Edward Said, *Orientalism* (New York: Random House, 1978), 206.

25. Ibid., 40, 206, 167.

26. Valerie Amos and Pratibha Parmar, "Challenging Imperial Feminism," in *Feminist Review* 17 (1984): 5–6.

27. Ibid., 9.

28. Ibid., 11, 17.

29. Abdul R. JanMohamed, "Humanism and Minority Literature: Toward a Definition of Counter-hegemonic Discourse," in *Boundary* 2 12.3 (Spring 1984): 282.

30. Spivak, "Questions of Multiculturalism," in *The Post-Colonial Critic*, 61–62.

31. Gilles Deleuze and Félix Guattari, "What Is a Minor Literature?" trans. Robert Brinkley, *Mississippi Review* 11 (Spring 1983): 13–33.

32. Ibid., 16–17.

33. JanMohamed, "Humanism," 297.

34. Chandra Talpade Mohanty, "Under Western Eyes: Feminist Scholarship and Colonial Discourses," in *Third World Women and the Politics of Feminism*, ed. Chandra Talpade Mohanty, Ann Russo, and Lourdes Torres (Bloomington: Indiana University Press, 1991), 59, 51.

35. Sara Suleri, "Woman Skin Deep: Feminism and the Postcolonial Condition," *Critical Inquiry* 18.4 (1992): 759.

36. Sara Suleri, *The Rhetoric of English India* (Chicago: Chicago University Press, 1992), 4.

CHAPTER 15

Redefining the Postcolonial Female Self

Women in Anita Desai's *Clear Light of Day*

Pushpa Naidu Parekh

The politics of theoretical and literary representation by international women of color in the last decade or two and its intervention in the diversifying context of feminist discourse invites and, in many cases, challenges theorists and practitioners to address the specific nature, method, and politics of these representational practices. In this context, to borrow Bapsi Sidhwa's terms, "third world, our world" women's voices interpellate postcolonial theories of cultures with diverse strategies that explore the praxis of cultural contact, difference, domination, and change.[1] Known and emerging Indian women writers have recently begun to be studied in the West within the rubric of International, Women's, or Postcolonial Studies. In the United States they are often viewed as representations of the marginal, and many write from the consciousness of displacing the center, whether of patriarchy, colonialism, or imperialism. Indian women writers—in the category of Asian women, Third World women, or women-of-color writers—have often been given this ambiguous space in the periphery of the dominant Euro-American curriculum.

The recent surge of Postcolonial Studies in American institutions verges on the dangerous brink of emphasizing and therefore privileging an artificial and ahistorical repositioning of ex-colonized women writers for the purpose of proving or debating, from intellectual and institutional grounds, certain theoretical assumptions regarding women's roles in cultural dynamics. Although the recognition of Postcolonial Studies in academia implies a refreshingly challenging force that pushes beyond the overt and covert manifestations of hegemonic practices, its revolutionary ramifications are still in the process of being constituted. Within one broad category, the discourses of nation or nationhood and decolonization have foregrounded various contentious forms of resistances and "decolonizations," depending on the specific politics of the subject position that is being confronted or contested. For postcolonial female subjects, the "politics" has often been layered and sedimented by the converging forces of oppression that Patricia Hill Collins refers to, in the context of black feminist thought, as the "interlocking systems of oppression" and the "matrix of domination."[2] Race, gender, class, caste, religion, sexual orientation, and age differences, as well as the politics of coloniality and postcoloniality, complicate the identification of women's issues. Writing from a certain location implies, for a postcolonial female writer, some combination of these positions in the overriding matter of social and cultural space as well as the contours of colonial and postcolonial histories.

Within the current debates over the ongoing processes of articulating decolonizations and feminisms, Anita Desai's observations, in an interview conducted by Feroza Jussawalla, reflect a criticism of the role of American institutions within the larger contradictions of capitalistic technocratic societies that engage in selective, self-serving forms of "multiculturism":

> The reason that *Baumgartner* has had any success over here is not because of its Indian material but because of its Jewish material. It's aroused a great deal of curiosity and interest among Jewish readers. It won a Jewish prize in fact, the Hadassah prize, and people are interested in the element of the war, the Nazis and then the Holocaust. India is really superfluous as far as American readers are concerned. . . . I don't think for Americans India has ever figured very largely in their imagination, except for a very limited area which is South Asian studies in a few of the universities.[3]

Desai's name began to be recognized in the United States academy only after the publication of *Baumgartner's Bombay* (1988), although she has been writing since the 1960s. Her previous works—*Cry, the Peacock; Where Shall We Go This Summer; Bye, Bye, Blackbird; Voices in the City*—won her the Sahitya Akademi Award in 1978 and the Guardian Award (United Kingdom) in 1983. *Clear Light of Day* and *Fire on the Mountain*, both written in the 1980s, deal with women's psyches and relationships, yet the fact that U.S. publishers and academicians ignored them is evidence of how and why Third World writers are or are not allowed into the larger arena of Western-centered academic machinery where current critical theory feeds on and is fed by the limited number of their texts that are published or even translated. Without diminishing the significance of Holocaust

experiences, Desai clearly sees that her novels on Indian contexts and even Indian women are still outside the scope of academic discussions of feminism. By
and large, Desai occupies a peculiar place even within the Indian academic
arena. Often viewed as a singular woman writer among giant male figures writing in English in the aftermath of India's independence—R. K. Narayan, Raja
Rao, Mulk Raj Anand, A. K. Ramanujan—Desai has a certain prominence, yet
her prose style and a Euro-Indian consciousness are constant reminders of the
hybrid space that she occupies. As she herself puts it, "My life was always made
up of Western and Indian elements."[4]

Offspring of a German mother and an Indian father, Desai learned early to
look at India with both intimacy and a "certain detachment." She invests her
literary world with the viewpoint of the insider and the outsider. This double
perspective translates into the defeatism and the exhilaration that exemplifies
the "Indian paradox," reflected particularly in the conditions of postcolonial
middle-class women protagonists as they accept or confront their destinies. The
women characters in *Clear Light of Day* illustrate this paradox. According to Desai, Tara personifies "the suffering of Indian women," and Bim, "women who
triumph": "They [Indian women] suffer in many ways—emotionally and
physically. Women who triumph are exceptional—women like Bim. That there
are such triumphs is another example of Indian paradox. In India you have
nothing in moderation, everything in excess—and that includes paradox."[5]

It is Desai's double perspective that creates the specific pattern of opposition,
conflict, and paradox in the lives of Third World women as they are explored
in her novels. Among the early post-independence writers writing in English,
Anita Desai made her mark as a unique artist with a psychological insight into
the inner world of the Indian woman.[6] Though referred to by some critics as
"the Virginia Woolf of India," she has resisted the labeling of her characters or
even herself as "feminist." Her uneasiness with Western-imposed categories,
reflected in the work of many Third World women writers, has turned to an
open questioning of a two-pronged phenomenon: the universalizing tendencies of Western-imported taxonomies together with the reifying tendencies of
colonialist discourses (such as the dialectics of binarism). This problematic is
of concern to postcolonial women theorists such as Gayatri Chakravorty Spivak, Chandra Talpade Mohanty, Sara Suleri, and Cheryl Johnson-Odim. Their
questioning is articulated through varying interpretations of alterity.

Desai, however, identifies certain crucial dilemmas of Third World women.
The term "Third World," as used by Chandra Talpade Mohanty and others, "foregrounds a history of colonization and contemporary relationships of structural
dominance between first and third world peoples."[7] Among these, as Johnson-
Odim points out, male-female opposition is not always the "primary locus

of the oppression of Third World women."[8] Desai, in portraying the ways in which women oppress other women, addresses the Third World women's dilemma in the Indian society: "Women are as responsible as men are for all those old orthodoxies and traditions having been kept alive through the generations. . . . I'm not sure if it's always an impulse to tyrannize, or whether it's simply fear of wrecking the traditions that they've lived by for so long." Whereas these traditions may subsume and silence some women, Desai presents the reality of the powerful women who are molded by these very conditions in strikingly different ways: "The powerful ones are so powerful they seem to make up in a way for all those who have no power."[9]

In my reading of the novel *Clear Light of Day*, the characters Bim and Tara represent two identities, among others, that define the postcolonial middle-class Indian woman: She is often the traditional woman who has found her own avenues to change and modernization, the elite woman who has liberated herself in the borrowed world of alien language and culture, or sometimes both identities in one. It is in the context of the heterogeneity of such characters that resistance to early feminist definitions of Third World women as a "homogeneous" group is being articulated by Indian women writers. Chandra Talpade Mohanty in "Under Western Eyes: Feminist Scholarship and Colonial Discourses," clarifies the problematics of Western feminist's "production of 'Third World Woman' as a singular monolithic subject." In her introduction to *Third World Women and the Politics of Feminism*, Mohanty explains her use of the term "Third World women" as an attempt to foreground an "analytical and political category" in order to "explore the links among the histories and struggles of third world women against racism, sexism, colonialism, imperialism, and monopoly capital" without essentializing "notions of third world feminist struggles."[10]

Resisting the categorization of the "marginal" woman, Gayatri Chakravorty Spivak, in a chapter of *In Other Worlds* titled "Explanation and Culture: Marginalia," deconstructs the polarities of masculinist-center and feminist-margin hierarchies: "The center itself is marginal," and she herself demonstrates this displacement of the privileged position "by not remaining outside in the margin and pointing my accusing finger at the center. I might do it rather by implicating myself in that center and sensing what politics make it marginal." As a deconstructivist she claims to "use herself . . . as a shuttle between the center (inside) and the margin (outside) and thus narrate a displacement."[11] In the chapter "Marginality in the Teaching Machine" of her later theoretical work, *Outside in the Teaching Machine*, Spivak articulates the need for vigilance against the Euro-American academic tendencies to prescribe and construct an "identifiable margin" that gains validation from the center. Moreover, as she observes, "the institutional 'dissemination of knowledge' . . . [continues] to determine and overdetermine the margin's conditions of representability," and "as teachers, we are now involved in the construction of a new object of investigation—'the third world,' 'the marginal'—for institutional validation and certification." The fact that "only such writers who write in the consciousness of marginality are christened as 'third world'" demonstrates that the margin is "being created to suit the institutional convenience of the colonizer."[12]

Theorists such as Spivak, Mohanty, and Suleri clarify that the center-margin displacement paradigm is different in First and Third World feminisms. Sara Suleri in *The Rhetoric of English India* cautions against some of the "governing assumptions" of the "discourse of colonial studies" which embed the "representation of otherness" in a "theoretical duality of margin to center." As she further demonstrates in her work, "the story of colonial encounter is in itself a radically decentering narrative that is impelled to realign with violence any static binarism between colonizer and colonized."[13] These theories are relevant to Desai's novels, particularly *Clear Light of Day*, in which she identifies certain crucial dilemmas of a specific class of the Third World (here, Indian and often caste Hindu) women in sociohistorical and political contexts. The exploration of women's identity in the context of class, caste, gender, and the politics of nation is both explicit and implicit; in either case, as my study indicates, Desai's women are engaged in defining themselves and their experiences in particular ways that problematize the very categorizing of postcolonial, Third World women.

Clear Light of Day is a complex novel about the psychological underpinnings that make or break human relationships. While the nation suffers partition, the Das family suffers division and separation. The details given place the family in the elite upper caste, headed by a father who owns a partnership in an insurance company. To his children he seems a distant figure clad in "his usual dark suit for the club, with a white handkerchief and a cigar in his breast pocket."[14] His Westernized attire and socializing, as well as the location of the Das residence "far outside the city, out in the Civil Lines where the gardens and bungalows were quiet and sheltered behind their hedges," indicate the socioeconomic benefits he enjoys along with his landowner neighbor, Hyder Ali, during the colonial era. Served by drivers and gardeners as well as Mira-masi, a widowed aunt ostracized by her in-laws and ultimately reduced to the status of an ayah, the Das family apparently parallels the outward elegance and ambience of an empire that is inwardly being eaten away by forces of neglect, illness, and madness. The contours of the family's history, however, trace the convoluted emergence of a multilayered reality of postcoloniality. Three of these layers reveal the nexus of politically significant issues in India today: the rise of Hindu-Muslim communalism; the forces of neocolonialism and the disparities of class; and the urgency of women's concerns. In the context of these layers and complex structures, essentializing definitions of "Third World" women as "singular monolithic subjects" are problematized.

At the center of the intense human drama, played out in the tensions of past and present, are the two sisters Bim and Tara. As a narrative of the emergence of the postcolonial "New Woman," the novel posits a clear move away from the discourses of binary categories and oppositional dialectics. Bim, the older sister, has stayed in the Old Delhi family home taking care of the alcoholic Aunt Mira and the autistic brother Baba; Tara, the younger sister, has escaped the dark memories of family breakups and nation partition through marriage to a diplomat. Tara's return home on a vacation from the United States becomes the occasion for unraveling the past and the unexamined contents of both family and national dysfunctionality in the context of transitional history and the intersection of the end of empire with the birth of Indian nationhood. Bim's and Tara's divergent journeys into the past are grounded in their own conflicted subjectivities, experiences as well as memories. At first, differences between them seem simplistically oppositional in the geopolitical sites (India and the United States), historical frames (past and present), and ideological positions (traditional and modern) they inhabit. Yet as the plot unravels, the inner journeys converge and project two possible realities. One is the complex psychic fragmentation of the postcolonial Indian woman as she encounters the possibilities for both subject formation and erasure within a historical frame where "nation" and "nationality" are to be understood "not as an essence" but, in Susie Tharu and K. Lalita's words, as "a *historically constituted terrain*, changing and contested and its citizen-subjects as subjects-in-struggle."[15] The other possible reality underscores the multifarious nature of the New Woman's identity as she shapes it into being, so that oppositionalities are coexistent in a complex, multidimensional whole.

Within the parameters of sociopolitical contours, however, the postcolonial "class privileged" Indian woman has faced a dilemma involving a sense of betrayal—both by colonialist powers that promised liberation through education yet confined her to an elite world, and by nationalists who claimed her services for political purposes. Neither seemed to place much value on her subjective experience of historical moments. Yet the Western-educated, middle-class women's voicing of this betrayal is often perceived by critics and scholars, particularly Marxist revisionists, as the peevish complaint of the elite who often benefited from this constructed class hierarchy. The rationale underscores the fact that the elite women at least are represented in the grand sweep of colonial history, which erased and "violently censured" a whole order of economically lower-class women in nineteenth-century Bengal. Yet these elite women, who were provided Western education, were used as instruments of silencing other women's voices—in the name, ironically, of women's emancipation. Sumanta Banerjee, in "Marginalization of Women's Popular Culture in Nineteenth Century Bengal," identifies the nonhomogeneous group of Bengali women in terms of caste as well as class differentials. "Women of rich families" and "women of the middle station" lived in the *andarmahal* or *zenana*, in secluded quarters; the "poor women" were "working women, either self-employed like *naptenis* (women from the barber caste), . . . sweepers, owners of stalls selling vegetables or fish, street singers and dancers, maidservants, or women employed by mercantile firms dealing in seed produce." The street singers, however, were Vaishnavites—worshipers of Vishnu—who represented cross-segments of social castes: "widows of kulin [caste] Brahmans who had nowhere to go, women who wanted to escape prostitution after having been seduced from their homes and deserted by their lovers, prostitutes who, after becoming old, had lost their occupations, or outcastes aspiring to independence and recognition." But class differential, Banerjee argues, did not mean separation among women until the Western education system was introduced to the upper- and middle-class women by reformist agencies in the hope of creating an educated intelligentsia. Before this, the popular culture of the poorer classes was accessible to women across all economic segments.[16]

The portrayal of the betrayed elite in Desai's novels is complicated by this psychic guilt of the betrayed who is also the betrayer of women's solidarity, particularly in formerly colonized regions of the world. In *Clear Light of Day* the divisive consciousness of the class-constructed woman is portrayed in the figures of the two sisters. Bim's anger at the denial of the self's worth, both from inside and outside, and Tara's sense of guilt can be seen as two levels of organizing experience and identity in the postcolonial female construction of self. Bim and Tara inhabit a space where privilege and agency for educated, upper-middle-class women is mounted on the silence and erasure of poorer and often socially ostracized women, such as the widowed Aunt Mira. Within a society constrained by caste, class, and patriarchy, operating on the principles of colonial institutions, the presence of some women implies the absence of many others.

Bim's and Tara's subjectivity also represents the process of redefining their female selves within the context of their personal and cultural history. Their personal history reveals unresolved conflicts with family members, constitutes a pattern of centripetal and centrifugal forces that characterize the overlapping circles of past and present time, and, in a larger context, shifts between the polarities of center and margin. Within this pattern, one or the other experiences either inclusion in or alienation from familial groupings and, eventually, meaningful solidarity collectives. Centered on male relatives such as Raja, Baba, or Bakul, the lives of the women and their internal struggles become peripheral;

it is only by re-focusing on the women's relationships to each other and their significance for both that the dynamics of the paradigm are shifted.

At the center of this pattern of family relationships and their forces is the recurring motif of imprisonment and exile that defines the women's destinies, experiences, dilemmas, and choices within the parameters of historical forces, social norms, traditions, customs, and the colonial hegemonic practices structuring their postcolonial reality. As each chapter reveals the memories of the past and their influences on the present, readers make the journey into the minds, hearts, and souls of the two women, each growing and developing in her own direction. Bim moves on the one hand toward self-assertion, intelligence, strong-mindedness, independence, education, and professionalism and, on the other, toward the past, the changeless—playing out the roles of caring sister, surrogate mother, and daughter in a family whose members are either slowly disintegrating or dispersing. Tara, the quiet, retiring one whose childhood is marked by passivity, fear, and isolation is, paradoxically, the one who chooses to escape from the confines of the past and saves herself from all that their Old Delhi house represents: decay, decadence, insanity, illness, and stasis. She moves toward affirmation of life and preservation of self, but she does so through the traditional mode of escape open to women—marriage. Both Tara and Bim incorporate past and present, change and tradition. Neither one is in herself "better" than the other; rather, they emphasize the connections between past and present and effect the breakdown of essentialist categories such as "traditional" and "emancipatory."

Bim's freedom of mind and spirit exile her mentally from the constraints of traditional social norms for women, such as marriage and dependence on a husband; she asserts indignantly to Tara, regarding the neighboring Misra sisters' early compliance with such norms, "Marriage isn't enough to last them the whole of their lives" (140). Defying the code of feminine self-consciousness, Bim shows no signs of inadequacy or uneasiness in the company of men; in contrast to the inferiority and helplessness exhibited by other women, Bim proves herself capable, intelligent, and hard-working, taking care of the family business as well as continuing with her teaching profession. Yet she journeys not into the far outer landscapes where heroic deeds are possible (as a child Bim had wanted to be a "heroine") but inward, into the dark, gloomy corners of a mind and heart racked by anger, bitterness, alienation, and hatred—the self-created imprisonment of emotions and intellect wherein she is, in her own words, like a "faded old picture in its petrified frame" (5).

Tara's physical and mental exile from the Old Delhi home is fraught with similar paradoxes. Through her husband, Bakul, "a diplomat in an Indian embassy," Tara experiences world travel and the comforts of a "neat, china-white flat in

Washington" (21). She becomes, under his supervision and training, "an active, organized woman" who molds herself to fit the needs of others. Ironically, Bakul's domineering influence and the tiring routine of keeping up the facade of a "modern" life-style bring Tara back to the Old Delhi home to question her relationship to Bim and the old roots. The evanescent glistening of the pearllike snail on the pathway of her childhood memories, defiantly triumphant like "an eternal, miniature Sisyphus" (2), symbolizes the enigmatic coexistence of illusion and reality, of movement and stasis, of past and present, of traditional and modern. Tara's return home, though for a short spell, begins a process of recognizing the irreducible complexities of life. Her borrowed existentialism, like the superficial Romanticism of their brother Raja, signifies the double-bind of the colonized subject. Within the confines of this hybridized reality, Bim's anger and cynicism are a rejection of all pretenses toward self-definition.

In such a context, home and past become conflicted realms in both their spatial (Old Delhi) and temporal (summer of 1947) dimensions. They are a source of comfort, like a snail's shell, as well as of conflict—an imprisonment of self like a "faded old picture in its petrified frame" (5). The psychic split finds expression in a trope of "illness": "It seemed that the house was ill, illness passing from one generation to the other so that anyone who lived in it was bound to become ill and the only thing to do was to get away from it, *escape*" (156). If Tara and Bim are envisioned as one person, their split psyches represent the multiple ways in which they claim their subjectivity through revisiting past histories and locations. Tara negotiates her precarious place in the landscape of cultural changes that violently thrust known epistemological frameworks into the wreckage of political turbulence and consequent social upheaval. Escape from illness is also an escape from the madness of history: At one level, this illness is exemplified in the destruction of traditional Indian kinship bonds. Parents who vaguely oscillate between their home and the club—a remnant of colonial encroachments—separate themselves from their children. The colonized world reinscribes the "familial disruptions" and dysfunctionalism of the Raj.[17]

Bim, whom Tara had envied for her independence and courage and who dreamed of becoming a "heroine," found that the dreams even of the courageous may end "at the bottom of the well—gone, disappeared" (157). Bim struggles as a strong, intelligent, self-questioning woman during the Hindu-Muslim conflicts of pre- and post-independence India. The stormy political and religious dissensions that threatened to devour the fledgling birth of a new, independent nation provide the background for the tumultuous inner landscape of Bim's mind. Tormented by Raja's betrayal of his bond to her as a sibling and her best friend, Bim remembers with painful intensity the summer of '47, when she had nurtured him back to health from tuberculosis. Feeding her anger and bitterness with a letter from Raja written as a benevolent landlord would write to his tenant, Bim unleashes her pent-up emotions in the presence of Tara: "Was he trying to make me thank him—go down on my knees and thank him for this house in which we all grew up?" (29).

Bim's anger and bitterness are the tangled edges of the past that confuse and disorient her relations in the present. But she is not the only one who is controlled by the past events and relationships. Tara is haunted by her inner guilt that in her eagerness to escape from the old house, she had abandoned Bim: "It was not spite or retaliation that made Tara abandon Bim—it was the spider fear that lurked at the centre of the web-world for Tara. Yet she did abandon Bim, it was true that she did" (134). Two specific past events fed this fear. The first was Bim's struggle with the alcoholic, widowed Aunt Mira, who was going insane as a consequence of a lifetime of blame and guilt for her young husband's death. In the final part of the novel, where the two sisters finally face the nature of their imprisonment and exile, Tara confesses her irreconcilable sense of guilt at having abandoned both Bim and Aunt Mira, even as Raja had done, leaving Bim alone to handle the family business and care for their autistic brother, Baba. Tara's guilt is concretized through the memory of the second event, the incident of the bees at the Lodhi Garden. Tara had run for her life while Bim struggled with the bees alone, in that summer of 1947, and Tara carries that guilt too into the present. In *The Women in Indian Fiction in English*, Shantha Krishnaswamy sees Tara's memory of the bee incident as "symbolic of her asking forgiveness for the greater abandonment of Bim forever."[18] It could also symbolize the imposed accusation of divided loyalties and the inner sense of guilt that entrap the emerging modern woman between the postcolonial politics of Third World feminism and a return to national roots. By contrast, Bim's sardonic criticism of Bakul's neocolonial stance quickly registers the fact that his return to India is a return to those comfortable zones where First World perceptions distort Third World realities. Through her resistance to the forces that could reinscribe her marginality as a "Third World" woman, Bim expresses her need for authentic validation of enduring ethical values, such as loyalty to one's family—especially Tara and Raja—and, by extension, to one's particular place in the nation. As Tara and Bim realize, the return is often a journey ramified with complex questions, doubts, and soul-searchings especially for women, who have endured centuries of specific forms of erasure, silencing, or even instrumentality in both colonial and postcolonial patriarchal structures.

In a present reunion marked by these tensions and unresolved conflicts, Bim and Tara find in each other the means to emerge from the darkness and chaos of the past. It is Tara who confronts Bim with the substance as well as the sterility of her anger and bitterness toward Raja and makes possible Bim's liberation from the past. Bim frees herself by tearing up Raja's letter, as Tara has suggested, thus ending her illusions about him and reviving her deep and abiding bonds with her family. No doubt the healing for both lay in time, seen as both the "destroyer" and the "preserver," as Bim recalls the words from Raja's copy of T. S. Eliot's *Four Quartets* (182). Ironically, their validation of their identities is colored with the language of the West's renowned male poet, who himself quoted liberally from Eastern philosophy. The distancing and mirroring of self through fluid replications of culture and gender boundaries is for the sisters both an act of agency and a surrender to historical destiny. But emphasis on only one factor distorts the truth, even as the blind imitation of Romantic poetry cheapens Raja's claims to creative talent. As agents who have actualized the influence of an otherwise passive passage of time, the two sisters are two women who come to grips with each other's individuality and the ineluctable forces of their relationship, two women who represent the diversities of complete women as well as the divided selves of a whole woman. Their danger is in remaining divided, fragmented. Such has been the condition of Aunt Mira, living the traditionally oppressed woman's life, and of their own mother, diligently following her husband to elite clubs. Bim and Tara, while in isolation from each other, have faced the same possibilities for becoming inadequate and insane, and thus social outcasts.

Throughout their childhood and adulthood, men—their father, Raja, Bakul—had occupied the central stage, minimizing the potentiality of one woman's importance for the other. But with the passage of time the two women, apparently dissimilar, become each other's healers. They are different in many ways; as Bakul characterizes them, Bim has the qualities of "decision, firmness, resolve," while Tara is "weak-willed and helpless and defeatist" (17–18). Yet in the end their differences help them complement each other. Bim's hardness is softened by Tara's quiet sincerity and patience, and Tara's weakness and guilt are eased by Bim's laconic reasoning: "It was all so long ago" (174). Bim realizes, with a growing gentleness toward Tara, what Tara herself had concluded, that "they were more alike than any other two people could be" (174). Thus, each sister makes it possible for the other to emerge from imprisonment and exile, to realize "the clear light of day." Bim's final thoughts evince this process of discovery. Within the context of postcolonial subject formation, the psychic split does not simply subsume all differences and conflicts; rather, differences and conflicts coexist within the parameters of the emerging "New Woman" identity. Tara and Bim go their separate ways, but they are no longer isolated from each other.

The postcolonial Indian woman has the potentiality to confront her own multiple or sometimes fragmented selves, and to find for each the counterpart that could make her whole again. Her cultural roots are rich, as are her intellectual insights and experiences, yet her traditions could oppress her and her new-found liberty could burden her. No one definition seems to identify her. Her class "elitism" is only one aspect of her wholeness, even as her Third World "otherness" is a partially seen reality. Acceptance of the two selves constitutes the process of "arriving" for postcolonial middle-class Indian women—but this "arriving" is often marked by anguish and anxiety, riddled with self-questioning and self-consciousness.

Anita Desai, herself a product of two cultures, envisions in her women characters the divisions as well as celebrations of dual or multiple identities that ramify the postcolonial Indian woman's definition of self. In exploring the psychic spaces within the minds of hitherto marginalized women, even in the canon of world literature, Desai contributes to the literary value of studying postcolonial women's texts. Her attempt to understand and fathom the female psyche, through her women characters, may assure her works a significant place in the area of Women's Studies as well. Yet Desai provides no overt political stance on women's problems; her works are often ambiguous in their criticism of colonial politics, because they reveal too often the tenacious hold of traditional practices that Western education has not eradicated, despite its claims to reform. In this contentious terrain of diverse and multiple locations, theoretical and literary representations by "native" and "diasporic" Indian women writers embody manifold constructions, definitions, and redefinitions of the postcolonial female self. Although their constructions impinge on specific political and socioeconomic machinery that defines their reality within the framework of society and culture, it is interesting and significant to note the dynamics of class and caste representationality. Revisionist historiography, whether from the perspective of subaltern or Third World feminist or nationalist politics, has rearticulated—through interventions in the debates on colonial agendas regarding female colonized subjects and claims of modernization—the constraints of reclaiming the heterogeneity of a precolonial past. Lata Mani, in "Contentious Traditions: The Debate on SATI in Colonial India," juxtaposes the historical contextualization of *sati* in nineteenth-century British colonial discourse (which privileged the "Brahmanic scripture" and its exegesis by court pundits who responded to questions posed by colonial officials) with "the continuing persistence of colonial discourse" in the Supreme Court decision regarding the Shahbano case of April 1985 and the consequent "nationwide controversy on the question of religious personal law and the desirability or otherwise of a uniform civil code."[19]

Women's emancipation by the beginning of twentieth century was clearly tied to an educational system that progressively displaced the social value and freedom of mobility of one class of women over another. The new form of women's emancipation was disseminated by patriarchally centered reformist groups, which were often allowed to operate because colonial officials saw them as inadvertently fulfilling the imperial agendas for Westernizing the native; however, a modified form of emancipation emerged through the collusion of English missionary practices and the patriarchal version of Hindu norms. This form denigrated and ultimately silenced the earlier overt, often bawdy and sensuous, yet tough and penetrating criticism of a male-controlled society articulated through folk performance, doggerel, street songs, and dances.

Class and caste intersections operate as significant constitutive forces in colonial and postcolonial representations of Indian women. They operate as material and symbolic registers of women's identity containment within both colonial and nationalist discourses. The physical and ideological distancing between the "elite culture in Bengal" of the *sambhranto* (the upper classes and castes) and the "popular culture" of the *itarjan*, (the lower classes) is traced by Sumanta Banerjee to the "progressive" mission of the colonial education system and the English-educated Bengali men who undertook the "cultural emancipation of women" through reform movements and, eventually, nationalist politics.[20]

My study confirms an aspect of Desai's work that is relevant in applying decolonization theories to literary representations of postcolonial women subjects. Desai's women are complex workings or even reworkings of women's identity at the interface of colonial and postcolonial cultural ambivalences. Because their political implications are embedded in but sometimes obscured by a prose style that derives from the Western literary tradition, Anita Desai appeals to a more traditional readership and is often ignored by radical feminist postcolonial critics. Her insight into the elite woman's psyche problematizes the reduplication of woman's role in the neocolonial marginalization of the less elite or socially ostracized woman. Her Aunt Miras never truly become subject agents. Their complexities are often absorbed in the oppositional binarism of a margin/center dialectic. Yet their presence, when imagined as enduring figures that shape the nature and direction of other women, locates the sources of women's solidarity in the spaces between the orbits of centrality and marginality. Therefore, to read Desai is to enter the particular vision of class-centered postcolonial women in the larger context of their subjectivity during complex phases of nation formation.

NOTES

1. Bapsi Sidhwa, "Third World, Our World," *Massachusetts Review* 29 (1988): 703.

2. Patricia Hill Collins, *Black Feminist Thought: Knowledge, Consciousness, and the Politics of Empowerment* (New York: Routledge, 1991), 222, 225.

3. Feroza Jussawalla and Reed Way Dasenbrock, eds., *Interviews with Writers of the Post-Colonial World* (Jackson: University Press of Mississippi, 1992), 168–69.

4. Ibid., 174.

5. Corine Demas Bliss, "Against the Current: A Conversation with Anita Desai," *Massachusetts Review* 29 (1988): 527, 524.

6. See Usha Bande, *The Novels of Anita Desai: A Study of Character and Conflict* (Delhi: Prestige Books, 1988); Meena Belliappa, *Anita Desai: A Study of Her Fiction* (Calcutta: Writer's Workshop, 1971); Jasbir Jain, "Anita Desai," in *Indian English Novelists: An Anthology of Critical Studies* ed. Madhusudar Prasad (Delhi: Sterling, 1982), 24–50; Jasbir Jain, *Stairs to the Attic: The Novels of Anita Desai* (Jaipur: Printwell, 1987); Seema Jena, *Voice and Vision of Anita Desai* (Delhi: Ashish, 1989); Asha Kanwar, *Virginia Woolf and Anita Desai: A Comparative Study* (Delhi: Prestige Books, 1989); Ramesh K. Srivastava, ed., *Perspectives on Anita Desai* (Ghaziabad: Vimal Prakashan, 1984); Ramesh K. Srivastava, "The Psychological Novel and Desai's Cry, The Peacock," in his *Six Indian Novelists in English* (Amritsar: Guru Nanak University, 1987), 275–98.

7. Chandra Talpade Mohanty, Ann Russo, and Lourdes Torres, eds., preface to *Third World Women and the Politics of Feminism* (Bloomington: Indiana University Press, 1991), x.

8. Cheryl Johnson-Odim, "Common Themes, Different Contexts: Third World Women and Feminism," in Mohanty, Russo, and Torres, *Third World Women*, 315.

9. Quoted in Jussawalla and Dasenbrock, *Interviews*, 165, 168.

10. Chandra Talpade Mohanty, "Under Western Eyes: Feminist Scholarship and Colonial Discourses," in Mohanty, Russo, and Torres, *Third World Women*, 333; Mohanty, introduction to Mohanty, Russo, and Torres, *Third World Women*, 4.

11. Gayatri Chakravorty Spivak, *In Other Worlds: Essays in Cultural Politics* (New York: Routledge, 1988), 107.

12. Gayatri Chakravorty Spivak, *Outside in the Teaching Machine* (New York: Routledge, 1993), 56, 58.

13. Sara Suleri, *The Rhetoric of English India* (Chicago: Chicago University Press, 1992), 1–2.

14. Anita Desai, *Clear Light of Day* (New York: Penguin, 1980), 64. Subsequent quotations are cited in the text by page number from this edition.

15. Susie Tharu and K. Lalita, "Literature of the Twentieth Century," in *Women Writing in India, 600 B.C. to the Present: The Twentieth Century*, vol. 2, ed. Tharu and Lalita (New York: Feminist Press, 1993), 53.

16. Sumanta Banerjee, "Marginalization of Women's Popular Culture in Nineteenth Century Bengal," in *Recasting Women: Essays in Colonial History*, ed. Kumkum Sangari and Sudesh Vaid (New Delhi: Kali for Women, 1989), 128–129, 134, 130.

17. Suleri, *Rhetoric*, 80.

18. Shanta Krishnaswamy, *The Woman in Indian Fiction in English* (New Delhi: Ashish, 1984), 274.

19. Lata Mani, "Contentious Traditions: The Debate on SATI in Colonial India," *Cultural Critique* 7 (Fall 1987): 154 (reprinted in Sangari and Vaid, *Recasting Women*). Shahbano Begum's legal case against her husband, Mohammed Ahmed Khan, seeking maintenance after their divorce, was settled by the Supreme Court of India on 23 April 1985. The court granted divorced Muslim women, traditionally placed under the protection of Muslim personal law, the right to lifelong maintenance through the exercise of a uniform civil code.

20. Banerjee, "Marginalization," 131.

CHAPTER 16

"Luminous Brahmin Children Must Be Saved"

Imperialist Ideologies, "Postcolonial" Histories in
Bharati Mukherjee's *The Tiger's Daughter*

Indrani Mitra

Few South Asian immigrant writers have commanded as much
critical attention as Bharati Mukherjee (only Salman Rushdie comes to mind)
or provoked as strong and disparate reactions in critics and readers. Two excerpts may illustrate the spectrum of Mukherjee criticism.

The first is from an essay on South Asian immigrant writing by Feroza Jussawalla: "Bharati Mukherjee definitely seems to have found her 'haven' in the
United States, but with this comes an obsequiousness, a pleading to be main-
streamed. . . . This new generation of South Asian writers are ex-colonials,
twice colonized, like the twice born Brahmins, oppressed by their European education and by their hunger to be Americanized.[1]

The second comment is from a review of Mukherjee's works by Polly Shulman: "It's not only the new-comers who have to learn new rules and ways of
thinking in these stories—Americans who love them also end up changing. . . .
In Mukherjee's books, everyone is living in a new world, even those who
never left home. As traditions break down, the characters must try to make lives
out of the pieces.[2]

If Jussawalla finds Mukherjee's assimilationist urge somewhat irksome, Shulman (and many would agree with her) discovers in these stories of immigrant
lives textual strategies that interrupt the self-absorbed passivity of mainstream
American culture with the distinct post-modern dialectics of center and margin, self and other, domination and subversion.

The multiplicity of critical perspectives calls for a reevaluation of Bharati
Mukherjee, especially of her place in the growing canon of "postcolonial"

literatures; more important, it necessitates a rigorous reexamination of the term "postcolonial" in its rapid deployment in scholarly and pedagogic exercises today. Mukherjee has herself claimed the label "postcolonial,"[3] and readers and critics have consented all too readily, pointing variously to the author's childhood in British India, her supposedly insider knowledge of a Third World" culture, her thematic preoccupation with immigrant identity crises, and her cultural critique of mainstream American life as signs of her "postcoloniality." This disconcerting range of meanings points to the ambiguity of the term "postcolonial" as a theoretical tool; more dangerously, the amorphous critical positions it generates speak of a crisis moment in the emergent field of Postcolonial Studies, one that perhaps signals the appropriation of its political content into the more domestic, poststructuralist preoccupations with identity and difference. My reading of Mukherjee's first novel, *The Tiger's Daughter*, is therefore framed by some of these larger issues in the politics of Postcolonial Studies.[4]

Those of us who teach and write in the gray zone now termed Postcolonial Studies no doubt agree that "postcoloniality" is at its very broadest a condition of existence that is anchored in a past of colonial domination and a present of ongoing struggles to overcome the legacies of that past at all levels. The difficulties posed by such open-ended definitions are immediately manifest in recent attempts to theorize the literary products of material conditions as global and varied as the legacies of colonialism. Theoretical studies such as *The Empire Writes Back*, whose editors—Bill Ashcroft, Gareth Griffiths, and Helen Tiffin—glibly include the American literary tradition as one more site of a "postcolonial" encounter with a dominant culture, warn of dangerous homogenizing tendencies.[5] This essay is an effort to retrieve the politics of "postcoloniality" by reconstructing the complex topography of colonized societies in which individual subjects are to be located. My reading of *The Tiger's Daughter* as "postcolonial" text rests on two thematic considerations: First, it examines the novel's formulation of East-West relations, both past and present; second, it attempts to uncover the textual ideologies encoded in the novelistic representation of one definitive moment in the history of contemporary India, the Naxalbari uprising of the 1970s.

This study, will, I hope, encourage another look at Mukherjee's place in the canons of "postcolonial" literatures. In their undoubtedly challenging task of defining this category, Ashcroft, Griffiths, and Tiffin point to the narrativizing of displacement—geographic, cultural, linguistic—as "a major feature of postcolonial literature."[6] So described, the emergent canon of "postcolonial" writing would certainly absorb Bharati Mukherjee's fiction, which overwhelmingly thematizes the postwar phenomenon of transcontinental migrations from the

former colonies to the metropolitan centers of the West and the consequent experiences of cultural contact and conflict.

Moreover, Mukherjee's own history—her birth in an upper-middle-class
Bengali family, early education in one of Calcutta's most reputed colonial
("English-medium") schools, and subsequent relocation in the West—play out
many of the psychosocial anxieties that are the legacies of colonialism. The
schizophrenic tensions of her colonial childhood she remembers in the opening pages of *Days and Nights in Calcutta*, a memoir written jointly with her Canadian husband, Clark Blaise. For Mukherjee, the cultural values learned during
early childhood in the extended family home in Ballygunj, a middle-class
neighborhood in Calcutta, were radically redefined when, with her father's increasing success as chemist and industrialist, the family moved to more exclusive, Westernized surroundings and even spent some time abroad. Bharati and
her two sisters were sent to the Loreto House Convent School, Calcutta's pres-
tigious colonial institution run by Irish nuns. Mukherjee recalls that even as a
child her "imagination created two distinct systems of cartography," accommodating in a fragile equilibrium the topography of the New Testament as well
as the multiheaded serpents and anthropomorphic gods of Hindu cosmology.[7]

Of course, in Mukherjee's case, the inscription of "home," already dislocated
in childhood by the imposition of an alien language and its associated value
system, is further complicated by the later events of her life: her training in the
writers' workshop in Iowa, marriage to a Canadian, fifteen agonizing years as
a minority person in hostile Canada, and ultimate adoption of the United States
as a naturalized citizen. In *Days and Nights in Calcutta*, Mukherjee reflects on the
alienation of the English-speaking expatriate writer: "I am a late-blooming
colonial who writes in a borrowed language (English), lives . . . in an alien
country (Canada), and publishes in and is read, when read at all, in another
country, the United States. My Indianness is fragile; it has to be fought for. . . .
Language transforms our ways of apprehending the world; I fear that my
decades-long use of English as a first language has cut me off from my *desh*
[country]" (170).

Mukherjee's self-definition as a "late-blooming colonial" has continued to resonate for many critics of "postcolonial" literatures; however, as my introductory
excerpts indicate, her status in this camp is decidedly ambivalent. Some of the difficulty arises from the writer's own sense of self. Mukherjee has in the past insisted on her recognition as an American writer, claiming an affinity with other
New World writers "whose parents and grandparents had once passed through
Ellis Island." More recently, she has situated herself in the American literary tradition but with a difference. Charting a dialectical relationship with the American mainstream, she offers to tell the epic tales of the "new-immigrants from

non-traditional immigrant countries" with an authority ostensibly founded on a shared history of marginality in a dominant culture.[8]

Through this decade-long process of unmaking and remaking the authorial "I," Mukherjee has continued to resist any attempt by critics to cast on her an Indian identity. She refuses to write the narrative of expatriation, she says. In her now famous essay on immigrant writing she denounces the chronic homesickness of self-conscious exiles such as Salman Rushdie and Amitav Ghosh. Of her Indian past she is willing to reclaim only a limited aspect. Her Indianness— a middle-class, Brahmin sensibility and the dual consciousness that is her colonial legacy—she describes as "a metaphor," an inner filter that colors the way she experiences the world. With India as a palpable material reality of 850 million lives she has severed all ties.

Mukherjee's conflicted relation with the country of her birth is worth investigating for a better understanding of her aesthetics, but I suggest that there are other compelling reasons for probing the actual moment of her rejection of India. What is the India that Mukherjee discards, and why? This essay explores these questions through a textual analysis of Mukherjee's first novel *The Tiger's Daughter*, a story which in my reading enacts the moment of the author's own categorical rejection of India. Since Mukherjee articulated this experience a few years later in *Days and Nights in Calcutta*, I find it useful to preface my analysis of the novel with a look at some significant passages in the autobiographical work, where Mukherjee narrates the intensely subjective history of her own psychological withdrawal from India.

The two texts are situated in analogous historical moments. *The Tiger's Daughter* (1971) is set in the Calcutta of the early 1970s, during the period that came to be known as the "Naxal times." *Days and Nights in Calcutta* (1977) records the author's brief personal experience of that period. The years 1967–73 have acquired a special significance in the history of modern India as the period of the Naxalite movement. A peasant uprising in the Naxalbari subdivision of North Bengal in the spring of 1967 initiated a period of organized armed struggle by landless farmers and itinerant farm workers against oppressive agrarian relations. A radical section of the Bengali communist intelligentsia provided the ideological leadership in the movement and later organized itself into the Marxist-Leninist (CPI-ML) Party. One of the more successful alliances between a radical urban intelligentsia and a militant peasantry, Naxalbari made an unforgettable impression on the sociopolitical consciousness of the country. Although the original uprising was quickly and brutally suppressed, the movement spread in a chain reaction to a number of surrounding areas. After Naxalbari, reflects Sumanto Banerjee, "nothing could ever be quite the same in the Indian countryside."[9]

The ideological nerve center of the movement and the training ground for its large student cadre, Calcutta in the 1970s was the site of numerous public demonstrations and labor strikes. The city produced a band of dedicated ac- tivists whose "bloodshed and heroism in the numerous battles fought in Cal- cutta and its suburbs in 1970–71 gave the [urban] movement its revolutionary aura." Although the movement attained its desired end in only a few pockets, and then only temporarily, its ideological impact was felt throughout the socio- political life of the country. The term Naxalite, Banerjee reminds us, "has be- come a part of common speech all over India, and along with 'Huk' of the Philippines, 'Al Fatah' of Palestine and 'Tupamaros' of Uruguay, has today found a place in the vocabulary of world revolution."[10]

Many of us who grew up in Calcutta in the 1970s knew ourselves to be in some way touched, perhaps transformed, by the storm of that revolution and the epoch of despair that followed. It is no surprise, then, that Bharati Mukher- jee was also changed in that climate; it is the nature of that psychological trans- formation that interests us here. Unexpectedly returning to India for an entire year in 1973 with her Canadian husband and two sons, Mukherjee found her- self in a Calcutta under siege. In *Days and Nights in Calcutta* she provides a telling impression of that year: "It was a year of protest marches and labor strikes and of heartbreaking letters in local newspapers. It was a year for predicting hor- rendous famines and economic collapses. Street people knifed each other over minor irritation. . . . Students rebelled against irrelevant syllabi and poorly de- vised examinations; in some examination halls, they stabbed to death defense- less proctors. . . . Cities changed their character" (167).

The revolutionary potential of the Naxalite movement and other anti-caste, anti-class movements of the time becomes diminished in Mukherjee's text to the disgruntled actions of peevish schoolboys. She remembers only a time of meaningless violence and crippling terror. The reductive move is abundantly clear in a remark a page later, which may serve as a commentary to the fore- going passage: "In India, history is full of uninterpreted episodes. . . . Events have no necessary causes; behavior no inevitable motive. Things simply are, be- cause that is their nature" (168). Effectively decontextualizing sociopolitical struggles for justice and liberation, Mukherjee represents, with a recognizable Orientalist slant, an essentialized India that must make even the least sensitive of her readers cringe.

In the moment of revolutionary struggles, Mukherjee's allegiance is clear. In Calcutta she experienced Naxalbari and its aftermath through the fragile lives of her former school friends, all members of a Westernized elite, then seemingly beleaguered in their graceful colonial mansions behind high garden walls that provided only an indifferent shield from the anger searing the city beyond. The brutal city, Mukherjee feared, would soon wipe out these last remaining spaces of beauty, good taste, and innocence. She admired her friends for their allegiance to the old city, their refusal to leave. For her, the unsung hero of the hour was not the dispossessed peasant or the militant worker but the upper-class housewife left alone to comfort an aging mother-in-law and young children through the days-long blockade of her home by the disgruntled employees of her industrialist husband. By her own admission, Mukherjee registered in Calcutta a Chekovian tragedy of a dying elite. If her sympathy is sometimes undercut by a mild censure of this naive upper class, it is because objective distance and superior education enable her to recognize the inevitability of their demise.

At the end of that year, Mukherjee made a telling choice: to be in the future merely "another knowledgeable but desolate tourist" in India. She knew that if she stayed, the country would "fail [her] more seriously than she had failed it by settling abroad" (284–85). The scenes of underdevelopment and the specter of violence had reduced India for her to "just another Asian country with too many agonies and too much passion" (285). Once again, the blatant Orientalist formulation—East/Asia = passion (West = reason would be the logical, if unstated, other term of the dichotomy)—cannot but leave her readers dismayed. Discarding the real India for (an)other India created daily in her imagination, Mukherjee underwent a symbolic rebirth from expatriate to immigrant in the United States. Keeping in mind her response to India, we can now turn to *The Tiger's Daughter*, written a few years before *Days and Nights in Calcutta* but situated in the same historical moment—Calcutta in the early 1970s.

The Tiger's Daughter is the story of Tara Banerjee Cartwright, born in Calcutta, educated at Vassar and Madison, and married to an American, David Cartwright. Tara returns to India after seven years to find the city of her childhood altered beyond recognition. (Even the most cautious poststructuralist critic can hardly fail to recognize the autobiographical traces in the novel's plot and in the conceptualization of its protagonist.) Against the backdrop of the riot-torn city, Tara reestablishes contact with one-time school friends, all members of Calcutta's Westernized upper class. In the idle chatter of these young people, in their melodramatic references to the "troubled times," she notices a frightening naiveté. Educated in the progressive institutions of the West, Tara alone seems to possess a deep understanding of the inexorable processes changing their world. In a curious reworking of the patriarchal imperialist mythology that had cast the white man as savior, Mukherjee's text brings the educated, emancipated Indian woman back from the West as the only remaining symbol of cultural progress in a moribund, tradition-bound society and, therefore, as the possible redeemer of the East. That Tara, too, is drawn into the effete, indolent climate and can neither communicate her knowledge nor effect positive change is not merely a reflection of the author's own distaste for upper- and middle-class Bengali culture; it is also the text's ideological judgment on the political climate of the 1970s, in which Mukherjee can see only the end of all order and the onset of total anarchy.

The Camac Street society to which Tara returns retains the traces of Bengal's colonial aristocratic culture. Tara's childhood home still manifests the "eclectic" meeting of two worlds, from the Italian tables in the entrance halls and the tiger skin decorating one wall (the trophy of a Banerjee ancestor's keen interest in the favorite imperial sport), the heavy imported furniture in the living room, and the deep canvas chairs on the balcony reflecting "the order and ease of British days" up to the marble prayer room on the third floor where the array of Hindu gods and goddesses are the objects of Tara's mother's constant preoccupation (30–34). In the city at large, the few remaining colonial institutions—the Rotary Club, the British Council, and, of course, the Catelli Continental Hotel—are the last social sites of this cultural encounter. The violence of colonialism is carefully written out of Mukherjee's text, which celebrates instead the exuberance of cultural interchange. If there is a critique of this society at all, it is merely a mildly censorious eyebrow raised at an anachronistic world that still lives "by Victorian rules, changed decisively by the exuberance of the Hindu imagination" (34).

The text's most telling sign of a decayed colonial culture is old Joyonto Roy Chowdhury, in blazer, ascot, and sockless sandals, keeping a protective vigil on the terrace of the Catelli Continental over the beautiful "Brahmin children" ("Brahmin" is the author's novelistic code for the upper class or caste), "the last pillars of his world," as they while away their days, impervious to the disappearing world around them (46). The old man's endless phrase games are an ironic commentary on the shallow lives these young people lead, clinging to the cultural and linguistic artifacts of the imperial West as the mark of their distinction in society.

As Joyonto knows and Tara will learn, theirs is a world under siege. Not surprisingly, the plot is framed by images of invasion. The opening of the novel calls attention to the somber doorman of the Catelli Continental, who keeps his solitary vigil over that precious symbol of a disappearing era, and the concluding scene returns to this man as he is clubbed down by the riotous mob. Of course, one discovers moments before the end that this last bastion of the *bhadralok* (Bengali gentleman) has finally fallen, for the Catelli is now owned by the grotesque Marwari industrialist Tuntunwalla. The novel's most compelling trope for the demise of an era is the "invasion" of the female body in the scene of Tara's seduction by the repulsive Marwari, the emblem of a new power structure in an anarchic regime (on this point, more later).

The text injects a tragic (almost cosmic) inevitability into the decline of the
Bengali elite by locating the story of the 1970s against a larger narrative of social and political change over the last century. It is not without significance that
even before it introduces Tara, the novel recalls the murder, nearly a hundred
years before, of Tara's great-grandfather Harilal Banerjee, the renowned *zamindar* (landowner) of Pachapara. Although Harilal's death signaled the end of an
epoch, and the landowning Banerjees were superseded by the "Jute Mill" Roy
Chowdhurys, representatives of a rising mercantile elite, the contours and
meaning of that change remained long unrecognized. The surviving members
of the landed aristocracy (Tara's grandfather, for instance) were easily absorbed
into the ranks of the rising mercantile and professional classes, and Bengal's cultural and economic prominence was unimpeded for another century. Yet the
text implies that the murder of a nineteenth-century *zamindar* by unknown as-
sailants signals the start of an inexorable cosmic process whose final, fatal form
is the riot-torn Calcutta of 1970.

The oppressive production relations under feudalism and later under mercantile and industrial capitalism that periodically led to peasant militancy and
labor unrest in India are left unexamined in Mukherjee's novel. Instead, the
sociopolitical history of Bengal for the last hundred years is narrativized as the
elegiac tale of the privileged class. The moments of change seem to be marked
by acts of violence against strong and innocent men. At his death the villagers,
his subjects, remember Harilal as "a good man, a strong man"; his successors,
the Roy Chowdhurys also produced "good and virile men" (7). In the novel's
present, Tara's father, Bengal Tiger Banerjee, continues the heritage of strength
and vision: "While the restive city forced weak men to fanatical defiance or dis-
honesty, the Bengal Tiger remained powerful, just and fearless" (9). Textual
ideology is nowhere more blatant than in this idealized portrait of the benevolent, paternal employer who, impervious to the pressures of the times, performs his duties, "working out medical and disability insurance for his workers, night classes in the factory for those who could not write or read" (9).
Social protest is decontextualized so that we merely hear of "angry, fanatical
faces," "unreasonable murders," "suspicious drownings," "bloody and muti-
lated bodies," without any reconstruction of the socioeconomic causes that
provoked such acts of violence.

Is it surprising, then, that the political situation of the 1970s, the background
of Tara's story, remains blurred in *The Tiger's Daughter*? The terms "Naxalbari" and
"Naxalite" never surface in the narrative. We hear, instead, of *goondahs* (hooli-
gans) and "burglars," of "rioters" and "demonstrators" and "marchers." The
closest the novel comes to applying a political label to the group is the generic
term "revolutionaries" or the absurdly comical "left-of-the-left" politicians. The

text does not permit a close look at the revolutionaries; we see them only as a "disorderly crowd" with no clear agenda beyond overturning cars and vandalizing the ritzy shopping district below the Catelli. From the safety of the hotel balcony, the marchers appear to Tara as "tourists" enjoying an unfamiliar sport or as "rebellious children rather than political militants," an impression that succeeds in trivializing the ominous slogan "Blood bath! Blood bath!" In the novel the revolutionaries have no political goal other than a vaguely articulated lust for revenge. One hears of gheraos (holdups) of industrialists and assassinations of landlords, but the text remains silent as to their social and political causes.

Ignoring the socioeconomic forces that erupted into the revolutionary situation of the 1970s, Mukherjee looks for answers in the psychological makeup of the upper-class Bengalis. In the young men of her circle—the soft, flabby Pronob and the shallow, pompous Sanjay—Tara notices a regrettable lack of the entrepreneurial energy that characterized empire builders of the past generation such as the Bengal Tiger. Their present descendants, the young people who had "inherited, not earned, their wealth" (45), are equipped neither to extend their empires nor to protect their world against the agents of destruction, figured in the novel by the riotous mob on the one hand, and on the other the crude Tuntunwalla, representative of a new race of unprincipled capitalists.

In a calculated distortion of history, the novel's concluding scene presents an unexpected alliance of two savage forces: between them, the bloodthirsty mob and the henchmen of the Marwari attack old Joyonto Roy Chowdhury, that human caricature of Bengal's elite colonial culture. This last scene is underlined by a grim sense of tragedy. The book ends with the death of Pronob, the most prominent member of Tara's circle, in a desperate act of martyrdom to save the old man. By granting Pronob this final, albeit futile, moment of heroism, the text manifests its ideological stance on the sociopolitical situation of the time. Within the terms of the novel, the decline of the Bengali elite—admittedly now effete and sterile—also signals the death of a grand humanist code of honor, decency, and chivalry. Joyonto Roy Chowdhury's delirious rambling at this point evokes a poignant sense of assault on innocence: "The year of the puppy is over, do you understand? The age of the snake is coming, but the boy doesn't know it yet" (208; emphasis added). But the poignancy is undercut by the knowledge that the Bengali upper class owes its present fate to its own spiritual sterility, its inability to produce in the current generation such men of vision and action as the Bengal Tiger.

Perhaps the single place of transformative politics in The Tiger's Daughter is the tacit recognition of the bankruptcy of an older, patriarchal social order founded on a belief in powerful men as producers and protectors. Through the life of Tara Banerjee Cartwright the text proposes a dual ideological project: to remake the Indian woman in a new mold fit for a changed, and far less stable, social environment; and to locate in this reconstructed figure a measure of promise and vision that might restore some of the lost vitality to an exhausted social class. Ultimately, the text can realize only part of this project.

In an interesting narrative complexity, the novel foregrounds the lives of women in the evolving history of changing modes of production in Bengal. The story of Tara is contextualized against the lives of Banerjee women from 1879 to the present. The brief history of the *zamindar* Harilal Banerjee's younger daughter, Arupa, testifies to the oppressive place of women in feudal patriarchy. In Harilal's granddaughter Arati, Tara's mother, we glimpse an emergent definition of femininity, produced under the pressure on the *bhadralok* of "progressive" Western (Victorian) models. "Trained in the minor decorative arts, to sing well, play the sitar, supervise cooks" (32), Arati combined the skills of modern home management with a limited desire for self-development through education. Yet in her we see the germ of a feminist consciousness. A practical sense acquired through reading and a budding awareness that "things were really bad for Bengali women" (48) bred in Arati the self-confidence to defy the authority of the patriarchal extended family and to make the first move toward a nuclear home founded on the "companionate" model of conjugal relations.

The boundaries of autonomous subjecthood for women in this variation of familial relations are evident, however, in the sentimental tableau of a relaxed summer evening when the Bengal Tiger sits in the center of his Sears, Roebuck garden swing with his wife by his side. For women like Arati, the limited quest for selfhood is still inscribed within the domestic space and critically hinges on the material prosperity of well-meaning husbands. In the unstable social climate of the 1970s, the text is unable to create even such a space of relative security for the present generation of women.

It is not quite accidental, then, that the story of Tara's return to Calcutta is prefaced with whispered reminders of the fate of Mrs. "General Pumps" Gupta, a recent victim of certain unspeakable deeds (rape?). The incident, recalled several times through the novel, sets the stage for the climactic acts of violation: the attack on Tara by a group of ruffians in Darjeeling, and finally, her seduction by Tuntunwalla. These instances of assault on upper-class women (the label "General Pumps" indicates the victim's class affiliations) no doubt serve a crucial purpose in the plot. In a curious adaptation of colonial narrative, in which the white woman inevitably fell prey to the native rapist, Mukherjee's novel undertakes another calculated distortion of history by casting the dominant, economically powerful group in the role of victim.

In the life of Tara, the novel explores the conflicted course through which the modern woman may map an identity in an uncertain environment where the older models are obviously exhausted. For Tara, the first step was taken when the Bengal Tiger, always a man of vision, decided to send his fifteen-year-old daughter to college in Poughkeepsie, New York, in explicit defiance of social convention. Unlike the previous generation of women who had reshaped their lives in the patriarchal care of fathers and husbands, the young Tara was left to carve her destiny in previously uncharted terrain. In the dormitory at Vassar she made the first move toward autonomous selfhood: She discovered that she had "started to think for herself" (11). The critical break with the past happened when this great-granddaughter of Harilal Banerjee, overcoming her fear of caste impurity and mlechha (nonbeliever) men, became the wife of David Cartwright in an alliance that required "no priests, no fires, and no blessings" (125).

Back in Calcutta, however, Tara discovers the young women of her circle still controlled by obsolete social conventions. The ultimate developmental goal that the novel posits for Tara is to be the bearer of progressive, Western ideas to a moribund society. Yet again, in an ideologically significant formulation, The Tiger's Daughter brings the West back into the life of the East with a new "civilizing" mission, but this time without the darker imperialist agenda. The two Western characters in the novel, the student civil rights activist and the social worker, are both in India "because India needs help. The third world has to be roused to help itself" (166). These latest representatives of the West, however, with their liberal-humanist agenda, are largely incomprehensible to a native population that still lives by Victorian rules. Therefore, in the "new" Bengali woman, with roots in both worlds, the text attempts to construct the ideal cultural ambassador.

Not surprisingly, then, Tara alone possesses an acute understanding of the changing times (old Joyonto Roy Chowdhury may be dismissed as a comic chorus in the work). It is Tara who sees in her father, the Bengal Tiger, a lonely "pillar supporting a balcony that had long outlived its beauty and its function" (29). Armed with a liberal education and Western notions of sexual emancipation, she alone notes with exasperated pity her woman friend's uncritical submission to a traditional marriage with a "foreign-educated and very brilliant boy" (127) from a compatible caste group. And it is she, again, who recognizes in the Marwari the real enemy of the bhadralok. But Tara can only suffer her vision; sinking into the same apathy, she can neither save herself nor communicate her understanding. Interestingly, perhaps predictably, her psychological regression is charted through the breakdown of her communication with David (the voice of the West?), her conscience in the novel. It is David who insists she "take a stand against injustice, against unemployment, hunger and bribery" (131). The disintegration of the person she had carefully constructed at Vassar and Madison is best evident in her inability to write a meaningful letter to David, to tell "this foreigner" she loved him very much. She recovers herself at the very end, but by then, of course, it is too late.

Narrative outcome in *The Tiger's Daughter* reinforces its ideological mission. Mukherjee's novel does not assume the task of illuminating the multiple struggles for social and economic justice in a "postcolonial" society, increasingly depleted of its resources in the present neocolonial phase. Rather, the ostensible project of the text is the dirge (Chekovian elegy) for an old-fashioned elite culture. Therefore, in the Calcutta of 1970, the site of one of the most powerful antifeudal, anticapitalist struggles of our time, the text fails to locate any regenerative energy. For Mukherjee, any residual hope is located only in the figure of the modern woman as she sheds the shackles of obsolete conventions and constructs an autonomous self. Of course, we must remind ourselves, the place of such subjective reconstruction can only be the West, more specifically the United States, where Mukherjee herself has found a hospitable climate for self-development. Indeed, the novel's concluding lines, the delirious rambling of old Joyonto Roy Chowdhury, may resonate with a wealth of meaning for Mukherjee's readers: "Dear Madam, you I shored against my ruins. Have you left? *Where are the jets?*" (209; emphasis added).

How, then, are we to read Mukherjee's first novel? Can we, perhaps, continue to read in it (as most critics, Jussawalla included, have done) only an early thematization of the author's preoccupation with questions of identity in the ex-colonial immigrant: "How does the foreignness of spirit begin?" Or should we, instead, search for textual traces that shed light on a moment in Mukherjee's own ideological formation as she turns from India, with scarcely concealed distaste, to a celebration of the United States as an unmarked, ahistorical utopia free of discriminatory politics, a place of infinite becoming: "It's not that in the United States ghastly things don't happen, but the muggings in the subways or the firmhandedness in the stores are random incidents, not a pattern of racial discrimination. There is a kind of curiosity and immigrant exuberance in the United States."[11]

My purpose in this reading of *The Tiger's Daughter* has been to situate Bharati Mukherjee ideologically in the complex landscape of modern India. In doing so I must acknowledge with appreciation recent critical attempts to undergrid Mukherjee's class affiliations and the ostensible neocolonialist agenda manifest in her writing.[12] Despite occasional pungent criticism, however, scholarly interest in Mukherjee's writing has continued to escalate in the past few years (the present author's not excepted). MLA conventions have seen numerous papers, sometimes entire panels, devoted to studies of her writing, and anthologies of critical essays have recently been produced. Sympathetic, adulatory readings of her "postcolonial" identity crises more than amply compensate for the occasional combative criticism. Even as a Munshi Premchand or a Saadat Hasan Manto remains permanently "out of print," Mukherjee reappears on bookstore shelves in new paperback editions; the economical Fawcett series alone would testify to her secure place in the reading lists of "postcolonial" or multicultural or world literature courses.

To return, then, to the framing concerns articulated at the opening of this essay: What does it mean for us as teachers and scholars to read Bharati Mukherjee (or Hanif Kureishi or V. S. Naipaul, for that matter) in the classroom as one more site of "postcolonial" struggles? In a recent engagement with the term "postcolonial," Ella Shohat has indicated that its relative neutrality, as compared to the radical alternatives of "neo-colonial" or "third-worldist," makes it a more palatable option for conservative college administrations.[13] More important for our purpose, the absence of analytical precision in the term has allowed a shift in the focus of Postcolonial Studies from the resistance literatures produced in the imperialist and neoimperialist sites of struggle to a more domestic celebration of cultural diversity and difference. Mukherjee's own roots in a former colony, which form the basis of her immigrant narratives of cultural contact and conflict, have merited her inclusion under the over-extended banner of postcoloniality. That her overt "Brahminical" allegiances (again, Mukherjee's own code for the upper class and caste) have received little critical attention is not without significance.

Nowhere is the politics of current academic practices better apparent than in course reading lists that absorb in one global sweep the fiction of a Bharati Mukherjee and the protest literature of a Sembene Ousmane or a Ngugi wa Thiong'o, with the dangerous consequence of diluting the political and ideological content of the latter two. In the Indian context, for instance, the current trend has meant a neglect of works produced in the caste, class, and sexual struggles of India and an unmerited absorption in the writing of certain segments of the diasporic population—educated, upper-class immigrants—in the metropolitan centers. Compare the paucity of critical interest in a Premchand or an Ismat Chugtai or a Manik Bandyopadhyay (to name just a few Indian writers available in translation) to the spurt of scholarly papers generated annually on the group Tim Brennan has called "the metropolitan celebrities."[14] Now, therefore, when it appears that the canon wars are for the moment out of the way and Postcolonial Studies here to stay, it is perhaps time to undertake a rigorous review of the term itself, and especially the academic practices to which it translates, before "postcolonial" becomes another "shapeless sack into which one could simply dump peoples, classes, races, civilizations and continents so that they might more easily disappear."[15]

NOTES

1. Feroza Jussawalla, "Chiffon Saris: The Plight of the South Asian Immigrant in the New World," *Massachusetts Review* 29.4 (1988–89): 591–93.

2. Polly Shulman, "Home Truths: Bharati Mukherjee, World Citizen," *Voice Literary Supplement*, June 1988, 19.

3. See, e.g., the Interview with Bharati Mukherjee in *Iowa Review* 20.3 (1990): 7–32.

4. Bharati Mukherjee, *The Tiger's Daughter* (Markham: Penguin, 1987), hereafter cited by page number in the text.

5. The following comment illustrates my point: "The first post-colonial society to develop a national literature was the USA. . . . In many ways the American experience and its attempts to produce a new kind of literature can be seen as a model for all later post-colonial writing" (Bill Ashcroft, Gareth Griffiths, and Helen Tiffin, eds., *The Empire Writes Back: Theory and Practice in Post-Colonial Literatures* [London: Routledge, 1989], 16). Calling the American experience postcolonial succeeds in obscuring not only the colonial reality of territorial occupation and prolonged political and economic domination but also the role of the United States in the colonial exploitation of other peoples.

6. Ibid., 8.

7. Clark Blaise and Bharati Mukherjee, *Days and Nights in Calcutta* (Garden City, N.Y.: Doubleday, 1977), 171 (hereafter cited by page number in the text).

8. Bharati Mukherjee, *Darkness* (Markham: Penguin, 1985) 3; Mukherjee, "Immigrant Writing: Give Us Your Maximalists!" *New York Times Book Review*, 28 August 1988, 1.

9. Sumanto Banerjee, *India's Simmering Revolution: The Naxalbari Uprising* (London: Zed Press, 1984), i.

10. Ibid., 209, i.

11. Mukherjee, quoted in Jussawalla, "Chiffon Saris," 591.

12. I have in mind the essays in *Bharati Mukherjee: Critical Perspectives*, ed. Emmanuel S. Nelson (New York : Garland, 1993). Of particular interest in the collection is Debjani Banerjee's "'In the Presence of History': The Representation of Past and Present Indias in Bharati Mukherjee's Fiction" (161–80), which points to Mukherjee's misrepresentation and misuse of critical moments in the history of modern India.

13. Ella Shohat, "Notes on the Post-Colonial," *Social Text* 31–32 (1992): 99–113.

14. Timothy A. Brennan, "India, Nationalism, and Other Failures," *South Atlantic Quarterly* 87.1 (1988): 135.

15. Regis Debray's comment in reference to the term "Third World" is quoted in Barbara Harlow, *Resistance Literature* (London: Methuen, 1987), 6.

CHAPTER 17

The Troubled Past

Literature of Severing and the Viewer/Viewed Dialectic

Huma Ibrahim

When one nation, albeit with great self-contained diversity, "chooses" to split into unequal halves, what questions are we forced to ask about the historical and social psyche of peoples who were part of an uneasy whole but whose severance led to a massive butchery of one another? At the theoretical level, this violence against so-called different religious groups has a long-standing history in the subcontinent, from nearly a thousand years of Muslim colonial rule to two hundred years of Western, primarily British, colonialism. The somewhat artificial sub-continental partition gives rise to a presupposition of what I call a viewer/viewed dialectic, but that dialectic never unveils the intricate dynamics of the violence or commences a dialogue about that same troubled past between peoples both connected and severed.

It is useful to employ the dichotomy of viewer/viewed in regard to the subcontinental partition, because Hindus, Muslims, and Sikhs have all taken turns being subject and object in relation to the violence that occurred—in other words, being viewers of the massacre as it is external to their own subjective reality and being viewed as the immediate victims of that same trauma. What I have called the viewer/viewed dialectic becomes a mechanism for evasion, for putting the blame on the other side and collapsing into a regressive sentimentality. In this essay, I explore where the specifics of this particular evasion of historical violence originate. The analogy of silence and the breaking of silence that comes to mind is the African American one. As recently as the 1980s and 1990s, prominent writers such as Toni Morrison and August Wilson have entered the process of "rememorying" the gender specifics of the violent past. This "story," as Morrison has said on the last page of her novel Beloved, is "not to pass on."[1]

The story must be told, however, and as Leslie Marmon Silko says, there must not be "any lies." The recounting or recoding of the violent subcontinental partition is necessary precisely because it provides a window into the complexities of imperial political agendas as well as other sources of internal animosities.

At the time of the partition, those on what was to become the Pakistani side of the subcontinent worried that the "British swine" would favor the Indians, for wasn't Nehru so thick with the Mountbattens that he was even said to be sleeping with the lady side of that contingent? and everybody knew how reserved and cool Jinnah could be, et cetera, et cetera. Here, I want to elaborate on the nervousness about a politically conscious analysis of the partition as an evasion of historical processes in which the colonial subject participates, imperialism notwithstanding. Even the findings documented by the historian Gyanendra Pandey become evasive about the actual violence.[2] Statistics such as those of the centuries-old slave trade tend to horrify at an emotional level but are not often translated to a historical analysis of oppression. Further, this sort of evasiveness constitutes another aspect of what has to become the dialectic of decolonization. In other words, the silence that claims an important part of the past must be addressed, and the partition itself, fraught with ambiguity, must become part of the sociohistoric dialogue between Indian peoples as well as the peoples of what became Pakistan in 1947. This essay attempts to bring people from both sides of the border onto common ground so that they can analyze a joint history of the oppression out of which the violence of partition emerged.

Gyanendra Pandey has talked about the violence in Indian history as a "known," the "contours and characters" of which are "simply assumed" and therefore "need no investigation." His observations are accurate in that there is great reluctance to explore the issue in detail, but I would argue that "historical discourse" on the partition has simply not "been able to capture and represent the moment of violence," even "with great difficulty."[3] I agree with Pandey's contention that the present-day violence between Muslims and Hindus in India is part of an aftermath of the animosities occurring during the partition, but unlike him, I argue that the very nature of the violation of loyalties and of the violence freezes the dialogue between Hindus and Muslims into what seems like an impossible impasse. I call this impasse the viewer/viewed dialectic because it is based on suspicion, lack of information, and only the beginnings of a dialogue between the two sides about the partition. Films such as M. S. Sathyu's *Garam Hawa* (Hot air) have been a little more successful in portraying the "collective insanity" of this region, but written accounts have continued to sentimentalize or evade the undigested history of violence.[4] Saadat Hasan Manto's brilliant short stories tend to describe, in minute detail, the situation the partition gave rise to, but no literary critic has so far engaged the theoretical aspects of the violence.[5] There is little theoretical analysis of how Pakistanis and Indians looked for new meanings in the new context that emerged out of a desire for decolonization, or of how the desire for decolonization was fragmented by brutal violence amongst the colonized. Pandey rightly suggests that the violence hijacked an "enormously powerful and noble struggle."[6] I believe it is important to confront the theoretical implications of this "hijacking."

On the Pakistani side of the border (with which I am more familiar, though I assume the same sort of suspicion of neglect and deceit on the other side of the border) there is to this day a belief that the Mountbattens went in a plane with Nehru all along the length of what was to become the border between Pakistan and India, deciding over cocktails who should have what. Since Jinnah was a Muslim and could not partake of alcohol, he was not invited.

Historical gossip aside, the literature about the experience of the partition often suggests a desire for one side to be understood as well as forgiven by the other. Implicit in these tentative attempts is the invoking of an audience that usually consists of people on the other side of the border. But it seems to me that these two "peoples" who are so eager to address each other are reluctant to come face to face in order to do so. This is a curious part of the colonial and postcolonial dialogue over which palls a heavy silence, the few nostalgic and sentimental attempts to describe a unity that no doubt once existed notwithstanding. Indeed, the very fact that the topic of the partition still constitutes a place in the postcolonial imagination is testimony to its importance to historical dialogue. Often, the extreme nostalgia with which Hindu-Muslim relationships are described becomes, then, another sort of evasion. I believe it is time to engage in a dialogue about history whose central characters are not the colonizer but rather the colonized nations. These two nations have to interrelate because the histories of India and Pakistan are interwoven, giving rise to what Wilson Harris has called the "cross cultural psyche."[7]

Many Indian and Pakistani writers of fiction have incorporated the events of 1947 in larger or smaller detail in their work, but I contend that since the experience was indigestible, the historical psyche that views the past is still embarrassed, grieved, and baffled by what it sees. I cannot speak for the schools in India, but this part of our history is certainly overlooked in the Pakistani school systems. Even though there are parents who talk about the "difficulties" and necessities of emigrating from one nation split into two, a large and audible silence structures itself around the partition. As in the 1989 Bhagalpur riots in India, after which "none of the surviving victims will talk about rape," silence obscures the details of the trauma of partition.[8]

Despite their exploration of the partition—through history, novels, plays, poems, short stories, and films—writers, historians, and filmmakers seem reluctant to theorize, partly because of the attachment they have to this severing and partly because the violence will not allow them to make it part of what inevitably becomes human historical experience. Instead, there is a great reliance on sentimentality. I believe that the reluctance to negotiate the violence of partition emotionally and historically can be dissipated only through an ongoing dialogue between these "warring factions." One sees either a tendency to overplay the emotionality of the severing of communities which was the partition or a kind of detached informational recording and recoding of horrendous events. Another omission, if one can call it that, is the lack of attention to the jubilation a whole India felt at the leaving of the British. Abdul Kalam Azad, a Muslim political leader of the time who was against the partition, said that "for the first time in Indian history the entire people was aflame with the desire for independence."[9] The joy must have been quickly replaced by horror at the mutual massacre of Sikhs, Hindus, and Muslims. And in the "fictional" writing there is only the trauma without any trace of the joy.

The unconcealed joy of the colonial over the terrible fight in the federal congress about partition from the 1930s on is part of the colonial quotient which is often left undiscoursed. But the British, gloating over the growing dissension between Muslims and Hindus, found the task of severing one nation unequally into two easier, for of course they left shortly after the partition for their own little island nation. And perhaps the massacres reinforced their rationale for having subjugated barbaric peoples. The problematics of Hindu-Muslim disunity, however, is made nostalgic through time, in spite of what we see today in Ayodhya and Bombay as a reenactment of what occurred in 1947. I believe that the Hindu-Muslim conflict in Bombay and other parts of the country is related in part to what sits as undigested history from 1947, which perhaps one needs to understand in order to analyze the current animosities.

Most of the "historical" accounts of that period have been written by retired officials who in their capacity as representive of one side or the other choose to make somewhat clumsy stipulations about why Hindus, Sikhs, and Muslims brutally attacked one another and mercilessly killed innocent victims, even though there is a comparative silence about the actual reactions to the butchery.[10]

A recent play performed in Washington, D.C., no doubt for area Indians and Pakistanis, was about an old Hindu woman who haunts the house in which she was born and raised; the house is in Lahore, which was to become Pakistan. Curiously, this play reflects a desire to bridge the gaps between these "two" peoples and recognize the links between them, but it insists on remembering only the heroism and not the sordidness, which is equally problematic. In the play, an Indian Muslim family from Lucknow, allotted this house, after their initial shock adopt this brave woman who has refused to go to India with her own family but remains firmly fixed in her nation and in her loyalty to geography. A little later she does offer to go to her family in India to avoid causing community animosity against the Muslim family, "the enemy" whom she has adopted as her own kin. Her new family bravely refuse, insisting on a conceptually new yet contradictory stand of their own as well as on her right to be in that house. The end of the play is heart-rending, since her refusal to forfeit her right to die in her own house results in a dilemma for the Muslim people. They have to bury her but have no recourse to Hindu burial customs, a situation that simply would not have occurred before partition. During her funeral procession, however, the local mullah or leader of the Muslims, who has decided to bury this Hindu woman, is killed by extremists, and that act encapsulates the icon of the partition: needless killing of "brothers" and, I might add without any exaggeration, sisters. Yet these situations represent varying degrees of animosity toward colonialism. Both the Muslims and the Hindus want to end colonialism, even as they destroy each other. The producers of this play wanted to extend the idea, already in existence, which "seeks to expose the dangerous games that anti-social forces play with human lives and emotions. It is not an issue of Hindus versus Muslims or India versus Pakistan but the problems perpetrated by a few opportunists."[11] The recent interfaith violence in cities such as Bombay suggests a different ontological structure and history. It seems to me that there remains some undigested aspect of coloniality which has never entered the realm of discourse, even though it is saturated by the sentimentality of loss.

The name of this play is interesting in itself. Written by a Muslim, Asghar Wajahat, it is called *Jisne Lahore Nahin Dekha O Janmya Hi Nahin* (Whoever hasn't seen lahore hasn't really been born yet). The title harks back to division, perhaps, and as the play shows, an artificial one. The first part is in Urdu, a language developed by the Great Mogul Akbar to reunify India and to accommodate his enormous armies, which came from many different parts of the subcontinent. This language was meant to suggest oneness, consolidation for a multicultural, multilingual continent. Urdu still enjoys resounding success in Pakistan. The second part of the title is in Punjabi, and it is in the Punjab that Lahore is situated. The title suggests geographical loyalties: Whoever has not seen Lahore, the capital of the Punjab for a long time, has not even been born yet.

Lahore was the first major city in the plains after Muslim colonial warriors from beyond the mountains crossed the Hindu Kush range of the Himalayas. Its link to history in the form of colonialism and resistance to that colonialism has been all too obvious to the Punjabis and others who have visited and lived in Lahore. The special mystique attached to its name has over many years been cultivated and nurtured by its changing residents. To this day one hears from residents who left in fear of religious discrimination that the only thing they miss in their lives is Lahore. "Lahore ki baat hi aure hey" (Lahore is unique), and something terribly essential is missing in any translation, for the suggestion that Lahore has a unique story reflects their emotional ties to the city that the dwellers had. The implication is that in exile from the city, strong ties to Lahore have grown sharper in focus.

One can say, of course, that this play was written for people who, as expatriates, are closer to the experience of the partition than people are nowadays in India and Pakistan, but I don't believe the issue is as simple as that. There are other writers, far more detached, in whose work the troubled psyche defends itself by remaining merely the observer. This is most clearly seen in Bapsi Sidhwa's The Bride.[12] In this novel, a child whose parents are killed on a train to Pakistan is rescued by a "tribal." This man raises her and in a moment of nostalgia marries her off to one of his tribe in the mountains, even though he himself has chosen to live in the city. His adopted daughter, acutely miserable in their mountain habitat, is rescued by a youthful member of the armed forces, but because of the disgrace she has caused her adoptive father's family she can never go back to see him again.

The massacre of a train full of Muslims going toward the newly formed Pakistan is self-consciously presented as a camera would view the scene, not clinically but certainly without much emotionally engaged investment. This detachment in Sidhwa's second novel is so deliberate that it tends to draw attention to itself. She is involved with the lives of the people on the train, talking at length about the pain of exile and uprooting and severing. But the moment the massacre begins, we as readers are no longer in the train but behind a bush located close by—out of immediate physical danger though certainly not so emotionally safe—viewing the massacre with horror but not as part of the event ourselves. The violence does not invade our immediate subjectivities. It is not that the camera of Sidhwa's interest shifts but rather that she is unable to negotiate her pain and the torture of "her" people. She is much more willing to engage with the travelers' experience of potential exile, an exile that takes on sinister ramifications, since not many of them survive.

Is it Sidhwa's fastidious interest that is under attack or her inability to watch as Sikander and Zohra and the rest of the people on the train get massacred? I believe it is Qasim's experience—Qasim, who jumps off the train seconds before the torture—that she is most able to identify with. This occurs for two important reasons. First, much of that experience was like a story of horror told and retold, with large parts left out, about relatives or other Muslims; second, most actual survivors wanted to view it as Qasim or Sidhwa do, from a safe distance. But interestingly enough, this collaborative genocidal attempt not only appears and reappears in literature of that period but tends to crop up again and again in "innocent" novels, whose thrust is quite remote from the subcontinental partition. It is almost as if the emotional focus of the new citizen of Pakistan and the newly decolonized citizen of both India and Pakistan was not "when the British bastards" were here but rather when a family moved to whatever location it chose for its safety. The dialogue tends to take place between Hindus and Muslims rather than with the colonizer. Of course, even though part of the focus should be on the British, the dialogue does belong primarily between Hindus and Muslims; this is certainly true today especially as we hover under the shadow of the bombings in Bombay emerging from Hindu-Muslim animosities. Still, it is worth stipulating that the struggle accounts for this concentration away from the actual liberation and independence from the colonizer and back into the domestic realm, for the struggle between Hindus and Muslims was always used divisively by the colonizers in order to maintain control over them.

The Bride is not really about the partition or its aftermath. It is really about the young girl who was rescued by a tribal man who later married her off to a nephew. The members of her new family brutalize her and she later escapes, but the novel ends with her going off with a new husband and not being able to see her father, the man who rescued her as a girl and raised her. Yet this novel begins with the partition!

Just as Sidhwa is detached about the violence while introducing the subject of partition, Khushwant Singh in A Train to Pakistan is heavily sentimental about the actual severing of the two peoples and blames the angry emotions of special groups for the violence.[13] This novel focuses on a village of both Sikhs and Muslim whose lives are completely disrupted by the partition and rumors of violence, even though they have lived amicably with each other for a very long time. Individual characters are not important, since there are so many inhabiting the pages of this novel. Moreover, the violence is entirely backstage. We do not know who is perpetrating it, just that it is happening, although there are rumors about who is responsible. This tactic tends to exonerate the little communities. Much as in Hitler's Germany, during the subcontinental partition "brothers" denounced each other for often extremely petty advantages, yet there are many stories of honor and integrity maintained despite temptations of obvious economic gain.

Salman Rushdie's Shame evokes national shame but is premised on the life of three sisters who raise one child. In this novel Rushdie writes at some length on the partition—but he does not focus on the massacres as historical, politi-

cal, and social realities with patterns of subjectively negotiated dialogues between the perpetrators of the violence and the receivers of that same violence.
Instead, what we have are mythologist possibilities of the partition scenario.
There is the abstract shame of Chunni, Munni, and Bunny who proceed to conceive a child out of wedlock, pretend that all three of them are pregnant with
this one child, and indeed raise him with the idea that all three are his mothers. But the real shame resides in the experiences and aftermath of the partition.
The personal history of Omar Khayyam and his mothers becomes the mythology that surrounds the desire for severing and violence. Without overtly mentioning the partition, Rushdie writes: "Wherever I turn, there is something of
which to be ashamed. But shame is like everything else; live with it for long
enough and it becomes part of the furniture." Rushdie talks about *sharam*
(shame) for the "unrepented past"; later, when he shows the young Omar
Khayyam exploring the *haweli* (household), he says, "No howls, no clanking
chains!—but disembodied feelings, the choking fumes of ancient hopes, fears,
loves; and finally, made wild by the ancestor—heavy, phantom oppressions of
these far recesses of the run-down building."[14] Like heavy chains there is a suggestion of unaccounted history, and what he is trying to do is break down the
viewer/viewed dialectic by deliberately talking about the issues of the unrepented historical past.

Anita Desai and Bapsi Sidhwa have both written, with interesting collaborative distance as well as involvement, of the 1946–47 tragedy of the peoples of
India and what was to become Pakistan. What Rushdie says about "off centering" us in his novel on national shame is entirely true, though in different ways
from Anita Desai's remarks in *Clear Light of Day*, an appropriate title for a book
that carefully conceals just what it sets out to reveal.[15] Rushdie's *Shame* interests
me perhaps more because of its title than its plot. For Rushdie, "off centering"
occurs when the author refuses to give us the real name of the geographical location in which his characters enact their drama. Rushdie writes, with an interesting balance of involvement and detachment, "The country in this story is
not Pakistan, or not quite. There are two countries, real and fictional, occupying the same space, or about the same space."[16] The title of the novel refers,
however obliquely, to the problems of sameness and difference as they collided
with a new space during the time that Hindus and Muslims and Sikhs perpetrated extreme violence on one another in the name of religion. The repetition
of "same"(ness) in the foregoing quotation begs to be read in different configurations. Which country, especially if the analogy is to the newly emergent
Pakistan and the severed India, is the fictional one and which the real one? What
does either "real" or "fictional" mean in this context? Rushdie states emphati-
cally that the country is "not Pakistan" and then immediately detracts by adding

"or not quite," which leaves enormous room for speculation. Even if one sets aside the question of "real and fictional," one is still confronted by two countries occupying the "same" subcontinental space, and certainly the trope of the merging of two countries is implied if not asserted.

Clear Light of Day focuses on how a Hindu family negotiates the reality of everyday life before the partition and how loyalties and emotions are disturbed and reconfigurated after the partition. There are four main characters, siblings, who live separate yet united lives in a Delhi torn by partition. Desai does not reveal and conceal locality and geography as Rushdie does. Her novel is based very clearly in Delhi, and her characters, both Muslim and Hindu, are part of the Old Delhi milieu at a particular time in history. The largest part of the novel is devoted to the time when the whole family split in two, in analogy with the nation. Another icon for the family/nation, however, is that of the cow, an ancient and sacred symbol for the mother, as the bride who just after child-birth drowns in a dead well no longer used by the family. Perhaps it is also the icon for the carefully anticipated and finally decolonized nation—the bride, so to speak, as symbol of the new nation which, the British having been ousted, should have been treated with joy and celebration. But instead, contempt and violence are heaped on her. She is not watched diligently, and as a result she drowns, and thus the drowned bride/cow becomes the icon for the continuity of violence between families/nations and religions that began with partition.

The events in the narrative point first toward a separation and then to the desire for reconciliation in this torn family/nation. The implications are perhaps similar to those in Jisne Lahore Nahim Dekha O Janmya Hi Nahin in that families fight and separate but must come together again. Because the partition was about violence, however, the reconciliation has to emerge from dialogue and the recognition of truths about members of the same family—truths that are extremely hard to negotiate within a family discourse. Perhaps historical theorists need an icon different from the family one developed by most writers who have fictionalized the partition.

Anita Desai tries to complicate the construct of the India-Pakistan partition in her novel. In Clear Light of Day, the cow was supposed to provide sustenance for the growing children, as decolonization was supposed to provide sustenance and rejuvenation for the country. But liberation for the new/old nation-state drowns in a stagnant well of desires and is never recovered. Two new nations were born, and in Desai's novel they are the symbol of new hope, just as the cow as a new bride brings her young progeny into the household. Yet both the nation and the cow, symbols of motherland and mother, are lost to the brutal dynamic that created both a separate Pakistan and a decolonized India. The wishes of a nation are drowned in violence, the cow unrecoverable in its silent decay. Loss and silence constitutes the foreground of individual and national hope. If one accepts the "necessity" of the severing of a nation, with the consequence that there is an abundance of bloodshed and that neighbors and friends become assassins, it is no wonder that the carcass of the cow—equivalent to the mother/bride of the nation—cannot be recovered. Instead, it sits in stagnant waters, festering in the historical consciousness of the severed family/nation. Both components of geographical division become unable to twist their way out of the viewer/viewed dialectic. This, in turn, gives rise to the state of indigestible historical and political consciousness in a way almost identical to that whereby decolonization contributed and gave rise to the violence that was the aftermath of the partition.

The somewhat accidental drowning of historical consciousness in stagnant waters is viewed not only with horror but with a participatory dread that cannot be exorcised. As the severed nation cannot forgive even as it tries to comprehend, neither can Bim forgive her brother Raja—not for joining the Muslim family and becoming one of them but for denying a historical dialogue that included not his role as her landlord but rather as a brother. At several halting points in Clear Light of Day, family members Mira- masi and Bim express fear about drowning in the well themselves. It is a curious desire for and identification with destruction, much as the massacres at partition must have been because they were so much like, without exaggeration, destroying members of one's own family. This identification of one individual member of the nation with another who is also victim can be perceived at its most profound level in Thich Thien-Tam's poem about Vietnamese sea pirates looting other Vietnamese as they tried to escape their land.[17] The poet says he is the sea pirate as well as the woman whom the pirate rapes. What was supposed to sustain one—the family/nation, the geography of one's environment—turned from its role as protector and instead threatened to drown the hopes of the new nation by brutalizing its members.

None of the characters in Clear Light of Day digest any of the stark and cruel historical reality of the partition but rather emulate it in their own lives and tend to slip into the personalized and overly sentimentalized past. Desai does exactly what Sidhwa did later in The Bride: she draws back from what is occurring at national levels by concentrating too closely on the less threatening reality of family turmoil, even though that turmoil always becomes an icon for the newly decolonized nation.

It is easy for Bim to transfer her national anger to Raja, and it is no coincidence that she chooses to teach history, since the Hindu-Muslim split is at the core of the separation from the beloved brother. She becomes a viewer. She sees Delhi burning but sees it only as a woman who is not directly involved in the slaughter; she goes up to the roof of her house and watches at a distance. Her alienation is based on her gender as well. Did the partition incorporate the wishes and necessities of women, or did it simply use the bodies of women to glorify the horror? A tale one still hears in Pakistan—and there are no doubt similar stories in India—tells of a very silent train that arrived from India with a cargo of the cut-up parts of women, indicative of partition's brutality against large numbers of Hindu, Muslim, and Sikh women. It is interesting to note the commonality between the alienated women who suffered considerably through the partition and the alienated response of these women writers.

Khushwant Singh's *Train to Pakistan* is an oversimplification of the sentiments of the experience of severing. In his novel all the violence is perpetrated by non-characters, by the amorphous violent lot who are "out there," off the scenes he carefully depicts. His characters who actually inhabit specific places, be they Hindus or Muslim or Sikhs, do not harm each other even for petty economic gains—as a lot of people did in that time—because the partition and the threat of violence brings out the best in them. Singh, through a saga of commonality and brotherhood, evokes the best that can be displayed by peoples and communities in transition, without taking account of the actuality of violence by the same people.

Sentiment did have a lot to do with the partition. As present-day Pakistanis and Indians will attest, Hindu and Muslim people were saved by each other in the war zones in times of extreme uncertainty. My father always remembered being saved by Ram, his Hindu friend, when they were all vacationing in Darjeeling, which was to become India. Later, when my mother, whose family had fled from Kashmir, was pregnant with her first child and craved *aam papad* (a sour-sweet snack), Ram sent it from India, for it was not available in Pakistan. This friendship too was severed, however, and contact "resumed" only thirty years later, after the death of my father. The complex analysis of the violence during partition has not yet come forth; the sentimentality has never been absorbed by the historical and political reality of what happened to the lives of the severed. They were forced to view each other as the enemy, and the hate festered because of stories of torture inflicted on one side or the other.

How was the individual's sentimentality going to be absorbed into the larger political consciousness of national reality? I don't think it is possible not to be alienated by the horrendously alienating experience of the partition at some level, not only because of severed emotional ties but also because a history that had become so tied had to be disentangled. No disentanglement can occur without pain. Responses to pain can be like Sidhwa's detachment, the deliberate stance of a viewer who is pained by what she views and creates distance between herself and what is viewed so as not to be a participant.

In *Clear Light of Day*, the family problems are patched up clumsily at the end when Bim tells Tara that Raja can come and visit her, but the national historical problems wait silently for a response. This novel was published in 1980—thirty-three years after the partition—yet Desai cannot talk about it with the clarity of day.

Anita Desai's *In Custody*, both film and book, has receded into the dialectics around the death of a language constructed by the Muslim colonial emperor, Akbar—a language considered, often erroneously, finer than Hindi.[18] This novel traces the journey of a Hindu who teaches and admires Urdu literature. He goes to interview the only living poet of Urdu who had great stature, but he is ineffectual and disappointed by the poet and his life. He is also unable to record anything because the machine keeps breaking down, and the man who is operating it seems as inept as the interviewer himself. Urdu is also glamorized in *Clear Light of Day* as a language representing cultural finesse. But again, even though it would be the colonial who would empower Urdu at the cost of Hindi, the mention of any violence is oblique. The death of Urdu is happening in India, partly out of the people's celebration of readopting and revaluing their own language, Hindi; thus, that death would represent decolonization in India. In Pakistan, by contrast, Urdu thrives as a literary language today. This linguistic ambivalence seems to perpetuate the viewer/viewed dialectic in that it dissipates dialogue instead of enhancing it.

Another aspect of what Homi Bhabha has called "ambivalence" is the way Sidhwa uses humor to camouflage her concerns about the terrors of the partition itself. Her book *Ice-Candy-Man*, published in 1988, only eight years after Desai's *Clear Light of Day*, is innovative in its view of the partition.[19] Like Desai she sets up a buffer zone of humor as well as a detached perspective on the partition. The main character is a child, Lenny, whose chief concern is her Hindu ayah (nanny), who is raising her but is later caught in a Muslim zone, Lahore, during the partition. Here the partition is viewed by a Parsee who has middle-class protection and does not cross any war zones or recently constructed borders. Despite some obvious problems, *Ice-Candy-Man* does tend to take the bull by the horns in ways that are important for the dialogue on the partition. It is not incidental that the novel was written four decades later. The young protagonist and recorder/recoder of history tends to view things more as pieces of information than as events that affect her personally.

The buffer zone allows both reader and writer a certain amount of disengagement from the actual historical brutality. The partition affects the child personally only because her Hindu ayah, the darling of a multiethnic community of men, is taken away from her, and it is Lenny who has unwittingly betrayed her to Ice-Candy-Man—or so it seems to her child's mind. The affliction of honesty is too much for her, and she begins the search for her nanny. This search, the central motif of this novel, seems to be for the other half, the loved or familiar one, which is central also to the whole Hindu-Muslim dichotomy. But the search for the other does not seem to transcend the viewer/viewed dialectic, and this in turn forces a separation entirely unnatural to the historical, political unity that existed previously between Hindus and Muslims. This is not to say that there were no religious or economic tensions but that Muslims and Hindus had earlier closed ranks in their attempt to decolonize India. It is inappropriate to sentimentalize the harmony between religious communities in India, but there was an acceptance of one another, and partition interrupted that. The cruelty that replaced the familiarity jarred every social and political relationship. It is no surprise that when Lenny finds the beloved ayah, her wishes for the ultimate reunion are shattered. The ayah, her faith in humankind destroyed, is only interested in being taken to her village across the border to the safety of her India. She has gone "dead inside," as uninterested in Lenny and uninterested in love and life as if she has decided to go back to the womb, having rejected the external world. When Lenny finds her (and it seems like a total indulgence for this middle-class brat to have found this unhappy, violated, and betrayed woman), she is living in Hira Mandi (diamond market), a euphemism for the prostitution area of Lahore, with Ice-Candy-Man, her pimp, swearing everlasting love to her.

For ayah, going back to India, or the womb, means a specific rejection, a denial of what has happened to her and a denial of the reasons she has become a mere pawn: that Ice-Candy-Man, who is a Muslim, suddenly has enormous power over her ultimately becomes unacceptable to her. Her inward journey is necessary because, like the nation, she needs to digest the experience and the extent of human cruelty and violence that her life and time have imposed on her and those like her. It is no coincidence that she is a poor woman; that is why she must suffer a situation that perhaps a middle-class Hindu woman caught in Pakistan could have avoided.

Hari, the male Hindu gardener, combats history by becoming Muslim, complete with circumcision; this act saves him from the brutality that the ayah is not spared. Unlike Hari, she cannot hide her Hinduness, cannot be circumcised. She has no recourse, mainly because she is a woman lost in the men's fight to win her favor as they "give birth" to a nation. She has almost no power to determine her history. Like the dead cow in the dead well, the ayah becomes a viewer of her own torn and battered life, which she does not choose and has no control over. Thus, her process of assimilating her history is one of withdrawal. She "goes dead inside" and demands only to be "taken home" to India.

Both Anita Desai and Bapsi Sidhwa, like the characters they create, come very close to real examination but shy away from it because the pain of the cruelty during partition has made them into viewers who are reluctant to engage with the past, reluctant to negotiate a brutal severing. Since this phenomenon of evasiveness seems to pervade especially the written literature on the partition, perhaps a multidisciplinary approach to the analysis of this troubled time would be an appropriate way to recode and reconfigure the violence that has remained unnegotiated at several levels. Such a reconfiguration would renegotiate the viewer/viewed dialectic in ways that can become meaningful for historians of that troubled time.

NOTES

1. Toni Morrison, *Beloved* (New York: Penguin, 1987), 337.

2. Gyanendra Pandey, "In Defense of the Fragment: Writing About Hindu-Muslim Riots in India Today," *Representations* 37 (Winter 1992): 27–55.

3. Ibid., 27.

4. *Garam Hawa*, dir. M. S. Sathyu, with Balraj Sahni, Geeta Siddarth, Jalal Agha, and Farouque Shaikh, Unit 3 MM, 1973.

5. See *Best of Manto*, ed. and trans. Jai Ratan (Lahore: Vanguard, 1990).

6. Pandey, "In Defense of the Fragment," 30.

7. See Wilson Harris, *The Womb of Space* (Connecticut: Greenwood Press, 1983), xvi–xx.

8. Pandey, "In Defense of the Fragment," 34.

9. Quoted in Hirendranath Mukherjee, *Was India's Partition Unavoidable? Slide-Down to Terrible Tragedy* (Calcutta: Manisha Granthalaya, 1987), 46.

10. See Amir Kumar Gupta, ed., *Myth and Reality: The Struggle for Freedom in India, 1945–7* (New Delhi: Manohar, 1987); Zahid Husain, *Rationale of Partition* (Karachi: Royal Book, 1990); H. M. Seervai, *Partition of India: Legend and Reality* (Bombay: Emmenem, 1989); Anita Inder Singh, *The Origins of the Partition of India* (London: Oxford University Press, 1987); Madanjeet Singh, *This Is My People* (New York: Rizzoli, 1990).

11. Program notes to Asghar Wajahat, *Jisne Lahore Nahim Dekha O Janmya Hi Nahin*, dir. Asghar Wajahat, Virginia High School Theater, 15 November 1993.

12. Bapsi Sidhwa, *The Bride* (London: Fatura Macdonald, 1987).

13. Khushwant Singh, *A Train to Pakistan* (New York: Grove Press, 1956).

14. Salman Rushdie, *Shame* (New York: Vintage Books, 1984), 20, 27.

15. Anita Desai, *Clear Light of Day* (New York: Penguin, 1980).

16. Rushdie, *Shame*, 23–24.

17. Thich Thien-Tam, poem read at the University of Hawaii, 1988.

18. Anita Desai, *In Custody* (New York: Penguin, 1984).

19. Bapsi Sidhwa, *Ice-Candy-Man* (London: Penguin, 1988).

PART V

EXPERIMENTAL CRITIQUES

CHAPTER 18

Jane Austen in Meerut, India

Amitava Kumar

Twelve sleeping pills in fancy packets of four each, made in Ulhasnagar, near Bombay. Brand name Somnorax. A supine king on each packet with hands beneath his head and eyes wide as chasms. And inscribed beneath him the lines from Shakespeare's *Macbeth*: "the innocent sleep, Sleep that knits up the ravell'd sleave of care."

A district collector recalls his youth in Azamganj where, enrolled in a Hindi-medium school, he waded through Wordsworth's *Prelude* on his own because knowing English, of course, gives one confidence.

An old man boasts that his granddaughter is doing her M.A. in English ("A very fine subject, Keats and Tennyson, very good—for girls especially"), only to be told, "You mean, it's a distinct advantage in the marriage market. Then your advertisement in the matrimonial columns can say 'convent-educated, M.A. in English,' and when you exhibit her in the drawing rooms of her husbands-to-be, she can, after singing the mandatory Tagore song, recite 'The Lady of Shalott.'"

And then there is Jane Austen in Meerut. One Dr. Prem Kishen of Meerut University has written a book on "E. M. Forster, India's darling Englishman—most of us seem to be so *grateful* that he wrote that novel about India." Dr. Kishen holds a Ph.D. on Jane Austen. The publisher of Dr. Kishen's book asks, "What is Jane Austen doing in Meerut?"

These diverse and deeply embedded uses of English and fictitious appeals to an obsolete canonicity are not exploited by Agastya Sen, the narrator of Upamanyu Chatterjee's novel *English, August*, in order to repeat the narrow, futile debates about the relevance of English in the Indian context.[1] Rather, the heterogeneity of the scenarios suggests not only a variety of uses but also a variety of languages, registers, and sociolects dividing and bringing into tension what could be only reductively described as English. In fact, Chatterjee's own very refreshing reliance on parody and references to bodily functions, chiefly sexual and scatological, produces a language that is far removed from the English of his bureaucratic superiors. Consider, for example, his happy overturning of the language of the bureaucracy: "Agastya was amused, among innumerable things, by officialese. No officer ever left, he always took his leave. None of them ever stayed a night somewhere, they always made night halts. Perhaps leave was actually a euphemism for arsehole, thought his irrepressible imagination: we shall make a night halt, sir, and there I shall take your leave, sir" (203).

The language of Agastya Sen, Chatterjee's reluctant hero, is mixed, far from rigid, not bound by the rules of propriety, and open to the fecundity of innovation. On the very first page of the novel, when Sen (August or English to his school friends who mock his love for everything Anglo) is told that he is going to be "hazaar fucked" at his new job as an administrator in rural India, he responds: "Amazing mix, the English we speak. Hazaar fucked. Urdu and American . . . a thousand fucked, really fucked. I'm sure nowhere else could languages be mixed *and* spoken with such ease" (1). As a matter of fact, I'm sure nowhere else in contemporary writing in English in India is there an effort to rely on this boisterous, blasphemous mixing of words and world views to lampoon the hollow pieties of post-independence India; for example, it would be quite impossible to find in the writings of Raja Rao or Anita Desai, anything like the description of the badly built statue outside the Gandhi Hall in Madna as "a statue of a short fat bespectacled man with a rod coming out of his arse" (21).

Near the middle of the novel the district administration's picnic trip to Gorapak has the makings of a Rabelaisian carnival that would have tickled Bakhtin: obese, male senior officials, each of whom the narrator fantastically crossdresses in a bra, travel through lines of shitting children, erotic scupltures and masturbatory fantasies, plentiful food, pot, slow and surreal masochism, temples where the sight of phallus worship is described as "a blue film," divinity tumbling from its sacred heights, literally in touch with the bodily and the profane: "There was a tube-light in the innermost sanctum directly above the black stone phallus of Shiv. There the wives came into their own. They took turns to gently smear the shivaling with sandlewood paste, sprinkle water and flowers over it, prostrate and pray before it, suffocate it with incense, kiss their fingers after touching it. Agastya found the scene extraordinarily kinky. Kumar beside him was breathing a little heavily" (128).

And yet, the reader is justified in asking, what is this irreverence and debunking in the interest of? or, put another way, what does this laughter hide? In *English, August,* the corrosive humor that erodes the decorum of authority is often unable to reach resources that would find strength beyond cynicism. The resources I have in mind are those of human solidarity and the unities of groups that in different measures are resisting power and its injustices. August is in touch with some reasons for his own isolation when he wonders what some-one else, one struggling for a living, would think of him and concludes, "Would probably just sneer, might even be envious, would say, a soft success story, the son of a Governor, Anglicized and megalopolitan, now in the Indian Administrative Service, all you have to do is recline and fart to earn your money" (224). My fastening rather simply on a class analysis in a "strident Marxist way" would no doubt only give August another chance to repeat his disapproval of a practice he despises; let me stay, then, with his laughter and watch and see who shares his jokes.

In his chapter "Rabelais in the History of Laughter," Mikhail Bakhtin writes, "True ambivalent and historical laughter does not deny seriousness but puri-fies and completes it. . . . Laughter does not permit seriousness to atrophy and to be torn away from the one being, forever incomplete."[2] It is true that Au-gust uses his laughter to empty that pompous space inhabited by his bosses, of-fering what Allon White has called in another context "both a critique of, and corrective to, the lie of pathos."[3] At the same time, it is unfortunately the fact that this laughter condemns to a silly seriousness all "subordinates." This is not ·so much a "politically correct" charge that there are jokes at the expense of Au-gust's servant-caretaker, Vasant; rather, the point is that the Vasants in this novel, consistently called "menials" and invariably "surly," are virtually always condemned to silence. The underpaid rickshaw wala who declined the little amount that August's friend paid him with the advice "When next your father farts, push that two-rupee note up his arse," and in a similar situation the Delhi taxi driver who "undid his pyjama and drawer strings, fisted his cock and said, 'This is what I think of you Government types'" (81, 146)—these offer a cou-ple of instances when this silence is broken but only by what is perceived as sullen meanness.

In the writings of Bakhtin, and sometimes in the recent reception of his work in the Western academy, there has often been an uncritical celebration of dia-logism and heteroglossia. One could justifiably qualify one's praise for the het-erogeneity and hybridity of the prose of English, August by recalling the critique advanced by writers such as Allon White and Ken Hirschkop of the tendency in Bakhtin to place novels in the street cultural traditions of the carnival: "The suggestion that medieval carnival and bourgeois realist novels are of a piece car-ries the assumption that dialogism, whether incarnated in the streets or the drawing rooms of the bourgeoisie, has the same signifying effects."[4] In our reading of English, August too, subversion cannot be too easily assumed, and cer-tainly not when it is in the parlor that all the games are being quietly played and the music of the streets firmly shut out. In other words, the tension between August's hip, hybrid English and his bosses' stuffy and dated officialese has to be seen as having more to do with conflict between two sections of the elite than with the fierce and elaborate drama of the battle between the rulers and the ruled.

Further, that elite is overwhelmingly male. The women included in the novel's cast make their appearance mostly as wives whose sole terms of definition are either sexy or not sexy. When a poor tribal woman called Para arrives at his office door to demand government intervention in the drought, we find our hero, August, distractedly listening to her while "revelling in a rare uncontrollable erection" (254). Again, we cannot clap our hands and shout that now desire runs riot in the Indian novel written in English (though when have the likes of R. K. Narayan ever written of masturbatory fantasies and dreams of lust?), because the debunking of prudish moralism in Chatterjee's writing is accompanied by a rather juvenile inattention to the politics of its privilege. When a friend has his hands cut off by enraged tribals because of his sexual involvement with the tribal woman who was his maidservant, August chokes out that "it was equally true that she liked the seduction" (262). The wrongdoers in this complicated scenario, as far as August is concerned, are largely the dogmatic, urban Marxist revolutionaries active in the area, complacently unaware of their own politics of representing those who cannot represent themselves. The point, of course, is that neither August nor the Marxists he dislikes can escape representation; if the Marxists he caricatures are oblivious to their own contradictory practices, August, too, is utterly disengaged from the burdens of organizing and developing solidarities.

In effect, I am faulting *English, August* for not presenting paths of action; like August, the novel loathes work and, again like him, is unable to distinguish between one task that it rightly sees as useless and another that it cannot even imagine. Far too easily is the question of multiple oppressions foreclosed in Chatterjee's discourse, and the brilliance and newness of the satirical wit notwithstanding, it is impossible not to conclude that the spaces he opens up are sealed all the more effectively.

In the past several years, much of the critical labor of Gayatri Chakravorty Spivak has been directed to the inclusion, in theory, of the task of "measuring silences."[5] The Indian writer in whom Spivak locates the painstaking attention to this task is Mahasveta Devi.[6] In order to suggest a possible and enabling departure from the foreclosed possibilities of *English, August,* I want very briefly to read Devi's writing too, except that with my own emphasis on the transgressions of the boundaries of novelistic performance, I will draw your eye to her more public, journalistic writing and her encounter with India's tribal population.[7]

In a report filed by Devi after police fired on a meeting of tribals, she poses the question, "What happens to the mothers, fathers, wives, children the killed persons leave behind?" and responds, "One simply does not know." Here, "knowing" involves the recognition of the conditions of silence. "Singhbhum is so like the white-haired woman collecting firewood in the jungles who never answers a stranger, never looks at anyone. Keeping the intruders into her grief beyond the barrier of immobile silence, she collects firewood." The difficulty of knowledge is articulated in the differences of gender, the hierarchies of rural and urban divides, the materiality of physical space, and the labor that is required to retrieve information. "Singhbhum is an unfathomable mass of untold miseries. It needs a lot of time, tenacity and toughness to unearth even the names of the officially dead there. It needs the stamina of being able to cover long distances on foot."[8] In other words, Devi's reading of the limits becomes a way of marking the plain struggle to cover and uncover distances—of places, of uneven distributions, and of repressive silencing.

On each rupee of land rent they pay to the government, Mahasveta writes in another report, the tribespeople in Singhbhum pay forty paise tax for education. But the people remain illiterate because often no school buildings exist and teachers from North India posted to the region are more devoted to the work of moneylending, doing business in land, and running shops. In the mode of what I would call a "contemporary subaltern historian," Devi quotes a song sung by the Mundari tribe, describing this situation: "Rando, Rando, come to the school! / Mata, Mata, where are you? / Rando and Mata and the other boys / Graze the cow, tend the goat. / The Masterji sits in his shop." Under these circumstances, it is not through the battles of curricular change in the structures of institutionalized learning, familiar to the Western(ized) academic, but through more marginal productions that oppositional knowledge is brought to the fore. Devi relies on a mother singing to her baby about a child who has become a worker at the *bhatta* (brick kilns) to introduce the reinvention of bonded labor among the tribal population: "My Bali could live on jungle fruits, / My Bali could live on jungle roots; / But trees do not grow saris, / So my Bali went to the bhatta, / So my Bali went." And Devi draws upon the current diaries of activists such as Purnendu Mazumdar, an organic intellectual in the Gramscian sense and a household name in the tribal villages, to present reports of tribal women who for a payment of a hundred or more rupees have been sold by their parents into sexual bondage to brick kiln owners: "A young Ho girl Joshin, aged sixteen, has been compelled to become the 'aurat' for the aged kiln owner Hidayat Ali at Gajpara in 24-Parganas, West Bengal. Joshin is Dibra Jamuda's daughter and she is from the village Dharamsai under Chakradharpur police station." It is thus that Devi constructs against the official history, which claims that the bonded labor system was abolished in November 1975, a detailed counternarrative linking voices and narratives, carrying accounts of what she calls "tales of woe and exploitation on the one hand; the pulse of resistance mounting on the other."[9]

These traits give strength to Devi's other writings too, her novels and plays, lending energy to the resistance of tribals and women. For example, in her play *Mother of 1084*, originally written as a novel, the mother is at once a locus of oppression and an evolving, changing agent of social protest. In the 1978 introduction to her collection of stories *Agnigarbha*, Devi wrote, "I desire a transformation of the present social system. I do not believe in narrow party politics. After thirty-one years of Independence, I find my people still groaning under hunger, landlessness, indebtedness, and bonded labour. An anger, luminous, burning, and passionate, directed against a system that has failed to liberate my people from these horrible constraints, is the only source of inspiration for all my writing."[10]

Even Upamanyu Chatterjee's August will recognize that in Devi's writings the hypocrisy and high speech of the bureaucratic and political elite are challenged by the laughter and tears of the disaffected poor whose idioms are drawn from folklore and common, everyday experiences.[11] For August, the Marxist lover of his friend Neera is only "a mouth spewing historical inevitability, with spectacles above it" (287). In Devi's writings, however, the figures of resistance are drawn in a complex relationship, rewriting traditional heroism and motherhood. As the critic Samik Bandyopadhyay explains:

> There is a continuum between Mahasweta Devi's mothers and leaders of men, between the cold, grasping awareness of the former shaping into resistance, or stopping at the very edge of defiance, and the evolving militancy of the latter. Right from Chandi, cast out by a superstitious community in *Bayen* (1971), to the tribal Naxalite, Draupadi, in the story named after her (1976), Mahasweta Devi's mothers are too earthy and emotionally charged to bear overtones of any mystical-mythical or archetypal motherhood. They are invariably located within a network of relationships defining their personalities into absolute clarity.[12]

As a way of noting the impulse present in Devi's journalism, but by returning to the fictive, this essay honors those that don't find a place in the narrative universe of *English, August*. To mark in solidarity the shifting but repeated space on the continuum of oppression and resistance, and as a tribute to writers, critics, mothers, sisters, and other activists, I offer my short story "The Monkey's Suicide." This story is set, like Devi's narratives, in small-town and rural eastern India. It finds in women, trapped in the ruins of a decadent and debauched patriarchal structure, the strength of ordinary survival and triumph. Its closing gesture links these women with other agents of resistance, thereby making overt what has remained implicit throughout: the process of finding in the politics of place (in Ara, a postcolonial, post-independence site of peasant resistance and class war in which women have played no small role) the possibility not only of sharing struggles but also of overturning extant divisions between private and public, the home and the world, the party and the family.

It may not be out of place to suggest here that my unconventional juxtaposition of "scholarly writing" and "short story" is designed to address and maybe even undo a series of oppositions between "Western" theory and "Eastern" storytelling, academic theorizing and popular narratives, and, more immediately, criticism and fiction. In that respect, this essay embodies the question, if not the crisis, facing the emergence of Postcolonial Studies: the negotiation of what have been called the divided locations and locutions. Although the dismantling of disciplinary boundaries remains a necessary gesture, that struggle does not of course exhaust the need to pull down many other social divisions. Interestingly, that appeal is perhaps repeated in the following story.

THE MONKEY'S SUICIDE

The red-bottomed monkeys still leave the branches of the huge tamarind tree and peel the oranges left unattended on the balcony of my now dead maternal uncle Lotan Mamaji's house. I was baptized me in my childhood with a tale of fear when one of them, a medium-sized young male, stole upon Mamaji's huge white bed and finding his pistol waved it ineffectually, they say, at my cousin born two months after me and still in her crib, before turning the pistol around and, with the primate brain moving the index finger to grip the pink-nailed thumb on the trigger, blew his brains out, splattering bits of meat over the pictures of the family patriarchs.

I was five months old then and when I returned to Lotan Mamaji's house three years later the monkeys were still there, removing pieces of dead skin—though my young cousin Chunni said it was lice—from each other's bodies while beneath the tamarind's branches, like sacks of rotting wheat, rested the mohallah's pigs actually black in color but often coated with the dry brown mud of my birthplace Ara. That summer

Chunni and I were quite taken with the pigs because they appeared in their loose packs, incessantly grunting, beneath the hole in the toilet, a wooden board placed a few feet above the ground, pushing their snouts inside the buckets under us. I was nineteen when lying drunk on a mattress where I would find him next morning sleeping in his own shit, Mamaji laughed at the old memory of my surprise at the sudden appearance of the pigs. I was afraid that my poor nephew would now forget to shit, he said, and his fairy father would again get a chance to lay some blame on my shoulders, but you have the courage of this soil. The pigs! Mamaji snorted and laughed till tears mixed with the red paan juice of the betel-leaf that bled from his mouth.

We had come as members of the baraat party of the bridegroom for a marriage in this village which was about four hours' drive from Ara. Our hosts had made available the one large hall that was all there was to the village high school; sixty of us, all men, of course, were to eat and sleep and while away our time for the next two days in this room surrounded on three sides by the monsoon rains which had filled the village with water and the unrelenting croaking of bull-frogs. Earlier I had watched my uncle take out the moist bundle of hundred-rupee notes from under his sweat-dreached kurta and singly offer them to the dancer who had been brought from Calcutta for ten thousand rupees. The elderly men from the district's Rajput families had at last been able to watch live the dances first performed by Meena Kumari on the silver screen in her husband Kamaal Amrohi's classic *Pakeezah* a few months before she died of alcohol overdose. The village had no electricity but a loud fuel-generator had been hired and transported from Ara. It lit three large bulbs that attracted moths and more than two hundred villagers who gathered around the steamy square that was the baraat gathering. The dancer didn't seem mindful of the rivulets of sweat flowing down her front and back, and she flashed her smile undampened by the expectation of the crowd that arose like a warm emanation and engulfed her and the tabla player. Mamaji was leaning on his left elbow, his back propped by a pillow, trying to hold steady his glass. With his right hand he would grasp at the dancer's hands or waist and slip in the notes clumsily, sometimes shoving the money in her blouse, at other times pushing it into the fold of her sari at the waist. And every time she bowed and salaamed, he smiled. Once, he allowed her to put a paan in her mouth which she had folded, after placing a clove and a cardamom in its leaf-folds with a great show of delicacy. After we had helped him to the high school hall which was still bare an hour after midnight except for an old man coughing in his sleep in the corner, Mamaji drew out his .38 and pushing its nozzle into my palm, said in a voice that was unnaturally soft, Son, if any of the bastards bother you, just shoot their mother-fucking heads off.

The medicine bottle that Mamaji had bought for his wife, Kanya, was still unopened and apparently not even moved from where it had been first set down on the windowsill four days ago, the day we had left Ara for the marriage in the village. I was sitting on the ground eating the rice and dal that my cousin Chunni had put in a plate before me; her other four sisters were not in the house, two of them at a neighbor's house and the other two playing in the dirt in the shade of the tamarind. Kanya, who was the youngest of my maternal aunts, did not speak much; today, as she waved the small palm leaf fan to cool herself and me, she spoke only to cut me short with a brief "I know, I heard about it" when I began telling her a bit about Mamaji throwing away the money for the bank loan repayment at the dance in the village. I had no sympathy for Mamaji but it was to lessen Kanya's misery, to somehow put everything that had happened in a space outside the normal and the sane, that I said, They had made him drink too much, I don't think he knew what he was doing.

Two sparrows flew into the verandah where I was eating and Kanya watched them for a moment before turning to look at Chunni, and I turned to her too and asked whether she had eaten. Chunni said, I ate after I returned from my classes. And I, trying to tease this cousin I had played with as a child, asked, And did you feed your mother?

You are such a clown, Chunni said, rocking on the heels of her feet. You jump off the train for a day and start ordering me around. She was smiling, her beautiful, uneven teeth lending loveliness to her small face that was more light-skinned than either Mamaji's or Kanya's. But there was no trace of humor on Kanya's face and even the oil she had freshly rubbed into her hair only added gloom to her appearance. I wanted to distract my aunt and so I asked her, Does Chunni take care of her younger sisters? Kanya slowly responded, The children know how to take care of themselves. She pointed at the bottle of medicine with her fan, and added, You made him spend sixteen, seventeen rupees to buy that medicine. You don't realize it but weak as I am, he needs that medicine more than I do. He is sick. And for me it would be medicine enough if he could stop doing what he is doing. I am ashamed to show my face to the people in this mohallah not because he drinks but because I have grownup girls in the house who have to hear the words their father screams as abuse every night from our own rooftop when he comes home and grownup girls, all girls, shouldn't have to hear all this.

Kanya was illiterate and Mamaji barely managed to make it through high school. They were married when they were young teens, twenty years ago, in Kanya's village which has a reputation for getting flooded every monsoon. The huts in the village are built high and narrow and they crowd together like a herd of goats marooned on an island. Kanya's brother had taken off his turban and placed it at my maternal grandfather's feet and begged him that he accept the proposal of marriage between his sister, Kanya, and Lotan Mamaji who was then in high school and away at that time in the ancestral village supervising the harvesting of wheat. My grandfather pitied the lad in front of him because he was fatherless, and on the following Tuesday which was an auspicious day he sent a Brahmin priest to Kanya's village to talk to others in the family and make sure that the girl had no physical disabilities. The brahmin returned with the gift of a yellow cotton dhoti and two betel nuts, out over eleven rupees, and a story about a tall, gentle girl who was respectful to all. Soon after that, on a day that my grandfather was to remember later as a sad one because his cow gave birth to a stillborn calf which was placed before its mother so that she would have its smell in her nostrils and then taken away to be quickly skinned and stuffed so that its mother's teats wouldn't dry and the carcass with stumpy, sewn-up legs could be produced before its blindfolded mother at milking time, on that very day after six in the evening, the shuttle train brought Kanya's brother and ten other members of his extended family for the tilak ceremony during which a new HMT wristwatch and five hundred and one rupees were put in Lotan Mamaji's palm to seal his engagement. Two months later, in spite of the squabble that broke out because one of the boats carrying the bridegroom's party overturned near the bride's hut and led to a minor incident of shooting and a lot of shouting, Lotan Mamaji and Kanya were married with the help of the same priest who had been impressed earlier in the year by the way in which Kanya had bent down to put at his feet the gift of the yellow cotton dhoti and then had stayed silent, communicating only with slight shakes of her head when asked questions about her education, skill at cooking, sewing, and her knowledge of the sacred gayatri mantra and the ingredients that would be necessary to prepare the panchamrit essential for the religious occasion of the Satyanarayankatha puja. A little after dawn, when Lotan Mamaji had put the red sindoor in the parting of Kanya's hair and the marriage ritual was finally over, the bridegroom's party was rowed, along with the bride who was sobbing because she was being parted from everything that had been her past, to the other side of the water-logged fields where a truck was waiting to trasport them to the railway station where the eight o'clock shuttle would take them to Ara.

The railway lines were only a stone's throw away from Lotan Mamaji's house, and if we waited a little, Kanya, Chunni, and I would have to pause in our conversation because the six o'clock shuttle would soon be coming into Ara station with its load of daily passengers, mostly office babus, students, petty traders, and loafers who came back to Ara from their business at the capital city, Patna. Kanya, my aunt, looked at me and smiled. So, now that you are studying in the big cities, will you marry someone you find there? Oh, aunty, I said, I have just begun my college education. So has she, Kanya replied, nodding toward Chunni, but everyone has been asking me why am I keeping a grownup daughter under my roof. People misunderstand things. Soon enough they will be thinking there is some defect in our daughter; you are old enough to understand how this world works. Do you know of anyone in your college who is of our caste and would be good enough to be the brother-in-law of a man like you? She smiled again, and I glanced at Chunni who still stood there, leaning against the pillar, and there was no shyness in her expression, and no unease either. Or maybe she was hiding her emotions, submitting to the anxieties of her worried mother. I'll ask my father, I said, because as a professor he gets to meet a lot of the youth you might find suitable.

An hour later when Lotan Mamaji came back from the town he produced from his bag two packets of green peas and grams which he declared he would quickly like to see fried with onions and green chilies for his nephew. When we were young, he remarked with gusto, his small eyes sparkling, we used to go to our maternal uncle's home only to eat. And now all those links are being broken, man is getting farther and farther from his own brother. Take your honorable father, for instance. The other day I went to ask for his help. I want him to put in a word with an official who was his student, but instead of doing a simple deed which will help me and my kids, he offered me a lecture on morality. Hell, if I was a Mahatma Gandhi wouldn't I have gone to the masses, or just gone on a fast, instead of baring my ass in front of my goddamned brother-in-law and getting kicked for it?

My aunt shook her head in disapproval and with a pleasantly mocking expression on her face commented, And even God knows that you don't need a lecture on morality. Kanya waited as Chunni brought us our plates of fried green peas and grams, and then said, Well, Manohar was suggesting earlier in the afternoon that his father could tell us about some suitable groom for Chunni. Lotan Mamaji nodded and said, Yes, but he isn't ever going to even speak to me straight. Why don't you go back together with Manohar when he returns home and talk to the great man? I am sure he will treat you differently. Yes? Kanya asked in response, and leave you here alone to do what you please with your drunken friends and terrify the kids out of their minds?

This was the first time that Kanya or anyone else had said anything so directly or explicitly to Lotan Mamaji in my presence, and yet my sense of surprise was quite exaggerated, I think, because the man who was here being accused was quite unfazed. In fact, he even appealed to what he was granting as my sense of objective wisdom. Have you ever heard anything like this? he queried, looking at me with his black beard tipped high so that I could see the gold chain around his neck with his mother's name inscribed on it. For the past three days and four nights, he went on, I was shitting in a motherfucking hellhole of a village and even entertaining my citybred nephew in that stable fit for animals. And why was I doing that? So that none of our caste brethren, not one person among our kith and kin can ever say that Lotan has turned his back on them. After all, it is not from America or Australia that we will bring a groom. It is among our own society that we will marry and live and die. And that is why I have been carrying this body that is no longer young through the tortures of marriages and social gatherings. But right here, in my own house, I get accused of criminal neglect. What do you think about this, he looked at me momentarily before throwing out the next question, and why aren't you eating? I replied I didn't want more, but as a way of addressing what had started this debate I volunteered that I would take the information from my father and quickly mail a letter to them. Yes, we know he is busy but it would be helpful if he kept this point in mind, Lotan Mamaji said. That was all that was said till he insisted that I eat some more and I replied that I had really had enough and I got up to put the plate back inside near the little tap that was only four inches above the ground because the pressure was so low in the small towns in our state. I got talking to my cousins, especially the kids whom I hadn't really had a chance to talk to and was quite sure I would be asked questions about when I returned home the next day. Ruby, the youngest one, talked about Mickey Mouse on her T-shirt as if he was a local boy fond of watching movies at Moti Talkies and playing cricket in the gullies. And what is he doing now? I asked her. She shifted her big, round eyes to look into the darkness outside and said decisively, He's at home with his mother. I took Ruby's hand and went looking for Kanya. She had just come out of the kitchen and was about to step out into the yard where we had been sitting. I asked Kanya what she was doing and she pointed at the plate and said, The fried green peas and grams. On ordinary days he eats and drinks in the town with his friends. Why do you think he brought these today? So that he can have them with his whiskey, though as an honor to you he will be drinking at home, and maybe it will also be quieter tonight. She then went out and I went back to talk to Chunni.

Chunni was alone in her room which actually wasn't a room at all; it had a narrow shelf-like structure because it had been designed as a storage space for grains, dried spices and pickles, and, in addition, when suspended from the iron hoops embedded in the wooden beams, milks and curds in earthen pots high enough to be out of reach of cats. Chunni was listening to Hindi film songs on the tiny Bush radio that Mamaji had presented to her when she passed her matric exams; she turned the volume down when she saw me at the door but we both listened to the songs together without saying much. One afternoon maybe five years ago, we were all in Ara and it was my birthday though that didn't matter much because I was suffering from dysentery, and there was a Mohammed Rafi song playing on the radio, the popular film hit about the quiet torments of a girl in love who was beautiful but dusky—*bahut khoobsurat magar sanwali si*—and from my mattress on the floor I had looked up and seen Chunni, her face a little shiny in the heat, reading a romance novel on her bed and ever since then that song passed through my mind whenever I thought of her. We used to tease Chunni about her affair with their neighbor's son who was in the army and posted far away in Tripura, but the truth was that Chunni had never exchanged more than a few words with that man, and anyway she was too young and he was interested only in taking a room in Hotel Raja and screwing women whose names he didn't know and actually whose names often changed. Tomorrow, before you go, Chunni spoke suddenly, I'll give you a letter to take to Patna. Chunni didn't say who this letter was for, but we both knew that it would be for my mother, the eldest member in my maternal family, and the letter would document, with a desperate weariness that was to be shared both by the reader and the writer, the latest misdeeds of Lotan Mamaji, his health, the worries surrounding my aunt Kanya, the state of the children. Earlier I had twice been the bearer of such a letter.

The shelves for the jars of spices and pickles were now stacked high
with literary magazines and college notebooks each singly covered with
newspaper. Chunni had bound her books in the more colorful foldouts
from the magazines and on the front cover of each book she had signed
her name. There was a thin layer of dust on the books and the shelves,
and the bed smelled slightly musty. But this was the world that was utterly hers; in this cramped, damp space she put a cover on things and
signed her name.

And though I might have brought in some adolescent sense of superiority in my own assessment because I had been successful at college
while Chunni had failed to get through the entrance exams for medical
schools, I was nevertheless struck by the change in this room one hot
May morning, two years later, soon after both of us had turned twenty-
one. I slid in a shiny metal trunk where Chunni's bed used to be, and
quickly took note of more than a dozen jars of mango and lime pickles
on the shelves, beneath them the dried peppers wrapped in white cloth,
and above them, hanging from the beams, the rancid pots of sour curds
and two huge clusters of bananas brought from Sonepur smelling of the
sweet, rotting sand beneath the river. I found Kanya and touched her
feet respectfully, and she said, It's nice that you came early.

In a room adjoining the verandah where it seemed I had sat only the
other day asking whether she took care of her sisters, Chunni sat utterly
still and silent in a circle of older female relatives and children. She wore
a simple yellow sari which had been washed in turmeric for good luck,
and her face took some of the color so that her complexion was that of
damp straw. When she saw me she smiled, and then began to sob
loudly. I held her close to me and with a faint attempt at wit said, Ah,
she was betting that I wouldn't be able to make it to her wedding. Behind me, Kanya waited for a minute and then turned away to hide her
tears by giving directions to the halwai who was preparing the sweet-
meats in a huge cauldron although the wedding was still three days
away.

Every time the trains whistled from the other side of the dry palm
trees we expected more relatives to arrive. Uncles who had aged since
the last marriage season because of painful engagements in prolonged
litigations in the civil courts, a widowed step-grandmother who always
made a grand appearance by hugging each of her surviving sisters and
wailing out the name-of-the-father-of-my-firstborn, cousins who had
got married in the last wedding season and now had come with their
newly born: they all came through the hours of the morning, hot after-

noons, and even the late nights, bringing with them memories, gifts, and a mixed sense of anticipation. My mother had found this occasion to be down with asthma, and Kanya would stop me as I hurried about trying to complete the million small chores that still remained to be completed and she'd say, We are taking care of her but you should go up to her and inquire whether she is okay. That evening, the night before the wedding, I helped my mother down the stairs and we sat on a string-cot while next to us, on the wooden platform that had been put together for the wedding, Lotan Mamaji was lying while a servant massaged his painfully swollen legs. The moon with the textured brightness of the scales of the rohu fish was already visible and the air was full of the scent of the beli flowers that was said to draw snakes. Kanya decided to massage my mother's legs and my mother protested, Oh, don't spoil me, you have been up night and day. You should rest and let Manohar do the son's duty.

When I laughed and began to play with my mother's toes, Kanya turned her sallow face to me. He has been doing the brother's duty day and night, she said, and added, Chunni will have courage because he is around. Quietly, I continued to knead my mother's feet and knew when I heard him sniff that Lotan Mamaji was crying. He tried to make light of it by beginning to talk of the stupid things I made him do when I was a boy but he couldn't go on, and hearing him cry my mother hushed him, telling him in a scolding voice that if he broke down how was Kanya going to bear it. I looked at Kanya sitting at the edge of the cot, her tall, thin frame erect, and her head quite still, her gaze fixed unwaveringly on her husband's face as he lay weeping on the platform where only a day later Chunni, without raising her eyes to look at him, would put a heavy garland of beli, marigold, and roses around the neck of her soon-husband-to-be. There was a look of profound sadness on Kanya's face because if she gave in she'd weep to the end of her days. At the hospital in Patna in July more than a year later, I would recall this moment as I tried to calm my mother who was hysterical beside Lotan Mamaji's dead body. I wanted to remind my mother of Kanya's grief as she sat on the other side, a spoon in her hand, maybe because she had first thought Mamaji had fainted again and she'd need to slip in the spoon quickly between his teeth before he had the chance to bite his tongue, and the stem of steel in her hand trembled as if she were using it to divine the signs of life in some deep place inside Mamaji's body that had for the past several years been closed to her. But I stayed silent, as I had done on that evening before Chunni's wedding, and shared what felt like solidarity with Kanya.

Two hours before the bridegroom's baraat party was to wind its way
up from the Republic Hotel, with the band playing Hindi film tunes
from the past two decades and the youth dancing and others shooting
their guns in the air, my father's car pulled up at the gate. He looked
handsome in his silk kurta and dhoti and when Lotan Mamaji hurried up
to meet him and touch his feet, my father said sharply, You are still going around in yesterday's clothes and we can already hear the baraat's
band at the corner. Mamaji turned to my mother and said, Didi, what
can I do to please him? My father smiled and asked Kanya with some
tenderness, You are happy now, aren't you? Kanya joined her hands together and replied that she'd be happy if everything went off well in the
next couple of days. Everything will be perfect, my father said to her
with assuredness, if Lotan remains in his senses. My mother clicked her
tongue to silence my father but he had already turned away after saying
what he had to, and I didn't raise my eyes to look either at Mamaji or
Kanya. My mother quickly said, Okay, let's speed things up, otherwise
we'll just be standing around and they'll be at our doorstep.

It was some time after midnight when I had brought back the hired
television and VCR from Hotel Republic, where we were showing our
guests the latest Bacchan starrer, *Muqaddar ka Sikander*, that I tiredly sat down
to eat and discovered that I had no hunger at all. I asked someone to see
if they could find me a cold drink and I fell down in a chair. The fellow
who was running the generator chose that moment to come to me to ask
whether he should pull the connection off from the lights outside. I
turned and watched the series lights, red and yellow, on the bushes and
the lower branches of the tamarind; then there were the lighted signs that
showed a coconut among mango leaves on the sacred kalash. I got up
and went inside where I knew the wedding rituals must be making their
tedious progress. There was a chorus of women's voices raised in protest
when I asked whether the outside lights could be turned off; if my
mother had her way the ongoing rituals would be accompanied also by
fireworks. I pressed Chunni's shoulder and asked whether she was okay;
her head was covered with a red veil and I could only see her nod. So I
went back out and sat among the lights which blinked emptily without
anyone to watch them. Maybe because that might have been the only occasion when I was alone in those few days, I allowed myself to break
down and shed tears at the thought of Chunni's leaving not only Lotan
Mamaji's house but also, it seemed, our childhood and shared youth.

The man that Chunni got married to that night, Rakesh, is a mining
engineer posted in a small, remote town south of Ara and I did not see

him much, much less get to talk to him, for a very long time except momentarily at Mamaji's funeral. It was about eight or nine years later, when I went to their town, Jamadoba, to write about the slayings of labor union leaders that I met Chunni and Rakesh again, and for the first time their five-year-old son, Suman. Their small flat in Jamadoba overlooked a broad ravine that once had been a mine but was now covered with greenery that joined, in the distance, undulating hills. Trucks of the Tata Corporation meandered in and out of those hills, and closer to us the cows and goats of the townspeople grazed amid the bushes. It was my second day of stay in Jamadoba and Rakesh had returned early from work with a bottle of rum and we cheerfully mixed it with water and some ice that we bought at the paan store down the street. I have dreams of going to the United States, Rakesh said, even if it is only for a week. I have been inside these mines for too long and I want to explore the outside world.

In his house there were tapes of Hemant and Lata whom Chunni loved, but also the tapes of Eric Clapton and Neil Diamond who for Rakesh represented the world he wanted to escape to. He dressed fashionably and even as we talked I noticed how he'd carefully bring his hair back, arranging it over his receding hairline. Even Ara or Patna would be much better than this place, Rakesh began saying after we had been drinking for a while, because here in this barrenness your dreams are buried. Chunni could hear us as she stood cleaning the fish she was going to cook tonight, but she said nothing and I didn't ask her for her views either. More to change the subject than anything else, I said, Ara . . . yesterday the train passed the house, you know, and it looked just so bare. Not that we usually saw people on the balcony and the stairs but yesterday it looked just so bare to me—Rakesh interrupted my repetitive description to say, Yes, let's talk about Ara and you will want to know what I mean by buried dreams. You know, my father-in-law, even when he drank and spent money in Ara was never so lost in his excesses as he was when he came down to the mining region, to Dhanbad for example, to look after his business. Here, he had quite a reputation. I am sure you know all that, but my point is that there is something in this place itself.

But I had no idea at all what Rakesh was saying about Lotan Mamaji and his reputation here. This place, Rakesh went one, is made of people who are utterly rootless. They all came from other regions and they survive here without ever trying to belong. All they do here is burrow holes in the ground like rats and scurry in and out of them. Rakesh pointed at the abandoned mines, where even though it had started drizzling some cows still grazed placidly, and said, It is in these holes that people find their real lives while above the ground they indulge in murder and loot. I stopped Rakesh and asked him whether Mamaji's investment in the transport industry was still paying off. Still? He threw that word at me as if I had asked the most stupid question. It had stopped paying off long before he died, Rakesh said with great emphasis, and the only reason he came to Dhanbad and spent months here was that he had a mistress, a common, middle-aged prostitute whom I never had the good fortune to meet. But I learned that he took care of her rent, though of course she had other means of paying it off. What Rakesh was saying was new to me, and I'm sure Chunni never wrote of this to my mother because I read all her letters and would have known. I was silenced by this disclosure and Chunni, when I looked at her, went on removing the scales from the fish; I took another sip of the rum and for some bizarre reason felt that the only intelligent question I could ask was, What were the dreams that Lotan Mamaji had buried here?

The question did not inspire Rakesh and he followed another train of thought. Let's take up the case of your father, he said to me and followed it with a long pause. Quite confident about taking up that case by himself, he went on, That man is someone I admire because he has stayed true to the dreams of his youth. He has worked hard and today can be proud of his achievements. His children are well educated, and he has traveled abroad and last but not the least has saved enough for his retirement. You wouldn't, he said conclusively, find that man here. Again, I was completely innocent of the knowledge that Rakesh was offering; I had no idea what had been my father's dreams in his youth, and I was certainly unaware of his savings. I shrugged and said, But he wouldn't appreciate our drinking this rum, so let's not talk about him. Tell me what you know about the work of labor unions in the mines. But Rakesh wouldn't talk much about that and he poured more rum and he and I started a discussion on the quality of the onions I had volunteered to chop for the fish curry.

It was the hum of the mosquitoes that woke me, I think, and I realized that the electric supply had failed again. The blades of the table fan behind my head were still and my back was turning the bed damp with sweat. I fanned my face with the magazine I had been reading before I fell asleep, but I soon tired of that and as no sleep was forthcoming I got out of bed. The door, I found, was already unlocked and on opening it I saw Chunni sitting with her head leaning against the wall on the stairs outside. I called out her name and she turned and wearily spoke up in a half-whisper, This happens so often. At least it's cool outside today. Sometimes it's like a furnace. The bricks on the stairs felt cool when I sat down and Chunni told me that the electricity had gone nearly an hour before. Rakesh, she said with a laugh, when he's drunk has a conversation with himself even when asleep. Maybe we should carry him out, I suggested, so that we can participate in it. Chunni quickly replied, No, let him be there. He will keep talking and if Suman wakes up he won't be afraid. She got up and said, I'll make some tea for you. It's cooler here, you keep sitting.

It was very difficult for me to accept Papa's death, Chunni was telling me after we had been talking on the stairs for an hour, and I blamed myself for not taking care of him. But as much as I found fault with myself, I was also very angry with the world because every face I saw was a lie. People had used Papa's drinking as an excuse to stay away from us, and they used his death to come back just once and then run away from us scared. That there were so many unmarried daughters in the house really worried them and they didn't want to enter through that door and accept our reality because they believed it would somehow make them look weak. But that's not how it was at all. The truth is that these people, and I mean our own uncles, aunts, and cousins, weren't really afraid they were weak; it was just that they were ashamed they were so strong. And they didn't care. When Papa died you were there, and you remember, don't you, that none of his brothers' sons would agree to light his pyre? Just because you'll have to observe some rules about the food you eat for a few days, you won't help cremate a dead man who didn't have sons!

The last words were spoken so sharply that I felt for a moment that Chunni was accusing me, but I knew too that her anger was not limited to a few men in the family and her anguish embraced the entire universe. I couldn't see Chunni's eyes very well in the darkness, but the shiny bindi on her forehead flashed even in the dim light when she moved her head. Chunni said, I am not trying to defend my father. You saw him during my marriage. He was trying to prove them wrong, those inside the family too who used to say that his daughters would be out on the streets soon. I was in a new place at my in-laws' and my mother and sisters didn't want to make me worried, but it is true that he very quickly grew worse after my marriage. He would tell my mother he missed me and would drink himself to oblivion; one night he cut his foot badly and the flesh didn't heal for months. He had made himself so sick the blood wouldn't clot. One day a fellow I knew in college found him unconscious in the Patna-Ara shuttle; he was lying in a stupor, his money gone, outside the toilet of the moving train. And then there was the whole business in Dhanbad. When Chunni paused, I wasn't sure I wanted to hear any more. I cleared my throat and said, Let it be.

No, you have to listen, Chunni insisted in the dark, so that the next time someone begins telling you about this, you won't give him the satisfaction of being a better man just because he is not like my father or knows more about him than you do. Oh god, she cried out with a desperation that I did not understand, and then went on with her story about Lotan Mamaji, especially during the last year when, till a few months before his death, he practically lived in Dhanbad. Chunni's bold insistence that I must listen to her brought up in my mind a memory of Kanya who, when I was perhaps sixteen or seventeen, had once begun telling me while I stood on the steps in Ara, on my way to the station, that I must tell my parents that Mamaji was not improving at all. I had lowered my eyes out of embarrassment because no one really spoke about these things, certainly not to us who were seen only as children, and Kanya had commanded me, it seemed, not to hide when she said, Look at me when I'm talking to you. These are the things he has been doing. He might listen to your mother, so go and tell them that I told you this.

Kanya had then put a fifty-rupee note in my breast pocket. I had said, No, don't do this. Although custom demanded that I be given some money before leaving my maternal uncle's home, I knew that there was no money to be spared in that house. That particular time, though, Kanya had said, You take this because I saved this for a long time for you. This is the first time you came to us after you started studying in the big cities. I want you to be happy, and when I can't afford it, of course, I won't be able to give you anything. Kanya had then kissed my forehead and said, Hurry or you'll miss the train. And that is how it came to be almost within a year or two; whenever I was leaving Ara I'd get up early when the smoke from the coal and dung fires had just begun to climb up from some of the houses in the mohallah and I'd leave without saying goodbye to anyone, still not having the courage to accept that Kanya would not be embarrassed because she couldn't afford any longer to slip some money in her nephew's pocket and give him her blessings.

Dawn was no more than half an hour away and soon we'd be able to make out the thin columns of smoke spreading over the tiled roofs of the miners' tiny quarters. The morning shift in the mines would begin soon and the straggly line of miners was already visible as it crossed the field in front of us to reach the bus stop on our right. I was still thinking of Kanya when Chunni touched my arm and said, Papa used to say that you had Ara in your blood, do you? I turned to look at Chunni in the pale morning light, her eyes bright beneath her black hair drawn in a bun. I said, You don't even look tired, and she replied, And it's obvious you can't see in this light. I laughed and extended my arm in front of me and groped down the stairs as if I were blind. Chunni enjoyed my performance but when I made it safely to the bottom of the stairs, she stopped laughing and repeated the question from where she was sitting, Do you have Ara in your blood, are you like Papa? I didn't know exactly what answer she had in mind but I replied truthfully, Oh, certainly, but having Ara in my blood also means being like others . . . and as, with my eyes shut and arms held in front of me I falteringly climbed the steps, I recited the names of those fighters who had been killed by the police in the villages around Ara, beginning with the peasant leader Jagdish Master, and when I reached the top I took Chunni's face in my hands and said, But most of all, it means being like Kanya and like my precious, precious sisters.

NOTES

1. Upamanyu Chatterjee, English, August: An Indian Story (London: Faber, 1988), 59–60, 95–96,166,170 (hereafter cited by page number in the text). For a sense of some of the old debates around the use of English in India, see Aspects of Indian English in Writing, ed. M. K. Naik (Delhi: Macmillan, 1979); The Other Tongue: English across Cultures, ed. Braj Kachru (Illinois: University of Illinois Press, 1982); Braj Kachru, The Indianization of English (Delhi: Oxford University Press, 1983), and Peggy Mohan's, review of Kachru's book in Seminar (May 1986).

2. Mikhail Bakhtin, Rabelais and His World, trans. Helene Iswolsky (Bloomington: Indiana University Press, 1984), 122–23.

3. Allon White, "Bakhtin, Sociolinguistics, and Deconstruction," in The Theory of Reading, ed. Frank Gloversmith (Sussex: Harvester Press, 1984), 132.

4. Ken Hirschkop, "Bakhtin, Discourse, and Democracy," New Left Review 160 (1986): 101. Hirschkop credits Allon White with this particular insight.

5. Gayatri Chakravorty Spivak, "Can the Subaltern Speak?" in Marxism and the Interpretation of Culture, ed. Cary Nelson and Lawrence Grossberg (Urbana: University of Illinois Press, 1988), 286.

6. Gayatri Chakravorty Spivak, In Other Worlds: Essays in Cultural Politics (New York: Methuen, 1987); see Spivak's translation of and commentary on Devi's short stories "Draupadi" and "Breast-Giver," 179–96, 222–40. Also see Spivak, "Who Claims Alterity?" in Remaking History, ed. Barbara Kruger and Phil Mariani (Seattle, Wash.: Bay Press, 1989), 269–92, which

includes a reading of Devi's short story "The Hunt"; and Mahasweta Devi, *Imaginary Maps: Three Stories*, trans. and intro. Gayatri Chakravorty Spivak (New York : Routledge, 1995). My spelling of Devi's first name is at variance with Spivak's phonetically more accurate transcription only for the sake of maintaining consistency with Mahasveta's own usage in her journalistic publications in India.

7. Devi told me in an interview (Calcutta, 26 June 1989) that she currently writes a regular column in Bengali for regional publications read in the tribal-populated areas of Bihar, West Bengal, and Orissa. Unfortunately, I have access only to her earlier journalism written in English.

8. Mahasveta Devi, "Witch-Sabbath at Singhbhum," *Economic and Political Weekly* 16.30 (1981): 1595–97.

9. Mahasveta Devi, "Contract Labour or Bonded Labour?" *Economic and Political Weekly* 16.23 (1981): 1012, 1011, 1013.

10. Quoted in Samik Bandyopadhyay's introduction to Mahasweta Devi, *Five Plays* (Calcutta: Seagull Books, 1986), ix.

11. Mahasveta has this to say in an interview (quoted in ibid., xvi): "In the last few years in my travels among the people, I've come across several traditional folk forms, like the *alkap*, with its rich treatment of social themes in an idiom of repartees—earthy, full of blood, and highly sophisticated forms that carry on easily from speech to singing. I have seen several such performances that project images of persecution. In the 1940s the Communist Party had instructed its cadres to locate and learn and revitalize all these forms, and made them a vehicle for both the people there, and the people here who would like to communicate with them. . . . I feel a crying need for a revival of that process."

12. Ibid., x.

CHAPTER 19

Border Crossings

Retrieval and Erasure of the Self as Other

Shantanu DuttaAhmed

For now I am hidden, nearly invisible in this dark that is the inside of the mango tree. Here it smells of a sweet ripening and camphor. In the topmost branches, the monkeys make sorrowful noises and shake the boughs. Just beyond the shadow-pool of the tree, the heat is strong enough to lean on. Through the chinks in the leaves, I can see the boy strip off his clothes and lie naked in the tall grass. He thinks he is hidden, but I can see him clearly—his brown body dappled by the sun—from where I am crouched, low and invisible in the shadows. Someone begins reciting a poem: it is my uncle "practicing his Wordsworth." The foreign words float out the window and evaporate in the heat; this climate cannot sustain them; they dissipate.

This labor, at least initially, must invoke memory, which is where the border dweller usually begins. For me, working from the shadows of the diaspora, the border does not mark a specific location so much as it does a material condition.[1] And if memory helps us frame the borderlands we do inhabit, then it seems that any field of inquiry within these parameters can potentially become charged with the personal. As a result, what is contained in these pages cannot be detached from me in any significant sense. Although the Western academy demands the impersonal skeleton only—the cool and immaculate bones presented as academic discourse—I must offer instead a cumbersome creature replete with flesh and blood, stumbling, circling, unable to roost: For me, there is indeed no place like home.

Often, the risks or value of such self-representation are overshadowed by its presumed arrogance: After all, what right have I to impose the personal? Patricia Williams has usefully noted that "the personal is not the same as 'private': the personal is often merely the highly particular . . . [which] we have lost the courage and the vocabulary to describe . . . in the face of the enormous social pressure 'to keep it to ourselves.'"[2] Thus against cultural opposition and even self-imposed silence Williams urges us to articulate the personal. This essay is about such speaking. Its discussion of visibility versus invisibility is not meant to be understood as an oppositional binary, or a closed nexus of ultimately fatal or polar choices, but rather as a recognition of fruitful tension—a place of infinite beginnings as opposed to epistemological closure.

Like many other writers working from the margins, Toni Morrison, in describing the genesis of Beloved, refers to her poetics as an act of "literary archeology" wherein memory facilitates the retrieval of lost narratives—those stories that have been disavowed by the hegemony and even repressed by the Self in willful acts of forgetting.[3] Similarly, Michael Frisch locates memory as a catalyst for identity: "Memory simply cannot exist without presuming the active verb, to remember. . . . *For all the dilemmas of subjectivity, then, the evidence of memory is indispensable*" (emphasis added).[4] Within Frisch's formulation, memory becomes teleologically driven, and the very act of remembering implicates subjectivity. More important, Frisch is concerned with the ensuing products of subjective consciousness, the "Public History" that memory makes possible. He articulates a trajectory for any act of retrieval at the border: Memory—History—Text. If Frisch's formulation is somewhat optimistic in suggesting too direct a correspondence between the three terms, he nevertheless isolates the teleological impulse behind acts of retrieval at the border. Caren Kaplan has also noted that Gilles Deleuze and Félix Guattari "use the term 'deterritorialization' to locate [the] moment of alienation and exile in language and literature";[5] she suggests that diasporic memory then becomes a redemptive psychic locus, and text the revisionist manifestation of the physical and historic displacement.[6]

For the deterritorialized, however, to remember is not necessarily to be renewed; memory is not an obliging muse, nor is it home. At best, memory can be the site of involved transactions where varying selves are dialogically reckoned with. But what of the texts that signify this re-membering, however momentary or accidental? What of its marking, like a buoy on the vast and treacherous oceans, the point at which we author our own words, articulate our differences, or even render ourselves (in)visible? Since attempts to speak from the margins are so often thwarted, doesn't every public word make it easier, at least more tempting, to resist those ubiquitous declarations on the death of the author? For those of us who have not written but have been written about and sometimes written upon—our bodies and stories owned by another—the negation of authorship is a luxury we cannot afford just yet.[7]

But as I argue, and even attempt to illustrate experientially, the transactional economies of memory as an act of retrieval, which then initiates the possibility of identity and/as the material production of texts, are vexed with problems concerning the controls exercised by and the expectations of the dominant culture. To begin with, as Kobena Mercer has written, "In a material context of restricted access to the means of representation, minoritized subjects are charged with an impossible 'burden of representation.'"[8] Such dilemmas of representation, which inscribe the slippage between the terms of the presumably safe trajectory of memory-history-text, render problematic what initially appears as a substantial and valid equation between the breaking of silence and the retrieval of visible identity. Presumably, at its most generous, this new visibility should allow me a politically viable identity or at least a utilitarian otherness. Once I am empowered to represent my own differences, shouldn't I be able to cross borders fearlessly and arrive on the other side intact?

Yet in my own experiences this has not been the case. Border crossings are always difficult, since the border almost by definition facilitates the production of the paradigmatic otherness insisted on by the metropolis. This singular, commodified otherness gives me a visibility that is frightening. Against this singularity I would propose instead the strategic deployment of self-erasure as a form of a programmatic invisibility—a tactical intervention[9]—which would suggest that otherness is in fact a negotiable and dynamic category on an epistemological as well as ontological level.[10] It is in fact disrupted selves, multiple selves, that the border posits rather than the singular, identifiable Other who is then configured in opposition to the Western subject. I should point out as well that my conception of otherness does not always signify within the expected quotidian parameters—metropolis/Third World, powerful/powerless, colonizer/colonized, and so on. What I am particularly interested in examining is the tension—political and psychic—by which the border Self is contained within an Other, or an otherness-of-the-self, if you will. This (dis)location of multiple selves within the border subject, however, is not an attempt to pathologize, along the lines of Western psychoanalytic ideology, a schizophrenic split within an otherwise unified subject. That is to say, this "splitting" of the Self (though I use the word with some hesitation, for as Trinh Minh-ha has written, difference or multiplicity can be that "which undermines the very idea of identity, deferring to infinity the layers whose totality form 'I'")[11] should be viewed as a product of colonization, displacement—in short, the material conditions of a diasporic ontology. Since the border subject has been historically represented as an alterity only, the possible expression of her ontological status is already materially split through that history and strategy of the production of otherness. Thus any attempts to reposition the Self must begin within that representational history. In other words, the border selves (the plural is intended) are literally lodged within this construct of a unitary Other—disrupted and displaced within its site of production.

Working out of a different though by no means wholly unrelated field of inquiry, Judith Butler, in revising Freud's theory of melancholic appropriation as a mimetic practice that is both a response to and a refusal of loss, suggests an alternative paradigm for conceptualizing Self and Other which might be useful in stirring up border trouble in the ways she advocates gender trouble. Using the work of psychoanalytic theorists Mikkel Borch-Jacobsen and Ruth Leys, Butler wants us to consider an identificatory mimetism that "*precedes 'identity'* and constitutes identity as that which is fundamentally 'other to itself.'" Butler believes that we insist on an impossible, unitary selfhood and accept too readily the impossible desires and the appropriative gestures of melancholia as proof of an Other external to us. She suggests instead that the "'Other' installed in the self thus establishes the permanent incapacity of that 'self' to achieve identity; it is . . . always already disrupted by that Other; the disruption of the Other at the heart of the self is the very condition of that self's possibility."[12] This disruption of the Self that Butler describes is in fact actualized through the representational strategies by which the Other has been inscribed in dominant culture, a representation that can affectively yield any self as its own other; *therefore, the border writer is able to accommodate differences within and resist an ontology solely based on binaries.* Subsequently, acknowledging our selves under such conditions becomes not so much a hierarchic enactment of difference as a recognition of these other-selves. Butler's performative strategies suggest a privileged position from which they can be enacted; I find her theoretical paradigm useful in articulating the disruption of the self that always already happens to the colonial subject *as a matter of historical record* and must be accounted for. To displace the phenomenon from the political matrix of deterritorialization results in the troubling move of locating an other within the self through self-reflexive gestures, as has become de rigeur in theorizing subjectivity.[13]

In the context of our discussion, then, to render a politically kinetic otherness we need to recognize that the terms "visible" and "invisible" are themselves valenced by the hegemonic culture and need to be rethought. Incorporating work done by Richard Dyer and Gayatri Chakravorty Spivak, Mercer has further written that "for all our rhetoric about 'making ourselves visible,' *the real challenge in the next cultural politics of difference is to make 'whiteness' visible for the first time,* as a culturally constructed ethnic identity." In an attempt to negotiate the conflicted borders of the visible and invisible, I must indulge in recalling two separate incidents, reminiscences of sorts; though they appear markedly different, both were inevitable and treacherous border crossings. In thus proceeding, I no doubt put myself in the egregious position of "telling tales in school," to paraphrase D. A. Miller's description of transgressing academic textual practices, and lay myself open to ensuing charges of sentimentality.[14] Nevertheless, since these particular memories were, not surprisingly, the catalysts for this essay, a telling of stories seems inevitable.

The first incident concerns a return trip from a San Diego conference. My partner was driving, and I was complacently smudged in my seat by a good lunch, a paper that had gone well, and a generous afternoon of margaritas. Oh, the pleasures of the predictable rocking of the car and the buttery warmth of the southern California sun! In fact, though my eyes were open, I was roaming the dark groves of my grandmother's house, watching the monkeys swing from branch to branch and forage for the last remains of late August fruit. It was then that I happened to see the traffic sign and was jarred to attention. Within the familiar rubrics of black on yellow, the diamond shape bordered by a thick, black band, was the silhouette of people in flight: linked arm in arm, the authoritative engine of the father pulling his family along in a determined course. The figures were slanted dramatically to the left, hair flying in the opposite direction, their separate bodies working as one organism in flight. Perhaps danger, desperation, and violence had created out of its chaotic windfall this unexpected unity—this family propelled by their will to survive, their collective muscular intensity coalesced into a singular organism. The sign is planted in the good, solid turf of the highway—beyond the paved strip the wheat grass dries to dense golden tufts, and embedded in it are the wicked glints of barbed wire.

Where is it that this family travels? Within the stark representational strategies of the sign they move undaunted to their destination, a direction as clearly marked as it is empirically diffused and mythically trenchant. This sign marks the location and the moment when the border is both a horrifically actual and a glittering psychic hinterland that positions the southwest corridor as explosive and dangerous, epitomizing a threat presumably so extreme that the possibility of intrusion is everywhere; the border becomes its own pure excess. At one point in "Traveling Cultures," James Clifford asks, in a no doubt well-intentioned if somewhat romantic mood, "How translatable is this place-metaphor of crossing? How are historical borderlands (sites of regulated and subversive travel, natural and social landscapes) like and unlike diasporas?"[15] I believe Clifford here articulates the supplementarity of the border, apprehends that moment of kinetic exchange between the psychic and the physical that the border not only transacts but is. But I wonder to what extent this place can ever be a metaphor for those who come from the shadows to cross it. And how does one answer Clifford's question while keeping in mind the realities of fences, bullets, food, flesh and bone? Consider even my own abstract paradigms: How do I play out the semantic tensions between visibility and invisibility here on a physical plane? How do I gamble on that moment of actual contact between body and fence, and ensure that the embrace will be tenacious enough to bleed me through to the other side so that I can arrive not just spirit (which this land disbelieves in) but flesh and bone as well?

The traffic sign generates that point of origin for colonial discourse which Homi Bhabha has described as the necessary "'fixity' in the ideological construction of otherness."[16] Here, such ideological fixity is concretized through the familiar rubrics of black and yellow into a signifier that spells privilege for those who know how to read it, for those of us who own or are traveling in cars, who are in a position to watch the intruders and perhaps even to prevent them from bursting open like pods of thistle on the barbed wire. But the sign, though ideologically fixed, can be affectively transitive, for in an instance it reverses my outward gaze: now I am the one being looked at. As we approach the checkpoint, the cars slow to a crawl under the direction of the border patrolmen. Occasionally, a vehicle is pulled out of the single file and directed to another area where three or four armed men scrutinize the passengers; then the car is either allowed to go on or told to stop, and a search ensues. My partner said to me: "Don't be alarmed, but I think because you're in the car, we will probably be pulled over." He said this gently, softly, but I could still hear the understandable agitation in his voice. A gay couple becomes wary of overt manifestations of the state, especially when such displays involve armed men in uniform. But in one of those proverbial split seconds that alter and define so much, it wasn't the state or its uniformed agents or any other as yet invisible threat that I responded to, but rather my partner's comments. He is a white, blond, blue-eyed Scandinavian; I am South Asian or, rather, nonwhite. At a border crossing my skin takes precedence; I become the unitary Other. My anger toward my partner was based on the privilege that allowed him to articulate his concern for me, however genuine. His words, said no doubt to calm me, perhaps even to protect me, became instead the rhythm, rhyme, and reason of every good colonial's cordially extended care.

Almost instantly I remembered a still, white-hot afternoon in India, the bullock cart overturned on the road and half-naked boys gathered around the groaning bull. My grandfather was standing with three sahibs I did not know, don't remember; they come back only as three very large and very red men with bushy mustaches. This was in the mid-1960s, and the three men were leftovers, icons. Perhaps they were living fearfully, knowing that their whiteness was slowly becoming visible, that we could now count them and, by quantifying, render them finite. But this is too easy an equation: Seeing does not always allow for revisionist possibilities; extended degradation casts its own patina on dark skin. While we could have said, there are three sahibs on a dirt road surrounded by a thousand dark figures, and so perhaps have begun a process of reconfiguration, the scene played out somewhat differently: A native official came up to the three white men and in an effort to calm their rising anger said in a distant sing-song, "Do not be angry, sahib, you know we cannot even fix a cart wheel without assistance, and this is so much more complicated." No doubt I have rearranged the words or perhaps even chosen some he did not speak, but I know I have the essence right. I am familiar with the glazed look in the eyes that is hardened and permanent obsequiousness, the indestructible legacy of the colonized, an inheritance that manifests itself as physically and as surely as the drunkard's shake or his red eyes. And now, almost thirty years later, I am still on that dirt road with that damned cart still to be righted. I am powerless, driving in the car with a sahib who has the power to say, "Don't be alarmed." If I say I am not, I would be lying. Of course I am alarmed, why shouldn't I be? There are white men with guns ahead of me. As surely and certainly as that road converging with the shimmering heat, this moment shifts, finds its own confluence in space and time, and our car is taken out of the line that is allowed to go forward. Instead, we are pulled—I am pulled—out into a semicircle. The man with the gun comes up close to the window, and I see myself reflected in his sunglasses; I doubt that his naked eyes would have revealed any secrets. He is in full control of all he possesses, including his gaze. I can only see my features dilated and unrecognizable on his convex and shimmery lenses: my dry-mouthed and resentful stare, my eyes like two blobs of dark jelly, sliding, indecisive. This time am I supposed to look the sahib straight in the eye? Suddenly, he motions us to continue, and in minutes the checkpoint is physically far behind me. I look at my partner, wanting to say something, but decide against it.

Recording the incident in my journal did not lay it to rest. This personal fragment, sharp and insistent as a shard of glass, was beginning to stick to things, cutting through the surface and becoming embedded in my readings, my work. I wanted to write it out so as to inscribe it as essential to my very existence. This insistence perhaps reflected a characteristic noted in the summary comment a professor had once made on my semester's work. His criticism boiled down to what he perceived as a constant attempt on my part to merge art and life; he implied that my academic work was doomed to failure unless I rid myself of this perverse urge to have art and life cross the borders, as it were, and occupy an unsanctioned space within the academy.

In a more formal letter meant for my files, the same professor had written what initially seemed at best a curious aside: "He is always very eager to please." I have read this letter several times, and that last sentence always calls me back, probably because I am unsure of exactly what it means or how such a statement is even relevant to an evaluation of my academic performance. At this point I should tell you that this professor is white and male, and I wonder if he as a white man is even aware of how a person of color would read his observation. Does his remark imply that he expects to be pleasured and is making note of my inclination to accommodate him? Or is his comment rather a generous gesture, condoning instead of punishing me for having failed somehow to please him yet wishing to note that I was eager nevertheless? Or is my "eagerness to please" just another marker of my race (being remarked upon by those that have the right to observe), an innate characteristic manifesting itself, needing comment—the sniveling monkey grubbing for rotten fruit? At any rate, such simian antics were recorded and deposited in my file during my tenure at the academy.

I suggest that these two observations of me—my presumably misdirected attempts to merge art and life, and my eagerness to please—are as relevant to a discussion of belonging and identity and erasure as was the more readily apprehensible experience at the border. No doubt the borders of the academy are less overtly demarcated; such crude signifiers as black and yellow signs or barbed wire have been thinned to invisibility, yet the border here is as rigidly fixed as any dangerous strip of Interstate 5. In fact, it is more dangerous because of the absence. When I cross this border, I have to make those split-second ontological revisions as surely as I do elsewhere. In this unmarked and treacherous terrain, what renders me suspicious, troublesome, and, most important, *ungrateful*? In short, what is defined as excess baggage? Every classroom, every office, every encounter—even with a familiar person—requires that I reinvent myself in order to survive.

Within the public discourse of the academy I am fetishized as the racial other, my mere presence becoming the proof of the achievement of its democratic ideals; privately, in more intimate encounters, I am asked to become white by praxis. In *White Mythologies* Robert Young has pointed out that this process of absorption is endemic to Western philosophy itself, and he describes it as "ontological imperialism," a transactional economy wherein "the other is neutralized as a means of encompassing it."[17] Similarly, bell hooks describes this ethnic cannibalism in an essay aptly titled "Eating the Other," and suggests that such seemingly desirous consumption, "with no apparent will to dominate, assuages the guilt of the past . . . [and] structures of domination [are] deflected by an emphasis on seduction and longing."[18] Thus overtly embedded in a narrative of desire, the consumption of the other is presented less as an act of political power than as the consummation of desire. In effect, through the recuperative and appropriative modes of capitalism, the other is purchased and absorbed into the academy. Once we are inside, this permission—indeed, this directive—to be white is deemed our greatest privilege.

Thinking white is transacted along lines not only of race but of gender and sexual orientation as well, for within the circuits of power, to be racially white is to be male and straight. To render myself visible, then, as a nonwhite—let alone as a gay, South Asian male—is to become the object of the gaze: I am, for all practical purposes, feminized. In his opposition to my attempted merger of "art and life," I wonder if my professor wasn't actually warning me about breaking the ultimate masculine code of the academy, for in "personalizing" myself, do I not engage in what must have seemed to him a dangerous and self-indulgent urge to feminize myself?

Although postmodernism attempts to relativize the centrality of Western culture in relation to non-Western "others," for those who have been denied memory, history, or text, the terms of the reconsideration are still valenced suspiciously. Young suggests that "contrary, then, to some of its more overreaching definitions, postmodernism itself could be said to mark not just the cultural effects of a new stage of 'late' capitalism, but the sense of the loss of European history and culture as History and Culture, the loss of their unquestioned place at the centre of the world." Gayatri Chakravorty Spivak has addressed the problem more cynically, pointing out that the attempts to decenter Western hegemony may instead imply pernicious attempts to reinstate it: "Some of the most radical criticism coming out of the West today is the result of an interested desire to conserve the subject of the West, or the West as Subject. The theory of pluralized 'subject-effects' gives an illusion of undermining the subjective sovereignty while often providing cover for this subject of knowledge."[19] At its simplest and perhaps even most amusing, the underlying assumption seems to be that the impossibility or failure of Western hegemony renders inoperant the concept of subjectivity itself. If the academy is currently engaged in refuting the explicit production of otherness, one of the problematic expressions of this egalitarian effort seems to be the negation of otherness as a category of analysis altogether.

Ironically, subjectivity can be had only by enrolling in the regime of the same, while on the most obvious level the self/other binary is used to signify difference. In effect, then, this is a pervasive economy of exchange—an otherness perpetually bartered, traded, to formulate a self. To paraphrase a popular song, the border dweller has been looking for subjectivity in all the wrong places. As (re)defined and rethought within poststructuralist and postmodernist practices, subjectivity still becomes articulated as a form of viable currency, which is then "mortgaged," in a Lacanian sense, to become a self. It seems to me, however, that the terms in which cultural studies question the concept of self and subjectivity do not adequately examine the self/other binary at its core, and the economy of exchange in which the binary is implicated. In other words, the selfhood that is available to the border dweller for purchase may not be worth having. Simply raising the issue of difference does not solve the representational fixity accorded the other, because issues of difference remain ideologically valenced. Similarly, revisioning representational dilemmas as praxis and sites of production-of-otherness, versus the identification of otherness, does not disrupt the relationships of power between observer and observed which make the self/other binary possible.

As work by Foucault on issues of sexuality and discipline has shown, the desired visibility of the other has been a pervasive impulse of metropolitan regimes. Visibility allows an actual site of initial control from which it can spread in ever widening networks of power. Foucault argues, for example, that an important aspect of panopticism was the near-universal applicability of its principles beyond the particulars of the prison. The panopticon is effective because it "automizes and disindividualizes power. . . . Any individual, taken almost at random, can operate the machine. . . . Similarly, it does not matter what motivates him: the curiosity of the indiscreet, the malice of a child, the thirst for knowledge of a philosopher who wishes to visit the museum of human nature, or the perversity of those who take pleasure in spying and punishing." Foucault presents a scene of surveillance where not only is the other under constant observation but, more important, the panopticon induces "in the inmate a state of conscious and permanent visibility."[20]

Acknowledging the debt to Foucault, though specifically addressing the homosexual body, Lee Edelman writes about the cultural imperative to view alien others as "inherently textual—as bodies that might well bear a 'hallmark' that could, and must be read." More important, Edelman also exposes the contradictions inherent in this regime of legibility, since textualizing and displaying the other can disrupt the very oppositional categories that the other is supposed to stabilize: "The historical positing of the category of the 'homosexual' textualizes male as such, subjecting it to the alienating requirement that it be 'read,' and threatening, in consequence, to strip 'masculinity' of its privileged status as the self-authenticating paradigm of the natural or the self-evident itself."[21] Like Edelman, Homi Bhabha notes that the same contradiction—the disruptions that ensue in the self as a result of producing a visible other—is endemic to the colonial encounter. Bhabha theorizes the production of otherness as a fetishistic impulse, an attempt to mask the perceived lack and difference of the colonial self. He argues that the fetish or stereotype of the native is "not a simplification because it is an arrested, fixated form of representation. . . . *The stereotype impedes the circulation and articulation of the signifier of 'race' as anything other than its fixity as racism.*"[22] Edelman and Bhabha's exposure of the contradictions inherent to producing a visible other is important to our project of reconfiguring the self/other binary because it allows for the reading of "race" itself as an imposed performance (of difference).[23] It is my contention that in attempting a tactic of absence or invisibility against the demands of a continual visibility, we need to deconstruct race but not otherness as an empirical category. I am arguing that "race" as a category is only relationally produced. Frantz Fanon states it succinctly: "Not only must the black man be black, he must be black in relation to the white man."[24] Henry Louis Gates, however, has pointed out that if race is an arbitrary signifier, a trope, it nevertheless is a powerful one; constructed against an invisible whiteness, *the otherness of what we mean by "race" is always residually intact in any deconstructions of it.* The other is continually implicated in economies of exchange that are attempts to stabilize metropolitan constructions. What I am proposing is the articulation of a politics that provides freedom from this exchange, that enables the other to occupy a material space from which to reconfigure by leaving that space empty. The other can best be present by being absent, being invisible.

Let me here answer at least those immediate charges I expect my comments to engender: Is this politics or mysticism? Am I in fact making impossible any kind of multicultural project that requires learning from others? Satya Mohanty has written in a recent essay that in discourses "where . . . skepticism is conjoined with relativism of some kind . . . we are left in the uncomfortable position of seeking a noncolonizing relationship with the other culture but accepting a theoretical premise that makes anything that can be called a relationship impossible."[25] But it seems to me that regardless of the theoretical sophistication or even sincerity with which we apprehend the other as alterity and allow for a genuine "play of difference," as Bhabha would say, the humanistic agenda behind such a beginning is inevitably to show how the other is after all the same. Richard Terdiman has pointed out, for example, that much of the revisioning of New Historicism relies on metonymy, a "trope of wholes and parts. Hence it always presumes or posits an organic system, whether we call this a 'totality,' a 'field,' an 'episteme,' a 'culture,' or a 'text.'" What Terdiman calls the "strategy" of New Historicism relies on showing how a closeup, a detail, makes sense within a broader context. Meaning is thus produced as a linking of disparate elements in a given field of view. But as Terdiman cautions, if a single fragment "can serve as a lever to unpack the meaning of a whole text or, indeed, of an entire society, this must be because the same structures of signification reproduce themselves indifferently in each. . . . However, such reproduction of the same can turn voracious. At the limit it can consume alterity completely." The logic and the politics of metonymy then accept alterity only as a means of demonstrating its nonexistence.[26]

A politics that allows for tactical invisibility as a way to maintain alterity is not one of correcting misrepresentations, false images, but rather one of questioning the substitution of images as programmatically useful.[27] Actually, what I am suggesting is hardly radical, for the colonial theater has been masquerades of absence anyway: The colonizer's impossible desire to see himself in the other and the other as himself frames the space and narrative of this consigned performance.[28]

If my titular reference to "self as other" suggests too great a compromise, a giving up of self to win an abject selfhood, let me say that what I am alternatively suggesting is an agitation and disruption of the binary on which the oppositional paradigm of self and other ultimately rests— hence my insistence on a perpetual retrieval and erasure of what we call self—to render the construct *en procès*. It seems possible that if we disrupt the Cartesian duality of self and other, the violence as desire of an empiricist ontology can itself be rewritten. In considering Butler's revisionist dynamics, can we not think of (re)membering itself and any ensuing retrieval as a point of erasure, since an act of retrieval also locates a moment of flux, an *other self*, that is not so much visible (thereby hegemonically fixed) as it is a point of infinite possibilities? In insisting on visibility during these moments of remembrance, do we not play upon ourselves the old trick of memory-as-home? when, in fact, memory is only a point of departure or reference—a sliding signifier that exhausts itself in diasporic connections (if one is lucky) and on an ordinary day dissipates to nothingness like words(worth) during a white-hot afternoon.

NOTES

1. Although borders are inarguably actual geographic sites of political transactions (consider for example the current efforts to enforce Proposition 187 in California), elastic applications of the term are nevertheless useful. As Gloria Anzaldua herself points out in the preface to her *Borderlands/La Frontera: The New Mestiza* (San Francisco: Aunt Lute, 1987): "The actual physical borderland that I'm dealing with in this book is the Texas-U.S. Southwest/Mexican border. The psychological borderlands, the sexual borderlands and the spiritual borderlands are not particular to the Southwest."

2. Patricia Williams, *The Alchemy of Race and Rights* (Cambridge, Mass.: Harvard University Press, 1991), 93.

3. Toni Morrison, "Site of Memory," in *Inventing the Truth: The Art and Craft of Memoir*, ed. William Zinsser (Boston: Houghton Mifflin, 1987), 109–26.

4. Michael H. Frisch, "The Meaning of History," *Radical History Review* 25 (1981): 17.

5. Caren Kaplan, "Deterritorializations: The Rewriting of Home and Exile in Western Feminist Discourse," in *The Nature and Context of Minority Discourse*, ed. Abdul R. JanMohamed and David Lloyd (New York: Oxford University Press, 1990), 358.

6. Memory as enabling a revisionist history is implicated in a complex debate over what Joan Scott has called "the evidence of experience," particularly as it is played out in essentialist or postmodernist terms. For a useful summary of the major debates surrounding this issue, see Joan W. Scott, "The Evidence of Experience," *Critical Inquiry* 17 (Summer 1991): 773–97; also Satya Mohanty, "The Epistemic Status of Cultural Identity," *Cultural Critique* (Spring 1993): 41–80.

7. Not surprisingly, the feminist response to the (somewhat sudden) death of the author has been ongoing and is richly invested in foregrounding issues of marginality as well. For example, in an article that usefully summarizes the feminist response to the issue, Cheryl Walker has suggested an alternative concept of authorship that "does not diminish the importance of difference and agency in the response of women writers to historical formations" ("Feminist Literary Criticism and the Author," *Critical Inquiry* 16 [Spring 1990]: 560.

8. Kobena Mercer, "Skin Head Sex Thing: Racial Difference and the Homoerotic Imaginary," in *How Do I Look?* ed. Bad Object Choices (Seattle, Wash.: Bay Press, 1991), 205.

9. I borrow the term "tactical intervention" from the subtitle of Rey Chow's book *Writing Diaspora: Tactics of Intervention in Contemporary Cultural Studies* (Bloomington: Indiana University Press, 1993), in which she notes Michel de Certeau's distinction between "strategy" and "tactic": "A strategy has the ability to 'transform the uncertainties of history into readable spaces.' The type of knowledge derived from strategy is 'one sustained and determined by the power to provide oneself with one's own place.' A tactic by contrast is a 'calculated action determined by the absence of a proper locus.' Betting on time instead of space, a tactic 'concerns an operational logic'" (16).

10. For an extended discussion on the importance of considering both the epistemological and ontological in contextualizing the self in cultural studies, see Elspeth Probyn, *Sexing the Self: Gendered Positions in Cultural Studies* (London: Routledge, 1993).

11. Quoted in Michele Wallace, *Invisibility Blues: From Pop to Theory* (London: Verso, 1990), 220.

12. Judith Butler, "Imitation and Gender Insubordination," in *Inside Out: Lesbian Theories, Gay Theories,* ed. Diana Fuss (New York: Routledge, 1991), 26, 27.

13. See Frances E. Mascia-Lees, Patricia Sharpe, and Colleen Ballerino Cohen, "The Postmodernist Turn in Anthropology: Cautions from a Feminist Perspective," in *Anthropology and Literature,* ed. Paul Benson (Urbana: University of Illinois Press, 1993), 225–48.

14. Mercer, "Skin Head Sex Thing," 206; D. A. Miller, *The Novel and the Police* (Berkeley: University of California Press, 1988).

15. James Clifford, "Traveling Cultures," in *Cultural Studies,* ed. Lawrence Grossberg, Cary Nelson, and Paula A. Treichler (New York: Routledge, 1991), 109.

16. Homi Bhabha, "The Other Question: The Stereotype and Colonial Discourse," *Screen* 24.6 (1983): 18.

17. Robert Young, *White Mythologies: Writing History and the West* (London: Routledge, 1990), 13.

18. bell hooks, *Black Looks* (Boston: South End Press, 1992), 25.

19. Young, *White Mythologies,* 20; Gayatri Chakravorty Spivak, "Can the Subaltern Speak?" in *Marxism and the Interpretation of Culture,* ed. Cary Nelson and Lawrence Grossberg (Urbana: University of Illinois Press, 1988), 271.

20. Michel Foucault, *Discipline and Punish: The Birth of the Prison* (New York: Vintage, 1979), 202, 201.

21. Lee Edelman, *Homographesis* (New York: Routledge, 1994), 6, 12.

22. Homi Bhabha, *The Location of Culture* (London: Routledge, 1994), 75.

23. The debates about deconstructing "race" are ongoing and extensive in both physical and social sciences as well as in cultural studies. For a summary of the central arguments, see Diana Fuss, "'Race' under Erasure?" in Fuss, *Essentially Speaking: Feminism, Nature, and Difference* (New York: Routledge, 1989), 73–96.

24. Frantz Fanon, *Black Skin, White Masks* (New York: Grove Weidenfeld, 1967), 110; see also Henry Louis Gates Jr., "Two Nations, Both Black," *Forbes*, 14 September 1992, 132–38.

25. Satya P. Mohanty, "Colonial Legacies, Multicultural Futures: Relativism, Objectivity, and the Challenge of Otherness," *PMLA* 110.1 (1995): 113.

26. Richard Terdiman, "The Response of the Other," *Diacritics* 22.2 (1992): 6.

27. See also Rey Chow on the inefficacy of merely substituting a presumably "correct" image for a "false" one, esp. chap. 2, "Where Have All the Natives Gone?" in her *Writing Diaspora*, 27–54.

28. For this idea, I am indebted to Peggy Phelan's work and her concept of "theatres of absence." About Jenny Livingston's film *Paris Is Burning*, Phelan writes: "In part a visual threnody for a pre-Aids culture, the film is nostalgic for a future her informants had dreamed of in a more vital past. The loss of that future haunts the speakers' dreams of economic success and idealized femininity. . . . The impossibility of realizing these dreams frames the space of this particular theatre. The balls documented in *Paris* are masquerades of absence" (*Unmarked: The Politics of Performance* [New York: Routledge, 1993], 94).

CHAPTER 20

I See the Glass as Half Full

Uma Parameswaran

So what is it like to be a woman, a South Asian, and a feminist in North America?[1] What is it like to be a nonwhite, non-Judaeo-Christian, non-male in academia? What is it like to be a Canadian writer who was born and educated in India?

Tropes and Trolls of Litcrit

Responding to this self-imposed framework, I sent an essay to the editors. In due time, after an exchange of cordial notes, came the formal acceptance in which I was asked (1) to shorten the essay somewhat and (2) to reinforce it with theories and other theorists on self-representational writing. I started with the easier task and made deletions and revisions. The new version pleased me. But a self-conscious scrutiny was revealing. I had edited out sections that consisted of personal anecdotes, and I had been pleased because the new version more closely approximated the depersonalized voice of authority institutionally favored by academia during my graduate years. So strong are the powers of early indoctrination. The old version and style had to be restored.

Turning to the task of identifying theoretical underpinnings, I realized I had embraced the feminist move toward I-centeredness and anecdotalizing without charting the coordinates of my own positioning. This called for some analytic introspection.

I see my current critical writing as a kind of metacriticism, a process that shares with the reader the steps whereby the critic explores, feels her way, bumps into walls, retracts, comes upon a scene that momentarily takes her into another space or upon a metaphor that impels her to pause, sit down, and enjoy where she is. The words have led me into a labyrinth. So what made me think of criticism as a labyrinth? I could try psychoanalysis and surface with pseudo-scientific data on my id and libido, or I could use common sense to look at what is encoded in these free associations: Labyrinth = Minotaur—Abhimanyu—gardens—Versailles.[2] Euro-classical—Hindu classical—Indian historical—personal symbol. The analysis of each of these terms could be endless, but what stand highlighted for me are the duality of my sensibility and my perception that the labyrinth is a garden. There is the duality of my Eurocentric academic training and my Hindu cultural roots; then there is the duality of patriarchal war game, or quest and sacrifice, motifs of Minotaur and Abhimanyu paired with the feminist affirmation of personal space and my personal symbol of Versailles. The associations are simultaneous, not sequential.

Indian classics and folklore tell us about labyrinths that were part of the architectural layout of pleasure gardens. I am in no panic to find the way out of the labyrinth. To adapt what Jane Tompkins says in "Me and My Shadow" about her stockinged feet,[3] I feel quite at ease here, wiggling the bare toes of my left foot, which is in a cast after a badminton court injury.[4] There are others walking around, with and without tour guides; maybe one or two will join me on this garden bench; in any case, the gatekeeper takes count at sunset, and airlift facilities are available. That is how far we have come on the shoulders of earlier feminists, some of whom entered the labyrinth, like Abhimanyu, before airlift facilities.

Language as Parole, not Langue

Nancy Miller uses a term that resonates for me, "personal criticism," which she defines as "an explicitly autobiographical performance within the act of criticism." "Narrative criticism" is a "mixed mode of autobiography and cultural analysis."[5] Paul de Man says in "Autobiography as Defacement," that an autobiographer can project a self-image only through language,[6] and Sidonie Smith follows up on this with, "Given the very nature of language, embedded in the text lie alternative or deferred identities that constantly subvert any pretensions of truthfulness."[7] I would add that both language and psychological processes have a part in all self-representation. I am interested in language as parole (communication) more than as langue (abstract system.) Feminist writing, be it critical, autobiographical, or fictional, tends toward the self-conscious mode, which is subjective by nature. But subjectivity does not exclude rational or analytic processes. A certain amount of editing takes place before the act of writing even in free-fall writing, and even more, it stands to reason, in any critical writing. Thus, the images and metaphors related to my Achilles tendon come naturally, but even so, they are the result of inner editing in that my mind has picked that particular personal event in my present life over many other events that might be more weighty but do not lend themselves as well to what I wish to communicate.

Different parts of what one says have different resonances for different readers. When I say "Achilles tendon," the sympathetic reader's mind translates it to her own personal equivalent, whereas the reader unsympathetic to my language or ideology translates the reference in a different way. Self-conscious reading generates intellectual and emotional responses that go beyond the literal veracity and conscious slanting of the writer. Thus, both writing and reading are self-conscious acts, though they need not always be so. Perhaps these two levels are encoded in Hinduism where the deity of wisdom is separate and distinct from the deity of learning.[8]

Labels and Lines

Postcolonial and feminist experience frequently run parallel and often intersect in the spirograph of our lives. Nobody likes labels, and yet we are labeled at every turn; moreover, in feminist discourse we label ourselves as a matter of principle, wearing our class, race, gender, political ideology, sexual orientation, or family tree on our sleeves. The key point is whether the label is given to us as in colonial and postcolonial contexts, or by us as in feminist practice. Who the "us" is or are is yet another morass, given our new debate in Canada on "Appropriation of Culture" about who can speak for whom. The issue is further complicated by the current yen to reclaim words (black, dyke, wog, subaltern), to wear with pride what Salman Rushdie calls "the demon-tag the farangis hung around [our] neck."[9] It is certainly possible and necessary to change usages and language; after all, it did not take long to educate people that when we said "Ms." we were replacing "Miss" and "Mrs." with a word that had parity with "Mr." But there are problems in replacements and reclamations arising from the question of who can speak for whom (as Rushdie found out). Toni Morrison puts a lilt into "niggah" that makes it sing, but I have serious qualms about calling anyone nigger or dyke or wog or WASP even if they call themselves so; the principle of respecting their preference conflicts with the principle of acceptable language. Further, if we accept the unrestricted fluidity of signifiers, we would need to define our terms at every turn to alert readers that when we say "abc" we mean "xyz," and that the word could well be "mno" in another place at another time. Even Rushdie's terms are outdated; blacks who were once Negroes are now African Americans (the latter part of that compound to be further changed with geographical locations).

Resisting labels is far more complex than changing usages because labels arise from perceptions of selves, one's own and others'. For South Asians, certainly, cultural constructs are significant. Cultural constructs have generated a deep divide between Western feminists and South Asian feminists, so deep that Madhu Kishwar has stated in an article in *Manushi* that she does not call herself a feminist: "I resist the label of feminism because of its overclose association with [the] Western women's movement. I have no quarrel with western feminist movements in their own context. . . . However, given our situation today, where the general flow of ideas and labels is one way—from west to east—in the overall context of highly imbalanced power relations, feminism, as appropriated and defined by the west, has too often become a tool of cultural imperialism."[10] Gayatri Chakravorty Spivak also speaks against this patronizing approach in "French Feminism in an International Frame."[11] As expatriates domiciled in North America, we too have to be wary lest we fall into that neoimperialist approach when discussing the role and plight of women in our original homelands. While acquiring the tools of scholarly discourse, we just might have let our cultural tendons atrophy and may be strutting on ankle supports fashioned by the tools.

Moreover, to add to this problem of possible distancing between us and our original homelands, we have a problem closer to home: whether we like it or not, in our own everyday lives we are drawn into the responsibility of resisting cultural imperialism without breaking the essential bonds of the women's movement. The growing rift between white and nonwhite feminists is a serious threat to solidarity.[12] A South Asian colleague who attended a recent Women's Studies conference talked jubilantly about the atmosphere at the plenary sessions where the room was filled with nonwhite faces. The theme of the conference was racism, and the answer to my next question confirmed what I had feared. Were there as many white women as this annual conference usually attracts? No. I hope that that was due to a phase of necessary regrouping and that the movement will be stronger for it. I hope the right analogy is to Women's Studies classes, which at present are and should be overwhelmingly female, and not to campus events on gender-related issues, which regrettably draw very, very few male colleagues.

It takes two to make a dialogue. Absenting oneself from possible dialogues is a neoimperialist strategy; shutting out possible dialogues is an older one. At another recent conference a speaker used what she saw as a humorous analogy about young Turks and old Turks, that young Turks who think they know everything usually grow up to be old Turks who have seen it all. During the discussion after the talk a woman rose and protested the usage, saying that she was from the Middle East and that speakers should be aware of minorities' feelings and possible overtones of racism. Soon after that I had my hand up with an innocuous comment in mind related to a central metaphor the speaker had used; she identified others who had their hands up—one in front of me, two practically on either side of me—but not me. Her "oversight" and my upraised hand were both so insistent that they were noticed by many, some of whom came to me later.

The speaker was perhaps on her guard; the other woman had looked like anyone else but had turned out to be a minority person and had taken offense where none was meant. Since I looked so obviously different, wearing a sari and with a bindi on my forehead, the speaker perhaps was apprehensive of yet another accusatory comment from a "visible minority" member. Of course, there is a remote possibility that she did not see me. But it seemed to me an example of an age-old imperialists' ploy now adapted for cultural imperialism: As long as one diverts possible dialogue, lines can be used to define and restrict the Other on one's own terms.

Ganga in the Assiniboine

So what is it like to be a writer, an academic, and a feminist in North America? I have managed fairly well on all fronts, I would say. Someone else might say I have failed. Both assessments would be both true and false. That everything can be seen in more than one way is something I learned long before the deconstructionist revolution. I learned it from trying to talk about India to my fellow Canadians, and that process has led me to my ideology of the half-full glass. India is the sound of spontaneous laughter, I say (knowing that laughter is one of the first luxuries many of us lose when we come as graduate students), and they say why? (seeing in their mind's eye the pavement dwellers of the cities, whose laughter I have heard and they cannot even imagine); it is gopurams and temple bells and flowers, I say, and they say how? (thinking of superstitions or of souls to be saved for Jesus); it is women topping most graduating classes in most professional colleges, I say, and they shake their heads (recalling dowry deaths and femicides).

Given India's diversity, anything one says of India is both false and true. Everything boils down to the old analogy of a glass half filled with liquid. The choice of responses, "the glass is half full" or "the glass is half empty," would tell us a lot about the respondent, even if it tells very little about the nature of the liquid or the shape and texture of the glass. Each response, however, is related to the way we live and act. There may be only one Truth, but we have to live in a plane of many truths. My truth is to see the glass as half full, which is not to deny that the glass is half empty.

I do not deny the existence of Mother Teresa's India; however, because we seem to hear only about that facet of India, for the last twelve years I have been producing a television show twice a month on the half-full glass: interviewing South Asian Canadians about their professions and careers; rummaging for slides, postcards, pictures in books; and then writing up scripts on the architectural monuments, art, music, crafts, dances, and mythologies of India.[13] So there I am, appearing week after week with an introductory blurb that over the years has included such phrases as "the acceptance, indeed the celebration of differences," "the contributions of South Asian–Canadians that help us stand tall." The response, especially of the younger generation, is that the show does indeed help them stand tall in their South Asian–Canadian identity.

But all hyphenated identities are a cross that gets heavier the further in time one travels from the original homeland. I carry India with me wherever I go, says Raja Rao somewhere. It is time to do more. My goal is to bring Ganga to the Assiniboine,[14] not only for Indo-Canadians but for all Canadians, so that the fund of Canadian allusions and sensibilities is extended, and readers recognize literary allusions to the river Gange and to the Krishna cycle of stories as readily as we, growing up in India, recognized allusions to the Jesus cycle of stories. As one of the characters in my *Trishanku* says,

> And I shall bring Ganga
> as Bhagiratha did of old,
> to our land
> our Assiniboine,
> and the flute player
> dark as kaya blossom
> shall dance on the waters of La Salle.[15]

Those who see the glass as half empty would say that will never happen because North American society is too racist, the white establishment too entrenched. There are statistics enough to support that argument. But I have Gandhi and my Romantic faith in the essential divinity of human nature to support me. In my lighter moments I postulate that numbers are in my favor. I said this about Rushdie's use of images of endless procreation and aromas in *Shame*, *Midnight's Children*, and *The Satanic Verses*:

> Good News's fertility and Shiva's potency are symptomatic of population boom. Outside Asia, the South Asian population is growing much faster than the white population. The masalas of India have found their way to all corners of these countries. In my fantasy, the conquering armies marching from immigrant Asian wombs will outnumber, outthink and outshine the others and take over. Not an unfit retribution for the races that have annihilated aboriginal cultures and peoples in five continents over the last five hundred years.[16]

On a more serious note, it is an exciting time to be in Canada, where we are shaping a new national culture that will be a composite of many heritage cultures, not the least of which will be the aboriginal culture that is experiencing a renaissance.

The Day My Achilles Tendon Snapped

Born in a Wordsworthian environment in central India and nurtured by the English Romantics, I found that my first reaction to postcolonial and feminist critical theories was one of exhilaration. "Bliss was it in that dawn to be alive, / but to be young was very heaven!" Edward Said's *Orientalism* (1978) and subsequent works spoke as Chapman's Homer spoke to Keats: "Then felt I like some watcher of the skies / When a new planet swims into his ken." The concept of the Other—of how colonizers shaped their views of the colonized by making them the Other, how they denigrated non-Western history and culture, how they turned into straw all that had been gold, and how we, the postcolonial generation, can invent new identities and histories—spoke directly to me. Later, in the mid-1980s, when I was initiated into feminist scholarship and read what Hélène Cixous says about "the other bisexuality" as "each one's location in self (*reperage en soi*) of the presence—variously manifest and insistent according to each person, male and female—of both sexes,"[17] I heard a clearer articulation of what I had written ("Feminine Sensibility in Raja Rao, Kamala Markandaya, and Pritish Nandy") for an MLA session in 1979, about the time Cixous's original French version would have appeared. The ideas were formulated from my own experience as a writer and instructor of creative writing.

Similarly, Lacan's modification of Freud's concept of "penis envy," whereby he formulates a symbolic order and the idea of the Imaginary as something that is beyond difference made far more sense than Freudian readings, but I questioned the Lacanian angle that the self does not exist prior to language.[18] Again, French feminist theorists such as Julia Kristeva opened up a new way of looking at identities and oppressions.[19] Works of such critics as Gayatri Chakravorty Spivak, Homi Bhabha, and Frantz Fanon in postcolonial literatures have changed our ways of reading and shaping literatures. Yes, I can see where the postcolonial and French feminist theorists are coming from, and I can see the linkages between female and colonial experience and the semiotics and symbolisms that they propound, though I protest many of their own and others' applications of their theories to art and literature. The day I read Kristeva's interpretation of Giovanni Bellini's Madonna and Child figures in Mary Jacobus's *Reading Woman* was the day my litcrit Achilles tendon snapped under the pressure of my growing dissatisfaction with the proliferation of theories.[20]

The violence of my reaction called for further analysis, and so I read Kristeva again. First, Kristeva's hyperbolic and highly emotive prose style puts my back up in the same way as do the staccato imperatives of the patriarchal style. Both have an edge of self-absorption that turns me off. Kristeva volleys far too many adjectives and subjective viewpoints at the reader. "There is a shiver of anguish in the child's hand," she says of one of the paintings, and of another, "Aggressive hands prod the stomach and penis of the frightened baby."[21] As Mary Jacobus points out, the paintings hardly call for such destructive associations.[22] For example, to support an infant with one hand across his chest and another under his buttocks is a practical pose and not one of obsessive sexuality.

Second, Kristeva's starting point is biographical, that the absence of the mother in Bellini's own childhood—of which, by Kristeva's own admission, very little is known—is the source of the predatory images in his paintings. If biography is at all relevant, it seems to me that Kristeva's interpretation of Bellini might owe more to her biography than to his.

Third, as I thought about the core of Kristeva's ideas concerning semiotic (or maternal) language and the symbolic (or paternal) language of signification, it struck me that cultural constructs just might turn a Kristevan reading on its head. In Hinduism the transformation of Sound-into-Word is initiated by a goddess, Akshara Lakshmi, and not by a patriarchal force. The male principle, Siva, is all encompassing but inert Essence; Shakti, the feminine principle, which is the power that gives form to the Essence, which by interacting with Siva gives rise to the manifested world of generation. Yet again, the moon symbol of female fickleness in the Western world is male in Hinduism.

Thus, theories can be exciting and give us different angles on the text or art being experienced, but in the final count, as with the response to a glass half filled with liquid, they tell us more about the critic than about the text or painting.

Activists and critics not only have the choice to focus on the filled or empty half of the glass but can also decide on the shape and color of the glass, as long as our common goal is to increase the quality and quantity of the liquid and not to play games of one-upmanship with our stemware. The glass into which Kristeva pours Bellini is not my preference, just as my glass may seem too rose-tinted for some others.

You Don't Have to See What I See

The other day at a party I met a woman, white and Winnipeg-born, who had been my student years ago. She told me how much she had enjoyed my class; she particularly remembered a text I had used in the course—Kamala Markandaya's *Nectar in a Sieve* (1954). She liked it, she said, because it was by a woman, by a non-Caucasian, and set outside the Western hemisphere. (In those days, we could teach only the old canon of literature, but as a quiet subversive I consistently included literature by women and by Indians).

Nectar in a Sieve provides an example of the difficulty of getting students to see the glass as half full. Given the material affluence of Canadian society and the prevalent stereotypes of different cultures, it is genuinely difficult for students to go beyond pity to recognize that the story is about the inextinguishable spark of the human will to survive, and to survive with dignity. Students tend to concentrate on the economic roots of Rukmini's sufferings in the novel, which they inextricably tangle with colonial oppression, and they overlook her indomitable strength and compassion. Similarly, the Muslim life-style so beautifully rendered by Attia Hosain in *Sunlight on a Broken Column* (1961) is quite beyond the average student's imagination, which is fed by media and sociological reports of women in Islam.

Many of these reports are true, as is the fact that the glass is half empty. But then, we also know that the glass is half full, which gives us the strength to contribute toward filling it to the top. We are activists, both in and out of the classroom. But sometimes it is disheartening, because in activist work there often seems to be no room for a half-full glass, all space being demanded by the halfempty one. When it was my turn to write an editorial for a *Contemporary Verse* 2 theme issue on children, I wrote the following prose poem:

> write she said about women writing children. but it is all already there i said, child in adult, adult in child, adult that never was child. write she said write an editorial on the theme. they've said it all already i said and so well. some women have children and some don't, some women want to bear children and some don't, some women don't want but do, some women want to but can't, some write because of children pulling at their heartstring some don't because of children pulling at their apronstring nonono apronstrings are out find new words patriarchal oppression gender role victimization, some spirits are stifled after they are born yesyesyes, some stifled before they are born nono let's not get into that. some beaten molested love-starved, yesyesyes, some degenerate cruel abusive, who's to blame. where are my children, i said, the sheer joy of hands holding talcsoft baby bottomswithout mememe looking atthroughintobehind? why aren't my children here? is there no poetry in dancing laughing children singing the sky into being? poetry yes but no poems for where we are in the sad waste of time before and after.[23]

But Don't Come between Me and My Glass

N.B.: Between the time I wrote the first version and this revision, the pyrotechnics of Naomi Wolf's recent *Fire with Fire* threatened to distort my words and intent. Enough to say that I dissociate myself from the shape, texture, and much of the contents of her glass.

All this endless talk about colonial and patriarchal oppressions, valorization and reification of the masculine, abuse of power and consequent loss of self-esteem in the victim, the scars etched forever and a day in the psyche of the colonized and of women bothers me because they often make the erstwhile-colonized and the female of the species out to be as weak and helpless as macho sexist racist masculinists do. Listening to some academic papers on Indian English literature, one would think India, Indians, Indian culture were totally crushed by the British; some of the applications of contemporary feminist literary criticism would have us conclude that patriarchy has totally crushed women's backbone, initiative, self-esteem, and so on, and so on. These interpretations are not totally false—the glass is half empty—but jargon often seems to take over and trivialize both real victimization and real heroism. Often a visceral experience of gut-wrenching victimization or of spirit-exalting achievement is replaced by a Halloween costume of litcrit gobbledygook. As a pluralist, I accept scholars' right to choose their glasses, but in the classroom, when I see such jargon influencing student responses, I feel constrained to step in with my half-full glass.

Links between the Native Renaissance and the Diaspora

Resistance and solidarity are strategies we can learn from the Native Renaissance now in progress in Canada. I see linkages between the two struggles—one waged by Natives and the other by us, the South-Asian diaspora in North America. Most relevant for us is that Natives—or First Nations, as some prefer to be called—do not recognize the boundary between the United States and Canada, a boundary drawn by white colonizers. I believe in national boundaries, since they are linked with Canadian sovereignty, which is sadly threatened by the free trade agreement between the two countries; however, I do believe that the South Asian diaspora in North America can and should assert and promote the commonalities that we share as writers, readers, academics, members of a common heritage culture.

The surge of interest in Native culture has generated problems very like the problems faced by feminists in their efforts to revise the canon and by post-colonials in their efforts to reinscribe and reinterpret history. Because they are of relevance to all minority cultures in a multicultural country such as Canada,

I have thought about the issue of "voice appropriation" and about its parallels for me as a writer and feminist teacher. I have more questions than answers because I am on both sides, being both an academic who must endorse the principle of uncensored research and a minority writer who is aware of the fallout from uncensored encroachments on cultural property. Though I unequivocally assert Natives' right to cultural property, as their oral tradition is often called, the multicultural reality of Canada is that there are far too many crossovers for other ethnocentered cultures to claim territorial rights, and also the bases of negotiation for an immigrant are different from those for a member of the First Nations. But, I repeat, I have more questions than answers. What follows are excerpts from entries (March to August 1992) in my ongoing journal on "cultural misappropriation." The segments in brackets are additions made for this essay.

Cultural Appropriation/Misappropriation: Journal of an Ongoing Journey

The baggage that has accreted around the terms "voice appropriation" and "cultural appropriation" has polarized people. To one constituency the terms signify censorship, and to the other they signify racial exploitation. Even more than "Who can speak for whom?" the issue is, "Who can speak about whom?" During the year (1992) commemorating five hundred years of resistance, I started my journey of questioning.

My journey, literal and figurative, started with a minority writers' conference where we first sat in a circle and listened to Native drummers. One of the organizers spoke about how it had been foretold that this land—Turtle Island, as it was called in her cultural lore—would one day be home to people of different colors. She talked about Turtle Island, about the wealth of traditional wisdom they once had, about depredations suffered at the hands of early traders and settlers, about the loss of land, of identity, of dignity. She stopped speaking and she cried. And then she went on. This wrongful appropriation must stop, and we will ensure that it stops by insisting that anyone engaged in literary exploration of any culture not one's own must seek permission. (Permission. I thought about this key word, which is also a key word in feminist language.) All who seek to write about the First Nations must first seek and obtain permission from the elders with offerings of sweet grass and tobacco, and certain promises. She stopped, tear-choked, several times.

Audience response. I had heard almost the same speech from the same person twelve months earlier when it was given to a large hall of academics, most of whom were white and male. The tension in the air was palpable in that auditorium, but they sat in tight-lipped silence, as white (mostly male) academics usually do. After the talk a few voiced their objection to her position, with tight-lipped formality as white (mostly male) academics are trained to speak. I found the situation hilarious—both the speaker's perfect sense for the dramatic and academia's response. But here, at this meeting where native drummers had opened our discussions, the response was quite different. One after another, individuals, most of them nonwhite and non-academic and nonmale, stood up and thanked her—for crying, for her openness, for affirming that emotion had a place in our discourse. Yes, we would support her in her stand. We would draw our line of resistance.

* * *

[At Toronto airport] I spoke to a stranger who was clearly headed for the same conference as I. We got to know each other a little more during the next two days. She was a researcher into Native culture; during and after last year's plenary on voice appropriation, she too had cried, but by herself under a tree outside the auditorium; she had decided she would abandon Native studies because she was white. A Native elder had recognized her and comforted her. Later, I came to know she was married to a Native and had several children by him. Is she or is she not eligible to do this research, I asked a First Nations spokesperson. The answer was no, she was not. I could partially empathize with the spokesperson's concerns. In any struggle of resistance, one has to draw a line and defend it; else, little by little one is pushed into retreat.

* * *

[At another conference session] I listened to another Native writer. She is in her sixties. She spoke in a soft voice, and very slowly. It was as if she took control of the space and slowly drew us into her world of sedate pace; her age and her gentleness compelled us in. She spoke to us of the wealth of Native stories, some of which she had collected and retold. Several times she said words to the effect, Please help us preserve them; take them with respect and write them down; please help us get them into written form so that posterity and the present can learn about us. It reminded me of words in a novel by S. S. Dhami, a South Asian Canadian novelist whose work Maluka is set in British Columbia of the 1920s. Maluka was told by his elders when he was a boy, "Write our story some day. . . . Say it like you saw with your eyes; say it like you heard us speak."[24] But Maluka was of their own blood, of the same race, I thought, and whites and nonwhites are not. We must defend our line of resistance.

* * *

[At another conference] I presented my paper on Reshard Gool's *The Nemesis Casket*. The nemesis casket, a metaphor for Canada as I see it, contained all kinds of records which each character had put in, stored, edited, excised, rewritten over the years. We loved that writer, our comrade, now dead. He was a Canadian whose ancestry could be traced to at least three different bloodstreams, three different races. He had appropriated voices from the country's mosaic and given it to the main characters, who were related in different ways as in a large family, another of his figurative devices. The writer's own life and novels moved toward synthesis, toward the concept of one culture, ultimately composite and Canadian however different and hybrid the roots—many-voiced, many-hued but composite and whole. When so many of us have so many bloodstreams in our veins, where does one draw the line for "appropriation," and why?

* * *

Blood lineage and only that gives one admittance to the inner circle, was the activist's message. Even if it is only one-quarter, eighths, sixteenths of one's bloodstream? Also, can one assume blood will not misrepresent, distort? Born in one of Britain's former colonies, I have first-hand knowledge of how grossly British texts and writings misrepresented and distorted other cultures during colonial times. As one living in North America, I regret and fear the neocolonialism of today where white researchers go to my native land for a few months, pick the brains of local scholars, and through this misappropriation make a name for themselves simply because they know how to handle academic jargon; they are aided by some publishers who assume that a white writer's work is more "objective" and worthy of publication than a nonwhite's.

But my newest regrets and fears concern those whom in my most generous moments I call victims of neocolonialism. At other times I have unprintable words for them. At a minority writers' conference I heard the following story separately from three different persons who were present when it happened: A member suggested that at the next round of group discussions we should break up into ethnocentric groups to discuss issues; one of the members, who left India in childhood, is reported to have said he didn't want to be in a roomful of bloody [East] Indians, who burnt their brides and killed their babies. By blood, he is an insider, but clearly his sensibilities and reasoning are as distorted with neocolonial, negative, sweeping generalizations about India as those of a blinkered, bigoted neo-Nazi. The Japanese Canadians have a word for second-generation immigrants: Nisei. I have long feared for the Nisei and Sansei from the country of my birth, cut off from their heritage and growing up in an environment that has the potential to be hostile; but now I realize I have reason to fear them for the harm they can do me, especially those *Issei and Nisei who are articulate and make a virtue of their ignorance.*

Insider, outsider, where do we draw the line, and how?

* * *

One of the perquisites of attending conferences is that one gets to meet professional colleagues who have become friends over the years. I met a friend who had recently come out. At some point, I talked to him about the course in Gay and Lesbian Studies offered at my university, and his face lit up. He could not even imagine anything like that being initiated where he was. It can be done, I said; he could write to the professors, whose names I could give him. No, he said, no, he was not ready for that. I said there was someone I knew in the room who had initiated a similar program at his university and I could introduce him to this person. No, no, he said, he was no good at making small talk on this issue. I know it is not easy to talk about it, I said, but there is strength in numbers and the other guy was right there. I pointed in his general direction. No, he said, some other time some other place. I have seen this guy over the years at various conferences, I said, usually alone—even this morning, for example, he was alone at breakfast. Where is he? he asked, where? And I saw in his face, his eyes, the deep concern that I have seen in mothers' eyes. I remember a childhood poem by Browning about a mortally wounded teenage soldier rushing to give Napoleon news of their success at Ratisbon. On hearing the good news, "the chief's eye flashed" with new plans but, on seeing the boy's blood, "softened, as sheathes a film the mother eagle's eye / when her bruised eaglet breathes." It was a beautiful moment that I had witnessed by happenstance.

But more often I have been eyed with suspicion in my attempts to erase some lines. For example, I was at a conference on South Asian culture. There were panel discussions on economic oppressions, racism in the workplace, intergenerational communication; there were poetry readings, plays, and video documentaries. The program was rich and the atmosphere electric. South Asian Canadian identity was coming into its own. I was barred from the lesbian discussion group, however, because of my heterosexuality. I teach lesbian texts and write with a lesbian sensibility, and I am concerned about South Asians being adversely targeted. But that was not enough. Someone snickered that maybe I was a lesbian in spirit? No one suggested that there might be validity in that position. There was at least one non–South Asian in the room, the partner of a South Asian; clearly one's sexual practice carried more weight than one's South Asian identity and sensibility in that conference called to promote South Asian culture. By the same token, I should have been barred from groups that discussed problems connected with low income, illiteracy, and racism in the workplace, for what experience of any significance do I personally have of any of these?

Insider, outsider, how do we draw the line, and why?

* * *

[I was in Ottawa for a meeting of writers.] There was to be a plenary session on "voice appropriation." The term is rather meaningless in the context of creative writing. The moment writers write, they appropriate, take over, a voice. Even in the most confessional of writings the narrative or recording voice is an appropriated voice, though some writers might genuinely think it is their own or might like readers to think so. Appropriation as a term has denotative problems. No wonder the air was tense. At one point—oh irony!—there was even some discussion on whether the media should be barred from sitting in on what might be an explosive discussion on fundamental freedom of expression! The National Council, in consultation with the Racial Minority Writers' Committee, had circulated a notice of motion on "cultural appropriation" and on "recognizing and affirming the responsibility and accountability that attend the freedom of imagination and freedom of expression." The long preamble covered and protected every aspect of a writer's freedom, but Eurocentric cultures seem to have a thing about so-called freedom of expression. It is a red flag that rouses some inner bull and sends them raging blindly.

Because the air was thick with tension the day before the debate, and because it was so important that the resolution be passed, I proposed a motion that enunciated the same principles but used the word "misappropriation" instead of "appropriation" because the latter had accreted too much polarizing baggage in the media debates of the preceding months. Since the original movers would not agree to this friendly amendment, in solidarity I withdrew the motion. Then someone else made a motion with the same substitution, and it was passed by an overwhelming majority.

The motion is simply a statement of a professional code comparable to the code of any other profession. Doctors take the Hippocratic oath. Engineers wear a steel ring, the metal of which is said to have come from a bridge that was improperly constructed and took many human lives when it collapsed; the ring is to remind engineers of their professional responsibility. So what is the problem with professional writers stating a commitment to responsibility and accountability regarding cultural property?

There is the other side, however, there is always the other side to every issue, several other sides. Who decides what is misappropriation? Who decides who can speak for whom or who can speak about whom? Further, several minority writers have said the "mis" makes the resolution so diluted as to be meaningless. A friend smilingly said I should next get Homi Bhabha and others to add the "mis" in future editions of their work. Meanwhile, the controversy hits closer to home. For example, some students genuinely cannot look beyond the fact that Gabrielle Roy is not Inuit and so they cannot appreciate the pathos and philosophy of her story, "The Satellites," about an Inuit woman. So what do we do? Erase all lines, those phallic symbols of patriarchal oppression? Better, bend them into circles.

For Crying Out Loud, Please Laugh

When I say for me the glass is always half full, I am enunciating an informed choice. In my poetry and fiction the glass is sometimes half full and sometimes half empty. But in my published works it is more often half empty. I always thought, with Shelley, that it was because "our sweetest songs are those that tell of saddest thought." But when I see the propensity of white editors and anthologists to choose the half-empty ones over the half-full ones, and find my lighter tales and poems promptly returned, I am not sure there isn't some neoimperialism at work that can admit the Other only when they come as suffering victims, alienated, marginalized, and so on. Let me resolve that this year I shall write and send out only humorous or celebratory poetry and fiction, even if I have to break my leg for it. Which I already have. As I've repeatedly brought to the reader's attention. See what I mean when I say self-representational writing is often self-conscious writing that edits itself into that circularity which is so instinctively and symbolically feminist?

NOTES

1. I use the term "North America" in the received sense of the geographic entity comprising Canada and the United States. I recognize that this marginalizes Mexico and the Caribbean countries, but I prefer "North America" to "Anglo-America" because as a Canadian I have serious problems with the latter. In Canada, the French and Native presences are not to be ignored, nor is the fact that we have two official languages, French and English. Further, we ought not to ignore our multicultural realities, in which equal status is to be given to all ethnic origins and all heritage languages promoted. "Anglo" thus becomes a very exclusive term for those of British cultural origins and for the English language. Given the choice of being consistent with the editors' usage in this volume or being consistent with my Canadian identity, I choose the latter. My thanks to the editors for allowing me to do so.

2. In the *Mahabharata*, Arjuna's son Abhimanyu was taught the secret of penetrating the maze-formations of war strategies and, in doing so, contributed to the Pandavas' victory over the Kauravas. But a curse on him made him forget the formula for the way out, and he died within the labyrinth.

3. Jane Tompkins, "Me and My Shadow," in *Gender and Theory: Dialogues on Feminist Criticism*, ed. Linda Kauffman (New York: Basil Blackwell, 1989).

4. I severed my Achilles tendon the week I revised the essay, and related allusions naturally knit their way into the revision. I let them stay, hoping the tendons will likewise knit themselves naturally into wholeness. A happenstance example of the combination of voice and editing that goes into self-conscious writing?

5. Nancy Miller, *Getting Personal: Feminist Occasions and Other Autobiographical Acts* (New York: Routledge, 1991), 1, 111.

6. Paul de Man, "Autobiography as De-facement," *MLN* 94.5 (1979): 919–30. Barbara Johnson's argument in "Deconstruction, Feminism and Pedagogy" (cited by Miller in *Getting Personal*, 15) that de Man's pronouncements lead to a patriarchal delegation of the personal as women's territory, and therefore usually devalued, is well taken, but language is our only tool of communication, and our struggle to resist devaluation too has to be fought through language.

7. Sidonie Smith, *A Poetics of Women's Autobiography* (Bloomington: Indiana University Press, 1987), 5.

8. It is interesting to note that the creation of both deities bypassed sexual union, and that the goddess of learning, Saraswati, is the daughter of the god Brahma, while the god of wisdom, Ganesha, is the son of the goddess Shakti.

9. Salman Rushdie, *The Satanic Verses* (London: Viking, 1988), 93.

10. Madhu Kishwar, "Why I Do Not Call Myself a Feminist," *Manushi* no. 61 (November–December 1990): 3.

11. Gayatri Chakravorty Spivak, "French Feminism in an International Frame," in *In Other Worlds: Essays in Cultural Politics* (New York: Methuen, 1987), 134–53.

12. When celebrating identity, I might use other terms such as "women of color" or "brown," but in political contexts of exclusion I use "nonwhite" as a more pertinent term.

13. I use the term "mythologies" consistently in my course outlines and classes—Hindu mythology, Aboriginal/Amerindian mythology, Judaeo-Christian mythology. All of them are true or all of them are false, take your pick.

14. I've been asked whether I think readers will comprehend these references to a river of India and a river (and Native people) of Canada. But that's my point—that readers have to work at understanding cross-cultural allusions.

15. Uma Parameswaran, *Trishanku* (Toronto: TSAR Books, 1988), 66.

16. Uma Parameswaran, "We/They Paradigm in Rushdie's *The Satanic Verses*," in *Us/Them: Translation, Transcription, and Identity in Post-Colonial Literary Cultures* ed. Gordon Collier (Amsterdam: Rodopi, 1993), 199.

17. Hélène Cixous, "The Laugh of the Medusa," trans. Keith Cohen and Paula Cohen, *Signs: Journal of Women in Culture and Society* 1.4 (1976): 884.

18. See Jacques Lacan, *Ecrits: A Selection*, trans. Alan Sheridan (New York: Norton, 1977).

19. See Julia Kristeva, *Desire in Language: A Semiotic Approach to Literature and Art*, trans. Thomas Gora, Alice Jardine and Leon Roudiez (New York: Columbia University Press, 1980).

20. Mary Jacobus, *Reading Woman: Essays in Feminist Criticism* (New York: Columbia University Press, 1986), no. 20.

21. Kristeva, *Desire in Language*, 254.

22. Jacobus, *Reading Woman*, 156.

23. Uma Parameswaran, editorial, *Contemporary Verse* 2 14.4 (1992): 5.

24. S. S. Dhami, *Maluka* (Bombay: Heinemann, 1987), 27.

ABOUT THE CONTRIBUTORS

Meena Alexander is professor of English and Women's Studies at Hunter College and the Graduate Center, City University of New York. Her poems and prose pieces have been translated into several languages, including Malayalam, Arabic, French, German, and Italian. Her current work includes *The Shock of Arrival: Post-Colonial Reflections* (1996); a novel, *Manhattan Music* (in press); and a volume of poems, *River and Bridge* (1996).

Deepika Bahri, assistant professor in postcolonial literature and theory at Emory University, has published articles in *Ariel, Studies in American Humor, and Mythes, croyances, et religion dans le monde Anglo-Saxon;* other essays are forthcoming in various collections. She is currently working on a book-length study of technology, culture, and postcolonialism.

Mahasveta Barua received her Ph.D. from Temple University and is currently an instructor at the University of Delaware. Her research is in the area of fables and epics, and she is preparing a book on Anne Finch's fables.

Ranita Chatterjee, born in Calgary, Alberta, is an instructor in the Department of English and the Women's Studies Program at the University of Utah. She is completing a dissertation on the libidinal dynamics of the writings of William Godwin, Mary Wollstonecraft, Mary Shelley, and Percy Shelley at the University of Western Ontario.

Samir Dayal, assistant professor of English at Bentley College, Massachusetts, is at work on a collection to be titled *Postcolonial Diaporas.* His recent writings have appeared or are forthcoming in collections and journals, including *Genders, College English, Cultural Critique,* and the *Journal of the Midwest Modern Language Association.*

Shantanu DuttaAhmed is a graduate student at the University of Southern California. His particular interest is in areas where race, ethnicity, and sexuality intersect. His current project, *Transactional Moments: Space, Identity, and the Diaspora,* traces the shift from organic to spatial metaphors of identity.

Huma Ibrahim is assistant professor of postcolonial literature and theory at American University in Washington, D.C. Her book *Bessie Head: Subversive Identities in Exile* is forthcoming, and she is working on a study of theoretical questions related to "Third World" women's desire within structures of nation-states.

Sohail Inayatullah, a political scientist, is currently a research fellow at the Communication Centre, Queensland University of Technology, Brisbane, Australia. Born in Lahore, he has lived in Kuala Lumpur, Islamabad, Bangkok, Geneva, Indiana, New York, and Hawaii. He is on the editorial board of the journals *Futures* and the *Journal of Future Studies*. He has written and published extensively on the politics of Islamic science, the thought of P. R. Sarkar, and South Asia's alternative futures.

Sukeshi Kamra is a professor of nineteenth-century British literature and postcolonial literatures at Okanagan University College in Canada. She has published a book on Rudyard Kipling and is currently working on the literature of the partition of India.

Amitava Kumar, who teaches Cultural Studies at the University of Florida, is also a columnist for *Samkaleen Janmat* (India) and a photographer for the New York–based co-op Impact Visuals. He has published in *Critical Quarterly*, *Minnesota Review*, *Modern Fiction Studies*, *Rethinking Marxism*, and other journals. He is preparing two books for publication, *Passport Photos* and *Poems for the I.N.S.* The short story "The Monkey's Suicide" included in his essay for this volume won the *Asian Age* Best Short Story of 1994 Award.

Sanjoy Majumder is visiting assistant professor of Film and Video Studies at Rosary College, Illinois. His research and teaching are in Third World cinema, cultural studies, video production, and film theory.

Binita Mehta is completing her dissertation, on the representation of India in French theater, at the City University of New York. Articles related to her area of study appear in *Francographies* 1995 and the *Dictionary of Literary Biography*.

Indrani Mitra is assistant professor of English, Mount Saint Mary's College, Maryland. Her research interests are in the literatures and cultures of India, Africa, and the Caribbean. She has recently published an article on feminism and nationalism in *Modern Fiction Studies* and is currently working on a book-length study of Indo-English women writers.

Uma Parameswaran is a professor at the University of Winnipeg, Canada. Her works of criticism, poetry, fiction, and drama include *Trishanku* (poems), *Rootless but Green Are the Boulevard Trees* (a play), and *The Perforated Sheet: Essays on Salman Rushdie's Art*. Her current research is in South Asian–Canadian literature.

Pushpa Naidu Parekh, assistant professor in comparative literature at Spelman College in Atlanta, teaches postcolonial, immigrant, and African literatures. She is currently coediting a sourcebook titled *Postcolonial African Writers* and preparing a work on British poets.

Amritjit Singh, professor of English at Rhode Island College, Providence, is the author of numerous articles and books and editor of collected essays in American, African American, and Indian literature. Most recently, he has published critical editions of Richard Wright's works and coedited *American Studies Today: An Introduction to New Methods and Perspectives* (1995), *Memory and Cultural Politics* (1995), *New Perspectives in Indian Literature in English* (1995), and *Memory, Narrative, and Identity* (1994).

Gayatri Chakravorty Spivak is Avalon Foundation Professor in the Humanities at Columbia University. She has published *Of Grammatology* (1976), a critical translation of Jacques Derrida's *De la Grammatologie*, and *Imaginary Maps* (1944), a critical translation of Mahasveta Devi's fiction. Her own books are *Myself Must I Remake* (1974), *In Other Worlds* (1987), *The Post-Colonial Critic* (1988), *Outside in the Teaching Machine* (1944), and *A Spivak Reader* (1995).

M. G. Vassanji was born in Nairobi, Kenya, was brought up in Tanzania, attended MIT and the University of Pennsylvania, and now lives in Toronto, where he edits the literary magazine the *Toronto Review*. In 1989 he was writer-in-residence at the International Writing Program of the University of Iowa. He is the author of five works of fiction, including *The Gunny Sack; No New Land; Uhuru Street*; and the *The Book of Secrets*, which won the Giller Prize for the best work of fiction in 1994.

Mary Vasudeva is on the board of directors for the Academic Excellence Foundation at Bowling Green State University, Ohio, and coordinates an outreach program for disadvantaged single mothers. She has just completed a dissertation on the usefulness of literature in creating a multicultural curriculum in the university and is preparing a review essay on Native American literary criticism for *College Literature*.

Gauri Viswanathan, associate professor of English and comparative literature at Columbia University, is the author of *Masks of Conquest: Literary Study and British Rule in India* (1989) and *Outside the Fold: Conversion, Modernity, and Belief* (forthcoming). She has also published widely on the overlapping cultural histories of England and India, religious identity, and colonial ideology.